TM

...For Dummies

BESTSELLING BOOK SERIES

References for the Rest of Us!®

Are you intimidated and confused by computers? Do you find that traditional manuals are overloaded with technical details you'll never use? Do your friends and family always call you to fix simple problems on their PCs? Then the For Dummies® computer book series from Wiley Publishing, Inc. is for you.

For Dummies books are written for those frustrated computer users who know they aren't really dumb but find that PC hardware, software, and indeed the unique vocabulary of computing make them feel helpless. For Dummies books use a lighthearted approach, a down-to-earth style, and even cartoons and humorous icons to dispel computer novices' fears and build their confidence. Lighthearted but not lightweight, these books are a perfect survival guide for anyone forced to use a computer.

Already, millions of satisfied readers agree. They have made For Dummies books the #1 introductory level computer book series and have written asking for more. So, if you're looking for the most fun and easy way to learn about computers, look to For Dummies books to give you a helping hand.

Wiley Publishing, Inc.

P9-CFO-303

Visual Basic® 6

FOR

DUMMIES®

by Wallace Wang

Wiley Publishing, Inc.

Visual Basic® 6 For Dummies®

Published by
Wiley Publishing, Inc.
909 Third Avenue
New York, NY 10022
www.wiley.com

For general information on our other products and services or to obtain technical support, please contact our Customer Care Department within the U.S. at 800-762-2974, outside the U.S. at 317-572-3993, or fax 317-572-4002.

Wiley also publishes its books in a variety of electronic formats. Some content that appears in print may not be available in electronic books.

Library of Congress Cataloging-in-Publication Data:

Library of Congress Catalog Card No.: 98-87098

ISBN: 0-7645-0370-7

Manufactured in the United States of America

15

About the Author

At the time of this writing, the author's body temperature was 98.6 degrees Fahrenheit, and he was breathing normally. But beyond the physical characteristics, the author of this book has also has written over a dozen computer books including *MORE Visual Basic For Windows For Dummies, Microsoft Office 97 For Windows For Dummies,* and *MORE Microsoft Office 97 For Windows For Dummies.* When he's not writing computer books, he does what other computer authors usually do and writes articles for computer magazines instead. He writes a monthly column for *Boardwatch* magazine and has written articles for *The Net* magazine as well.

When not writing computer books, he often refers to himself in the third person singular form, such as in this current sentence. While such self-referential sentences tend to look authoritative and profound when appearing in print within a book's "About the Author" page, they tend to make people stare in a most peculiar way when spoken out loud in public. Not many people introduce themselves at parties as "Hi, his name is Wallace," and this author, of course, is no exception.

In his spare time, Wallace can often be seen watching the demolition crews knock down the buildings in San Diego that used to house his former employer. Wallace's only regret is that the demolition crews didn't start much earlier when his former boss and coworkers would still have been inside.

Dedication

This book is dedicated to all the wonderful people I've met during my mad pursuit in the world of stand-up comedy:

Budd Friedman, for giving me my first national TV appearance on his show *A&E's Evening at the Improv.*

Mark Kuker, for offering delightfully strange, one-nighter gigs in Ruidoso and Deming (home of the annual duck races), New Mexico. Mark and his wife Amanda are two of the best people a comedian could ever hope to work for.

Steve Schirripa and Don Learned, for giving me my first Las Vegas gig at the Riviera Comedy Club, located in the Riviera Hotel & Casino. The next time you're in Las Vegas, drop by, see a show, and dump some money in the Riviera Casino slot machines. Who knows? Maybe you'll win enough money to buy yourself a new computer.

Patrick DeGuire and Dat Phan who helped me put together Top Bananas, our company devoted to booking the three of us in corporate comedy events around San Diego. Thanks also goes to Fred Burns, Leo (the man, the myth, the legend) Fontaine, Ron Clark, Dante, Frank Manzano, Chris (the Zooman) Clobber, Bob Zany, Tony Vicich, and George Hirschmann.

Final thanks go to Gene Perret, Linda Perret (and the rest of the whole happy Perret clan), Liz Sage, and everyone else who has helped me navigate my way through the minefield of inflated egos and hair-trigger temperamental personalities known as show business.

Author's Acknowledgments

Nobody writes and publishes a book without the help of other people, and this book is no exception. It goes without saying (although I'm going to say it anyway) that two of the most important people responsible for this book are Matt Wagner and Bill Gladstone of Waterside Productions. Thanks guys. I'd give you more than your usual 15 percent cut but if I did, then I wouldn't have anything left over to pay for my groceries.

Two other people who deserve thanks include Brian Kramer of IDG Books Worldwide, Inc., and Allen Wyatt of Discovery Computing, Inc.

Next, I have to acknowledge Cassandra (my wife) along with Bo, Scraps, Tasha, and Nuit (my cats) for their support during the long hours I've spent glued to my computer instead of doing anything else around the house.

A final acknowledgment goes to the friendly people at Complete Design & Remodeling including Wes McKusick and Tom DeLisle who did all the remodeling of my new house while I just wrote them checks.

Publisher's Acknowledgments

We're proud of this book; please register your comments through our online registration form located at www.dummies.com/register.

Some of the people who helped bring this book to market include the following:

Acquisitions, Editorial, and Media Development

Project Editor: Brian Kramer

Acquisitions Editor: Sherri Morningstar

Copy Editor: Patricia Yuu Pan

Technical Editor: Allen Wyatt

Media Development Editor: Marita Ellixson

Associate Permissions Editor: Carmen Krikorian

Editorial Manager: Leah P. Cameron

Media Development Manager: Heather Heath Dismore

Editorial Assistant: Donna Love

Production

Project Coordinator: Karen York

Layout and Graphics: Traci Ankrom, Lou Boudreau, Kelly Hardesty, Angela F. Hunckler, Jane E. Martin, Brent Savage, Michael A. Sullivan, Dan Whetstine

Proofreaders: Kelli Botta, Michelle Croninger, Rachel Garvey, Sandra Wilson, Janet M. Withers

Indexer: Sherry Massey

Special Help

Tim Gallan

General and Adminstrative

Wiley Technology Publishing Group: Richard Swadley, Vice President and Executive Group Publisher; Bob Ipsen, Vice President and Group Publisher; Joseph Wikert, Vice President and Publisher; Barry Pruett, Vice President and Publisher; Mary Bednarek, Editorial Director; Mary C. Corder, Editorial Director; Andy Cummings, Editorial Director

Wiley Manufacturing: Carol Tobin, Director of Manufacturing

Wiley Marketing: John Helmus, Assistant Vice President, Director of Marketing

Wiley Composition Services: Gerry Fahey, Executive Director of Production Services; Debbie Stailey, Director of Composition Services

Contents at a Glance

Cartoons at a Glance

By Rich Tennant

"Kevin here heads our Windows software development team. Right now he's working on a spreadsheet program that's sort of a combination of Lotus 1-2-3 and FrankenWolf."

page 7

Real Programmers don't like to be bothered when they're working.

page 53

"SO I SAID, 'WAITER! WAITER! THERE'S A BUG IN MY SOUP!' AND HE SAYS, 'SORRY, SIR, THE CHEF USED TO PROGRAM COMPUTERS'. AHH HAHA THANK YOU! THANK YOU!"

page 207

"It's been reported that we went a little crazy trying to bring this product to market on time..."

page 309

"HOLD ON, GREG! Those are some MONSTER nose hairs you've got there. Here, use my...
"...SWISS ARMY MOUSE!"
*TRACKING DEVICE AND PROGRAMMER'S AID

page 441

Real Programmers hate decaffeinated coffee.

page 327

THE GREAT THING ABOUT OBJECT-ORIENTED PROGRAMMING IS, IT'S MADE SOFTWARE DEVELOPMENT AS EASY AS PUTTING ONE FOOT IN FRONT OF THE OTHER.

page 353

You're NOT A CYBERHOLIC... if you look for the Soup of the Day in the Format menu.

page 161

"WE SHOULD HAVE THIS FIXED IN VERSION 2."

page 409

Fax: 978-546-7747
E-mail: richtennant@the5thwave.com
World Wide Web: www.the5thwave.com

Table of Contents

· ·

Introduction

● ●

*W*elcome to computer programming using Visual Basic 6. If you've ever tried to program before but found the whole endeavor too complicated, relax. If you can doodle mindlessly on a scrap of paper, you can write a program in Visual Basic 6. (Seriously!)

Unlike other programming books you may have picked up (and immediately dropped due to their excessive bulk and weight), this book uses the unconventional approach of talking about programming in plain English. Besides using honest-to-goodness English explanations, this book also provides interesting programming trivia, a CD-ROM loaded with tons of sample programs, and step-by-step instructions for writing programs in Visual Basic 6.

Contrary to popular belief, programming doesn't have to be difficult — it actually can be lots of fun. As a reminder to enjoy yourself, this book keeps up a spirit of playfulness. After all, that's why most people buy a computer in the first place — to have fun. (Admit the truth. Does anyone really buy a computer just to balance a budget?)

About This Book

Think of this book as a friendly guide and reference to Visual Basic 6 programming for Windows 95, 98, and NT. Although Visual Basic isn't hard to understand, remembering all the petty details needed to write programs can be confusing and difficult. Some sample topics you find in this book include the following:

- ✔ Saving your program
- ✔ Designing a user interface
- ✔ Creating pull-down menus
- ✔ Killing bugs in your program
- ✔ Printing out stuff

Although many people think that programming a computer requires years of advanced mathematics and technical training, relax. If you can tell someone how to get to your house from work, you can certainly tell a computer what to do. The purpose of this book isn't to cram your brain full of technical details and explanations. The purpose of this book is to show you all the steps you need to write a Visual Basic program and to give you the know-how and confidence to write with Visual Basic.

How to Use This Book

This book shows you step-by-step how to create a real-life working Windows program using Visual Basic. You figure out how to design your own user interfaces and then write BASIC code to make your program respond to any action taken on the user interface (such as clicking buttons and pressing certain keys).

All code appears in monospaced type, like this:

```
Printer.DrawWidth = Value
```

Due to the margins in this book, some long lines of code wrap to the next line. The underscore character at the end of a line means that the code continues onto the next line:

```
Sub Form_MouseUp(Button As Integer, Shift As Integer, X _
             As Single, Y As Single)
```

On your computer, you can also choose to type these wrapped lines as a single line of code.

Visual Basic doesn't care if you type everything in uppercase, lowercase, or any combination of both. However, to make what appears on your screen correspond to the figures in this book, use uppercase and lowercase, as shown throughout the book's examples.

You may also run across a few cryptic-looking tables such as:

Object	Property	Setting
Form	Name	frmHello
	Caption	Hello, world!
Option2	Name	optSmile
	Caption	I'm okay.

When you're designing a user interface (explained in more detail in Chapter 3), you'll need to define the properties of each object (such as a command button or check box). The preceding table tells you the name of the object to modify (such as Form or Option2), the specific properties to change (such as Name or Caption), and the exact value to use in each particular property (such as frmHello or optSmile).

To test your understanding of the topics covered, I sprinkle simple quizzes throughout this book. Rather than focus on making people miserable, these multiple-choice quizzes emphasize boosting your self-esteem. All choices but one will be so outrageously wrong that choosing the right one will be easy. Not only will these questions teach you something, but you'll have a good chuckle reading the wrong choices as well.

Foolish Assumptions

Assuming that you already know how to turn a computer on and off and use a mouse and a keyboard — and that you want to write your own programs for fun, profit, or work (work isn't always fun or profitable) — you're ready to start finding out how to program in Visual Basic 6.

In addition to your computer, you also should have a copy of Visual Basic 6 and a desire to know how to use the program. In case you're still feeling self-conscious about your programming abilities, consider Albert Einstein (the famous physicist who came up with the theory of relativity). Einstein once had an elementary-school teacher who thought he was such a slow learner that he must be retarded.

Perhaps in response to this, Albert Einstein said, "Imagination is more important than knowledge." (Some people claim that Einstein also said, "If my elementary-school teacher is so smart, where is his Nobel Prize?" However, this latter statement has yet to be confirmed.)

So if you have an imagination, a personal computer, and Visual Basic 6, you already have more than enough to get started writing programs in Visual Basic 6 right away.

How This Book Is Organized

This book contains nine major parts. Each part contains several chapters, and each chapter contains several modular sections. Anytime you need help, just pick up this book and start reading. Following is a breakdown of the nine parts and what you'll find in them.

Part I: Creating a Visual Basic 6 Program

Part I contains a brief introduction to all the major features of Visual Basic 6. If the thought of programming a computer makes you break out in hives, this is the place to relieve your anxieties and to boost your self-esteem.

Part II: Creating User Interfaces

A user interface determines what your program looks like. This is the fun part, where you can make your program look as ugly or as beautiful as you want. In Part II, you doodle circles, draw lines, and scribble all over the screen. In fact, if you try doing this without a computer, people may think that you've lost your mind and reverted to kindergarten finger painting.

Part III: Making Menus

In Part III, you get to create fancy pull-down menus that you see all the expensive programs using these days. If you want your program to impress your friends and influence people, this is where you find out how to create such a program.

Part IV: The Basics of Writing Code

In Part IV, you discover how to write honest-to-goodness BASIC programs that the computer can understand and obey. Although you may already know how to tell your computer what to do (using four-letter words), this is where you find out how to tell your computer what to do using the BASIC language.

Part V: Making Decisions (Something You Stop Doing When You Get Married)

Part V is where you find out how to tell your computer to make up its own mind and do something useful instead of relying on you to do everything. For those of you raising children, you may find this idea of self-reliance particularly appealing.

Part VI: Getting Loopy

Loops are another way of telling your computer to repeatedly do something until it gets the job done right. In Part VI, you encounter different ways to make your computer repeat itself.

Part VII: Writing Subprograms (So You Don't Go Crazy All at Once)

Many people panic at the thought of writing a large program. In Part VII, you discover the secrets to maintaining your sanity while writing many little programs that work together to create one huge program.

Part VIII: Database Files and Printing

I name Part VIII "Database Files and Printing," but don't let the title intimidate you. Database files are nothing more than special ways that computers organize information. People store their information in drawers, folders, and closets; computers use databases. No big deal. You also find out how to print all your valuable programs on paper for the whole world to see and admire.

Part IX: The Part of Tens

Part IX contains miscellaneous information that you may find useful and interesting, including tips about add-ons for Visual Basic and where to find more information about Visual Basic programming.

Icons Used in This Book

This icon signals technical details that are informative (and sometimes interesting) but not necessary. Skip these sections if you want.

This icon flags useful or helpful information that makes programming even less complicated.

Don't pass these gentle reminders — they signify important information.

Be cautious when you encounter this icon. This icon warns you of things that can ruin your day if you're not careful.

Step-by-step instructions and explanations dealing with code follow this icon.

This icon means you can check out the accompanying CD-ROM for useful software and code files (which you can load directly into Visual Basic rather than typing everything from scratch).

This icon highlights new features found only in Visual Basic 6. If you already know how to use a previous version of Visual Basic, search for these icons. You can discover right away how to use the new Visual Basic 6 features.

Where to Go from Here

In case you're asking yourself where to go from here, the obvious answer is to turn the page and start reading. Don't worry. Computer programming in Visual Basic 6 can be as fun as playing with an Etch-A-Sketch (except you can actually draw circles in Visual Basic 6). If people accuse you of goofing off when you should be working, you can impress them with your new knowledge about Visual Basic 6 programming — and then tell them where *they* can go from here.

In an effort to spread Visual Basic to the masses, Microsoft sells several different editions of Visual Basic: the Learning Edition, the Standard Edition, the Professional Edition, and the Enterprise Edition. If you have either the Learning Edition (a crippled, inexpensive version designed to get the program into the hands of programmers as inexpensively as possible) or the Standard Edition of Visual Basic, you may not be able to use all the examples I describe in the later chapters of this book.

Part I
Creating a Visual Basic 6 Program

"Kevin here heads our Windows software development team. Right now he's working on a spreadsheet program that's sort of a combination of Lotus 1-2-3 and FrankenWolf."

In this part . . .

Writing your own program isn't hard. If you've always been curious about computer programming but were intimidated by the hard-to-read books, less-than-useful software, or obtuse and convoluted "explanations" from "experts," then this book is for you.

Rather than impress you with mathematical proofs and theoretical background about computer programming, this book (with the help of Visual Basic) lets you jump right in and start finding out about programming on your own computer all by yourself.

So grab some snack foods, a few carbonated beverages, a comfortable seat, and get ready to program your computer and make it finally do what you want it to do. . . .

Chapter 1
How Visual Basic Works

*T*he whole purpose of writing a program is to make your computer do something useful. People often spend thousands of dollars for one of these machines, so it's important that the computer does something more than consume electricity and take up space on a desk.

Before you delve into the world of programming, keep two thoughts in mind. First, anyone can write a program. Programming is just a skill, much like swimming, sailing, or shoplifting. If you've ever taught yourself a new hobby or skill, you can teach yourself how to write a program without an extensive mathematics background or a fancy college degree that puts you in debt for the next ten years.

Second, the key to programming is defining exactly what you want your program to do. Defining what you want your program to do is half the battle (a battle that governments and large corporations routinely lose all the time). The other half of the battle involves taking the time to write your program and making sure it works correctly. (This part of the battle is another place where governments and large corporations fall flat on their faces on a fairly regular basis.)

You can write a program to make your computer do anything you want, short of launching nuclear missiles at your next-door neighbor. (Of course, if you write a program for the Air Force's computers, you may even be able to do that.)

Writing a Visual Basic Program

There is no single correct way to write a program. Theoretically, you can use a million different ways to write a program correctly, just as you can travel from New York to Los Angeles a million different ways. Some people may fly, others may take a train or drive; the more adventurous may walk, hitchhike, or hijack a vehicle. Similarly, you can write the same program a million different ways. However, no matter how you write the program, the result can always be the same.

As a programmer, your job is to write a program that works correctly and is easy to use. If your program doesn't work, nobody can use it (although you often can sell a few thousand copies to unsuspecting individuals first). If your program isn't easy to use, nobody will want to use it, even if it works perfectly.

Testing whether your program works is usually simple enough. If your program is supposed to print mailing labels but erases the computer's hard disk instead, then your program obviously doesn't work correctly.

However, determining whether your program is easy to use is a bit more difficult. What you may consider easy to use may be almost impossible for someone else to understand.

To create programs that everyone can understand how to use, Visual Basic helps you to easily produce windows, pull-down menus, dialog boxes, and command buttons. These features are the same ones found in Windows 95/98/NT programs. Visual Basic helps you write programs that look and act like other programs on the market.

Making your program look and act like an existing program can help others learn your program faster. For example, most people can drive a Toyota or a Ford without any problems; the steering wheel and brakes always look and work the same way, even if the windshield wipers and horn may not. The same goes for programs. Pull-down menus contain a program's numerous commands, and you can always use the mouse to highlight and choose commands or objects. So while each program may work differently, they all look and work in similar ways.

The Visual Basic development cycle

Before writing a Visual Basic program (or any program for that matter), get away from your computer and plan your program using an old-fashioned paper and pencil. After you know what you want your program to accomplish and how you want it to look, then you can start writing your program. Skipping this crucial first step is like building a house without blueprints. You can do it, but it will probably take you longer.

TECHNICAL STUFF

Why programs don't work (Part I)

Writing a program that works 100 percent correctly all the time is mathematically impossible. First of all, if you write a program that works 100 percent correctly today, there's no way you can guarantee that it will work 100 percent correctly on future computer brands, models, processors, and accessories. As a result, you can never guarantee that your program will work correctly on all types of computers unless you exhaustively test every possible computer configuration in the world.

Second, not only do you have to test your program with the latest and greatest products (including the ones invented after you wrote your program), but you also have to consider the virtually infinite number of possibilities that your program must face during everyday use.

For example, your program needs to behave correctly if the user presses any key and then clicks the mouse anywhere on the screen. What if the user clicks the mouse by mistake while tapping a key? What if the user pounds the keyboard in frustration? What if another program happens to interfere with the computer's memory, thus affecting your program? What if . . . (well, you get the idea).

Unless a programmer can plan for an infinite number of possible problems and situations that a program may face during its existence, then writing a program that works 100 percent of the time is impossible.

What's scarier is that this scenario holds true for every computer operating system in the world (such as Windows 95/98/NT). Therefore, you'll always be writing programs to run on an operating system that doesn't work 100 percent correctly either. This situation is like building a house on a foundation of quicksand and then wondering why your house keeps falling apart.

Because no one has an infinite amount of time to test an infinite number of possible problems, computer programs always (yes, always) will have bugs that keep them from working 100 percent correctly. That includes every program you write and every program that Microsoft's millionaire programmers may write. That's why when you write a program, set aside plenty of time for testing so you can kill any potentially fatal bugs before you give your program to someone else.

So the next time you're using a program that doesn't work right, now you'll know that it's not your fault; it's the programmer's fault.

Writing a Visual Basic program requires nine steps — three steps fewer than those required to overcome an addictive habit. The first eight steps are what programmers call the *development cycle*. The ninth step is what programmers call *job security*.

1. Decide what you want the computer to do.

2. Decide how your program will look on the screen. (The appearance of your program is its *user interface*.)

3. Draw your user interface using common parts such as windows, menus, and command buttons. (The parts of a user interface are *objects* or *controls*.)

4. Define the name, color, size, and appearance of each user interface object. (An object's characteristics are its *properties*.)

5. Write instructions in BASIC to make each part of your program do something. (BASIC instructions are *commands*.)

6. Run your program to see if it works.

7. Cry when your program doesn't work perfectly. (Required.)

8. Fix any errors (or *bugs*) in your program.

9. Repeat Steps 6 through 8 over and over again until you get tired of searching for more bugs.

Although you don't have to memorize these nine steps, you do have to follow them. Shortcuts aren't an option. Trying to skip from Step 1 to Step 4 is like trying to start a car by using the gas pedal but forgetting to turn the ignition key. You can try it, but you're not going to get anywhere.

Believe it or not, Step 1 is actually the hardest and most important step of all. After you know exactly what you want your program to do, it's just a matter of finding ways to do it. Persistence and creativity are helpful, as are lots of caffeine-laden beverages and plenty of sleepless nights in front of the computer screen.

Making a neat user interface

The user interface is what someone sees when your program is running. Every program has a user interface in one form or another. Some programs have elaborate, colorful windows, while other programs have a sparse appearance — as if the programmer were afraid that screen phosphor may be in short supply one day.

A Visual Basic user interface consists of forms and objects. A *form* is nothing more than a window that appears on the screen. Most Visual Basic programs have at least one form, although most programs likely will use several forms.

Objects are items that appear on a form (see Figure 1-1), such as a command button, scroll bar, option button, or check box. An object lets the user give commands to your program. If you really wanted, you could create a program with only one form and no objects, but it wouldn't be very useful or interesting.

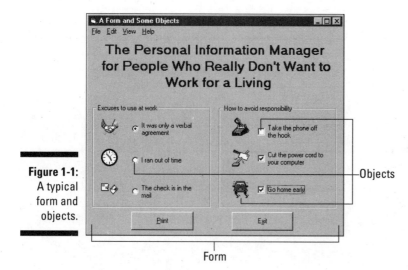

A Form and Some Objects
File Edit View Help

The Personal Information Manager
for People Who Really Don't Want to
Work for a Living

Excuses to use at work

- It was only a verbal agreement
- I ran out of time
- The check is in the mail

How to avoid responsibility

- Take the phone off the hook
- Cut the power cord to your computer
- Go home early

—Objects

Print   Exit

Form

Figure 1-1:
A typical
form and
objects.

Defining properties to make your user interface unique

After you create a form and draw some objects on it, the next step is to define the properties of each form and object. An object's *properties* determine the object's name, color, size, location, and appearance on the screen.

Different objects have different properties. Each time you draw an object on a form, Visual Basic assigns default property values, which define a generic object that no one can really use. If you want to customize an object, you need to define one or more properties for each object that your program uses. Chapter 3 provides a quick introduction to changing an object's properties.

Writing BASIC code

When you're happy with the way your program looks, the next step involves writing BASIC commands (also known as *code*) to make your program actually work. (Don't worry. If you change your mind and want to edit the appearance of your user interface, you can go back and alter it at any time.)

REMEMBER

The whole purpose of Visual Basic code is to tell objects on a form what to do when the user does something. For example, if the user clicks on an OK or Cancel command button, nothing happens unless you've written BASIC commands to tell your computer exactly what to do.

Why programs don't work (Part II)

Most programs are written by professional programmers who may have studied programming for years. Does this mean that every program they write will always work? Of course not. This is the world of computers where nothing works right, remember?

Besides the fact that the skill level among professional programmers can vary widely, professional programmers are often called upon to write programs for tasks that they don't understand themselves. For example, programmers may know nothing about accounting yet be hired to write a program to control a bank's electronic-fund-transfer system. Likewise, programmers with no skill or experience in flying may be hired to write a program to control the landing, takeoff, and flight of a 747 jumbo jet. Programmers with no knowledge of medicine may be required to write a program to control a medical instrument that administers doses of radiation to cancer patients. How can you work in a field where you have no experience and still get paid a lot of money? Easy, you become a programmer.

Hiring a programmer with no knowledge of the task she's trying to solve is like hiring a translator to translate Greek into French without that person's knowing how to read or write in either language. Given this paradox in the programming world, is it any wonder that planes crash, banks lose money, and hotels can't keep our reservations straight?

Any time a user presses a key, moves the mouse, or clicks the mouse button, it's called an *event*. Whenever an event occurs, your BASIC commands tell the computer, "Hey stupid, something just happened. Let's do something about it!"

Essentially, writing a Visual Basic program means drawing your user interface and then writing BASIC code to make it work. If you can handle these two steps without losing your mind, you can start writing your very own programs using Visual Basic. Chapter 4 provides a short introduction to writing real-life BASIC code.

Chapter 2

Using the Visual Basic User Interface

In This Chapter

▶ Loading Visual Basic

▶ Getting to know the Visual Basic user interface

▶ Opening, closing, and moving windows around

▶ Quitting Visual Basic

*B*efore diving into the depths of Visual Basic programming, take a deep breath and examine the program's user interface. After all, if you don't know how to use the Visual Basic user interface, you won't be able to write your own Visual Basic programs.

To use Visual Basic, you need to know the following three functions:

✔ How to load Visual Basic from Windows 95/98/NT

✔ How to use Visual Basic to write your own programs

✔ How to exit out of Visual Basic

Loading Visual Basic

To load Visual Basic, just follow these simple steps:

1. **Click on the Start button of the Windows 95/98/NT taskbar.**

   A pop-up menu appears.

2. **Click on Programs, click on the Microsoft Visual Basic 6 folder (or the Microsoft Visual Studio folder), and then click on Microsoft Visual Basic 6.**

   Visual Basic displays a New Project dialog box, as shown in Figure 2-1.

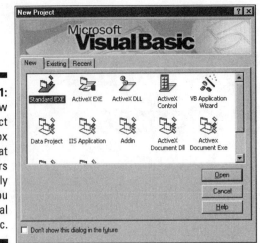

Figure 2-1:
The New
Project
dialog box
that
appears
immediately
after you
load Visual
Basic.

To load Visual Basic quickly, create a desktop shortcut by following these steps: Right-click on the Windows desktop, click on New, click on Shortcut, click on the Browse button, search for the VB6.EXE file, click on the Next> button, type **Visual Basic 6**, and click on the Finish button.

After the New Project dialog box appears, you have two options. You can

- ✔ Start writing a brand new program.
- ✔ Load an existing program so you can modify it.

Starting a new program

After you have the New Project dialog box displayed, you have several choices as to the type of program you want to create. (The Learning and Standard Editions of Visual Basic do not display all the following types of programs in the New Project dialog box.)

- ✔ **Standard EXE:** Creates a stand-alone program that you can copy, give away, or sell to others. Examples of stand-alone programs are Microsoft Word, Lotus 1-2-3, and Netscape Navigator. Stand-alone programs have an .EXE file extension.

- ✔ **ActiveX DLL:** Creates a file that has a .DLL file extension. ActiveX DLL files are not meant to be used by themselves. Instead, these types of files contain subprograms designed to function as building blocks when creating a stand-alone program.

✔ **ActiveX EXE:** Creates a file that has an .EXE file extension. Unlike a stand-alone EXE file, an ActiveX EXE file is designed to work as an OLE server, which is nothing more than a program designed to share information with another program.

✔ **ActiveX Control:** Creates a file that has an .OCX file extension. Unlike an ActiveX DLL or ActiveX EXE file, an ActiveX Control file usually provides both subprograms and a user interface that you can reuse in other programs.

✔ **ActiveX Document DLL:** Creates a file that has a .DLL file extension. An ActiveX Document DLL file is designed to help you run programs on a Web site.

✔ **ActiveX Document EXE:** Creates a file that has an .EXE file extension. An ActiveX Document EXE file can display a Visual Basic form within an Internet Web browser.

✔ **AddIn:** Enables you to create an addin program specially designed to work with the Visual Basic user interface.

✔ **VB Application Wizard:** Helps you create a skeleton Visual Basic stand-alone EXE program quickly and easily.

✔ **Data Project:** Creates a program for devising a database report, which lets you see your database information in a pretty and organized way.

✔ **DHTML Application:** New to Visual Basic 6, this program creates a DHTML (Dynamic HyperText Markup Language) document suitable for posting on a Web site.

✔ **IIS Application:** Creates a file for use with Microsoft Internet Information Server — another new Visual Basic 6 feature.

To choose one of these options from the New Project dialog box, just click on the option you want and click on OK.

If you choose File⇨New Project (or press Ctrl+N), Visual Basic displays a New Project dialog box that does not contain the Existing or Recent tabs.

Creating ActiveX, DHTML, IIS, and Data Project files is fairly advanced, so don't worry about such files until you figure out how to create a simple (Standard EXE) Visual Basic program first.

Loading an existing program

Most of the time you are going to want to load an existing program so you can modify it. To load an existing program, click on the Existing tab. Visual Basic displays folders so you can choose the specific Visual Basic program you want to load.

If you want to load a program that you've loaded in the past, click on the Recent tab. Visual Basic politely displays a list of all the programs you recently loaded. Just click on the Visual Basic program you want to edit and then click on Open.

If you choose File➪Open Project (or press Ctrl+O), Visual Basic displays an Open Project dialog box that does not contain the New tab.

If you click on the File menu, Visual Basic kindly displays a list of programs that you last edited. By clicking on one of these program names, you can load the program without going through the Open Project dialog box.

Welcome to the Visual Basic User Interface

After you decide to start a new Visual Basic program or edit an existing one, the Visual Basic user interface appears in its full glory. Of course, before you can draw your program's user interface and write BASIC code, you have to know how to use the user interface of Visual Basic itself. The eight main parts of the Visual Basic user interface appear in Figure 2-2, although all parts don't necessarily have to be visible at any given time.

- ✔ **Pull-down menus:** Provide access to every available Visual Basic command, although these menus can be confusing and intimidating to use.

- ✔ **Toolbar:** Displays icons that represent the most commonly used Visual Basic commands — which may still be confusing and intimidating to use.

- ✔ **Toolbox:** Displays the types of objects (such as a command button or check box) that you can draw on a form. The Toolbox may not list all possible objects you can draw on a form. To get a complete list of objects you can display in your Toolbox, press Ctrl+T.

- ✔ **Project explorer:** Lists all the files that make up a single Visual Basic program.

- ✔ **Properties window:** Displays the properties of the currently selected form or object.

- ✔ **Form layout window:** Enables you to arrange the location where your forms appear on the screen.

- ✔ **Form:** Provides a window where you can draw objects to design your program's user interface.

- ✔ **Immediate window:** Enables you to debug your Visual Basic program.

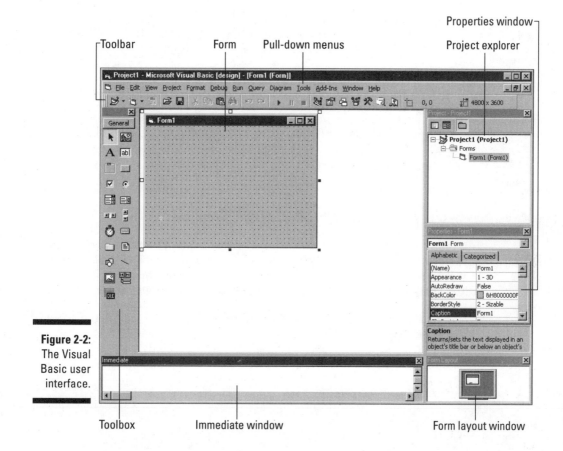

Toolbar   Form   Pull-down menus

Properties window

Project explorer

Figure 2-2:
The Visual
Basic user
interface.

Toolbox   Immediate window   Form layout window

When you're designing your user interface, you use the Toolbox to draw objects on a Form. After you draw your objects, the next step is to customize the appearance of each object by using the Properties window. Finally, after you're happy with the way your program's user interface looks, you can define the location of the interface on the screen by using the Form layout window.

To see more of the Visual Basic user interface, change your screen resolution by following these steps:

1. **Click on the Start button on the Windows 95/98/NT taskbar.**

2. **Choose Settings⇨Control Panel.**

   A Control Panel window appears.

3. **Double-click on the Display icon.**

   A Display Properties window appears.

As an alternative to Steps 1 through 3, just point the mouse cursor anywhere on your Windows 95/98/NT desktop, click the right mouse button, and click on Properties.

4. **Click on the Settings tab.**

5. **Click on the <u>D</u>esktop area horizontal scroll bar and drag the slider toward the right.**

   The screen resolution (such as 800 x 600 pixels) appears underneath the horizontal scroll bar.

6. **Click on OK.**

Closing and opening windows

If the Visual Basic user interface seems cluttered, don't be afraid to modify it. Because most parts of the Visual Basic user interface consist of windows, you may want to close them to give yourself more screen space. Then, when you need to use the interface windows again, just open them back up again.

To close a window in the Visual Basic user interface, click on the Close box of the window you want to close.

To open a window and make it appear in the Visual Basic user interface, choose View and then click on the window you want to open, such as the Code or Properties window.

Resizing and moving your windows

Rather than close a window and make it disappear completely, you may prefer to resize or rearrange the window instead.

To resize a window, move the cursor over the edge of the window until the cursor turns into a double-headed arrow. Next, hold down the left mouse button, drag the mouse, and release the left mouse button when the window is the shape you want the window to be, as shown in Figure 2-3.

To move a window, move the cursor over the title bar of a window, hold down the left mouse button. Drag the mouse and then release the left mouse button when the window is in the desired location.

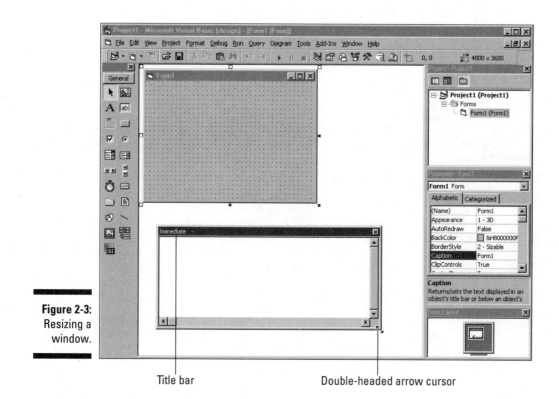

Title bar   Double-headed arrow cursor

Docking your windows

With so many windows cluttering up the screen, you can see how easily the
windows overlap one another and just get in the way. To help solve this
problem, Visual Basic offers a docking feature.

Docking simply means that Visual Basic neatly stacks your windows to one
side of the screen. To dock (or undock) a window, follow these steps:

1. **Move the mouse cursor over the title bar of the window you want to
   dock (or undock).**

2. **Double-click the left mouse button.**

   Visual Basic automatically docks (or undocks) your chosen window.

In case you don't want Visual Basic to dock (or undock) your windows at all,
you can turn off the docking feature. To turn the docking feature on or off for
a particular window, follow these steps:

1. **Choose Tools⇨Options.**

   An Options dialog box appears, as shown in Figure 2-4.

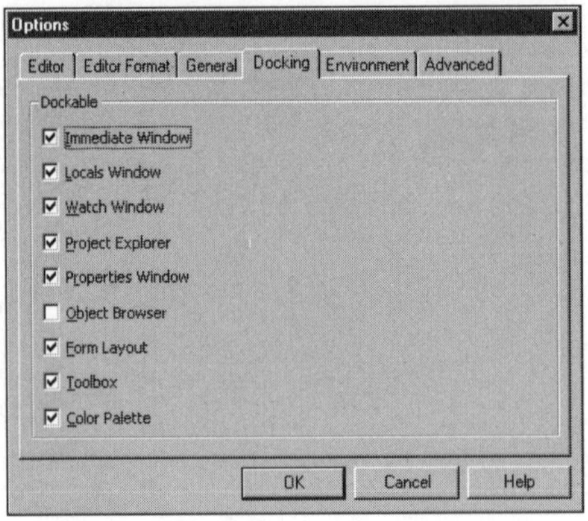

Options

Editor | Editor Format | General | Docking | Environment | Advanced

Dockable

☑ Immediate Window

☑ Locals Window

☑ Watch Window

☑ Project Explorer

☑ Properties Window

☐ Object Browser

☑ Form Layout

☑ Toolbox

☑ Color Palette

OK   Cancel   Help

Figure 2-4:
The Options
dialog box.

2. **Click on the Docking tab.**

3. **Click on a check box to place a check mark in or remove a check mark from that check box.**

   A check mark means that the docking feature is turned on for that particular window. An empty check mark means that the docking feature is (surprise!) turned off.

4. **Click on OK.**

Quitting Visual Basic

No matter how much you may love using Visual Basic, eventually you need to turn off the computer and go to sleep (or at least pass out on the keyboard for an hour or two). To exit Visual Basic, use one of these three methods:

✔ Choose File⇨Exit.

✔ Press Alt+Q.

✔ Click on the Close box of the Visual Basic user interface window.

If you haven't saved the currently displayed Visual Basic program, Visual Basic displays a dialog box, giving you one last chance to save your work before the material is gone for good. Just click on Yes to save your work (or No to lose any changes you have made since the last time you saved the file).

As long as your computer hasn't crashed, Visual Basic smoothly exits and dumps you back to the Windows 95/98/NT desktop.

Chapter 3

Designing Your First User Interface

· ·

In This Chapter

▶ Understanding the common parts of a user interface

▶ Drawing a user interface

▶ Changing the properties of your user interface

· ·

As I discuss in Chapter 1, you must go through a number of steps in order to create a Visual Basic program from start to finish. While the earliest of these steps deal with designing and creating the user interface, this chapter focuses on the fundamental steps in writing a Visual Basic program:

    ✔ Drawing the user interface

    ✔ Defining the user interface properties

    ✔ Writing BASIC code

So before you can write your first program in Visual Basic, you need to know how you can create a user interface.

Common Parts of a User Interface

Despite the different varieties of user interfaces available, most graphical user interfaces share similar features such as displaying text or pictures in a *window*. A window can fill the entire screen or just part of it. Two or more windows can appear on the screen at the same time, either overlapping like cards or side by side like tiles. For some odd reason, Visual Basic calls a window a *form*.

When you first create a form, it's entirely blank. To make your form useful, you have to draw *objects* on the form. An object can be a command button, a text box, a picture, or an option button. The user communicates with your program by clicking, typing, or manipulating the objects displayed on a form.

A short history of user interfaces

In the old days of computers (back in the '50s), using a computer meant opening up the computer and rearranging some wires. Not only did you have to know how to program a computer to use it, but you also had to know how to connect the computer's wires together without electrocuting yourself in the process.

To use a computer in the '60s, you had to type commands to punch holes in cards and then feed the stack of punch cards into the computer. Because typing commands perfectly on cards wasn't something that most people considered exciting, using a computer was slow, tedious, and boring.

In the '70s, scientists connected a TV set to the computer and called the whole thing a computer terminal. For the first time, you could type a command directly into the computer and the computer could respond right away. This was the first attempt at creating a user interface that people could actually use and understand.

Of course, these first crude user interfaces consisted of nothing more than a blank screen and a blinking dot, called a cursor. To get the computer to do anything, you had to type the proper commands. Unfortunately, if you didn't know the right commands to type, the computer would refuse to work and make you feel stupid. Once again, using a computer became slow, tedious, and boring.

In a desperate attempt to make computers simpler to use, computer programmers soon invented something called a *graphical user interface* or *GUI* (pronounced "gooey"). Basically, a GUI displays menus and icons that the user can choose by clicking on commands with the mouse.

Apple Computer created the first commercial GUI when it introduced the Macintosh, but Microsoft quickly created its own GUI (dubbed Microsoft Windows). Unfortunately, GUIs can still make a computer slow, tedious, and boring to use, so when this happens, blame the computer industry. This won't solve any problems, but at least you can make yourself feel better emotionally for a minute or two.

By themselves, objects do absolutely nothing but look nice. To make them functional, you have to write BASIC code (which you can read about in Chapter 4).

Drawing objects with Visual Basic

To draw objects on a form, you need to use the Toolbox, which normally appears on the left side of the screen (unless you move it somewhere else). The Toolbox contains little drawings that represent the various objects you can draw on a form, as shown in Figure 3-1.

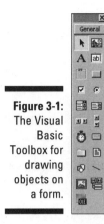

Figure 3-1:
The Visual
Basic
Toolbox for
drawing
objects on
a form.

To draw any object on a form, you always have to follow these steps:

1. **Click on the object in the Toolbox to tell Visual Basic what you want to draw on a form.**

2. **Move the mouse pointer onto the form where you want to draw the object.**

3. **Hold down the left mouse button and drag the mouse to draw your chosen object on the form.**

As a fast way to draw an object on a form, just double-click on an icon in the Toolbox and Visual Basic draws your chosen object in the center of the form automatically.

The two ways to create a user interface

When you want to create a user interface with Visual Basic, you can either:

✔ Use the VB Application Wizard to create a user interface for you automatically

✔ Create your own user interface from scratch

So which way is better? If you need to create a Windows 95/98/NT program that offers standard File, Edit, Window, and Help pull-down menus, let Visual Basic create your user interface for you automatically.

However, if you're just creating a simple program that doesn't need pull-down menus, creating your own user interface all by yourself is going to be easier.

Whichever way you decide to create a user interface, you can always add, delete, or modify your user interface at a later date.

Designing your user interface is a lot like doodling. Although Part II of this book explains more about using specific objects and how they work, for now just remember two things: All programs need a user interface, and Visual Basic uses forms and objects to help you create a user interface quickly and easily.

Drawing your first user interface from scratch

In case you don't feel like going through the following 14 steps, the enclosed CD-ROM has the HELLO1.VBP file stored in the Chapter 3 directory for you to examine and study.

To get acquainted with Visual Basic right away, the following are some steps you can use to create a real-life user interface from scratch:

1. **In Windows 95/98/NT, start Microsoft Visual Basic if you haven't done so already. If Visual Basic is running already, then choose File⇨New Project.**

   Visual Basic displays a New Project dialog box, asking you what type of program you want to create.

2. **Click on the Standard EXE icon and click on Open.**

   Visual Basic displays a blank form titled Form1. (If you want Visual Basic to create a user interface for you automatically, click on the VB Application Wizard icon at this step, but don't click on the icon now. The end of this chapter explains how to use the VB Application Wizard.)

3. **Move the mouse cursor over the bottom right corner of the form (directly over the small rectangle, called a *handle,* that appears in the center of the right edge) so the mouse cursor turns into a left and right pointing arrow. Hold down the left mouse button and drag the mouse to make the form larger.**

4. **Choose View⇨Toolbox to make the Toolbox appear on the left side of the screen.**

   (Skip this step if the Toolbox is visible already.)

5. **Click on the Command button icon in the Visual Basic Toolbox, as shown in Figure 3-2.**

Command button icon

Text box icon   Option button icon

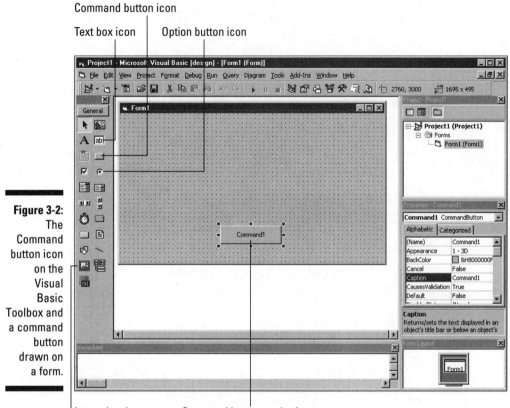

Figure 3-2:
The
Command
button icon
on the
Visual
Basic
Toolbox and
a command
button
drawn on
a form.

Image box icon   Command button on the form

6. **Move the mouse over the form, then drag the mouse to draw a command button such as the one shown in Figure 3-2.**

7. **Click on the Option button icon in the Toolbox and draw an option button.**

   Repeat this process two more times to draw three option buttons, as shown in Figure 3-3.

8. **Click on the Image box icon and draw an image box.**

   Repeat this process two more times to draw three image boxes, as shown in Figure 3-4.

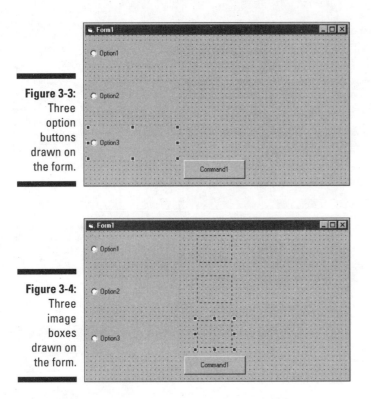

Figure 3-3:
Three
option
buttons
drawn on
the form.

Figure 3-4:
Three
image
boxes
drawn on
the form.

9. Click on the Text box icon and draw a text box.

Repeat this process two more times to draw three text boxes, as shown in Figure 3-5.

Figure 3-5:
Three text
boxes
drawn on
the form.

10. **Choose File⇨Save Form1 or press Ctrl+S.**

    A Save File As dialog box appears, asking what you want to name the file. (You may want to click on the Save In list box to choose a specific folder to save your Visual Basic project and forms.)

11. **Type HELLO and select Save.**

    This action saves your form in a file called HELLO.FRM.

12. **Choose File⇨Save Project.**

    A Save Project As dialog box appears, asking what you want to name your project.

13. **Type HELLO and click on Save.**

    This action saves your entire Visual Basic project in a file called HELLO.VBP.

14. **Choose File⇨Exit (or press Alt+Q) if you want to exit from Visual Basic.**

Congratulations! You've just created a generic Visual Basic user interface. If your user interface looks a little less than impressive, this is because you haven't customized the user interface for your program.

To customize a Visual Basic user interface, you have to define the properties for each object on your forms.

Defining the Properties of Your User Interface

Drawing your user interface creates the initial appearance of your Visual Basic program. To finish defining your program's user interface, you next have to define the properties for each object on your user interface.

But do you really need to define these properties? Yes and no. Visual Basic automatically sets default property values for all the objects on your user interface. However, these default values make your program look pretty ugly. So if you want to make your user interface more attractive, you must define the properties for your objects.

While each object typically has 10 to 30 different properties that you can change, you don't have to modify every single property. Most of the time, you just need to modify two or three properties of each object.

What properties do

Before you change the properties of any object, you may want to know what the heck properties do in the first place. Essentially, *properties* define the characteristics of an object such as its name, size, shape, and color on the screen.

The name of an object is for your convenience only. Visual Basic automatically gives all objects boring names like Text1 or Command3. However, when you need to refer to specific objects, it's much easier if you have descriptive names for each object used by your program.

An object's size, location, and color define its appearance on the screen. The whole purpose of an object's appearance is to make your user interface look pretty.

Changing property settings

You can change the property settings of an object at two separate times:

- ✔ During design time
- ✔ During run time

Design time is when you're drawing your user interface but before you actually run your program.

Most of the time, you want to change an object's property settings at design time. The most important property to change at design time is the name of the object.

Run time is when your program uses BASIC code to change an object's properties while your program is actually running. Of course, before your program can change an object's properties, you have to write BASIC code that tells your program exactly which object's properties you want to change.

Changing a property during run time enables you to create animation or display messages on the screen, such as error messages, program status messages, or warning messages alerting the user that the computer is going to blow up in ten seconds.

Changing property settings at design time

Several properties are assigned to every object, as shown in Figure 3-6. To change the property of an object, make sure you have a form displayed within Visual Basic and then follow these steps:

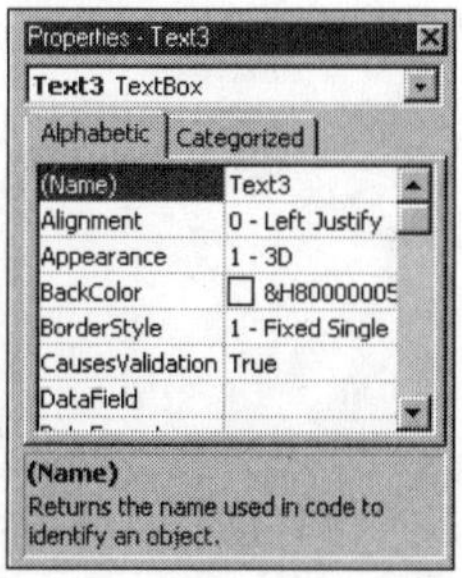

Figure 3-6:
The
Properties
window
showing
multiple
properties
for the
Text3 text
box.

Properties - Text3	☒
Text3 TextBox	▾

Alphabetic | Categorized |

(Name)	Text3	▲
Alignment	0 - Left Justify	
Appearance	1 - 3D	
BackColor	☐ &H80000005	
BorderStyle	1 - Fixed Single	
CausesValidation	True	
DataField		▼

(Name)
Returns the name used in code to
identify an object.

1. **Click on the object whose properties you want to change.**

2. **In the Properties window, click on the property that you want to change.**

   If the Properties window is not visible, press F4 to make the window appear.

3. **Type or choose a new setting for the property.**

Simple, don't you think? When you need to change multiple properties for one or more objects, this book displays a table similar to the following:

Object	*Property*	*Setting*
Form	Name	frmHello
	Caption	Hello, world!

The following steps detail what this table is telling you to do:

1. **Click on the Form object.**

2. **Click on the Name property in the Properties window.**

3. **Type** frmHello **to change the value of the Name property.**

4. **Click on the Caption property in the Properties window.**

5. **Type** Hello, world! **to change the value of the Caption property.**

Defining the properties of your first user interface

In case you don't feel like following the next 17 steps, the enclosed CD-ROM has the HELLO2.VBP file stored in the Chapter 3 directory for you to examine and study.

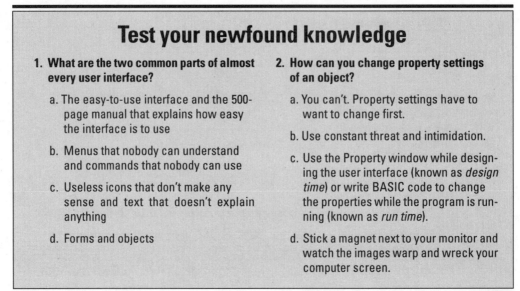

To define the properties of your user interface, follow these steps:

1. **In Windows 95/98/NT, start Microsoft Visual Basic.**

   Visual Basic displays the New Project dialog box. If Visual Basic is already running, choose File➪Open Project.

2. **Click on the Recent tab.**

3. **Click on the HELLO file (which is the HELLO.VBP file) and click on Open.**

   Visual Basic loads your HELLO.FRM form on the screen.

4. **Click on Option1 to highlight the option button, which causes little rectangles to appear around the edges of the option button.**

5. **Click on the Properties window, click on the Name property and type** optGrin. **Click on the Caption property and type** I'm happy!

6. **Click on the Image1 image box. (This appears near the top of the form.)**

7. **Click on the Properties window, click on the Name property and type** imgGrin.

8. **Click on the Properties window and click on the three dots (...) in the Picture property.**

   Visual Basic displays a Load Picture dialog box.

9. **Open the Icons folder. (You may have to dig through the Graphics folder in your Visual Basic folder to find the Icons folder.) Next, open the Misc folder within the Icons folder.**

   Visual Basic displays a Load Picture dialog box as shown in Figure 3-7.

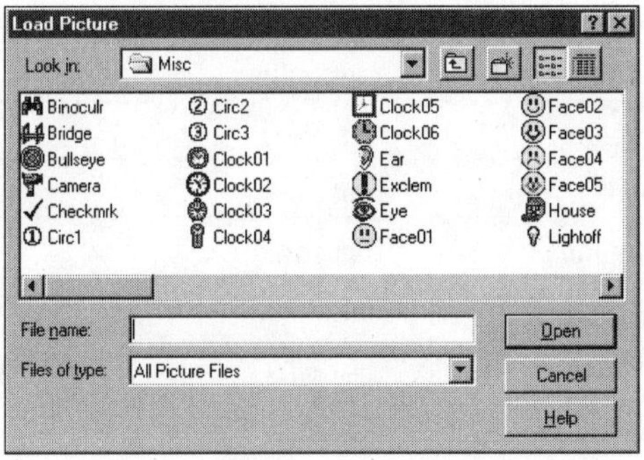

Figure 3-7:
The Load
Picture
dialog box.

10. **Double-click on the FACE03 icon.**

    Visual Basic displays a really happy face in the image box.

11. **Click on the Visible property and then click on the downward-pointing arrow and choose False.**

12. **Click on the Text1 text box.**

13. **Click on the Border Style property and then click on the downward-pointing arrow and choose 0-None.**

14. **Click on the Name property and type** txtGrin.

15. **Double-click on the Text property and then press Backspace to clear the Text property so no text appears.**

16. **Finish changing the properties for the rest of the objects according to Table 3-1.**

17. **Choose File⇨Save Project to save all your changes.**

Congratulations! You just defined all the necessary properties for your first user interface.

Table 3-1	Properties to Change to Finish Designing Your User Interface	
Object	*Property*	*Setting*
Form	Name	frmHello
	Caption	Hello, world!
Option2	Name	optSmile
	Caption	I'm okay.
Option3	Name	optFrown
	Caption	I'm sad.
Image2	Name	imgSmile
	Picture	FACE02
	Visible	False
Image3	Name	imgFrown
	Picture	FACE01
	Visible	False
Text2	Name	txtSmile
	Border Style	0-None
	Text	(Empty)
Text3	Name	txtFrown
	Border Style	0-None
	Text	(Empty)
Command1	Name	cmdExit
	Caption	Exit

Letting Visual Basic Create a User Interface Automatically

If you actually went through the steps to create a user interface from scratch, you can see how tedious and time-consuming this process can be. Because computers are supposed to save you time (so you have more time to play computer games), Visual Basic offers a VB Application Wizard.

The VB Application Wizard creates a skeleton program complete with pull-down menus, toolbars, and dialog boxes. If you want to create a program that requires a user interface similar to Microsoft Word, Excel, or PowerPoint, you can save time by letting the VB Application Wizard make your user interface instead.

To see how the VB Application Wizard works, follow these steps:

1. **In Windows 95/98/NT, start Microsoft Visual Basic. (If you already have Visual Basic running, choose File⇨New Project.)**

   Visual Basic displays the New Project dialog box.

2. **Double-click on the VB Application Wizard icon.**

   The Introduction window of the Application Wizard appears, as shown in Figure 3-8. This window asks for a profile to use. *Profiles* are skeleton settings so you can customize the VB Application Wizard. For now, just keep the profile option as (None).

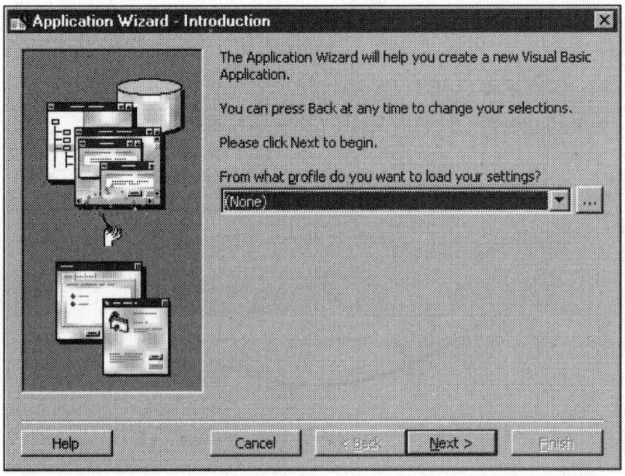

Figure 3-8: The Application Wizard– Introduction window.

3. **Click on Next>.**

   The Application Wizard – Interface Type window appears, as shown in Figure 3-9.

4. **Click on the Multiple Document Interface (MDI) option button and click on Next>.**

   The Application Wizard – Menus window appears, as shown in Figure 3-10. (If you want, click on a different option button for Step 4 to see what a Single Document Interface [SDI] and Explorer Style user interface look like.)

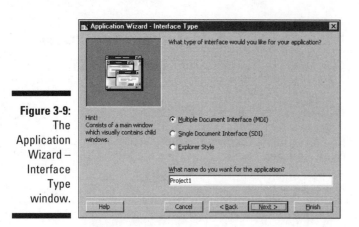

Figure 3-9:
The
Application
Wizard –
Interface
Type
window.

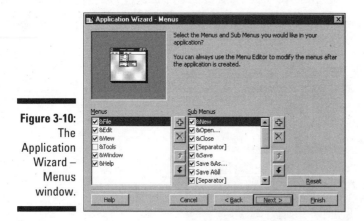

Figure 3-10:
The
Application
Wizard –
Menus
window.

5. **Click on Next> to accept the default selection.**

The Application Wizard – Customize Toolbar window appears, as shown in Figure 3-11. By dragging and dropping icons, you can create your own toolbars.

6. **Click on Next> to accept the default selection.**

The Application Wizard – Resources window appears, as shown in Figure 3-12.

Resource files can help you develop foreign language versions of your program. Rather than force you to retype your program's text (such as menus and dialog box captions) in different languages, a resource file stores the information in a separate file so you can just use a different resource file for each foreign language.

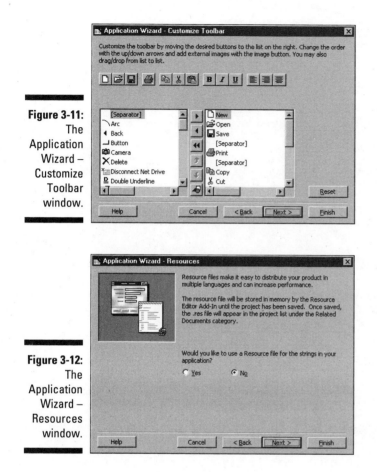

Figure 3-11:
The
Application
Wizard –
Customize
Toolbar
window.

Figure 3-12:
The
Application
Wizard –
Resources
window.

7. Click on Next> to accept the default selection.

The Application Wizard – Internet Connectivity window appears, as shown in Figure 3-13. This is where you can specify whether you want your program to be able to access the Internet.

8. Click on Next> to accept the default selection.

The Application Wizard – Standard Forms window appears, as shown in Figure 3-14.

9. Click on the About Box check box and then click on Next>.

The Application Wizard – Data Access Forms window appears, as shown in Figure 3-15. This is where you can specify what type of database files you want your program to use.

Figure 3-13:
The
Application
Wizard –
Internet
Connectivity
window.

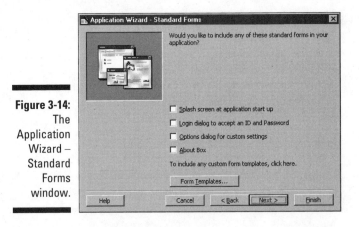

Figure 3-14:
The
Application
Wizard –
Standard
Forms
window.

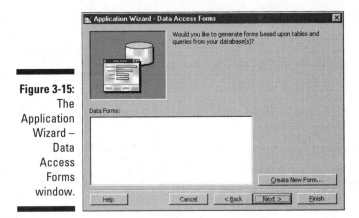

Figure 3-15:
The
Application
Wizard –
Data
Access
Forms
window.

10. Click on Next> to accept the default selection.

The Application Wizard – Finished! window appears, as shown in Figure 3-16.

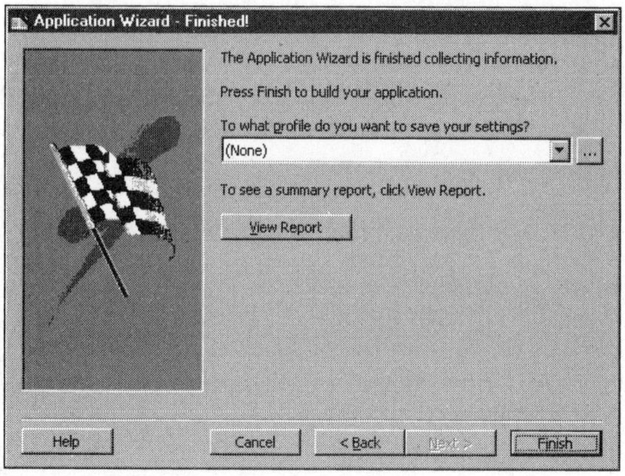

Figure 3-16:
The
Application
Wizard –
Finished!
window.

11. Click on the Finish button.

Visual Basic displays an Application Created dialog box.

12. Click on OK.

13. Press F5 to run the skeleton program that the VB Application Wizard created for you.

The program appears, as shown in Figure 3-17.

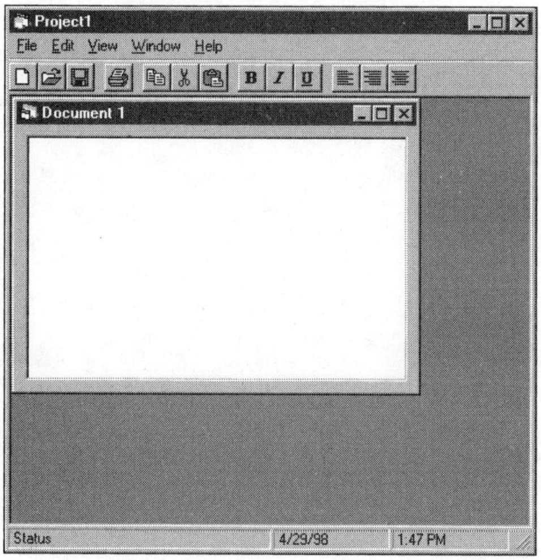

Figure 3-17:
The
skeleton
program
created
by the
Application
Wizard.

14. **Choose Help⇨About.**

    An About Project1 dialog box appears.

15. **Click on OK.**

16. **Click on any icon on the toolbar or on any of the pull-down menus to see what happens.**

17. **Choose File⇨Exit when you're done playing around with this skeleton program.**

18. **Choose File⇨New Project.**

    A dialog box appears, asking if you want to save your newly created user interface.

19. **Click on No.**

As you can see, the VB Application Wizard can quickly create a user interface that includes pull-down menus and a toolbar. However, you still need to customize the user interface and write BASIC code to make the program do anything worthwhile. The VB Application Wizard simply gives you a head start in creating your user interface.

Chapter 4

Writing BASIC Code

*T*o have your computer do anything, you have to give it step-by-step instructions. If you skip a step or give unclear instructions, your computer doesn't know what to do. (Actually, the computer knows what to do — it just doesn't do what you want it to.)

✔ Programmers call a single instruction a *command*. A typical BASIC command looks like the following:

```
Taxes = Income * FlatTaxRate
```

✔ You call a series of commands *code*. A typical series of commands looks like this:

```
Income = 90000
FlatTaxRate = .95
Taxes = Income * FlatTaxRate
```

✔ A collection of code that makes your computer do something useful (such as play a game, calculate your taxes, or display flying toasters on your screen) is called a *program*.

If you want to speak the language of programmers (even though programmers are notorious for never saying much of anything), you have to know programming etiquette.

You never write a program; you write code. Heaven forbid if you say, "Let me look at your series of commands." Cool programmers are likely to blush at your faux pas. Instead, you ought to say, "Let me look at your code."

What Is BASIC Code?

To get your computer to do anything, you have to give the machine instructions that it can understand. Because you're using Visual Basic, you have to use the BASIC programming language.

Like all computer languages, BASIC has special commands called *reserved keywords*. Some examples of reserved keywords are as follows:

Loop	Function	Sub	End
Do	Integer	Case	If
Else	Select	Then	For

BASIC code consists of nothing more than BASIC reserved keywords creatively strung together to form a program. Whenever the computer sees a reserved keyword, the computer automatically thinks, "Oh, this is a special instruction that I already know how to obey."

A program can be as short as a single reserved keyword or as long as several million reserved keywords. Short programs generally don't do anything more interesting than display something such as `Hello, world!` on the screen. Long programs usually do much more, but these programs are often as confusing to read as an IRS tax form.

Theoretically, you can write one long program consisting of a million or more reserved keywords. However, any programmer attempting to do so is likely to go insane long before completing the task.

Writing a program one step at a time

To make programming easier, most programmers divide a large program into several smaller ones. After you finish writing each of the smaller programs, you paste the pieces together to make a complete program.

- When you divide a large program into several smaller ones, these smaller programs are *subprograms.* In Visual Basic lingo, subprograms are *event procedures* (although some programmers may call them *subroutines*). Visual Basic also has special subprograms called *functions,* which you can read about in Chapter 29, and *general procedures,* which you can read about in Chapter 27.

- Procedures tell each object on your form how to react to something that the user does. Each object can have zero or more procedures that tell the object how to respond to the user.

One event procedure may tell the computer what to do if the user clicks on an object (such as a command button) with the mouse. Another event procedure may tell the computer what to do if the user presses a certain key while the object is highlighted.

Not every object needs event procedures. The only objects that need event procedures are those that the user can click on or choose in some way, such as command buttons, check boxes, or radio buttons.

Choosing objects and events

Before you can write an event procedure for an object, you have to tell Visual Basic

✔ The name of the object to use
✔ The event you want the object to respond to

Visual Basic gives you two ways to choose an object:

✔ The simplest way is to click on an object (such as a command button) on your form and press F7 (or just double-click on the object in the first place) to switch to the Code window. Visual Basic then kindly displays the most likely procedure that you need for that object.

✔ The second way is almost as easy. Each time you draw an object on a form, Visual Basic stores the name of that object in a list called the *Object list,* as shown in Figure 4-1. The Object list appears at the top of the Code window. To open this list, press F7. Next, scroll through the Object list until you find the object for which you want to write a procedure.

To choose an event to use, click on the Procedure list, which also appears at the top of the Code window next to the Object list. The Procedure list contains all possible events that you can write a procedure to respond to.

Just scroll through this list until you find the event for which you need to write a procedure. The most common event to use is the Click event.

After you choose an object from the Object list and an event from the Procedure list, Visual Basic displays the first and last lines of the procedure. You're now ready to start writing code for this procedure.

Object list box   Procedure list box

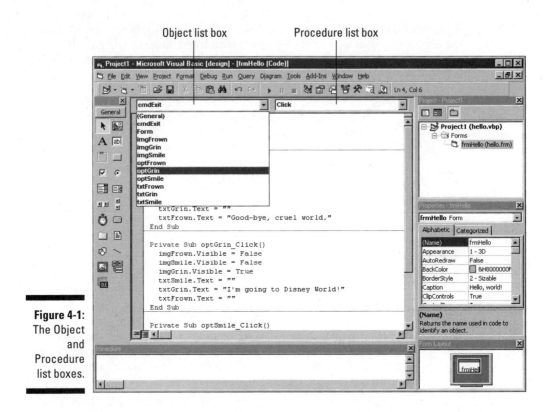

Figure 4-1:
The Object
and
Procedure
list boxes.

Writing Visual Basic Event Procedures

Before you can write a Visual Basic event procedure for an object, you have to draw the object on a form first.

Next, you have to change the properties of each object to give them unique names you can remember. If you don't do this, you're stuck with the generic names that Visual Basic provides by default for everything, such as Option1 or Text3.

Do you know what happens if you write an event procedure for a particular object and then later change that object's name? Visual Basic gets confused and thinks that you've created a brand-new object, which means that the renamed object won't have any event procedures attached to it. So if you're going to rename an object, do this renaming before you write any event procedures for that object.

To write a Visual Basic event procedure, click on the object that you want to write an event procedure for and then open the Code window. (To open the Code window, press F7, choose View➪Code, or double-click on the object.) After the Code window appears, you can start typing your procedure or code. Figure 4-2 shows the Code window.

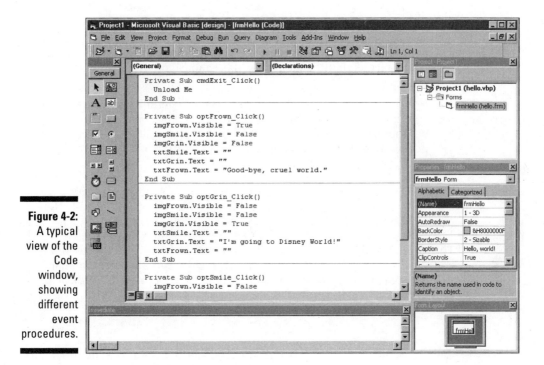

Figure 4-2:
A typical
view of the
Code
window,
showing
different
event
procedures.

But wait! Visual Basic doesn't just display a blank window. Visual Basic automatically types `Private Sub`, which is followed by the object's name, an underscore, an event (such as `Click`), and a set of parentheses `()` that may be empty or that may contain stuff inside of it. (You can find out more about the stuff inside of parentheses in Chapter 28.)

If you click on an object named cmdExit and then open the Code window, Visual Basic displays the following:

```
Private Sub cmdExit_Click()
End Sub
```

✔ The first line of this Visual Basic procedure begins with Private Sub, which is short for a subprogram that belongs exclusively to a specific object. In this case, the subprogram belongs to the object named cmdExit.

✔ Next, Visual Basic types your object's name. If you forgot to change the name property of your object, Visual Basic uses a default name such as Text2. Otherwise, Visual Basic displays your object's name (for example, cmdExit).

✔ Following your object's name is an underscore, which separates your object's name from its event. An *event* is something the user does to communicate with the computer. In this example, the event is Click, which means that the user clicked the mouse on the object named cmdExit.

✔ Next comes an empty set of parentheses. Sometimes, the parentheses contain data that the subprogram uses from the routine that called this subroutine. An empty pair of parentheses says that this subprogram does not need any special data passed to it from another part of your program.

Translating this procedure into English, the first line means, "This is a subprogram for the object named cmdExit, and the subprogram tells the computer what to do if the user clicks on the cmdExit object."

The last line of this Visual Basic event procedure consists of two words: End and Sub. This line tells the computer, "This is the end of all the commands that belong in this subprogram." Rather than type all that, Visual Basic uses the simpler

```
End Sub
```

Right now, this Visual Basic procedure does nothing. To make the procedure do something, you have to add commands between the first line and the last line. Before you start adding commands, you need to know what BASIC commands (also known as *code*) can do.

Test your newfound knowledge

1. What are reserved keywords?

a. Words you say when you have a reservation in a fancy restaurant where water costs $25 a glass.

b. What shy people want to say.

c. Special instructions that every programming language has.

d. Words that you want to say to the face of someone you don't like.

2. How can you write a large program without losing your mind?

a. Divide the program into subprograms, otherwise known in Visual Basic as procedures (such as event or general procedures).

b. Watch others write the program and then steal their homework.

c. You mean I actually have to write a program?

d. If you're thinking of writing a large program, you've probably already lost your mind.

What can BASIC code do?

BASIC code is generally used to do the following:

- Calculate a result
- Modify the properties (appearance) of another object

If you want to calculate the number of people who live in wooden cabins, subscribe to *Soldier of Fortune,* and own cats, Visual Basic can calculate this as long as you provide all the necessary data.

After you calculate a result, you probably want to show the result on the screen. To do so, you have to modify the properties of an object on your user interface. For example, if you want to display a message on the screen, you first need to draw a text box object on a Visual Basic form.

You then have to name this text box with something such as txtMessage. Finally, to display anything in this text box, you have to modify the Text property of the txtMessage text box, such as:

```
txtMessage.Text = "This is hard to explain."
```

This command displays the message This is hard to explain. in the txtMessage text box on the screen, as shown in Figure 4-3.

Of course, Visual Basic code can't change all the properties of an object. You can only change some properties (such as the object's name) during design time by using that object's property window.

How a Visual Basic event procedure works

In Visual Basic, the instructions in an event procedure run only when a specific event occurs, such as when the user clicks on an object. The same set of instructions can run over and over again each time the user clicks on an object. The only time a Visual Basic program ends is when an object's procedures specifically tell the program to end.

As an example, look at the simplest Visual Basic procedure that is necessary for every program to stop completely. For a simple "Hello, world!" program, this procedure looks like the following:

```
Private Sub cmdExit_Click()
   Unload Me
End Sub
```

Text box   Text property

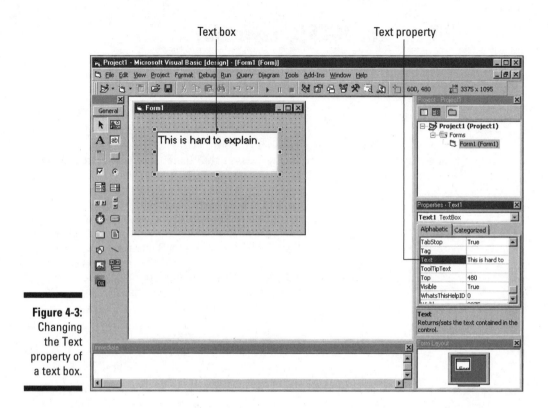

Figure 4-3:
Changing
the Text
property of
a text box.

The code in this procedure contains a Visual Basic reserved keyword called Unload and a variable called Me. The Me variable represents the form, so this procedure tells Visual Basic, "Unload the currently displayed form from memory." Because this program only consists of one form, this command effectively stops the program from running.

This procedure runs only when the user clicks on the cmdExit object. If you look at the cmdExit object on your user interface, you see that the object is a command button labeled Exit.

As an alternative to using the command Unload Me to end a Visual Basic program, you can also use the command End instead, like in the following:

```
Private Sub cmdExit_Click()
    End
End Sub
```

So which method should you use? The End command forces your program to stop running immediately, which can be like stopping your car by crashing it into a wall. For a gentler, kinder approach to stopping your program, Microsoft wholeheartedly recommends that you use the Unload Me command instead.

If you run this program, the following is what happens:

1. Visual Basic displays your user interface on the screen, including a command button named cmdExit. This name does not appear on the user interface. Instead, the command button's Caption property appears, which is the word Exit.

2. Clicking on the Exit button causes Visual Basic to ask, "Hey, what's the name of this object on which the user just clicked?"

3. In a huff, Visual Basic quickly notices that the Exit button's name is cmdExit.

4. Then Visual Basic asks, "Are there any instructions here that tell me what to do if the user clicks on the cmdExit object?" Happily, Visual Basic finds the `Private Sub cmdExit_Click()` procedure.

5. Visual Basic then examines the first instruction of the `cmdExit_Click()` procedure. In this case, the instruction is `Unload Me`, which tells Visual Basic to unload the form. Because this is the only form in the program, this effectively stops the program.

6. Visual Basic stops running the program and removes it from the screen. Naturally, all this happens in the blink of an eye, and your computer looks as though it's responding instantly.

Writing BASIC Code for Your First Visual Basic Program

For those who just like jumping right into the program without typing all the BASIC code, load the HELLO.VBP program from the enclosed CD-ROM in the back of the book.

Because experience is always the best teacher, the following steps show you how to write real-life BASIC code that you can use to impress your friends. You can find out how to write BASIC code for the HELLO.VBP program in Chapter 3.

Don't worry about understanding everything you're typing. The purpose of this exercise is just to show you how simple creating a program in Visual Basic can be.

1. **Start Microsoft Visual Basic if you haven't already done so. (Or choose File ⇨Open Project.)**

   Visual Basic displays a New Project or Open Project dialog box.

2. **Click on the Recent tab, click on HELLO, and click on** <u>O</u>**pen.**

   If the HELLO.FRM form does not appear on the screen, click on the frmHello form in the Project Explorer window and click on the View Object icon. (You can skip this step if you already have the form displayed on the screen from Chapter 3.)

3. **Click on the optGrin option button displayed in the upper-left corner of the form. (This is the button that says "I'm happy!")**

4. **To Open the Code window, press F7 or choose** <u>V</u>**iew**➪<u>C</u>**ode.**

5. **Type in the** `Private Sub optGrin_Click()` **procedure so that it looks like the following:**

```
Private Sub optGrin_Click()
   imgFrown.Visible = False
   imgSmile.Visible = False
   imgGrin.Visible = True
   txtSmile.TEXT = ""
   txtGrin.TEXT = "I'm going to Disney World!"
   txtFrown.TEXT = ""
End Sub
```

6. **Click on the downward-headed arrow in the Object list box at the top of the Code window and then choose the optSmile object.**

   Visual Basic displays an empty `Private Sub optSmile_Click()` procedure.

7. **Type in the** `Private Sub optSmile_Click()` **procedure so that it looks like the following:**

```
Private Sub optSmile_Click()
   imgFrown.Visible = False
   imgSmile.Visible = True
   imgGrin.Visible = False
   txtSmile.TEXT = "Hello, world!"
   txtGrin.TEXT = ""
   txtFrown.TEXT = ""
End Sub
```

8. **Click on the downward-pointing arrow in the Object list box at the top of the Code window and then choose the optFrown object.**

   Visual Basic displays an empty `Private Sub optFrown_Click()` procedure.

9. **Type in the** `Private Sub optFrown_Click()` **procedure so that it looks like the following:**

```
Private Sub optFrown_Click()
   imgFrown.Visible = True
   imgSmile.Visible = False
   imgGrin.Visible = False
   txtSmile.TEXT = ""
   txtGrin.TEXT = ""
   txtFrown.TEXT = "Good-bye, cruel world."
End Sub
```

10. Click on the Object list at the top of the Code window and then choose the cmdExit object.

Visual Basic displays an empty `Private Sub cmdExit_Click()` procedure.

11. Type in the `Private Sub cmdExit_Click()` procedure so that it looks like the following:

```
Private Sub cmdExit_Click()
   Unload Me
End Sub
```

12. Press F5 to run your program or choose Run⇨Start.

If you typed everything correctly, Visual Basic displays your user interface on the screen, as shown in Figure 4-4.

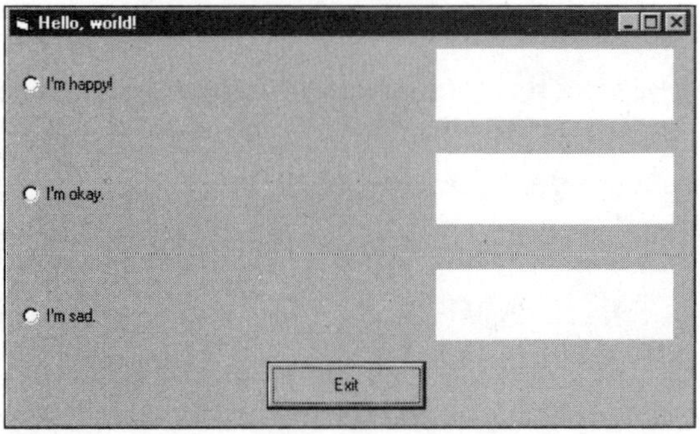

Figure 4-4: The Hello World! program.

13. Click on the option button next to the label "I'm sad."

Visual Basic displays a face on the screen, along with the message `Good-bye, cruel world`, as shown in Figure 4-5.

14. Click on the option button next to the label "I'm okay."

Visual Basic displays a smiley face on the screen, along with the message `Hello, world!`, as shown in Figure 4-6.

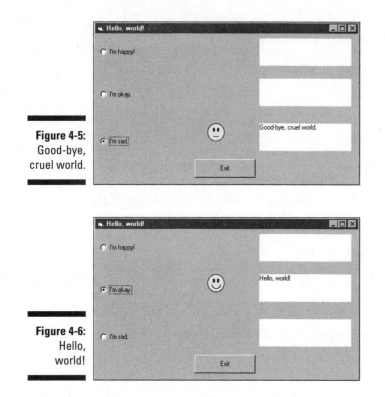

Figure 4-5:
Good-bye,
cruel world.

Figure 4-6:
Hello,
world!

15. Click on the option button next to the label "I'm happy!"

Visual Basic displays a really happy face on the screen, along with the message I'm going to Disney World!, as shown in Figure 4-7.

16. Click on the command button labeled Exit.

Visual Basic quits running your program and returns you to Visual Basic.

You finally completed the Hello, World! example. Now, you can see how you can use Visual Basic to create a friendly user interface quickly and easily.

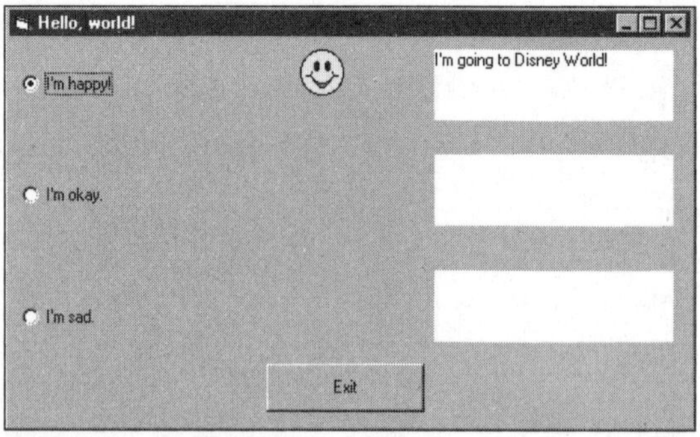

Figure 4-7:
I'm going to
Disney
World!

Part II
Creating User Interfaces

Real Programmers don't like to be bothered when they're working.

In this part . . .

A user interface allows other people to use your program. The clumsier the user interface, the harder your program is to use. So if you make your user interface simple and logical, you can bet that more people will be able to use your program.

This is the fun part of the book. You aren't forced to type any bizarre code, comprehend arcane commands, or memorize ridiculous keystrokes. In this part of the book, you get to doodle on your computer screen while actually finding out how to write your own programs at the same time.

Chapter 5

User Interface Design 101

To make oneself understood to the people, one must first speak to their eyes.
—Napoleon Bonaparte

First of all, nobody really wants to use your program. Most people would rather play at the beach, watch TV, or make out. However, people do want the results that your program can produce. If they could get these same results by other means with less work, they would. But because they can't, they're willing to use your program.

This means that people really want your program to read their minds and then magically do all their work for them automatically. Because that's not possible, the best you can hope for is to make your program as easy to use as possible. If a completely incompetent moron (your boss) can use your program, then most other people are going to be able to use your program as well.

Before You Create Your User Interface

Creating a user interface doesn't mean just slapping together some pretty pictures in a colorful window and hoping that the user can figure out how your program works. Your program's user interface must make your program easy to use. To help you create a user interface, here are some points to keep in mind.

Know your user

Before designing your user interface, ask yourself who is going to use your program. Are your typical users data-entry clerks who understand computers, or managers who understand only paper procedures and are learning to use a computer for the first time?

When you decide who your users are, design your user interface so that it mirrors the way the users already work, regardless of whether the user interface seems totally inefficient or alien to anyone else. Accountants readily accept spreadsheets because the row-and-column format mimics green sheets of ledger paper. Likewise, typists prefer word processors because a word processor mimics a blank sheet of paper.

But imagine if all word processors looked like spreadsheets with rows and columns. Any typist trying to use this kind of word processor would quickly feel lost and confused (although accountants may feel right at home with such a word processor).

The more a programmer understands the user, the more likely the interface is going to be used and accepted. The only person the user interface really has to satisfy is the user.

Orient the user

Not surprisingly, people get lost wandering through today's supermalls, which contain multiple levels and two different time zones. How do you feel when you have no idea where you are and no idea where you can go from your current position?

This feeling of helplessness is the reason why lost kids cry uncontrollably and confused computer users curse under their breath. (This is also the reason why malls install directories with the big red X that says, "You are here.")

A good user interface must orient people so that they know where they are in your program and how to get out if they want. Some user interfaces display a message at the bottom of the screen, such as "Page 2 of 5." In this case, the user knows exactly how many pages are available for viewing and which page currently appears on the screen.

Your user interface is a map to your program. Make sure that your user interface shows just enough information to orient users but not too much to confuse them.

Make the choices obvious

In addition to letting users know where they are in a program, a good user interface must also make all choices obvious to the user. If your user interface displays "Page 4 of 25" at the bottom of the screen, how can the user know what to do to see the next or previous page? One solution may be to show forward- and backward-pointing arrows in each bottom corner of the page. Another solution may be Next Page and Previous Page buttons. Figure 5-1 shows some possible solutions.

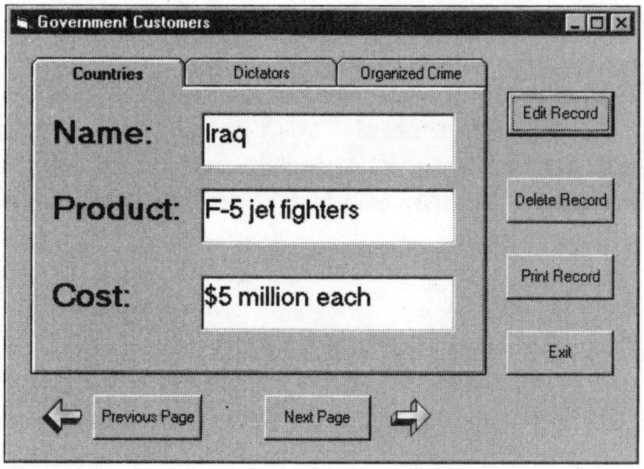

Figure 5-1:
Making the
choices on
a user
interface
obvious.

Government Customers	□ X

Countries	Dictators	Organized Crime	

Name:	Iraq	Edit Record
Product:	F-5 jet fighters	Delete Record
Cost:	$5 million each	Print Record
		Exit

⇐ Previous Page   Next Page ⇒

As long as your program shows the user which options are available next and which keys to press or where to click the mouse, the user feels a sense of control and confidence when using your program.

Be forgiving

The key here is useful feedback. If your program takes an arrogant attitude and displays scolding messages like "File MPR.DLL missing" whenever the user presses the wrong key or clicks the mouse in the wrong area, the user may feel intimidated if your program doesn't explain what the error message means and how he or she can avoid the error in the first place.

So be kind. Have your program hide or dim any buttons or menu commands that are unavailable to the user. If the user does press the wrong key or click the mouse in the wrong area, have your program display a window and explain what the user's options are. Users love a program that guides them, which means you can spend a lot less time answering phone calls for technical support.

Keep it simple

Most programs offer users two or more ways to choose a specific command. You can click on a button, choose a command from menus, or press certain keystroke combinations (Ctrl+F2, for example). Of these three methods, clicking directly on the screen is the easiest procedure to remember and pressing bizarre keystroke combinations is the hardest.

Make sure that commonly used commands can be accessed quickly through a button or a menu. Not all commands must be or need to be accessed through a keystroke combination.

Although keystroke combination commands are faster to use, these commands are harder to learn initially. Make keystroke combinations easy to remember whenever possible. For a Save command, Ctrl+S is easier to remember than something totally abstract like Shift+F12. People can easily remember that S stands for Save, but who has any idea what F12 represents?

Designing Your Visual Basic User Interface

When you write a Visual Basic program, you first have to design the user interface. Essentially, a Visual Basic user interface consists of objects that you place on the screen and arrange in some semblance of organization so that the screen looks pretty.

The common elements of a Visual Basic user interface appear in Figure 5-2 and consist of the following:

- ✔ Forms (also known as windows)
- ✔ Buttons (such as command buttons and radio buttons)
- ✔ Boxes (such as text boxes and check boxes)
- ✔ Labels
- ✔ Pictures (such as icons and graphics)

To design your user interface, follow these steps:

1. **Create a form.**
2. **Choose the object you want to draw from the Toolbox. (See Table 5-1.)**
3. **Draw the object on the form.**

Icons   Label   Form

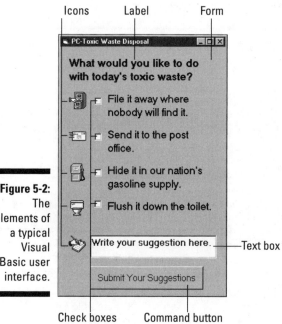

Figure 5-2:
The elements of a typical Visual Basic user interface.

Text box

Check boxes   Command button

Table 5-1	Tools in the Visual Basic Toolbox	
Icon	*Tool Name*	*What This Tool Does*
	Pointer	Selects objects
	Picture box	Draws a box to display graphics
A	Label	Draws a box to display text
abl	Text box	Draws a box that can display text and let the user type in text
xy	Frame	Groups two or more objects together
	Command button	Draws a command button
✓	Check box	Draws a check box
⦿	Option (or radio) button	Draws a radio button
	Combo box	Draws a combo box

(continued)

Table 5-1 *(continued)*

Icon	Tool Name	What This Tool Does
	List box	Draws a list box
	Horizontal scroll bar	Draws a horizontal scroll bar
	Vertical scroll bar	Draws a vertical scroll bar
	Timer	Places a timer on a form
	Drive list box	Draws a drive list box that displays all the disk drives available
	Directory list box	Draws a directory list box that displays a directory on a particular disk drive
	File list box	Draws a file list box that displays files in a specific directory
	Shape	Draws a geometric shape such as a circle or a square
	Line	Draws a line
	Image box	Draws a box to display graphics
	Data control	Draws a control to link a program to a database file
	OLE	Draws a box to insert an OLE object

Drawing an object

To draw any object, follow these steps:

1. **Click on the icon in the Visual Basic Toolbox that represents the object you want to draw (command button, picture box, label, and so on).**

2. **Move the mouse to the place on the form where you want to draw the object.**

   The cursor turns into a crosshair shape.

3. **Click and drag the mouse to where you want to draw your object and then release the mouse button.**

If you want to draw an object on a form in a hurry, double-click on the object's icon in the Toolbox. For example, if you want to draw a command button quickly, just double-click on the command button icon in the Toolbox, and Visual Basic draws the command button for you automatically.

Using the Properties window

After you draw an object on a form, the next step is to define the properties for that object. To define an object's properties, you have to use the Properties window. In case the Properties window doesn't appear on your screen, you can make the window appear by using one of the following three commands:

- ✔ Press F4.
- ✔ Choose View⇨Properties Window.
- ✔ Click on the Properties Window icon in the toolbar.

The Properties window can display properties in two ways, as shown in Figure 5-3:

- ✔ **Alphabetical:** Lists an object's properties alphabetically from A to Z.
- ✔ **Categorized:** Organizes properties into categories, such as properties that affect an object's appearance, behavior, or position on the screen.

After you open the Properties window, follow these steps to view the properties of any object in your Visual Basic program:

1. **Choose one of these methods to open the Project Explorer window:**

   Press Ctrl+R.

   Choose View⇨Project Explorer.

   Click on the Project Explorer icon in the toolbar.

2. **Click on a form name in the Project Explorer window that contains the object whose properties you want to examine and then click on the View Object icon.**

View Object icon

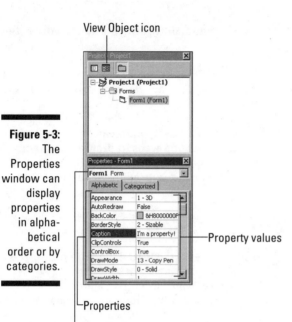

Figure 5-3:
The
Properties
window can
display
properties
in alpha-
betical
order or by
categories.

Property values

Properties

Object list box

3. **Click on the downward-pointing arrow of the Object list box in the Properties window and choose the object whose properties you want to examine.**

4. **Double-click on the property name that you want to change.**

If you click on an object displayed on a form, the Properties window automatically displays all the properties for that object.

Naming objects

Every object you draw has a Name property, which Visual Basic uses to identify the object. (That's the same reason your parents gave you a name — so people don't say, "Hey, you!" all the time to get your attention.) If you click on the Alphabetic tab in the Properties window, the Name property appears as (Name) at the top of the list.

Every Visual Basic object must have a unique name. If you try to give the same name to two different objects, Visual Basic complains and refuses to let you make such a horrid mistake.

When you create an object, Visual Basic automatically gives your object a boring, generic name. For example, the first time you create a command button, Visual Basic names the button Command1. The second time you create a command button, Visual Basic names this new button Command2, and so on.

The name of an object never appears on the screen. Names can be up to 40 characters long, but they cannot contain punctuation marks or spaces. You can name your objects anything you want, but Microsoft recommends that Visual Basic programmers all over the world use Visual Basic three-letter prefixes, as shown in Table 5-2. If everyone in the world uses these prefixes, it makes modifying another person's Visual Basic program easier to read.

Table 5-2	Suggested Prefixes When Naming Objects	
Object	**Suggested Prefix**	**Example Name**
Check box	chk	chkYourZipper
Combo box	cbo	cboBLT
Command button	cmd	cmdOpenSesame
Data	dat	datFanOverThere
Directory list box	dir	dirTree
Drive list box	drv	drvLikeMad
File list box	fil	filDocuments
Form	frm	frm1040Tax
Frame	fra	fraGroupedButtons
Horizontal scroll bar	hsb	hsbTemperature
Image	img	imgPeace
Label	lbl	lblFakeName
Line	lin	linBorder
List box	lst	lstCandidates
Menu	mnu	mnuHamAndEggs
Picture box	pic	picPrettyPictures
Radio button	opt	optStation101
Shape	shp	shpUpOrShipOut(circle, square, oval, rectangle, rounded rectangle, and rounded square)
Text box	txt	txtReadStuffHere
Vertical scroll bar	vsb	vsbMoneyWasted

To change the name of an object, follow these steps:

1. **Click on the object that you want to name.**

   Handles appear around the object. (To name a form, click anywhere on the form, but do not click on any objects on the form.)

2. **Open the Properties window.**

   To do so, press F4, choose View⇨Properties Window, or click on the Properties Window icon on the toolbar.

3. **Double-click on (Name) and type a new name.**

Creating captions for objects

In addition to a name, most (but not all) objects also have a caption. An object's caption appears as text on the screen. Some captions are shown in Figure 5-4.

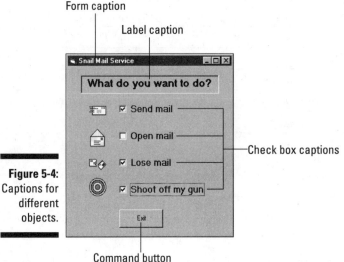

Form caption

Label caption

Check box captions

Figure 5-4:
Captions for different objects.

Command button

By default, an object's caption and name are the same until you change them. So the moment you draw a check box on a form, the check box's caption is something dull like Check1, and the check box's name is also Check1.

The caption for a form appears in the title bar of that form. The caption for an object (such as a command button, label, or text box) appears directly on that object while a caption for a check box or radio button usually appears to the right of the check box or option button.

Captions are meant to help the user figure out how to use your program. A caption can be blank or up to 255 characters long, including spaces, punctuation marks, and four-letter words. The following are valid captions:

✔ Hello

✔ Hello, buddy!

✔ Do I really know what I'm doing?

To change the caption of an object, follow these steps:

1. **Click on the object whose caption you want to change so that black handles appear around the object.**

   (To select a form, click anywhere on the form, but do not click on any objects on the form.)

2. **Open the Properties window (by pressing F4).**

3. **Double-click on the Caption property and type a new caption.**

   Notice that Visual Basic displays your caption on the screen as you type.

Adding hot keys to a caption

Besides looking pretty and displaying information to the user, captions can also be used to create *hot keys* so that the user can choose an object without having to click on the object with the mouse.

To add a hot key to a caption, you have to put the ampersand character (&) into an object's caption. You may be wondering, "Why the heck do I want to use an ugly symbol like that?" The answer is to give users yet another way to choose an object on your user interface.

For example, to push a command button, users can either:

✔ Click on the command button with the mouse.

✔ Press Tab until the command button appears highlighted and then press the spacebar or Enter (real obvious, huh?).

However, if you use the ampersand in the command button's caption, the user can push that button by pressing Alt plus whatever letter the ampersand is in front of. For example, if a command button has a caption of &Exit, it appears in the command button with the E underlined, as in Exit. To push this button, you can simply press Alt+E. If the command button has a caption of E&xit, however, the caption appears in the command button with the x underlined, as in Exit, and you can use Alt+X to press this command button (see Figure 5-5).

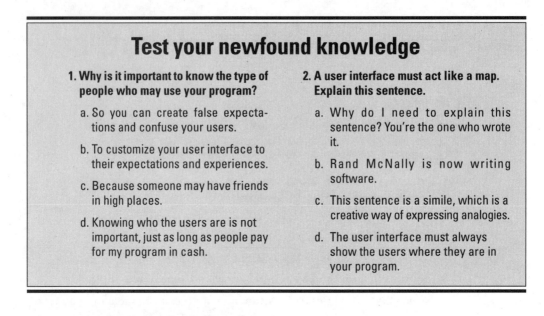

Test your newfound knowledge

1. Why is it important to know the type of people who may use your program?

a. So you can create false expectations and confuse your users.

b. To customize your user interface to their expectations and experiences.

c. Because someone may have friends in high places.

d. Knowing who the users are is not important, just as long as people pay for my program in cash.

2. A user interface must act like a map. Explain this sentence.

a. Why do I need to explain this sentence? You're the one who wrote it.

b. Rand McNally is now writing software.

c. This sentence is a simile, which is a creative way of expressing analogies.

d. The user interface must always show the users where they are in your program.

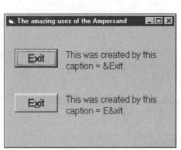

Figure 5-5: Two command buttons illustrating the use of the ampersand.

Changing the font of an object's caption

When you create a caption, Visual Basic displays your caption on the screen in a plain type style. For you creative types who want to make your captions look spiffier, you can change the font, type style, and size of captions to give them more pizzazz.

Fonts are different ways to display text. Normally, Visual Basic uses the MS Sans Serif font, but you can use any font stored in the memory of your computer. (MS Sans Serif is similar to the Helvetica font, and the Visual Basic MS Serif font is similar to the Times Roman font.)

To change the font of a caption, follow these steps:

1. **Click on the object whose caption you want to modify.**

2. **Open the Properties window (by choosing View⇨Properties Window).**

3. Double-click on the Font property.

Visual Basic displays a dialog box of all the fonts you can use, as shown in Figure 5-6.

4. Click on the font you want and click on OK.

Visual Basic immediately changes the font of the caption.

Fonts give you a chance to be creative, but they can also disorient the user, especially if you choose bizarre fonts that don't look like anything normally found in nature. To avoid confusion, let Visual Basic use the default font of MS Sans Serif, unless you have a really good reason to use a different font.

If you choose a really bizarre font, that font may not exist on other people's computers. When using fonts, try to use the most common ones found on all computers or else your program's captions may look really weird.

Changing the size of an object's caption

You can also change the size of your caption by making it smaller or larger to fit inside your object. Depending on the font you choose, Visual Basic gives you a variety of font sizes to choose from.

For example, if you choose the MS Sans Serif font, Visual Basic gives you the following choices of font sizes:

- 8
- 10
- 12
- 14

✔ 18

✔ 24

Obviously, the more font sizes you use, the odder your captions look. The best approach is to use one size to avoid confusing the user any more than you have to.

To define the font size of your captions, follow these steps:

1. **Click on the object whose font size you want to modify.**
2. **Open the Properties window (by clicking on the Properties Window icon on the toolbar).**
3. **Double-click on the Font property.**

   Visual Basic displays a dialog box like the one shown in Figure 5-6.
4. **Choose the font size you want to use and click on OK.**

Changing the type style of an object's caption

If changing the font and size of your captions isn't enough excitement for one day, Visual Basic also lets you change the type style of your captions. The number of available type styles depends on the font you're using for your caption.

For example, if you choose the MS Sans Serif font, Visual Basic gives you the following choices of type styles:

✔ Regular

✔ _Italic_

✔ **Bold**

✔ _**Bold Italic**_

✔ <u>Underline</u>

✔ ~~Strikeout~~

These different type styles are shown in Figure 5-7. If you want, you can even combine two or more type styles for extra emphasis.

To set different font styles, follow these steps:

1. **Click on the object whose caption you want to modify.**
2. **Open the Properties window (by pressing F4).**

3. **Double-click on the Font property.**

   Visual Basic displays a dialog box like the one shown in Figure 5-6.

4. **Click on the font style you want to use and click on OK.**

   Visual Basic immediately changes the caption's appearance.

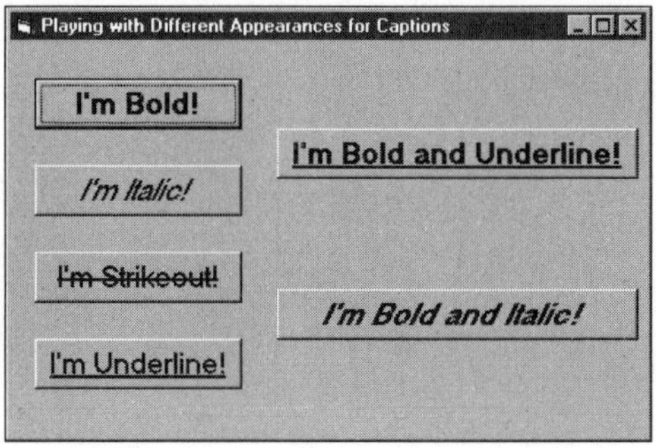

Figure 5-7:
Displaying
different
type styles
on a
command
button.

Changing the background and foreground colors of captions

Captions normally appear in boring black, white, and shades of gray. To make your captions stand out more colorfully, you can change the background and foreground colors. The BackColor property of an object represents the object's background color, and the ForeColor property represents the foreground color, as shown in Figure 5-8.

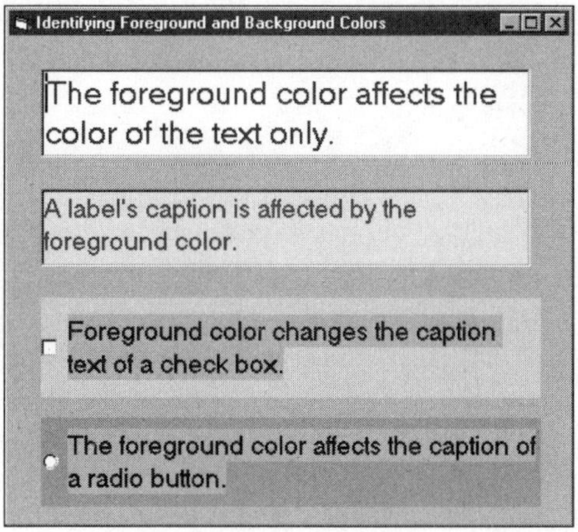

Figure 5-8:
The letters
appear
in the
foreground
color.
Everything
else
appears
in the
background
color.

Unlike other types of objects, command buttons have only a BackColor property. The BackColor property simply changes the color that surrounds the caption when the command button is highlighted.

To change the color surrounding an object's caption, follow these steps:

1. **Click on the object whose background color you want to change.**

2. **Open the Properties window (by pressing F4).**

3. **Double-click on the BackColor (or ForeColor) property and click on the Palette tab.**

   Visual Basic displays a color palette.

4. **Click on the color you want.**

   Visual Basic instantly obeys.

Moving objects on the screen

Objects can appear anywhere on a form. Visual Basic provides two ways to define the position of an object on the form:

 ✔ Use the mouse.
 ✔ Change the Left and Top properties in the Properties window.

To change the position of an object using the mouse, follow these steps:

1. **Click on the object you want to move so that black handles appear around the object.**

2. **Position the mouse over the object (not over one of the object's handles). Then hold down the left mouse button and move the mouse to where you want the object to appear.**

3. **Release the mouse button.**

In case you haven't figured out by now what is happening, when you create and place an object for the first time, that position is where Visual Basic displays the object. Use the mouse whenever you want to move an object quickly without regard to exact placement on the screen.

For more precise measurements when moving an object, use the Properties window and type in values for the Left and Top properties.

For objects, the Left property measures the distance from the left edge of the form to the left edge of the object. The Top property measures the distance from the top of the form to the top of the object.

For forms, the Left property measures the distance from the left edge of the screen to the left edge of the form. The Top property measures the distance from the top of the screen to the top of the form.

To change the position of an object using the Properties window, follow these steps:

1. **Click on the object you want to move so that black handles appear around the object.**

   (If you want to change the position of a form, click anywhere on the form so that handles appear around the edges of the form.)

2. **Open the Properties window (by pressing F4).**

3. **Double-click on the Left property and type a new value.**

4. **Double-click on the Top property and type a new value.**

Deleting objects off the face of the earth

Sometimes you draw an object and then decide that you don't need it after all.

To delete an object, follow these steps:

1. **Click on the object you want to delete.**

2. **Press Delete or choose Edit⇨Delete.**

If you press Ctrl+Z right after you delete an object, you can undelete the object you previously deleted.

Copying objects because you're too tired to draw new ones

After you draw an object that is the exact size you need, you may want to make a copy of the object rather than create a new one and go to the trouble of resizing it.

To copy an object, follow these steps:

1. **Click on the object you want to copy.**

2. **Press Ctrl+C, choose Edit⇨Copy, or click on the Copy icon.**

3. **Press Ctrl+V, choose Edit⇨Paste, or click on the Paste icon.**

   Visual Basic displays a dialog box that asks whether you want to create a control array. If you know what a control array is and want to create one, click on Yes; otherwise, click on No. Visual Basic displays a copy of your object in the upper-left corner of the form.

A *control array* lets you create two or more objects that share the same name. That way, two or more objects can share the same event procedure. If none of this makes any sense to you, just pretend this paragraph doesn't exist or refer to the latest edition of *MORE Visual Basic For Dummies,* which explains what control arrays are and why you might want to use them.

4. **Move this copy of the object anywhere on your screen.**

Selecting more than one object to move, copy, or delete

Before you can move, copy, or delete any object, you have to select the object by clicking on the object. However, if you want to move, copy, or delete more than one object at the same time, you have two choices:

✔ Use the mouse to select multiple objects.

✔ Click on multiple objects while holding down Ctrl or Shift.

To use the mouse to select multiple objects, follow these steps:

1. **Position the mouse at the upper-left corner of the group of objects you want to select. (But don't position the mouse directly over any of the objects you want to select.)**

2. **Hold down the left mouse button while you drag the mouse to the lower-right corner of the group of objects you want to select (see Figure 5-9).**

   Visual Basic displays a dotted line around all the objects you select.

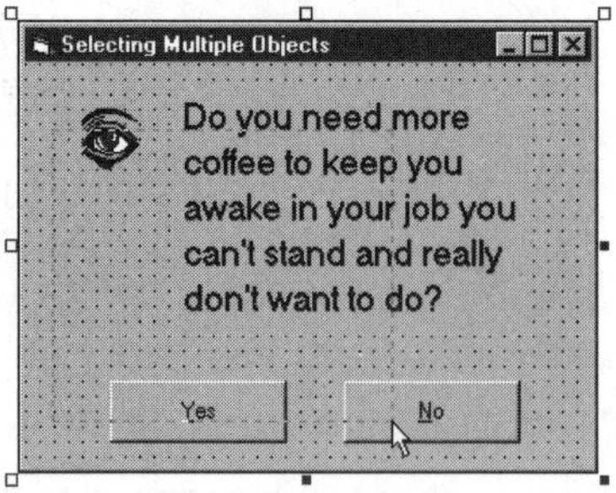

Figure 5-9:
Selecting
multiple
objects with
the mouse.

> **Selecting Multiple Objects**
>
> Do you need more coffee to keep you awake in your job you can't stand and really don't want to do?
>
> Yes   No

3. **Release the mouse button.**

   Visual Basic displays a gray rectangle around all the objects you select.

To click on multiple objects while holding down Ctrl or Shift, follow these steps:

1. **Click on the first object that you want to select.**

   Visual Basic displays black handles around the object.

2. **Point to the second object that you want to select.**

3. **Press Ctrl or Shift while you click on the second object.**

   Visual Basic displays gray rectangles around this object and each of your previously selected objects.

4. **Repeat Steps 2 and 3 until you select all the objects you want.**

Changing the size of objects

After creating an object, the next step is to define the object's size, which is a topic most men tend to exaggerate. Visual Basic provides two ways to change the size of an object:

🖙 Use the mouse.

🖙 Change the Height and Width properties in the Properties window.

To change the size of an object using the mouse, follow these steps:

1. **Click on the object that you want to resize.**

   Little black handles appear around the edges of the object.

2. **Move the mouse to the edge of the object until the mouse pointer turns into a double-headed arrow, as shown in Figure 5-10.**

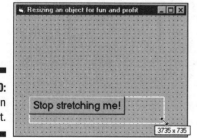

Figure 5-10:
Resizing an object.

3. **Hold down the mouse button and drag the mouse. When the object is in the shape you want, release the mouse button.**

To change the size of a form using the Properties window, follow these steps:

1. **Click on the object you want to resize.**

2. **Open the Properties window (by pressing F4).**

3. **Double-click on the Height property, type a new value, and press Enter.**

4. **Double-click on the Width property, type a new value, and press Enter.**

Use the mouse method when the exact size of your object isn't crucial. Change the Height and Width properties manually when you want absolute precision or when you feel like being picky about details that nobody else cares about.

Defining the TabIndex property of your objects

The TabIndex property determines the order in which Visual Basic high-lights buttons when the user presses either the Tab, up-arrow, down-arrow, right-arrow, left-arrow, or Shift+Tab keys.

- ✔ The Tab, down-arrow, and right-arrow keys highlight the object with the next-highest TabIndex value.

- ✔ The Shift+Tab, up-arrow, and left-arrow keys highlight the object with the next-lowest TabIndex value. To highlight option buttons, you can use only the up, down, right, and left arrow keys, but not the Tab or Shift+Tab keys.

- ✔ The spacebar or Enter key selects a highlighted object.

Some objects, such as image boxes and menu objects, don't have a TabIndex property, so you can't highlight them by pressing any keys.

An object with a TabIndex property set to 0 appears highlighted as soon as your program runs. If the user presses Tab, the object with a TabIndex property of 1 is highlighted next, and so on.

The first object that you create has a TabIndex property of 0. The second object that you create has a TabIndex property of 1, and so on.

The only way to highlight an object stored inside a frame (see Chapter 6) is to press Tab or to click on the object with the mouse. After an object inside a frame is highlighted, pressing the up-, down-, left-, and right-arrow keys only highlights other command buttons or objects in that frame.

Although most users use a mouse to highlight and select objects, some users may not. For those rare instances, the keyboard is the only way these behind-the-times people can select the objects on your user interface.

To change the TabIndex property of an object, follow these steps:

1. **Click on the object that you want to modify.**
2. **Open the Properties window (by pressing F4).**
3. **Double-click on the TabIndex property and type a number (such as 1 or 4).**

Whenever you change the TabIndex property of a button, Visual Basic automatically renumbers the TabIndex of your other buttons. Thus, you can never assign two buttons identical TabIndex values.

If you have created lots of objects, you can set the TabIndex properties for them quickly and easily by following these steps:

1. **Click on the object that you want highlighted last (the object that is to have the highest TabIndex property value).**
2. **Open the Properties window (by pressing F4).**
3. **Click on the TabIndex property and type** 0.
4. **Click on the object that you want highlighted second to last.**
5. **Repeat Steps 2 through 4 until you set the TabIndex properties for all your objects to 0.**

If you follow these steps, the last object you click on has a TabIndex of 0, the second-to-last object you click on has a TabIndex of 1, and so on.

For some reason if you don't want the user to be able to highlight an object by pressing the tab key, you can set that object's TabStop property to False.

Dimming objects

If you don't want the user to press a particular object (such as a command button, a check box, or an image box), you can dim the object, as shown in Figure 5-11. A dimmed object tells the user, "Sometimes you can click on this object but not right now. So there."

To dim an object, follow these steps:

1. **Click on the object that you want to dim.**
2. **Open the Properties window (by pressing F4).**
3. **Click on the Enabled property and set it to False.**

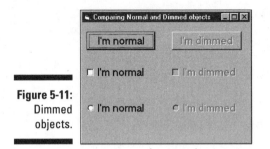

Figure 5-11:
Dimmed
objects.

A dimmed object doesn't do anything, so if you want to undim it during run-time events, you eventually have to use BASIC code.

To give you a sneak preview of the incredible power of BASIC code, here's how BASIC undims and dims a button. To undim a button, set the button's Enabled property to True. The following example undims a command button named cmdExit:

```
cmdExit.Enabled = True
```

To dim a button using BASIC code, set the button's Enabled property to False. The following example dims a command button named cmdExit:

```
cmdExit.Enabled = False
```

You can dim and undim buttons using BASIC code while your program is running. That way, you can dim and undim buttons in response to whatever the user is doing (typing, moving the mouse, pounding helplessly on the keyboard, and so on).

Making objects invisible

Rather than dimming an object (which essentially taunts the user because the object is there but unavailable), you can make objects disappear completely.

To make an object disappear, follow these steps:

1. **Click on the object you want to disappear.**

2. **Press F4 or select Properties from the View menu to open the Properties window.**

3. **Click on the Visible property and set it to False.**

You can also make an object disappear using BASIC code. To do so, set the object's Visible property to False. The following example makes a command button named cmdNew disappear:

```
cmdNew.Visible = False
```

Like dimmed objects, invisible objects are useless unless you can make them visible once in a while. To make an object appear again, you have to use BASIC code to set the object's Visible property to True. The following example makes a command button named cmdNew appear:

```
cmdNew.Visible = True
```

Adding Tooltips to an Object

Despite the standard user interface of Windows 95/98/NT, many people may still have no clue what the different objects of your program actually do. Rather than click on these unmarked objects at random (and risk wrecking their data), most people sit paralyzed with fear and wind up never using many parts of a program at all.

To overcome this hesitation, all of your objects can display tooltips. A *tooltip* is nothing more than brief text that explains what a particular object does. The tooltip remains invisible until the user moves the mouse cursor over the object and leaves the mouse hovering there for a few seconds. Then your Visual Basic program can spring to life and display the tooltip text, as shown in Figure 5-12.

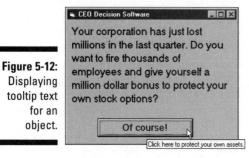

Figure 5-12:
Displaying
tooltip text
for an
object.

To create tooltip text for your objects, follow these steps:

1. **Click on any object on your form.**

2. **Open the Properties window (by pressing F4).**

3. **Double-click on the ToolTipText property.**

4. **Type the brief explanation that you want to appear whenever the user leaves the mouse cursor over the object.**

Doing Caption Changes for Yourself

The following sample program lets you change the caption on the form by typing a new caption in a text box and by clicking on the cmdCaption command button. Just create a user interface according to Table 5-3 and see for yourself the amazing power of Visual Basic.

Table 5-3	Properties to Change for CAPTION.VBP	
Object	*Property*	*Setting*
Form	Caption	The Incredible Changing Caption
	Height	3885
	Width	4680
Label1	Name	lblHeadline
	Caption	This caption can be changed by clicking on the command button below.
	Height	600
	Left	240
	Top	360
	Width	4000
Label2	Caption	Type a new caption here:
	Height	300
	Left	120
	Top	1680
	Width	1935
Text1	Name	txtCaption
	Height	495
	Left	2280
	Multiline	True
	Text	(Empty)
	Top	1560
	Width	1935

Object	Property	Setting
Command1	Name	cmdCaption
	Caption	Change Caption
	Height	495
	Left	1200
	ToolTipText	Click here to change the caption.
	Top	2640
	Width	2175

For those of you who don't like typing, you can examine the CAPTION.VBP program on the enclosed CD-ROM.

```
Private Sub cmdCaption_Click()
    lblHeadline.Caption = txtCaption.Text
End Sub
```

When you run this program, just type a new caption in the text box and click on the command button labeled Change Caption. Visual Basic immediately displays your newly typed text in the top label.

Chapter 6

Forms and Buttons

● ●

In This Chapter

▶ Creating forms and drawing borders

▶ Choosing the order in which forms are displayed

▶ Creating buttons

● ●

*T*he main part of a user interface is a window, which Visual Basic calls a form. A Visual Basic program needs at least one form, but most programs use two or more forms.

For example, a typical program uses one form to display a list of command buttons on which to click. If the user clicks on a command button, a second form appears displaying information such as names, addresses, and telephone numbers of people who owe you money.

The CD-ROM at the back of this book contains a simple Visual Basic program that shows how to change the background of a form. Feel free to experiment with this program and modify it so you can see how you can easily change the appearance of a form.

Creating a Form

Visual Basic provides two ways to create a form for your program:

▸ Create a blank form

▸ Use a form template

Creating a blank form is handy when you want to design the appearance of the form all by yourself. As a quicker way of creating forms, you can use a *form template,* which provides pre-designed forms for displaying a Tip of the Day, Web Browser, or Splash Screen window in your program.

If you use a form template, you still have to customize the form for your program, but at least you won't have to waste time drawing objects on the form from scratch. Figure 6-1 displays several of the more common form templates that Visual Basic can create for you:

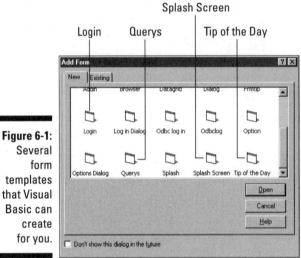

Figure 6-1:
Several
form
templates
that Visual
Basic can
create
for you.

- ✔ **Form:** Creates a blank form.
- ✔ **Dialog:** Creates a skeleton of a dialog box with an OK and Cancel command button.
- ✔ **About Dialog:** Displays information about your program.
- ✔ **Log in Dialog:** Forces users to type a User ID and password before they can use your program.
- ✔ **Options Dialog:** Displays a dialog box with tabs, allowing your program to offer options for customizing your program.
- ✔ **Splash Screen:** Displays the name of your program along with a logo whenever your program loads.
- ✔ **Tip of the Day:** Provides tips for using your program.
- ✔ **ODBC Log In:** Displays options for connecting your program to a database.
- ✔ **Web Browser:** Adds a Web browser to your program.
- ✔ **VB Data Form Wizard:** Automatically creates a form to display and edit database information.

To create a form for your program, follow these steps:

1. **Choose Project⇨Add Form (or click on the Add Form icon on the toolbar and click on Form, as shown in Figure 6-2).**

   An Add Form dialog box appears.

2. **Click on an icon in the Add Form dialog box, such as the Form (which adds a blank form), Web Browser, or Splash Screen, and click on Open.**

Saving forms

After you create a form, you may want to save the form (if not for religious purposes, then at least for practical ones) so that you don't have to create the form all over again later. To save a form, Visual Basic gives you two choices:

- ✔ Choose File⇨Save Form
- ✔ Press Ctrl+S

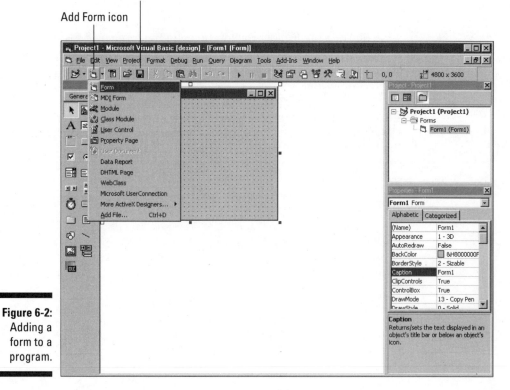

Save Project icon

Add Form icon

Figure 6-2:
Adding a
form to a
program.

If you have two or more forms displayed on the screen and you want to save changes to all your forms at once, choose File⇨Save Project or click on the Save Project icon (see Figure 6-2). This command automatically saves every file (listed in the VBP project file) that makes up your entire Visual Basic program.

Get into the habit of periodically saving your forms. If your computer fails, the power goes out (but doesn't get your hard drive), or terrorists raid your home and riddle your computer with bullets, you lose only the changes that you've made since you last saved the form.

Viewing different forms

Most Visual Basic programs that you create need two or more forms. To keep multiple forms from cluttering up your screen, Visual Basic kindly displays only one form at a time.

So if you want to switch to a different form to look at, follow these steps:

1. **Choose one of the following to switch to the Project Explorer window:**

    • Choose View⇨Project Explorer

    • Press Ctrl+R

    • Click on the Project Explorer icon in the toolbar

2. **Look for the Forms folder, as shown in Figure 6-3. If a plus sign appears to the left of the Forms folder, click on the plus sign.**

    Visual Basic displays a list of all the forms that make up your program.

3. **Click on the form that you want to view and then click on the View Object icon in the Project Explorer window (or just double-click on the form name).**

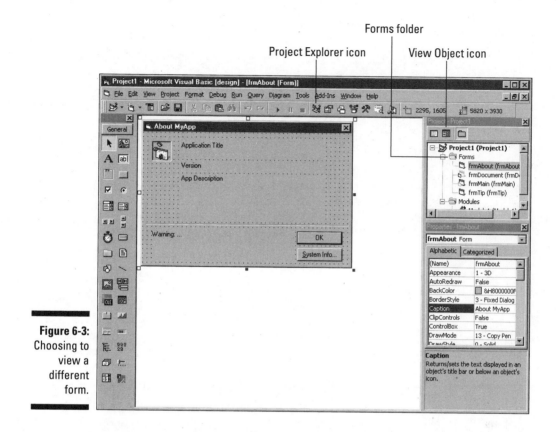

Forms folder

Project Explorer icon   View Object icon

Figure 6-3:
Choosing to
view a
different
form.

Positioning a form with the Form Layout window

The Form Layout window lets you decide where your forms initially appear on the computer screen when the program actually runs, as shown in Figure 6-4. In case you can't see the Form Layout window, choose one of the following:

- View⇨Form Layout window
- Click on the Form Layout window icon on the toolbar

Form Layout icon

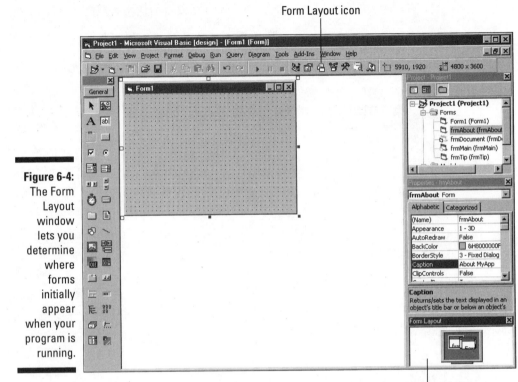

Figure 6-4:
The Form
Layout
window
lets you
determine
where
forms
initially
appear
when your
program is
running.

Form Layout window

The Form Layout window displays your forms within a tiny computer screen. To move a form's position, follow these steps:

1. **In the Form Layout window, move the mouse cursor over the form that you want to move.**

   The mouse cursor turns into a four-way pointing arrow.

2. **Hold down the left mouse button and drag the mouse to move the form to its new position.**

3. **Release the left mouse button.**

No matter where your form may appear on the screen while you're editing it, the Form Layout window controls the real position of your form when your program runs.

For a quick way to adjust the position of a form within the Form Layout window, right-click on a form, highlight Startup Position, and then choose an option from the pop-up menu as shown in Figure 6-5. As another alternative, you can change the StartUpPosition property directly within the Properties window.

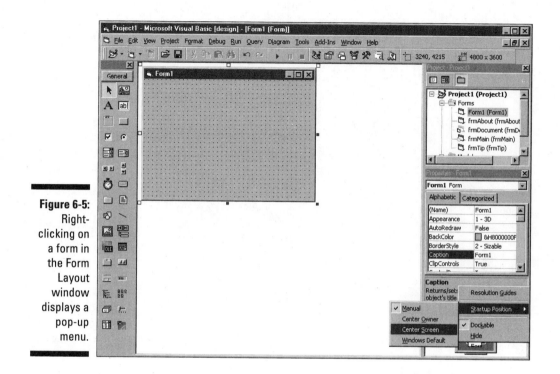

Figure 6-5:
Right-clicking on a form in the Form Layout window displays a pop-up menu.

Drawing borders around forms

Borders make forms look pretty, and they also give nations something to argue about. By changing the BorderStyle property, forms can have one of six types of borders, as shown in Figure 6-6.

In addition to making your forms look pretty, each border style also affects whether the user can move or resize the form.

- ✔ The 0 - None style doesn't display a border around your form, but any objects your form contains can still be seen. A user cannot move, resize, or minimize this type of form.

- ✔ The 1 - Fixed Single style displays a Control box, title bar, and Close box. Users can move, but not resize, this type of form.

- ✔ The 2 - Sizable style is the default style. This style displays a Control box, a title bar, Minimize and Maximize buttons, and the Close box. Users can move, resize, and minimize or maximize this form.

- ✔ The 3 - Fixed Dialog style displays a Control box, a title bar, and a Close box. Users can move this form but cannot resize, minimize, or maximize this form style.

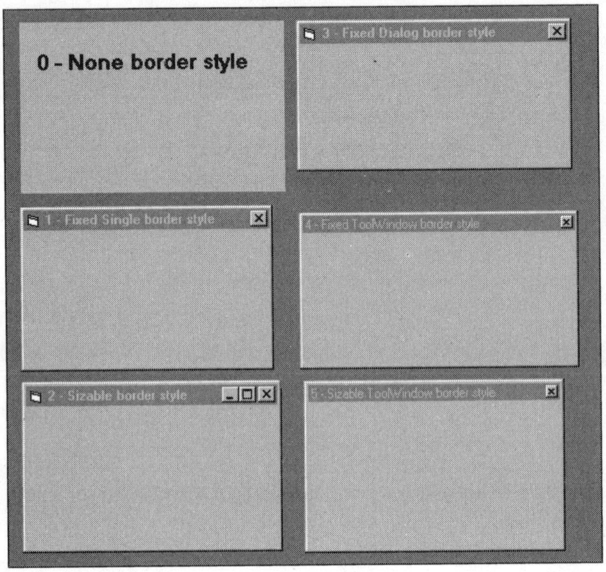

Figure 6-6:
The six
different
border
styles for
your form.

✔ The 4 - Fixed ToolWindow style displays a title bar and Close box. Users can move this form but cannot resize, minimize, or maximize this style of form.

✔ The 5 - Sizable ToolWindow style displays a title bar and Close box. Users can move and resize this form.

To change the borders around your form using the Properties window, follow these steps:

1. **Click anywhere on the form where there is not an object.**

2. **Open the Properties window (by pressing F4).**

3. **Click on the BorderStyle property.**

4. **Choose one of the following:**

    - 0 - None

    - 1 - Fixed Single

    - 2 - Sizable

    - 3 - Fixed Dialog

    - 4 - Fixed ToolWindow

    - 5 - Sizable ToolWindow

Minimizing and maximizing forms

Forms can cover part of the screen or the entire screen. Any form that hogs the whole screen is considered maximized. At the other extreme, forms can be shrunk and displayed on the screen as icons. A shrunken form is considered minimized. Any form that just covers part of the screen is considered normal. Anyone who thinks that computer programmers invent too many definitions is also considered normal. Figure 6-7 shows all three sizes of forms.

If you define a BorderStyle of 0 - None, 1 - Fixed Single, 3 - Fixed Dialog, 4 - Fixed ToolWindow, or 5 - Sizable ToolWindow, you cannot minimize or maximize a form.

To display a form as normal, minimized, or maximized while your program runs, follow these steps:

1. **Click anywhere on the form. (Do not click on any objects on the form.)**

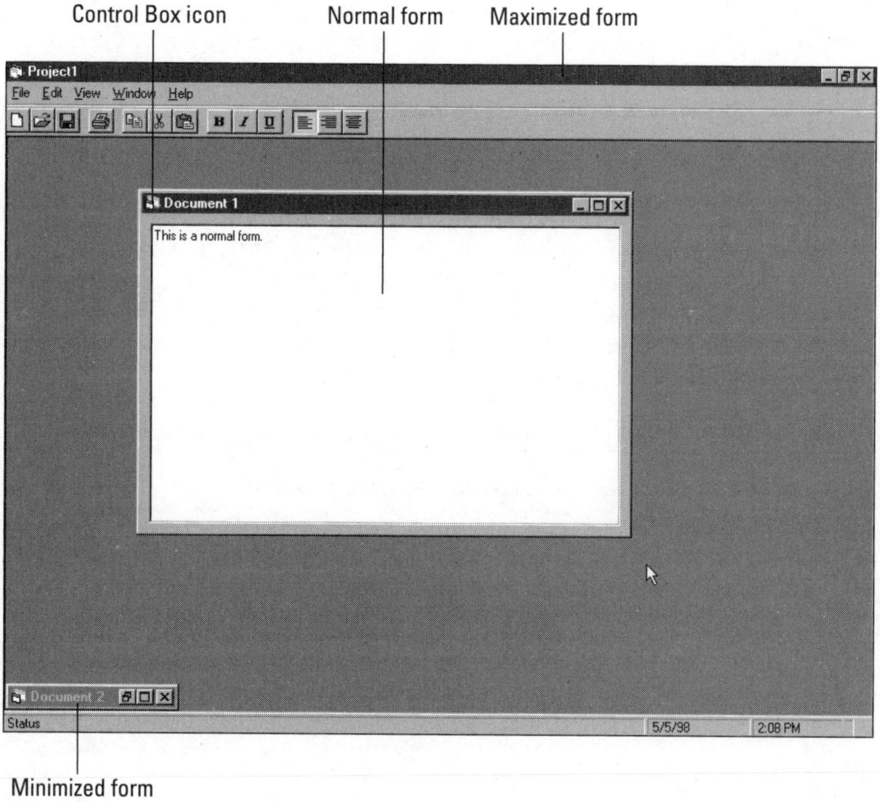

Control Box icon   Normal form Maximized form

Project1

File Edit View Window Help

Document 1

This is a normal form.

Figure 6-7:
Minimized,
maximized,
and normal
forms.

Document 2

Status 5/5/98 2:08 PM

Minimized form

2. **Open the Properties window (by pressing F4).**

3. **Click on the WindowState property in the Properties window.**

4. **Choose one of the following:**

   - 0 - Normal
   - 1 - Minimized
   - 2 - Maximized

You can also give the user the option of minimizing or maximizing a form. To do so, your form needs to display Minimize and Maximize buttons.

To display Minimize and Maximize buttons on a form, follow these steps:

1. **Click anywhere on the form where there are no objects.**

2. **Open the Properties window (by pressing F4).**

3. **Click on the MinButton (or the MaxButton) property in the Properties window and choose True or False.**

Depending on the border style you choose for your form, the default setting for the MinButton and MaxButton settings may be True or False.

Removing forms

Occasionally, you may decide you don't want a particular form as part of your Visual Basic program after all. To remove a form from a Visual Basic project, follow these steps:

1. **Choose one of the following to switch to the Project Explorer window:**

   - Choose View⇨Project Explorer
   - Press Ctrl+R
   - Click on the Project Explorer icon in the toolbar

2. **Click on the form you want to remove.**

3. **Choose Project⇨Remove or right-click on the form name and choose Remove.**

If you remove a form that you've previously saved, the form still exists on your hard disk; it just isn't part of your Visual Basic project anymore. To physically remove all traces of a form out of existence, use Windows Explorer and delete the form file.

The Control Box

Users can move or resize a form by using the mouse. To minimize or maximize a form, simply click the Minimize or Maximize button. For those users who haven't caught up with current technology or refuse to use a mouse, each form also provides a control box, as well.

If you choose a BorderStyle of 0 - None, 4 - Fixed ToolWindow, or 5 - Sizable ToolWindow, you won't see a control box icon on your forms.

To activate the control box menu while a program is running, click on the control box icon with the mouse pointer or press Alt+spacebar. A menu appears, which lets the user move, resize, minimize, or maximize a form.

Removing a control box

A control box appears on all forms. But if you think that the box looks really ugly and want to remove it, follow these steps:

1. **Click anywhere on the form (except where you find objects on the form).**

2. **Open the Properties window (by pressing F4).**

3. **Click the ControlBox property in the Properties window.**

4. **Choose True or False.**

   Depending on the border style you choose for your form, the default value may be True or False.

Displaying icons as the control box on forms

Icons are special graphics symbols with the ICO file extension. Normally, Visual Basic displays the control box of a form with a default icon that looks like a sail flapping in the wind (see Figure 6-7). If you don't like this icon, you can customize the icon. To change an icon with the Properties window, follow these steps:

1. **Click anywhere on the form, but not on any objects on the form.**

2. **Open the Properties window (by pressing F4).**

3. **Double-click on the Icon property in the Properties window.**

   Visual Basic displays a Load Icon dialog box.

4. **Choose the icon you want to use and click on Open.**

Choosing Which Form Visual Basic Displays First

When your program runs, the first form your program displays is generally the first form you've created. To make another form appear first, follow these steps:

1. **Choose Project➪ProjectName Properties (where ProjectName is the name of your Visual Basic project).**

   Visual Basic displays a Project Properties dialog box.

2. **Click on the General tab.**

   Visual Basic displays the Project Properties dialog box, as shown in Figure 6-8.

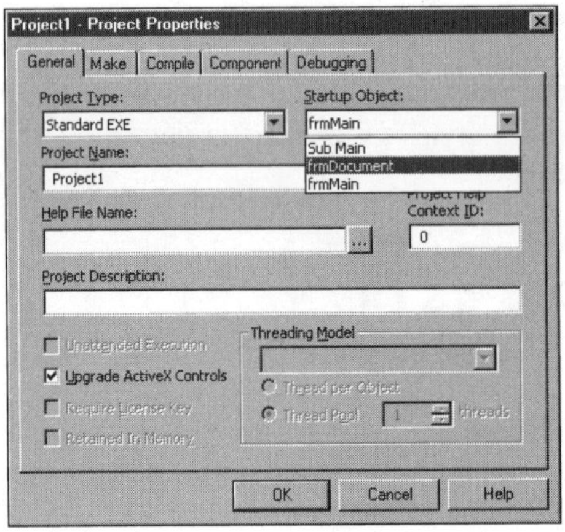

Figure 6-8:
Choosing the first form to appear with the Project Properties dialog box.

3. **Click on the downward-pointing arrow of the Startup Object list box to display a list of all the forms for your project.**

4. **Choose the form you want to display first and click on OK.**

Defining Units of Measurement on a Form

The reason to have a form is so that you can have a place onto which you can put objects. You may notice, therefore, that every form always displays a grid to help you align objects.

By default, each form uses a unit of measurement called a *twip,* which sounds like something Elmer Fudd says. ("I'm tying stwing acwoss this path so that wabbit will twip ove wit. Eh, eh, eh, eh, eh.")

In case you actually care, 1,440 twips equal 1 inch. If you don't like using twips as your preferred unit of measurement, Visual Basic offers seven options:

- ✔ Twips (1,440 twips = 1 inch)
- ✔ Points (72 points = 1 inch)
- ✔ Pixels (The number of pixels that equals 1 inch depends on your monitor's resolution.)
- ✔ Characters (A character is $1/6$ inch high and $1/12$ inch wide.)
- ✔ Inches (1 inch = 1 inch — amazing, don't you think?)
- ✔ Millimeters (25.4 mm = 1 inch)
- ✔ Centimeters (2.54 cm = 1 inch)

Hard-core programmers may be happy to know that Visual Basic even lets you create your own customized coordinate system. If you're thinking about doing that, you probably need to read a book with a title like *Visual Basic For Hard-Core Programming Geniuses* instead of this book. For the rest of us, the seven available units of measurement in Visual Basic are more than sufficient.

To change your form's grid scale, follow these steps:

1. **Click anywhere on the form. (Do not click any objects on the form.)**

2. **Open the Properties window (by pressing F4).**

3. **Click on the ScaleMode property.**

4. **Click on the downward-pointing arrow to display a list of all the different measurement units you can use.**

   Figure 6-9 shows this list.

5. **Select the unit of measurement you want your form to use.**

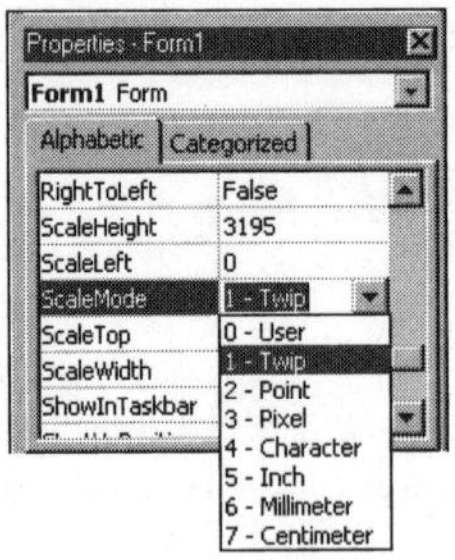

Figure 6-9:
Choosing a
grid scale.

Pushing Your Buttons

Pushing a button is a simple task that anyone can do. Even children can push buttons, which gives them the power to throw a hot dog in a microwave oven and shout with glee when the meat explodes before their eyes.

Everyone uses buttons. Your disk drive probably has a button that you press to eject a floppy disk. Your monitor has a button to turn the screen's power on and off. Even your mouse has a button (or two or three).

Because buttons are so familiar and easy to use, programs often display buttons on the screen that you can push with a mouse. Instead of forcing you to wade through various menus to find the right command, buttons conveniently display your options right before your eyes. All you have to do is figure out which button you want to press.

Buttons are a feature of nearly every program. Therefore, the rest of this chapter is all about making, modifying, and pushing your own buttons.

Types of buttons

Essentially, a button is nothing more than an area on the screen that the user can click with the mouse. When pushed (clicked on), a command button rushes off and performs a command. (That's why they call them *command* buttons.) Visual Basic lets you create two types of buttons: command buttons and image buttons.

A *command button* displays a caption or an optional icon. This caption can be as unimaginative as OK, Cancel, or Quit. Or the caption can represent a particular command, such as Erase File, Next Screen, or Lose Mr. Johnson's Airline Reservation.

Command buttons often appear in dialog boxes where the program displays a message, such as, "Do you really want to erase your IRS tax files to avoid criminal prosecution?" The available choices may be Yes and No.

Unlike a command button that can display both captions and icons, an *image button* can display only a picture.

The advantage of image buttons is that they can be smaller than command buttons. The disadvantage is that unless the user knows which command each image button represents, the user has no idea how to use your image buttons. Command buttons and image buttons are shown in Figure 6-10.

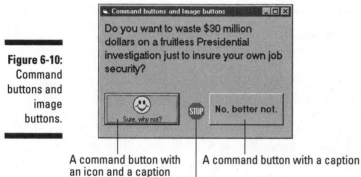

Figure 6-10: Command buttons and image buttons.

A command button with an icon and a caption   A command button with a caption

An image button

Because image buttons aren't as self-explanatory as command buttons, a good idea is to type a brief description of the image button's purpose in the ToolTipText property (see Chapter 5).

For example, if the only way to exit your program is to click an image button that shows an open door, people may not understand the connection and may wind up turning off their computer to exit your program instead. (And then they probably aren't going to use your program again, either.)

Creating buttons

To create a command button, follow these steps:

1. **Click on the Command Button icon in the Visual Basic Toolbox.**

2. **Move the mouse to the place on the form where you want to draw the command button.**

3. **Press and hold the left mouse button and drag the mouse to form a command button box.**

4. **Release the left mouse button to complete the operation.**

   Visual Basic displays a boring label like Command1 in the command button.

Although command buttons are the easiest for users to see and click on, you may want to use an image button to give users the option of clicking on a picture to create multimedia programs. To create an image button, follow these steps:

1. **Click on the Image Button icon in the Visual Basic Toolbox.**
2. **Drag the mouse to the place on the form where you want to draw the image button.**
3. **Open the Properties window (by pressing F4).**
4. **Double-click on the Picture property.**

   Visual Basic cheerfully displays a Load Picture dialog box.

5. **Load any graphics file (bitmap, icon, or metafile).**

   Visual Basic displays this graphic as your image button.

After you create a command or image button, you still have to write BASIC code to make the button do something when the user clicks on it.

Displaying pretty icons on command buttons

Although most command buttons simply display a caption, such as OK, Cancel, Yes, No, or Blame It On Your Parents, you also can display icons on command buttons. Pictures can help clarify a command button's purpose. For example, rather than just having a command button display a caption that says "OK," you can also display a green traffic light picture on the command button.

To make a command button display an icon, you can define the following properties:

  ✔ Style (Choose 1 - Graphical)
  ✔ Picture (Defines the icon that appears on the command button)
  ✔ DownPicture (Defines the icon that appears when the user clicks on the command button)
  ✔ DisabledPicture (Defines the icon that appears when the command button is dimmed)

The DownPicture and DisabledPicture properties are optional if you want to display an icon on a command button.

To display a picture on a command button, follow these steps:

1. **Click on the command button on the form that you want to display a picture.**

2. **Open the Properties window (by pressing F4).**

3. **Click on the Style property, click on the downward-pointing arrow, and choose 1 - Graphical.**

4. **Double-click on the Picture property.**

   Visual Basic displays a dialog box.

5. **Click on the picture you want to use. (You may have to dig through the Graphics folder to find a picture to use.) Click on Open.**

6. **Double-click on the DownPicture property to define a picture to appear when the user clicks on the command button.**

7. **Click on the picture you want to use. (You may have to dig through the Graphics folder to find a picture to use.) Click on Open.**

8. **Double-click on the DisabledPicture property to define a picture to appear if the command button appears dimmed.**

9. **Click on the picture you want to use. (You may have to dig through the Graphics folder to find a picture to use.) Click on Open.**

Changing the size of an image button

Visual Basic lets you freely draw an image box of any size that you want; however, if your graphics image is too big for your image button, the graphics image appears cut off.

To make your graphics image change size when you change the image button's size, you need to change the value of the image box Stretch property to True. (The default value of the Stretch property is False.)

For example, in Figure 6-11, the image box in the upper-left corner has the Stretch property set to False, so no matter how large you make the image box, the graphics image remains the same size. The other three image boxes have their Stretch properties set to True; therefore, the graphics image adjusts in size when you change the size of the image box.

Figure 6-11:
How the
Stretch
property
affects the
size of
graphics in
image
boxes.

Creating a default command button

The *default command button* is the one button that users can choose by pressing the Enter key right away as soon as the command buttons appears on the screen. A default button is the most likely choice for the user to choose.

For example, if the user gives a command to launch nuclear missiles at another nation, a dialog box may pop up asking, "Wouldn't you rather play a nice game of chess?" If the default button was Yes, the user can mindlessly hit Enter and save the world from nuclear destruction.

Only command buttons can be default command buttons. Image buttons can never be default command buttons because Visual Basic says so.

You can use two ways to create a default command button:

✔ Set the command button's TabIndex property to zero. This highlights the command button designated as the default button.

✔ Set the Default property on the default command button to True. This works only if no other object has a TabIndex value of zero.

To create a default command button using the TabIndex property, follow these steps:

1. **Click the command button that you want to be the default button.**

2. **Open the Properties window. (Press F4, choose <u>V</u>iew⇨Properties <u>W</u>indow, or click on the Properties Window icon on the toolbar).**

3. **Click on the TabIndex property and type** 0.

If no other command buttons on your form have a TabIndex property of zero, you can create a default button by setting the Default property of a command button to True.

To create a default command button using the Default property, follow these steps:

1. **Click on the command button that you want to be the default button.**

2. **Open the Properties window (by pressing F4).**

3. **Click the Default property and set the value to True.**

4. **Make sure that no other objects on the form have a TabIndex of zero.**

What happens if one command button has a TabIndex of zero but another command button has a Default property that is set to True? The default command button is the one with the TabIndex of zero. So there.

Defining the Cancel button

When users bang on Esc, they usually want to cancel their last command or exit out of the program. Any button that lets the user do this needs to be designated the Cancel button. Only one command button can be defined as the Cancel button. (Another good name for the Cancel button is the Panic button, but that destroys the image of programming as a fine science rather than an incoherent art.)

To create a Cancel command button, follow these steps:

1. **Click the command button that you want to be the Cancel button.**

2. **Open the Properties window (by pressing F4).**

3. **Click the Cancel property, set the value to True, and change the button's caption to "cancel" or something similar.**

Grouping command buttons

Occasionally, you may want to group related command buttons on the screen to give the illusion of organization, as shown in Figure 6-12.

To create a group of command buttons, follow these steps:

1. **Click on the Frame icon in the Visual Basic Toolbox.**

2. **Move the mouse to where you want to draw the frame.**

3. **Hold down the mouse button and move the mouse to draw a frame.**

4. **Click on the Command Button icon in the Visual Basic Toolbox.**

5. **Move the mouse inside the frame to where you want to draw a command button.**

6. **Hold down the mouse button and move the mouse to draw your command button inside the frame.**

7. **Repeat Steps 4 through 6 until you draw all the command buttons you need or until you decide that the time has come to do something else.**

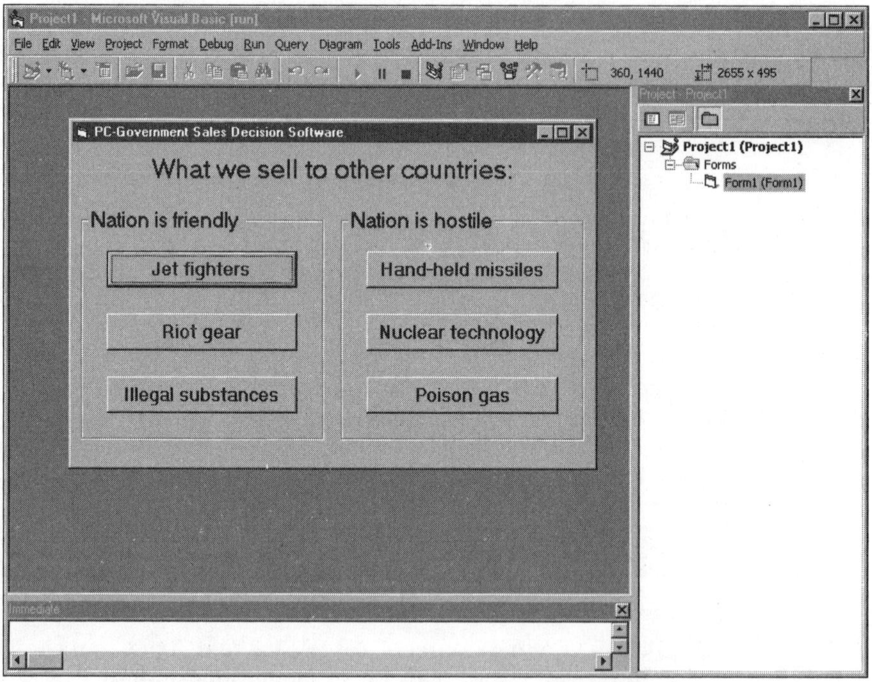

Figure 6-12:
Grouping
command
buttons.

After you draw a command button inside a frame, the button remains forever trapped inside the frame. When you move the frame, all command buttons inside move along with their host frame.

You cannot create a command button outside a frame and then try to move the button inside a frame, so don't bother trying.

If a command button exists outside of a frame, click on it, choose the Copy or Cut command, click inside the frame so the frame's handles appear, then choose the Paste command. This lets you copy or cut a command button from outside a frame and put it inside the frame.

As a final modification for grouped command buttons, set the TabStop properties of all grouped buttons to False. Next, set the TabStop property of the first command button to True. That way, if a lame user presses Tab, only the first command button in a group becomes highlighted.

Test your newfound knowledge

1. Why do command buttons have names and captions?

a. So you have twice as many chances to call them a four-letter word.

b. The name is a bad word you can call the command button, and the caption is there so that you can write a funny punch line.

c. The name identifies the command button, and the caption is what actually appears on the screen.

d. Because Visual Basic says so, and any product sold by Bill Gates can't be wrong because he's a billionaire.

2. Why do you want to group buttons together in a frame?

a. To keep them from escaping into the wild.

b. So related commands are easy to find on the screen.

c. To make understanding what your program is supposed to do harder for anyone.

d. No reason, except to cause more confusion to people trying to learn how to program a computer for the first time.

To turn off the TabStop properties for a group of buttons, follow these steps:

1. **Click any command button within the frame, except for the first command button.**

2. **Open the Properties window (by pressing F4).**

3. **Click on the TabStop property and set the value to False.**

4. **Repeat Steps 1 through 3 until the TabStop property for all the command buttons (except the first command button) has been set to False.**

5. **Go to the kitchen and reward yourself with a Twinkie for your good deed.**

Chapter 7

Boxes and Buttons for Making Choices

*I*n school, multiple-choice tests were always easier than essay tests because you could substitute guessing for thinking and still get a decent grade. However, students aren't the only ones who don't want to think if they can avoid doing so. Most users are the same way — they want choices clearly laid out in front of their eyes. That way, they can make wild guesses and be on their merry way.

Visual Basic provides several ways to offer choices to users: check boxes, radio buttons (also called option buttons), list boxes, and combo boxes. Check boxes let users choose one or more options. Radio buttons let users choose only one option. List boxes and combo boxes offer users multiple choices.

The CD contains a Visual Basic program that shows how check boxes, radio buttons, list boxes, and combo boxes work. Feel free to modify the source code and see what happens.

Creating Check Boxes and Radio Buttons

Check boxes get their name from those silly questionnaires that ask, "Check all that apply," as in:

Why do you want to work here? (Check all that apply.)

- ❑   I need the money.
- ❑   I want to participate in employee theft.
- ❑   I want a place where I can steal more office supplies.
- ❑   I need a safe place to hide from the police.

Radio buttons get their name from those old AM car radios that let you push a button to change stations quickly. Just as you can listen to only one radio station at a time, radio buttons let you choose only one option at a time. The following is an example of radio buttons.

What is your sex? (Choose only one.)

- ◯   Male
- ◯   Female
- ◯   Ex-male (surgically a female)
- ◯   Ex-female (surgically a male)

Aligning your boxes and buttons

Check boxes and radio buttons are usually left-aligned, which means they look like the following:

- ❑   This is left-aligned.

For some odd reason known only to those few programmers who actually use aligning options, you can also right-align check boxes and radio buttons.

     This is right-aligned.   ❑

To left-align or right-align a check box or radio button, follow these steps:

1. **Click on the check box or radio button that you want to align.**
2. **Open the Properties window. (Press F4, choose <u>V</u>iew⇨Properties <u>W</u>indow, or click on the Properties Window icon on the toolbar.)**
3. **Click on the Alignment property and set the value to 0 - Left Justify or 1 - Right Justify.**

Grouping check boxes

Check boxes rarely appear by themselves. Usually, two or more check boxes huddle together like frightened farm animals. The best way to isolate groups of check boxes is to use a frame. Frames visually separate different groups of check boxes. To create a group of check boxes, follow these steps:

1. **Click on the Frame icon in the Visual Basic Toolbox, as shown in Figure 7-1.**

2. **Move the mouse to where you want to draw the frame.**

3. **Hold down the left mouse button and move the mouse to draw a frame.**

4. **Click on the Check Box icon in the Visual Basic Toolbox.**

5. **Inside the frame, move the mouse to where you want to draw a check box.**

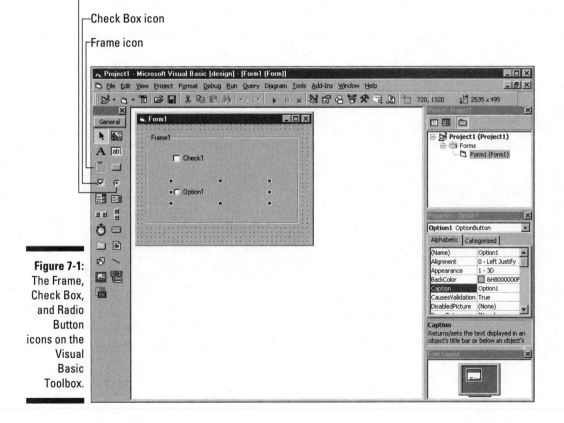

Figure 7-1:
The Frame, Check Box, and Radio Button icons on the Visual Basic Toolbox.

6. Hold down the left mouse button and move the mouse to draw your check box.

7. Repeat Steps 4 through 6 until you've drawn all the check boxes you want inside your frame or until you decide the time for a break has arrived.

As a final modification to a group of check boxes, set the TabStop properties of all grouped check boxes to False. Next, set the TabStop property of the first check box to True. That way, when someone presses the Tab key, only the first check box in that frame becomes highlighted.

To turn off the TabStop properties for a group of check boxes, follow these steps:

1. Click on any check box or radio button within the frame, except the first check box.

2. Open the Properties window. (In other words, press F4, choose View➪Properties Window, or click on the Properties Window icon on the toolbar.)

3. Click on the TabStop property and set the value to False.

4. Repeat Steps 1 through 3 until the TabStop property has been set to False for all but one of the check boxes.

Grouping radio buttons

If the radio buttons on a form are not grouped inside a frame, Visual Basic assumes that all radio buttons appearing on the same form belong to the same group. Thus, even if two radio buttons have nothing in common with each other but they appear on the same form, only one of the radio buttons can be chosen at any time. Figure 7-2 shows that only one radio button can be selected in each group of radio buttons.

If you need to display two or more groups of radio buttons, you have to group them within a frame. Otherwise, Visual Basic lumps all the radio buttons in a single group, which means that only one radio button can be chosen at any given time. To create a group of radio buttons in a frame, follow these steps:

1. Click on the Frame icon in the Visual Basic Toolbox.

2. Move the mouse to where you want to draw the frame.

3. Hold down the left mouse button and move the mouse to draw a frame.

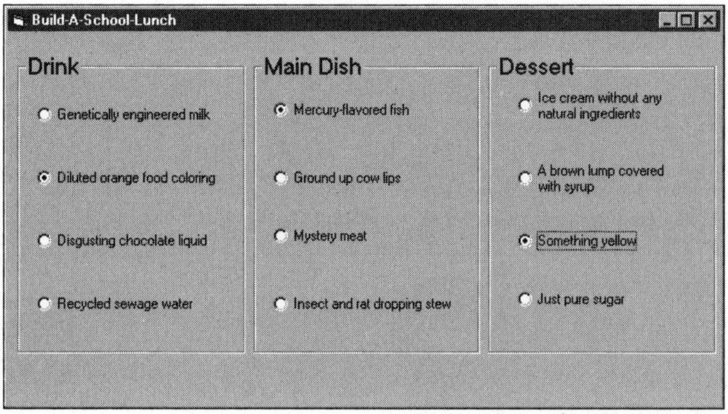

Build-A-School-Lunch

Drink
- ○ Genetically engineered milk
- ● Diluted orange food coloring
- ○ Disgusting chocolate liquid
- ○ Recycled sewage water

Main Dish
- ● Mercury-flavored fish
- ○ Ground up cow lips
- ○ Mystery meat
- ○ Insect and rat dropping stew

Dessert
- ○ Ice cream without any natural ingredients
- ○ A brown lump covered with syrup
- ● Something yellow
- ○ Just pure sugar

Figure 7-2:
How radio buttons affect one another on a form.

4. **Click on the Radio Button icon in the Visual Basic Toolbox.**

5. **Inside the frame, move the mouse to where you want to draw a radio button.**

6. **Hold down the left mouse button and move the mouse to draw your radio button.**

7. **Repeat Steps 4 through 6 until you've drawn all the radio buttons you want inside your frame or until you have to go to the bathroom.**

After you draw a radio button inside a frame, the button remains trapped inside that frame forever. When you move the frame, all radio buttons inside move along with their host frame.

Adding icons to check boxes and radio buttons

Normally, check boxes and radio buttons display only a caption; but if you want to get fancy, you also can display icons on your check boxes and radio buttons, too.

To make a check box or radio button display an icon, as shown in Figure 7-3, you must change the following properties as explained below:

✔ **Style:** Choose 1 - Graphical

✔ **Picture:** Defines the icon that appears on the check box or radio button

✔ **DownPicture:** Defines the icon that appears when the user clicks on the check box or radio button

✔ **DisabledPicture:** Defines the icon that appears when the check box or radio button is dimmed

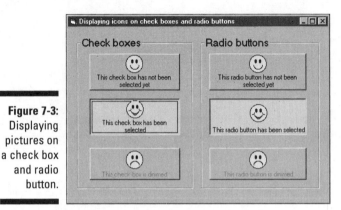

Figure 7-3:
Displaying
pictures on
a check box
and radio
button.

For some odd reason, Visual Basic makes check boxes and radio buttons with pictures appear like command buttons. Make sure that you take this strange appearance into account, or else both you and your users may mistake a check box or radio button for a command button instead.

To display a picture on a check box or radio button, follow these steps:

1. **Click on the check box or radio button on the form that you want to display a picture.**

2. **Open the Properties window. (Press F4, choose View▷Properties Window, or click on the Properties Window icon on the toolbar.)**

3. **Click the Style property, click the downward-pointing arrow, and choose 1 - Graphical.**

4. **Double-click on the Picture property.**

   Visual Basic displays a dialog box.

5. **Click on the picture you want to use. (You may have to dig through the Graphics folder to find a picture to use.) Click on Open.**

6. **Double-click on the DownPicture property to define a picture to appear when the user clicks on the command button.**

7. **Click on the picture you want to use. (You may have to dig through the Graphics folder to find a picture to use.) Click on Open.**

8. **Double-click on the DisabledPicture property to define a picture to appear if the command button appears dimmed.**

9. **Click on the picture you want to use. (You may have to dig through the Graphics folder to find a picture to use.) Click on Open.**

Offering More Choices with List Boxes and Combo Boxes

When you have only a few choices, check boxes and radio buttons work nicely. If you have ten or more choices, however, bombarding the user with a screen full of check boxes or radio buttons can be intimidating and ugly. To present many choices to the user in a clear and helpful manner, Visual Basic provides two alternatives to check boxes and radio buttons: list boxes and combo boxes.

List boxes display long lists of options from which users can choose. If users want to choose something that isn't on the list, too bad. They can't.

Combo boxes also display long lists of options for the user to choose. The difference is that combo boxes also let the user type a choice if the selection the user wants cannot be found on the list. Figure 7-4 shows an example of a list box and a combo box. Notice that the combo box displays items only if you click on the down arrow; the list box always displays items.

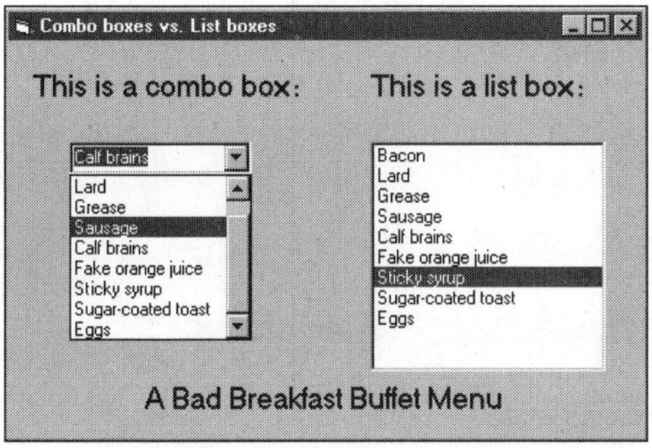

Figure 7-4:
Comparing
a list box
with a
combo box.

Creating list boxes and combo boxes

List boxes are like fast-food menus. You can choose only what's on the menu because the folks working there don't know how to handle special requests. Combo boxes are like fancy restaurants where you have a choice of ordering off the menu or saying, "I know this is a vegetarian restaurant, but I want the cook to grill me a steak anyway."

To create a list box, follow these steps:

1. **Click on the List Box icon in the Visual Basic Toolbox.**

2. **Move the mouse to the place on the form where you want to draw the list box.**

3. **Hold down the left mouse button and move the mouse to draw the list box.**

Visual Basic displays one list box with a dull caption such as List3.

4. **Repeat Steps 1 through 3 until you've drawn all the list boxes you need.**

To create a combo box, follow these steps:

1. **Click on the Combo Box icon in the Visual Basic Toolbox.**

2. **Move the mouse to the place on the form where you want to draw the combo box.**

3. **Hold down the left mouse button and move the mouse to draw the combo box.**

Visual Basic displays one combo box with a dull caption such as Combo1.

4. **Repeat Steps 1 through 3 until you've drawn all the combo boxes you need.**

Combo box styles

A combo box lets you type a choice or select one from the displayed list. For added variety, three styles of combo boxes are available, as shown in Figure 7-5:

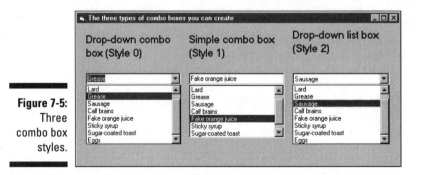

Figure 7-5:
Three
combo box
styles.

✔ Drop-down combo box (Style 0, the default)

✔ Simple combo box (Style 1)

✔ Drop-down list box (Style 2)

The drop-down combo box lets users type an item. If users have no idea what to type, they can click the downward-pointing arrow to the right of the combo box, and the combo box politely displays a list of possible choices. Visual Basic always creates this type of combo box unless you change the Visual Basic Style property.

The simple combo box always displays the list on the screen but also gives users the choice of typing an item.

Unlike the other two combo box styles, you must draw the full size of a simple combo box style so the user can see the items stored in the combo box.

The drop-down list box is actually a list box and always displays a range of choices, but you can't type anything of your own.

If you don't want the user to type anything into a combo box, set the combo box's Style property to 2 - Dropdown List.

At this point, you may be asking, "Wait a minute. Why do I want to create a combo box and then turn it into a stupid list box?" Unlike ordinary list boxes, a drop-down list box doesn't display the list on the screen until the user clicks on the arrow to the right of the box. This type of list box is useful when you need to conserve screen space.

Test your newfound knowledge

1. What is the main difference between a check box and a radio button?

a. You can choose one or more check boxes but only one radio button.

b. Radio buttons tune in to your favorite radio station, but check boxes are places where you save canceled checks.

c. I don't know. Aren't you supposed to be the teacher with all the answers?

d. Everything is one, man. Like, the answer is all in your point of view.

2. What is the major difference between a list box and a combo box?

a. A combo box gives you a choice of typing an item or choosing one from a displayed list. A list box forces you to choose an item from a displayed list.

b. A list box is spelled L-I-S-T, but a combo box is spelled C-O-M-B-O.

c. Combo boxes are cooler than list boxes because a combo box tends to be more confusing to the average user.

d. No difference. In fact, two out of three French chefs think that they both taste exactly like butter.

To define the style for a combo box, follow these steps:

1. **Click on the combo box that you want to change.**

   (This assumes that you've already created the box.)

2. **Open the Properties window. (Press F4, choose <u>V</u>iew⇨Properties <u>W</u>indow, or click on the Properties Window icon on the toolbar.)**

3. **Click on the Style property.**

4. **Click on the arrow in the Settings Box to display your list of choices.**

   (Hey, what do you know? The Settings Box is an example of a drop-down list box!)

5. **Click on the combo box style you want.**

Adding Items to List Boxes and Combo Boxes

After you create your list box or combo box, you have to fill up your box with items. (Otherwise, you have no real point in creating a list box or combo box, now do you?) Visual Basic gives you two ways to add items to a list box or combo box:

- ✔ Use the List property in the Properties window.
- ✔ Use BASIC code.

To add items to a list box or a combo box using the List property, follow these steps:

1. **Click on the list box or combo box that you want to add items to.**

2. **Open the Properties window. (Press F4, choose <u>V</u>iew⇨Properties <u>W</u>indow, or click on the Properties Window icon on the toolbar.)**

3. **Double-click on the List property.**

   A drop-down text box appears.

4. **Type the first item you want to appear in your list box or combo box. Next, press Ctrl+Enter.**

   Repeat this step for each item you want to add.

5. **Press Enter.**

When typing items in the List property, make sure that you press Ctrl+Enter in between each item. The moment you press Enter, Visual Basic assumes you're done typing items in the List property.

If you want to use BASIC code to add items to a list box or combo box, the secret BASIC command to use is AddItem. So if you want to add the item "Pick me" to a list box named lstCommands, here is the magic BASIC code that you use to do so:

```
lstCommands.AddItem "Pick me"
```

You can add items to a list box or combo box any time your program is running, but the most common time is when the form containing the list box or combo box first loads.

To add items to a list when a form loads, follow these steps:

1. **Click on the form in the Project Explorer window.**

2. **Click on the View Code icon.**

3. **Click in the Object list box and choose the form name.**

   Visual Basic displays the following procedure:

```
Private Sub Form_Load()
End Sub
```

4. **For each item you want to display in a list box or combo box, use the AddItem secret command.**

   For example, if you had a list box named lstToDo and a combo box named cboHideIn, the Sub Form_Load( ) procedure may look like the following:

```
Private Sub Form_Load()
  lstToDo.AddItem "Call stockbroker"
  lstToDo.AddItem "Make airline reservations"
  lstToDo.AddItem "Act normally until noon"
  lstToDo.AddItem "Steal $250,000"
  lstToDo.AddItem "Fake headache"
  lstToDo.AddItem "Leave work early"
  lstToDo.AddItem "Go to airport"
  cboHideIn.AddItem "Acapulco"
  cboHideIn.AddItem "Rio de Janeiro"
  cboHideIn.AddItem "Paris"
  cboHideIn.AddItem "Tokyo"
  cboHideIn.AddItem "New York"
  cboHideIn.AddItem "Bangkok"
End Sub
```

This procedure adds these items to the lstToDo list box and to the cboHideIn combo box whenever the first form of your program loads. See Figure 7-6 for an example of the result.

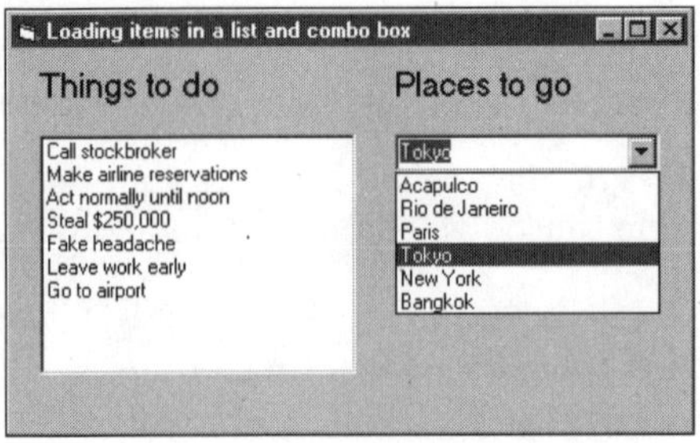

Figure 7-6:
What the lstToDo list box and the cboHideIn combo box look like when the Form_Load procedure fills them with information.

> **Loading items in a list and combo box**
>
> **Things to do**   **Places to go**
>
> Call stockbroker   Tokyo
> Make airline reservations   Acapulco
> Act normally until noon   Rio de Janeiro
> Steal $250,000   Paris
> Fake headache   Tokyo
> Leave work early   New York
> Go to airport   Bangkok

Highlighting default items

The purpose of list boxes and combo boxes is to provide users with choices. To make choosing items even more mindless and thus more efficient from the user's point of view, combo boxes can display default items. (With list boxes, the first item is the default item.) A *default item* is the item that the computer assumes the user wants unless instructed otherwise. (For a default item to be the least likely choice doesn't really make much sense.)

To create a default item for a combo box, follow these steps:

1. **Click on the combo box for which you want to assign a default item.**

2. **Open the Properties window. (Press F4, choose <u>V</u>iew⇨Properties <u>W</u>indow, or click on the Properties Window icon on the toolbar.)**

3. **Click on the Text property.**

4. **Type the item that you want to appear as the default item in this combo box.**

If you set a combo box's Style property to 2 - Dropdown List, you can define a default item by using BASIC code to set the ListIndex property to a value such as 0 (to make the first item the default item):

```
cboHideIn.ListIndex = 2
```

When a user clicks on the combo box, the default item is highlighted. (See Figure 7-6.)

If you don't define a default item, Visual Basic displays the combo box's generic name (Combo1, Combo2, and so on) as the default item. Because this looks very ugly and amateurish, you should always define a default item for your combo boxes.

Sorting items in a list box or combo box

The order that you add items to a list box or combo box is the order in which the items appear. For a little variety, Visual Basic lets you sort items in two ways:

- ✔ Alphabetically
- ✔ Any way you want

When Visual Basic sorts a list alphabetically, the list is sorted without regard to whether items are capitalized or not. For example, Visual Basic considers "Your Momma" and "YOUR MOMMA" to be identical.

To sort items in a list box or combo box alphabetically, follow these steps:

1. **Click on the list box or combo box in which you want to display items alphabetically.**

2. **Open the Properties window. (Press F4, choose View⇨Properties Window, or click on the Properties Window icon on the toolbar.)**

3. **Click on the Sorted property and set the property to True.**

Visual Basic always sorts items with the A's on top and the Z's at the bottom. You cannot sort items in descending order, with the Z's on top and the A's at the bottom (unless, of course, you flip your monitor upside down).

If alphabetic sorting isn't what you want, you have to sort items one-by-one yourself. Visual Basic assigns an index number (which is just an ordinary number such as 1 or 3) to each item in a list.

The first item in a list is assigned an index number of 0, the second item is assigned an index number of 1, the third item is assigned an index number of 2, and so on, as shown in Figure 7-7. (If you've ever been in a European elevator where the ground floor is labeled 1, the first floor is labeled 2, and the second floor is labeled 3, you are going to recognize the confusing way that Visual Basic assigns index numbers.)

Index=5(Bangkok)

Index=4(New York)

Index=3(Tokyo)

Index=2(Paris)

Index=1(Rio de Janeiro)

Index=0(Acapulco)

Figure 7-7:
How Visual
Basic
assigns
index
numbers to
items in a
list box or
combo box.

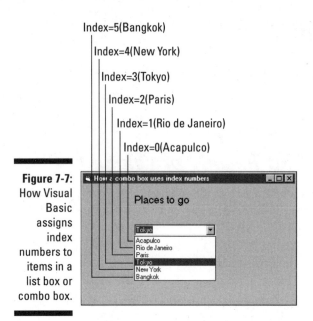

To put an item at the top of a list, you still have to use the magic AddItem
BASIC command in the following way:

```
cboHideIn.AddItem "Harare", 0
```

If you omit the index number, Visual Basic adds items to a list in one of two
ways:

✔ If the Sorted property of the list box or combo box is False, the item
goes to the bottom of the list.

✔ If the Sorted property of the list box or combo box is True, the item
goes in the correct alphabetic order.

Figure 7-8 shows how Visual Basic places "Harare" in alphabetical order in
the sorted list and at the end in the unsorted list if you omit the index
number.

If you set the Sorted property of a list box or combo box to True and add
items by using index numbers, Visual Basic adds the item according to the
index number and does not sort the newly added items alphabetically.

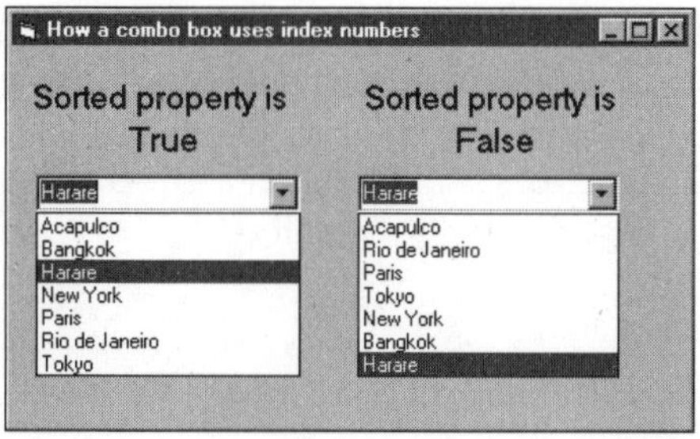

Figure 7-8:
Adding an
item to a
sorted and
unsorted
list box.

Removing items from a list box or combo box

Adding items and sorting them may make your lists look nice, but wiping out an item to satisfy that destructive urge that everyone experiences once in a while is more fun.

Visual Basic gives you two ways to remove an item from a list:

- ✔ Use the `RemoveItem` BASIC command to remove items one at a time.
- ✔ Use the `Clear` BASIC command to wipe out an entire list at once.

To use the `RemoveItem` BASIC command, you have to know the index number of the item you want to remove. For example, to remove the item with an index number of 5 that's located in a list box named lstToDo, use the following BASIC command:

```
lstToDo.RemoveItem 5
```

To use the `Clear` BASIC command to wipe out an entire list in a single blow, you need the name of the list box or combo box that contains the list you want to kill. To wipe out the entire contents of a combo box named cboHideIn, use the following BASIC command:

```
cboHideIn.Clear
```

Before using the `Clear` BASIC command, make sure that you really want to wipe out an entire list.

Displaying check boxes in your list boxes

When you display items in a list box, you can also display them as check boxes (see Figure 7-9). By using check boxes, you can check off items in a list box such as to-do lists, grocery lists, or lists of New Year's resolutions that you never plan to complete.

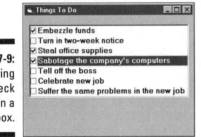

Figure 7-9:
Displaying check boxes in a list box.

To display check boxes in a list box, follow these steps:

1. **Click on the list box where you want check boxes to appear.**

2. **Open the Properties window. (Press F4, choose <u>V</u>iew⇔Properties <u>W</u>indow, or click on the Properties Window icon on the toolbar.)**

3. **Click on the Style property and choose 1 - Checkbox.**

To figure out which item a user may have chosen in a checked list box, you have to use BASIC code. Remember that items in a list box are assigned a number. The top item is given an index number of 0, the second from the top a number of 1, the third from the top 2, and so on. Knowing this, you have to write an event procedure that tells you which item was just checked (or unchecked). To do this, you have to use the event procedure attached to your list box such as:

```
Private Sub List1_ItemCheck(Item As Integer)
GlobalVariable = Item

' This will print the item checked (or unchecked)
Print Item
End Sub
```

The moment someone checks (or unchecks) an item in a checked list box, the ItemCheck event procedure runs and the Item variable tells you which item was checked (or unchecked). So if the top item is checked (or unchecked), the ItemCheck event procedure assigns the number 0 to Item.

Then you have to assign your own variable to Item so you can tell the other parts of your program which list box item got checked (or unchecked). From there, you have to write BASIC code to figure out what to do if someone checks or unchecks an item.

Creating Multiple Column List Boxes

For aesthetic purposes — or just because you're bored and want to goof around — you can display multiple columns in a list box. Visual Basic provides three types of multiple columns, depending on the value defined by the Column property:

- ✔ **Value 0:** A single column list with vertical scrolling (the default appearance of list boxes)

- ✔ **Value 1:** A single column list with horizontal scrolling (but no vertical scrolling)

- ✔ **Any value greater than 1 in number:** A multiple column list of two or more columns with horizontal scrolling (but no vertical scrolling)

These styles are illustrated in Figure 7-10. To change the way a list box displays items in columns, follow these steps:

1. **Click on the list box that you want to modify.**

2. **Open the Properties window. (Press F4, choose View⇨Properties Window, or click on the Properties Window icon on the toolbar.)**

3. **Click on the Columns property and type 0, 1, or any number larger than 1.**

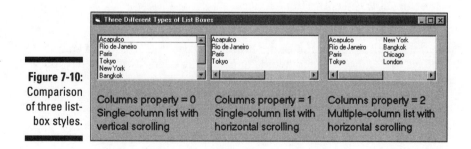

Figure 7-10: Comparison of three list-box styles.

Making Listed Items Look Pretty

To spice up your lists and make them look a little less like boring shopping lists, Visual Basic lets you change the font, type style, and size of your list's items.

Fonts are different ways to display text. Normally, Visual Basic uses the MS Sans Serif font, but you can use any font stored in the memory of your computer. (MS Sans Serif is similar to the Helvetica font, and the Visual Basic MS Serif font is similar to the Times Roman font.)

To change the font of items that appear in a list box or combo box, follow these steps:

1. **Click on the list box or combo box whose font you want to modify.**

2. **Open the Properties window. (Press F4, choose View⇨Properties Window, or click on the Properties Window icon on the toolbar.)**

3. **Double-click on the Font property.**

   Visual Basic displays a Font dialog box.

4. **Click on the font you want and click on OK.**

   Visual Basic immediately changes the font in the list box or combo box.

Be careful when you use fonts. Novices often get carried away and use so many bizarre fonts that all semblance of normality is lost. Unless you have a really good reason to use different fonts, let Visual Basic use its default font of MS Sans Serif.

You can also change the size of your items, making them smaller or larger. However, the larger the type size is, the larger your list box or combo box must be to show the entire item at once.

The larger the font size, the more the items in your list boxes and combo boxes stand out. Usually, the best method is to use one size for all your list boxes or combo boxes to avoid confusing the user any more than you have to.

To define the font size, follow these steps:

1. **Click on the list box or combo box whose font size you want to modify.**

2. **Open the Properties window. (Press F4, choose View⇨Properties Window, or click on the Properties Window icon on the toolbar.)**

3. **Double-click on the Font property.**

Visual Basic displays a Font dialog box.

4. Click on the font size you want and click on OK.

Visual Basic immediately changes the font size of the list box or combo box.

Besides changing the font and size, you can also change the font style and display text in **bold**, *italics*, underline, or ~~strikeout~~. To set any one or more of these font styles, follow these steps:

1. Click on the list box or combo box whose fonts you want to modify.

2. Open the Properties window. (Press F4, choose View⇨Properties Window, or click on the Properties Window icon on the toolbar).

3. Double-click on the Font property.

Visual Basic displays a Font dialog box.

4. Click on the font style you want and click on OK.

Visual Basic immediately changes the font style of the list box or combo box.

The more attractive you make your list boxes and combo boxes, the more likely the user is going to notice the boxes, at least (if not use them). Just remember that you want to make your program easy to use, not a work of art. If you want to get creative, take up finger painting. If you want to create useful programs and make millions of dollars, make your programs easy, fun, and simple to use.

Chapter 8

Text Boxes for Typing and Showing Words

In This Chapter

▶ Creating text boxes

▶ Filling text boxes and hiding passwords

▶ Using different fonts, sizes, type styles, and colors

Despite the growing acceptance of icons and graphical user interfaces, not all choices can always be offered through command buttons, radio buttons, or combo boxes. Sometimes your program may need to display a word, sentence, paragraph, or entire novel on the screen. And sometimes the user may want to type in a good word or two as well.

So what's the solution? Combo boxes work with words or short phrases, but if your program needs to display a chunk of text or if the user needs to type in a substantial amount of information, a *text box* can make your job a whole lot easier.

Text boxes have two purposes in life:

✔ To show text on the screen

✔ To let the user type text into the program

Text boxes are among the most flexible programming objects because you can display instructions in a text box and the user can type a reply using ordinary words. If you use enough text boxes in your programs, you may help increase literacy among our population today.

The Visual Basic program enclosed on the CD-ROM provides a simple example of using a text box for accepting a password. Dig into the source code and play around. At the very least, you may mess up the program but still learn something in the process.

Creating a Text Box

Text boxes are like miniature word processors but can display only one font, one size, and one type style (such as bold or italics). So if you want to display multiple fonts in a text box, give up that thought right now because you can't.

When a user types text in a text box, the following keys work:

- **Delete:** Erases the character to the right of the cursor
- **Backspace:** Erases the character to the left of the cursor
- **Shift+Arrow:** Highlights a block of text
- **Ctrl+Left arrow:** Moves the cursor one word to the left
- **Ctrl+Right arrow:** Moves the cursor one word to the right
- **Home (or Ctrl+Home):** Moves the cursor to the beginning of the line
- **End (or Ctrl+End):** Moves the cursor to the end of the line
- **Shift+any movement key (such as Home):** Highlights text
- **F11 or F12:** Doesn't do a thing and is about as useful on your keyboard as wisdom teeth in your mouth

To create a text box, follow these steps:

1. **Click on the Text Box icon in the Visual Basic Toolbox.**
2. **On the form, move the mouse where you want to draw the text box.**
3. **Hold down the left mouse button and draw the text box.**

   Visual Basic displays your text box with default text inside, such as Text1.

4. **Repeat Steps 1 through 3 until you've drawn all the text boxes you need or until you find something else to do.**

Putting pretty borders around text boxes

Normally, Visual Basic displays a single line around a text box, defining the boundaries of that text box. If you want to keep your users guessing where a text box is, you can remove this border. Figure 8-1 shows a text box with and without a border.

To change the borders around a text box, follow these steps:

1. **Click on the text box whose border you want to change.**

2. **Open the Properties window. (Press F4, choose <u>V</u>iew⇨Properties <u>W</u>indow, or click on the Properties Window icon on the toolbar.)**

3. **Click on the BorderStyle property and choose one of the following:**

   - 0 - None
   - 1 - Fixed Single

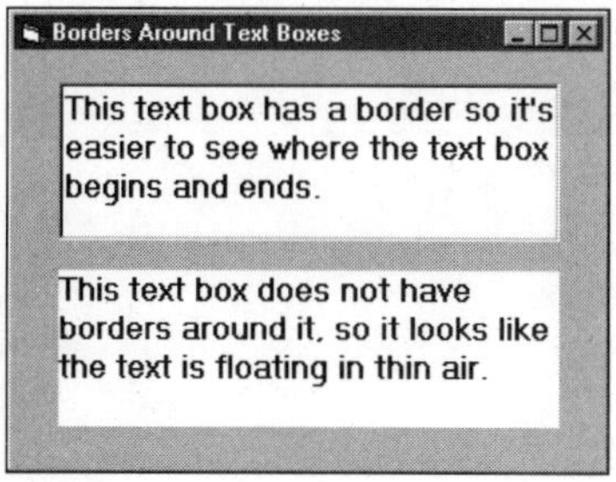

Figure 8-1:
A bordered
text box
and an
unbordered
text box.

Borders Around Text Boxes

> This text box has a border so it's easier to see where the text box begins and ends.

> This text box does not have borders around it, so it looks like the text is floating in thin air.

Displaying words in a text box

After you create a text box, the next step is to put some text in the box. By default, Visual Basic displays the text box's name in the text box, such as Text1.

Changing the Text property of a text box does not affect the Name property of the text box. So if you want your text box to display something more exciting than Text1, you have to change the Text property.

The Text property can contain anything from a blank line (which means your text box appears empty) to ordinary text, to a mass of incomprehensible text that resembles a typical computer manual. Figure 8-2 shows how the Text property determines what appears inside a text box.

To change the Text property of a text box, follow these steps:

1. **Click on the text box whose Text property you want to change.**

2. **Open the Properties window. (Press F4, choose <u>V</u>iew⇨Properties <u>W</u>indow, or click on the Properties Window icon on the toolbar.)**

3. **Double-click on the Text property (or just click once on the Text label) and type whatever text you want to appear in your text box.**

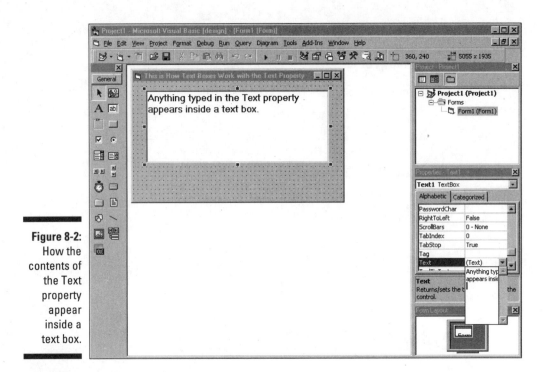

Figure 8-2:
How the contents of the Text property appear inside a text box.

If you want to change the contents of your text box while your program is running, you have to use BASIC code such as

```
txtMessage.Text = "This will now appear in the text box."
```

Whenever you change the Text property of a text box, the new contents of the text box completely wipe out the previous contents of the text box.

Aligning text in a text box

To make a text box look nice and organized, Visual Basic can align the text as left-justified, right-justified, or centered, as shown in Figure 8-3.

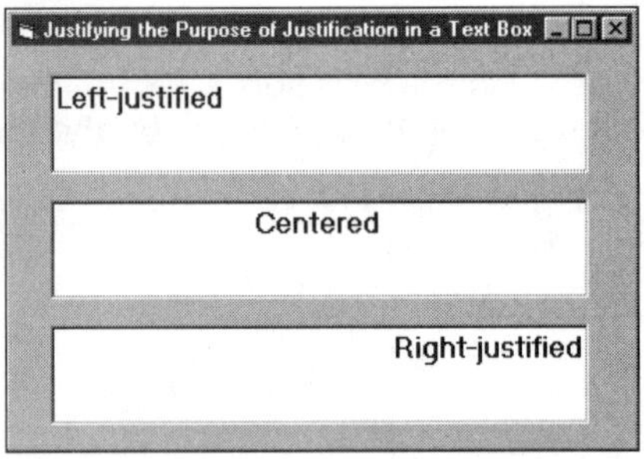

Figure 8-3:
Comparison of left, right, and center justification.

To align text in a text box, follow these steps:

1. **Click on the text box whose text you want to align.**

2. **Open the Properties window. (Press F4, choose <u>V</u>iew⇨Properties <u>W</u>indow, or click on the Properties Window icon on the toolbar.)**

3. **Click on the MultiLine property and set the value to True.**

   If the MultiLine property is set to False, Visual Basic ignores any changes you make to the Alignment property.

4. **Click on the Alignment property and choose one of the following:**

   - 0 - Left Justify

   - 1 - Right Justify

   - 2 - Center

Changing the Alignment property doesn't align the text until you first change the text box's MultiLine property to True.

Word-wrapping text boxes

In addition to displaying text that the programmer typed into the Text property, a text box also lets users type in their own text. By default, a text box is pretty stupid at handling text. If you type text into a text box, the text box cheerfully displays the text as one huge line that scrolls endlessly out of sight. To make a text box wrap words within the box's boundaries like in a word-processor program, you have to set the text box's MultiLine property to True.

To set the MultiLine property to True for a text box, follow these steps:

1. **Click on the text box where you want to use word-wrapping.**

2. **Open the Properties window. (Press F4, choose <u>V</u>iew⇨Properties <u>W</u>indow, or click on the Properties Window icon on the toolbar.)**

3. **Click on the MultiLine property and set the value to True.**

When a text box has a MultiLine property of True, the text box word-wraps text within the boundaries of the text box, as shown in Figure 8-4. If you change the width of a text box while your program is running, the text box automatically word-wraps the text within the new size of the text box. Now, don't you think that what computers can do nowadays is amazing?

How Word-Wrapping Works in a Text Box

This is why you need word-wra

See how word-wrapping neatly
displays text on multiple lines?

Figure 8-4:
Word-
wrapping in
a text box.

Adding horizontal and vertical scroll bars in text boxes

Word-wrapping is a fine way to display text within a text box, but if the text box isn't tall enough, the text box can't display all the text you may type in. To solve this problem, you may also have to add *horizontal* or *vertical scroll bars,* as shown in Figure 8-5.

Playing with Scroll Bars in Text Boxes

Watch this text scroll out of sigh

This text box uses vertical
scroll bars so viewers can
see more text than the text
box can display at once.

Figure 8-5:
Horizontal
and vertical
scroll bars
in text
boxes.

Be careful! If you add a horizontal scroll bar to a text box, that turns off all word-wrapping. When a text box uses horizontal scroll bar, the only way a user can type on the next line is to press Enter.

Adding a vertical scroll bar lets users type and display more text than the text box can display. With vertical scroll bars, users can press PageUp or PageDown to display text in a text box.

To add scroll bars to a text box, follow these steps:

1. **Click on the text box in which you want to add scroll bars.**

2. **Open the Properties window. (Press F4, choose <u>V</u>iew⇨Properties <u>W</u>indow, or click on the Properties Window icon on the toolbar.)**

3. **Click on the ScrollBars property and choose one of the following:**

    • 0 - None

    • 1 - Horizontal

- 2 - Vertical

- 3 - Both (horizontal and vertical scroll bars)

Vertical and horizontal scroll bars work only if you have set the text box's MultiLine property to True. (Otherwise, there's no point in having scroll bars remain if you can't display more than one line of text.)

Making a Password Text Box

In case you work for the CIA, FBI, NSA, DIA, IRS, or any organization that spends lots of money, buries itself in secrecy, and hides behind a three-letter acronym, you may be interested in the ability of Visual Basic to create special password text boxes.

Rather than display ordinary text, *password text boxes* mask any text you type into a text box with a single character, such as an asterisk (*). Figure 8-6 shows how the password "Top Secret" appears as only asterisks in the "CIA Software (Top Secret)" text box.

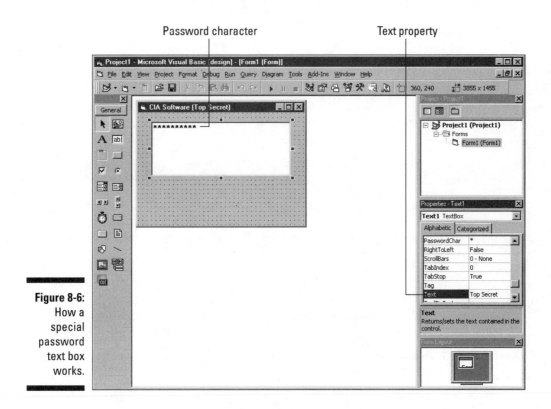

Figure 8-6: How a special password text box works.

To create a password text box, you need to define the character that the text box displays when someone types in text. To do this, you need to follow these steps:

1. **Click on the text box that you want to turn into a password text box.**

2. **Open the Properties window. (Press F4, choose <u>V</u>iew➪Properties <u>W</u>indow, or click on the Properties Window icon on the toolbar.)**

3. **Click on the MultiLine property and set the value to False.**

   Always set the MultiLine property of a password text box to False, otherwise the password text box can't mask any typed characters. This is the Visual Basic way of saying that passwords can't be so long that they require two or more lines to write.

4. **Click on the PasswordChar property and type the masking character, such as an asterisk.**

   The masking character can only be a single character.

Limiting the Length of Text

To prevent people from getting too wordy, you can set the maximum length of text for a text box. This way, people can't type rambling essays about what they did last summer in your text boxes.

To define the maximum number of characters that a text box can accept from the user, change the MaxLength property. If the user tries to type any characters beyond the MaxLength limit, Visual Basic beeps and accepts no more.

(Alas, Visual Basic doesn't have a minimum length property. For ordinary text boxes, this isn't a problem, but if you're creating a password text box, you can bet that at least one bozo is going to choose a one-letter password that some hacker can easily guess.)

To define the maximum length of characters that a text box accepts, follow these steps:

1. **Click on the text box whose maximum character length you want to define.**

2. **Open the Properties window. (Press F4, choose <u>V</u>iew➪Properties <u>W</u>indow, or click on the Properties Window icon on the toolbar.)**

3. **Double-click on the MaxLength property and type any number greater than zero.**

   A value of zero effectively means that no limit to the number of characters a user can type in a text box exists.

Changing Fonts, Sizes, and Type Styles

Visual Basic normally displays text in a text box using the MS Sans Serif font, but if you want to exercise your creativity, you can choose any font stored in the memory of your computer. (The MS Sans Serif font is similar to the Helvetica font, and the Visual Basic MS Serif font is similar to the Times Roman font.)

To change the font used in a text box, follow these steps:

1. **Click on the text box whose font you want to change.**

2. **Open the Properties window. (Press F4, choose View⇨Properties Window, or click on the Properties Window icon on the toolbar.)**

3. **Double-click on the Font property.**

   Visual Basic displays a font dialog box.

4. **Click on the font you want and click on OK.**

   Visual Basic immediately changes the font in the text box.

Be careful when using fonts. Beginners often get carried away and choose really bizarre fonts that confuse more than they clarify. Unless you have a really good reason to use a different font, just use the default font, MS Sans Serif, for most of your work.

You can also change the size of your text, making your text smaller or larger. Of course, the larger the type size of your text, the larger your text box must be to show the entire text. The larger the font size, the less text you can display. To avoid confusing the user any more than necessary, use one font size for all your text boxes.

To define the font size for a text box, follow these steps:

1. **Click on the text box whose font size you want to modify.**

2. **Open the Properties window. (Press F4, choose View⇨Properties Window, or click on the Properties Window icon on the toolbar.)**

3. **Double-click on the Font property.**

   Visual Basic displays a font dialog box.

4. **Click on the font size you want and then click on OK.**

   Visual Basic immediately changes the font size of the text displayed in your chosen text box.

Test your newfound knowledge

1. Give two uses for text boxes.

a. To store letters from your Scrabble game and to contain words that may win you a million dollars on Wheel of Fortune.

b. To display text on-screen and to let users type text into a program.

c. To store all the computer books that you buy but never read, and to make cardboard forts that your children can hide in.

d. To use as a litter box and to give your cat something to read.

2. If a text box has the PasswordChar property set to * (asterisk) and the MaxLength property set to 10, what happens?

a. I have to flip back through the pages of this book to find the answer, so wait while I do that.

b. I'm not sure, but whatever happens must be important because this question is listed here.

c. This defines the secret password that is needed to break into the Pentagon's computers.

d. The text box accepts a maximum of 10 characters and displays an asterisk (*) in place of an actual typed character.

Changing the font and type size of text can be fun so Visual Basic also gives you additional ways to change the appearance of your text to display **bold**, *italic*, or ~~strikeout~~. To choose a font style, follow these steps:

1. **Click on the text box whose font that you want to modify.**

2. **Open the Properties window. (Press F4, choose <u>V</u>iew⇨Properties <u>W</u>indow, or click on the Properties Window icon on the toolbar.)**

3. **Double-click on the Font property.**

   Visual Basic displays a font dialog box.

4. **Click on the font style you want and click on OK.**

   Visual Basic immediately changes the font style of your chosen text box.

Coloring Text Boxes

If you loved the idea of writing in different colors with crayons when you were a kid, then you are going to love the idea of coloring your text boxes using Visual Basic.

Normally, Visual Basic displays text in black against a white background. For more creativity, you can change the foreground and background colors of your text boxes, as shown in Figure 8-7.

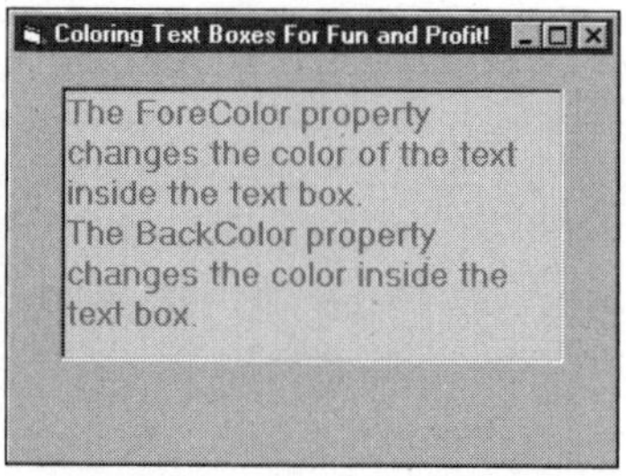

Figure 8-7:
Background
and
foreground
colors of a
text box.

The ForeColor property changes the color of the text inside the text box.
The BackColor property changes the color inside the text box.

The color inside the text box *(background color)* is defined by the BackColor property. The color of the text itself *(foreground color)* is defined by the ForeColor property.

To change the background or foreground color of a text box, follow these steps:

1. **Click on the text box whose background or foreground color you want to modify.**

2. **Open the Properties window. (Press F4, choose <u>V</u>iew⇨Properties <u>W</u>indow, or click on the Properties Window icon on the toolbar.)**

3. **Double-click on the BackColor or ForeColor property and click on the Palette tab.**

   Visual Basic displays a color palette.

4. **Click on the color you want.**

   Visual Basic immediately changes the color of your chosen text box.

By changing the color of your text boxes, you can highlight certain information and make it easier for the user to see (or ignore). Just remember that too many colors can be distracting and that some people may be color-blind, which means they won't experience the full effect of your program if they can't see the text displayed in certain colors. Remember, use colors sparingly.

Chapter 9
Scroll Bars and Labels

· ·

· ·

*N*ot all choices in life can be divided into neat categories like check boxes, radio buttons, or list boxes. Sometimes users may need to make choices that require a wide range of gradual adjustments.

Think of adjusting the volume on a stereo. If the only three choices you have are soft, medium, and loud, you can't adjust the volume to your taste. That's why most stereos let you turn a knob or press a button that gradually adjusts the volume higher or lower.

For minute measurements, or for moving through long lists of information, use scroll bars. Although text boxes, forms, and list boxes have built-in scroll bars, you can create separate scroll bars on your own. Figure 9-1 shows the different parts of a scroll bar.

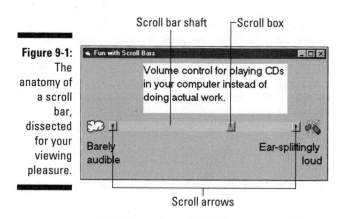

Figure 9-1:
The anatomy of a scroll bar, dissected for your viewing pleasure.

The CD-ROM contains a Visual Basic program showing how a vertical scroll bar works. Study the source code and modify it to see what happens.

Creating Scroll Bars

Visual Basic lets you create two types of scroll bars: horizontal scroll bars and vertical scroll bars. Horizontal scroll bars point left and right, just like the fast-forward and rewind buttons on your VCR or tape player. Vertical scroll bars point up and down, just like the volume control on some stereos.

To create a scroll bar, follow these steps:

1. **Click the Horizontal or Vertical Scroll Bar icon in the Visual Basic Toolbox.**

2. **Move the mouse cursor on the form to where you want to draw the scroll bar.**

3. **Hold down the left mouse button and move the mouse to draw the scroll bar, then release the left mouse button.**

4. **Repeat Steps 1 through 3 until you draw all the scroll bars you feel like making.**

If you double-click on the Horizontal or Vertical Scroll Bar icon in the Visual Basic Toolbox, Visual Basic creates a scroll bar on a form right away.

Setting scroll bar maximum and minimum values

Scroll bars are actually graphical representations of numeric values. The value of a scroll bar can range from –32,768 to 32,767. These numerical values can represent anything you want, such as measurements or quantities.

By default, Visual Basic sets the maximum value to 32,767 and the minimum value to 0. On horizontal scroll bars, the maximum value is represented when the scroll box is at the rightmost position on the scroll bar. The minimum value is represented when the scroll box is at the leftmost position on the scroll bar.

On vertical scroll bars, the maximum value is represented when the scroll box is at the bottommost position on the scroll bar. The minimum value is represented when the scroll box is at the topmost position on the scroll bar.

Obviously, the default values of 32,767 and 0 may be too extreme for most programs. To define a smaller range of values, you have to change the scroll bar's Max and Min settings.

To change the Max and Min settings for a scroll bar, follow these steps:

1. **Click on the scroll bar whose Max and Min values you want to change.**

2. **Open the Properties window. (Press F4, choose <u>V</u>iew⇨Properties <u>W</u>indow, or click on the Properties Window icon on the toolbar.)**

3. **Double-click (or click once) on the Max property and type a new value.**

4. **Double-click (or click once) on the Min property and type a new value.**

If the Min value is larger than the Max value, the scroll bar acts topsy-turvy. In this case, the scroll bar represents the maximum value at the leftmost or topmost position and the minimum value at the rightmost or bottommost position.

Where does the scroll box appear in my scroll bars?

By default, Visual Basic assigns scroll bars the value defined by the Min property (such as 0). This means that if your Max and Min values are positive, the scroll box always appears in the topmost position in a vertical scroll bar and the leftmost position in a horizontal scroll bar, as shown in Figure 9-2.

By default, the scroll box represents the minimum value of the scroll bar. However, if you want your scroll bars to display a default value of something other than the minimum value, you have to change the scroll bar's Value property.

To change the scroll bar's value, follow these steps:

1. **Click on the scroll bar whose value you want to change.**

2. **Open the Properties window. (Press F4, choose <u>V</u>iew⇨Properties <u>W</u>indow, or click on the Properties Window icon on the toolbar.)**

3. **Click on the Value property and type a new value.**

   Visual Basic dutifully changes the scroll bar's value while you watch.

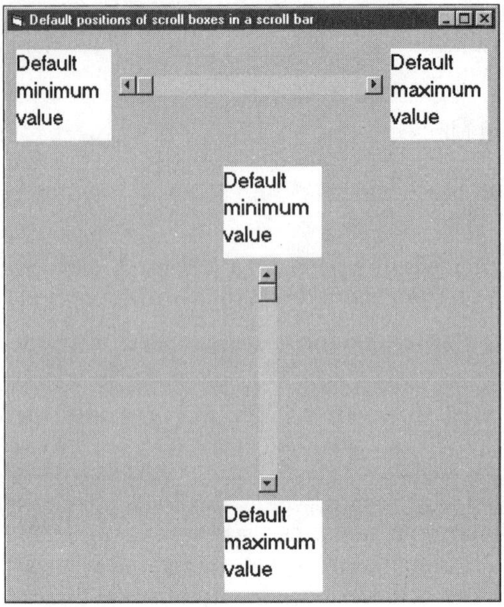

Figure 9-2:
Default
position of
the scroll
boxes.

Moving the scroll box

The scroll box represents the current value of the scroll bar. To move the scroll box, users can do any of the following:

✔ Drag the scroll box within the scroll bar.

✔ Click on the scroll arrows at each end of the scroll bar.

✔ Click in the area between the scroll box and each scroll arrow.

Each time the user clicks the scroll arrows, the scroll box moves a certain distance. By default, this distance is 1. Therefore, if your Min value is 0 and your Max value is 12, you have to click on the scroll arrow 12 times to move the scroll box from one end of the scroll bar to the other.

To modify the distance the scroll box moves when the user clicks on a scroll arrow, follow these steps:

1. **Click on the scroll bar that you want to modify.**

2. **Open the Properties window. (Press F4, choose View⊅Properties Window, or click on the Properties Window icon on the toolbar.)**

3. **Double-click (or click once) on the SmallChange property and type a new value.**

Likewise, each time the user clicks on the scroll bar shaft (in the area between the scroll box and the scroll area), the scroll box moves a certain distance. By default, this distance is 1, which means that if the Min value is 0 and the Max value is 5, you have to click five times to move the scroll box from one end of the scroll bar to the other.

To modify the distance the scroll box moves when the user clicks on the scroll shaft, follow these steps:

1. **Click on the scroll bar that you want to modify.**

2. **Open the Properties window. (Press F4, choose <u>V</u>iew⇨Properties <u>W</u>indow, or click on the Properties Window icon on the toolbar.)**

3. **Double-click (or click once) on the LargeChange property and type a new value.**

The values for LargeChange and SmallChange can vary between 1 and 32,767. The smaller the value, the smaller the distance the scroll box moves. The larger the value, the larger the distance the scroll box moves.

Here's some information you may never use: You can set LargeChange or SmallChange to values greater than the Max value. This just means that when the user clicks your scroll bar, the scroll box immediately jumps to one end of the scroll bar.

Test your newfound knowledge

1. When can you use a scroll bar?

a. When you want to give the illusion of complexity.

b. When the user needs to choose a range of values.

c. When you need to rewrap toilet paper that your cat unrolled onto the floor.

d. When nothing else seems to work, and you've run out of ideas on how to make your program easier to use.

2. What are the three ways to move the scroll box within a scroll bar?

a. Press the arrow keys, flip the mouse upside down, or unplug the computer.

b. Telekinesis, verbal threats, or pushing the scroll box with your finger.

c. The scroll box never moves. This is a trick question, right?

d. Drag the scroll box with the mouse, click the scroll arrows, or click the scroll bar shaft inside the scroll bar.

Creating Labels

For pure decoration, you can sprinkle labels on any of your Visual Basic forms. Labels simply identify the objects on your form. In real life, you see labels all the time, such as the label MEN or WOMEN on a restroom door, FIRE EXTINGUISHER over a fire extinguisher in a public building, or POWER next to your monitor's on-and-off button. Labels simply call your attention to something you may otherwise overlook.

REMEMBER

Both text boxes (see Chapter 8) and labels can display text on-screen. The main difference is that the user can modify the text inside a text box but can't modify text inside a label.

TIP

Psst, although users can't modify text in a label, BASIC code can modify the text inside a label. In this way, your labels can display changing messages to the user, such as "Sorry, that option isn't available at this time," "Now printing page 2 of 9," or "What are you, stupid or something?" Figure 9-3 shows some everyday examples of labels.

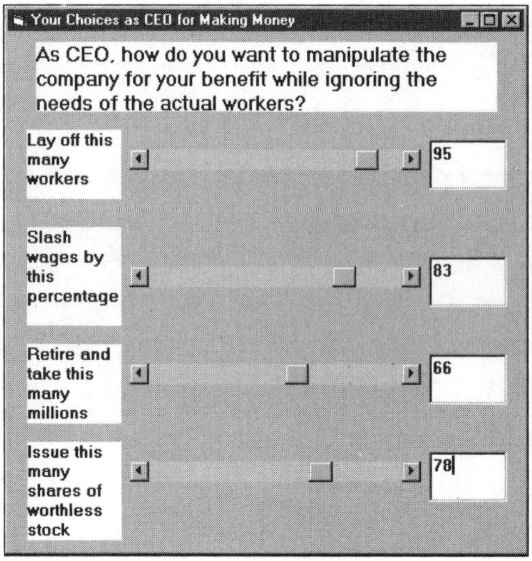

Figure 9-3:
Using labels in a real-life program.

To create a label, follow these steps:

1. **Click on the Label icon in the Visual Basic Toolbox.**

2. **Move the mouse cursor on the form to where you want to draw the label.**

3. **Hold down the left mouse button and move the mouse to draw the label. Release the left mouse button.**

   Visual Basic draws a label with a boring caption, such as Label2.

4. **Repeat Steps 1 through 3 as often as necessary for each label you want to draw.**

If you double-click on the Label icon in the Visual Basic Toolbox, Visual Basic creates a label on a form right away.

Putting pretty borders around labels

Normally, labels don't display any visible borders. However, you may want to put a boundary around a label to make the label easier to see. Visual Basic gives you two choices for label borders: a fixed single line or nothing at all, as shown in Figure 9-4.

Figure 9-4:
A bordered
label
and an
unbordered
label.

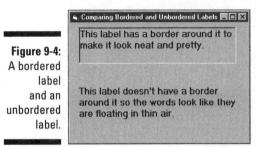

To create a border around a label, follow these steps:

1. **Click on the label whose border you want to change.**

2. **Open the Properties window. (Press F4, choose <u>V</u>iew⇨Properties <u>W</u>indow, or click on the Properties Window icon on the toolbar.)**

3. **Click on the BorderStyle property and choose one of the following:**
   - 0 - None
   - 1 - Fixed Single

Changing the size of labels

The size of a label on the screen determines the length of the caption (text) that the label can display. If a label is too small, part of the caption is cut off.

Note that the label caption (the text) doesn't change in size when you change the size of a label. To change the size of a label's caption, you have to change the Font property.

You may not know how much room your captions need, but to keep adjusting the width and height of your labels can be a real pain. Because computers are good at doing things that people don't want to do, Visual Basic can take care of this mundane task.

Visual Basic automatically can adjust the size of a label to fit any caption you stick inside of the label. Such *automatic adjusting labels* are perfect for displaying messages whose length may vary. Figure 9-5 shows the difference between an automatic adjusting label and one that refuses to change size at all.

Figure 9-5:
Comparison
of an
automatic
adjusting
label and an
ordinary
label.

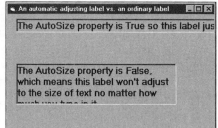

An automatic adjusting label grows or shrinks horizontally to match the length of the label's caption. So if you have a really long caption, the label cheerfully expands in size and disappears off the right side of the screen. To make an automatic adjusting label word-wrap text, you have to set the label's WordWrap property to True.

To create an automatic adjusting label, follow these steps:

1. **Click on the label that you want to automatically adjust to the size of its caption.**

2. **Open the Properties window. (Press F4, choose <u>V</u>iew⇨Properties <u>W</u>indow, or click on the Properties Window icon on the toolbar.)**

3. **Click on the AutoSize property and choose True.**

The advantage of automatic adjusting labels is that you can use BASIC code to give a label captions of various sizes without ever worrying that a particular caption isn't going to fit. The disadvantage is that you don't have control over the label's maximum size. If you're not careful, a label can get too big and cover other parts of your user interface.

Aligning text within a label

To make your label captions look nice and organized, Visual Basic offers three options for aligning captions, as shown in Figure 9-6:

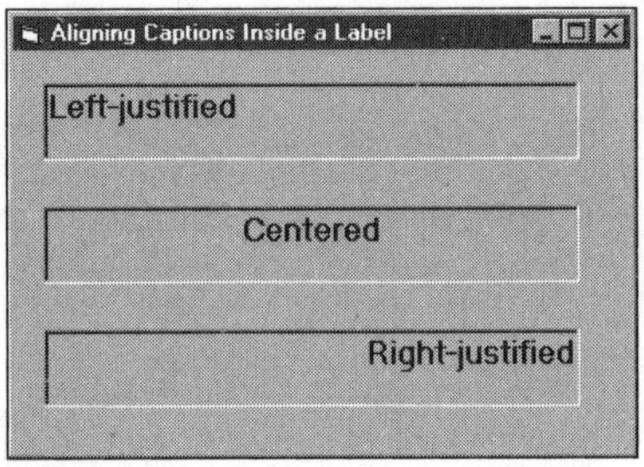

Figure 9-6:
Three ways
to align
captions in
a label.

Aligning Captions Inside a Label
Left-justified
Centered
Right-justified

✔ Left-justified

✔ Right-justified

✔ Centered

To align a caption in a label, follow these steps:

1. **Click on the label whose caption you want to align.**

2. **Open the Properties window. (Press F4, choose View⇨Properties Window, or click on the Properties Window icon on the toolbar.)**

3. **Click on the Alignment property and choose one of the following:**

   • 0 - Left Justify

   • 1 - Right Justify

   • 2 - Center

Word-wrapping labels

If you set a label's AutoSize property to True, the label expands horizontally as long as you keep stuffing it with text. However, if you want a label to expand vertically instead, you have to set both the label's AutoSize and WordWrap properties to True.

Setting both the AutoSize property and the WordWrap property to False means that long captions may be cut off at the bottom if your label isn't tall enough, as shown in the first example in Figure 9-7.

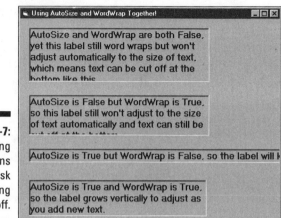

Figure 9-7:
Long
captions
run the risk
of being
cut off.

Setting AutoSize to False and WordWrap to True has the same effect as setting both AutoSize and WordWrap to False, as shown in the second example in Figure 9-7.

Setting AutoSize to True and WordWrap to False means that the label expands horizontally to fit an entire caption. However, the label shows only one line of the caption, as shown in the third example in Figure 9-7.

Setting both AutoSize and WordWrap to True means that the label grows or shrinks vertically to fit a caption, as shown in the fourth example in Figure 9-7.

To set the WordWrap property for a label to True, follow these steps:

1. **Click on the label in which you want to use word-wrapping.**

2. **Open the Properties window. (Press F4, choose View⇨Properties Window, or click on the Properties Window icon on the toolbar.)**

3. **Click on the WordWrap property and set the value to True.**

When creating labels that adjust to the size of a caption, be careful that your labels don't accidentally *grow* over and cover up other parts of your user interface. Otherwise, you may really confuse someone who is trying to use your program.

Chapter 10

Pretty Pictures and Objects from Geometry

. . . .

. . . .

You can sprinkle labels and pictures on any of your Visual Basic forms. Although pictures can make your forms look nice, they also can be an actual part of your program.

For example, a picture on the front of a road map showing a smiling gas station attendant with the label "Always Trust Your Car to the Man Who Wears the Star" is superfluous and decorative. However, a road map using pictures to show city highways and major side streets can be integral and necessary.

If you sprinkle plenty of labels and pictures in your user interface, your program is going to be easier to use and understand. After all, that's the purpose of creating a user interface in the first place.

Creating Pictures

Visual Basic provides two ways to display pictures on the screen:

✔ In a picture box

✔ In an image box

Use a *picture box* to display graphics or to group buttons together. Use an *image box* to display graphics or to create image buttons. To create a picture box or image box, follow these steps:

1. **Click on the Picture Box or Image Box icon in the Visual Basic Toolbox.**

2. **Using the mouse, hold down the left mouse button on the form and drag to where you want to draw the picture box or image box, and draw the box by dragging the mouse.**

3. **Repeat Steps 1 and 2 until you draw all the picture boxes or image boxes you need.**

If you double-click on the Picture Box or Image Box icon in the Visual Basic Toolbox, Visual Basic draws the picture box or image box on the form for you automatically. After drawing a picture box or image box, its size will likely change depending on the size of the graphic image you want to put in it.

Displaying pictures in picture boxes or image boxes

After you create a picture box or an image box, putting a picture in the box is only natural. (Why else do you create the box?) Picture boxes and image boxes can display three types of graphics images:

- ✔ **Bitmap files:** (BMP or DIB file extensions) Consist of patterns of dots, or *pixels,* which are the types of files created by paint programs, such as Microsoft Paint. If you enlarge a bitmap image, the image tends to look grainy and ugly.

- ✔ **Icon files:** (ICO file extensions) Special kinds of bitmap files with a maximum size of 32 x 32 pixels.

- ✔ **Metafiles:** (WMF file extensions) Images created by lines and geometric shapes that most people have forgotten about since high-school geometry. These types of files are created by draw programs, such as CorelDRAW.

To load a picture in a picture box or image box, follow these steps:

1. **Click on the picture box or image box into which you want to load a graphics file.**

   (This assumes that you've already drawn the picture box or image box on a form. Otherwise, draw the picture box or image box as explained in the Creating Pictures section.)

2. **Open the Properties window. (Press F4, choose View⇨Properties Window, or click on the Properties Window icon on the toolbar.)**

3. **Double-click on the Picture property in the Properties window.**

   Visual Basic displays the Load Picture dialog box, as shown in Figure 10-1.

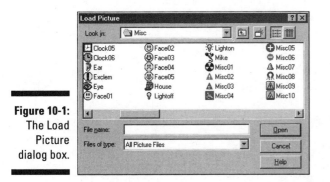

Figure 10-1:
The Load
Picture
dialog box.

4. Click on the picture file you want to load.

Visual Basic instantly loads the picture in the picture box or image box.

In addition to loading pictures by using the Properties window, you also can load and remove pictures while your program is running (during *runtime*). To load a picture into a picture box or image box, use the following LoadPicture command:

```
imgGreeting.Picture = LoadPicture("c:\graphics\martian.bmp")
```

The LoadPicture command specifies the exact drive, directory, and file to store in the Picture property of a picture box or an image box.

To remove a picture from a picture box or image box during run time, use the LoadPicture command as follows:

```
imgGreeting.Picture = LoadPicture("")
```

This statement essentially loads a blank image into the Picture property of a picture box or image box.

Putting nifty borders around picture boxes and image boxes

To define the edge of your picture box or image box, Visual Basic can display a border. By default, neither type of box displays a border. To change the border around a picture box or image box, follow these steps:

1. Click on the picture box or image box whose border you want to change.

2. **Open the Properties window. (Press F4, choose <u>V</u>iew⇨<u>P</u>roperties <u>W</u>indow, or click on the Properties Window icon on the toolbar.)**

3. **Click on the BorderStyle property and choose one of the following:**

   0 - None

   1 - Fixed Single

Changing the Size of Picture Boxes or Image Boxes

Generally, the size of picture boxes or image boxes has no effect on the size of the graphics image that the picture box or image box displays, with two exceptions:

✔ Metafile graphics always change size to fit within a picture box or an image box.

✔ If an image box's Stretch property is set to True, bitmap and icon graphics change size to fit within the image box.

Changing the size of graphics images

Bitmap and icon graphics appear in their original size no matter what the size of the picture box or image box (unless the Stretch property is set to True). Therefore, if you create a huge picture box but load in a tiny bitmap graphics image, all you see is a tiny bitmap graphics image with lots of empty space around the image.

Unlike bitmap or icon graphics, metafiles expand or shrink to fill an entire picture box or expand to their original size to fill an entire image box. To change the size of a metafile, just change the size of the picture box or image box holding the metafile.

If you use a picture box, you can never (and I mean never) change the size of bitmap or icon graphics. On the other hand, if you use an image box, you can change the size of bitmap or icon graphics by changing the image box's Stretch property. To change the size of bitmap or icon graphics in an image box, follow these steps:

1. **Click on the image box whose Stretch property you want to change.**

2. **Open the Properties window. (Press F4, choose <u>V</u>iew⇨<u>P</u>roperties <u>W</u>indow, or click on the Properties Window icon on the toolbar.)**

3. **Click on the Stretch property and set the value to True.**

After an image box has the Stretch property set to True, you can adjust the size of bitmap or icon graphics just by changing the size of the image box. (Isn't it amazing what $2,000 computers can do?)

Automatically changing the size of picture boxes

If you're too busy to bother creating and adjusting the size of your picture boxes, let Visual Basic do such formatting automatically. All you need to do is set the AutoSize property to True. The moment you load the bitmap or icon graphics image into a picture box, the picture box immediately shrinks or expands to fit tightly around the graphics image (shown in Figure 10-2), just like shrink-wrap around a box of floppy disks. To make a picture box automatically adjust its size around a graphics image, follow these steps:

1. **Click on the picture box whose AutoSize property you want to change.**

2. **Open the Properties window. (Press F4, choose View⇨Properties Window, or click on the Properties Window icon on the toolbar.)**

3. **Click on the AutoSize property and set the value to True.**

Figure 10-2:
Comparison of picture boxes with the AutoSize property set to True and False.

Coloring Picture Boxes

Visual Basic usually displays a plain gray background in picture boxes. If your graphics images fill up the entire picture box, the background color is irrelevant. But if the graphics image isn't big enough, the background color can be seen.

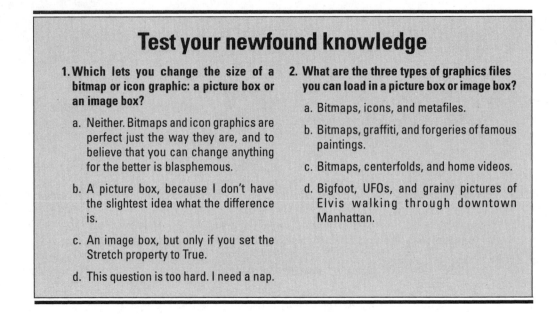

The background color is defined by the BackColor property. With a tasteful background color, you can highlight your graphics and make them more colorful.

To change the background color of a picture box, follow these steps:

1. **Click on the picture box whose background color you want to change.**

2. **Open the Properties window. (Press F4, choose View⇨Properties Window, or click on the Properties Window icon on the toolbar.)**

3. **Double-click on the BackColor property in the Properties window and then click on the Palette tab.**

4. **Click on the color you want.**

   Visual Basic instantly obeys.

Lines, Circles, and Other Nightmares from Geometry

What performs absolutely no useful function except a decorative one? If you answered, "The vice president of the United States," you're close, but the real answer is the parts of a user interface that make the interface look more attractive.

The prettier something looks, the friendlier people feel toward the pretty something, which explains why physically attractive people can go through life without having to pay their own bills. So if you make your user interface pretty, the likely consequence is that more people are actually going to try to use your user interface.

Visual Basic provides seven objects for adding visual makeup to your user interface, as shown in Figure 10-3. These objects are as follows:

- ✔ Lines
- ✔ Squares
- ✔ Rectangles
- ✔ Ovals
- ✔ Circles
- ✔ Rounded rectangles
- ✔ Rounded squares

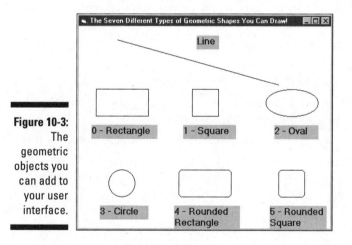

Figure 10-3: The geometric objects you can add to your user interface.

Creating lines

Lines are useful for underlining or separating items on the screen. To create a line, follow these steps:

1. **Click on the Line icon in the Visual Basic Toolbox.**

2. **On the form, move the mouse to where you want the line to start.**

3. **Hold down the mouse button and move the mouse to where you want the line to end.**

4. **Release the mouse button.**

If you double-click on the Line icon in the Visual Basic Toolbox, Visual Basic draws a line on the form for you automatically.

Creating circles and rectangles

Circles and rectangles can enclose and separate items on the screen. Or they can be an excuse for doodling on company time when the boss thinks that you're really writing a program. To create a circle or rectangle, follow these steps:

1. **Click on the Shape icon in the Visual Basic Toolbox.**

2. **On the form, move the mouse to where you want the top-left corner of the circle or rectangle to appear.**

3. **Hold down the left mouse button and move the mouse to where you want the bottom-right corner of the circle or rectangle to end.**

4. **Release the mouse button.**

   At this point, Visual Basic displays a rectangle on the screen. If that's what you want, stop right here; otherwise, continue to Step 5.

5. **Open the Properties window. (Press F4, choose View⇨Properties Window, or click on the Properties Window icon on the toolbar.)**

6. **Click on the Shape property and click on the arrow in the Settings Box.**

   Visual Basic displays a list of shapes to choose from:

   0 - Rectangle

   1 - Square

   2 - Oval

   3 - Circle

   4 - Rounded Rectangle

   5 - Rounded Square

7. **Click on the shape you want to create.**

Changing the color of lines and other shapes

Visual Basic usually draws lines, circles, and rectangles by using a solid black line. Although boring ol' black is okay for most purposes, sometimes a little color can spice up your user interface. You define the color of a line by using the BorderColor property. To change the line color of a line or shape, follow these steps:

1. **Click on the line or shape whose line color you want to change.**

2. **Open the Properties window. (Press F4, choose View⇨Properties Window, or click on the Properties Window icon on the toolbar.)**

3. **Double-click on the BorderColor property in the Properties window and click on the Palette tab.**

4. **Click on the color you want.**

   Visual Basic instantly obeys.

Changing the thickness of lines

Lines can be from 1 to 8,192 in thickness. (The numbers are relative and not related to an actual unit of measurement.) Any line thicker than 100, however, tends to look like a fat sausage on the screen. To change the thickness of a line, follow these steps:

1. **Click on the line or shape whose line thickness you want to change.**

2. **Open the Properties window. (Press F4, choose View⇨Properties Window, or click on the Properties Window icon on the toolbar.)**

3. **Double-click on the BorderWidth property and type a new value.**

   Visual Basic immediately changes the thickness of your line.

4. **Marvel at the wonder of technology and how one day you are going to be able to tell your children, "When I was going to school, we had to draw lines using an Etch-A-Sketch. You kids have line drawing so easy with computers and everything."**

Changing the appearance of lines, circles, and rectangles

Visual Basic usually draws lines, circles, and rectangles with a solid line. Although a solid line is easier to see, you may want to create special effects that look like perforations on a page or Morse code. Visual Basic provides the following seven line styles, some of which appear in Figure 10-4:

✔ Transparent

✔ Solid (the default)

✔ Dash

✔ Dot

✔ Dash-Dot

✔ Dash-Dot-Dot

✔ Inside Solid

Figure 10-4:
Examples of
available
line styles.

If the thickness of a line is greater than 1, the only BorderStyle settings you can use are 1 (Solid) and 6 (Inside Solid). If you use a different BorderStyle setting, nothing happens and you may think that Visual Basic is broken.

To confuse matters even more, the appearance of a line is determined by the *BorderStyle* property. Normally, you think of a border as something surrounding an object. But in the Visual Basic world of twisted logic, the BorderStyle defines the appearance of a line. To change the appearance of lines by themselves or lines that make up your circles or rectangles, follow these steps:

1. **Click on the line, circle, or rectangle whose appearance you want to change.**

2. **Open the Properties window. (Press F4, choose <u>V</u>iew⇨Properties <u>W</u>indow, or click on the Properties Window icon on the toolbar.)**

3. **Click on the BorderStyle property and choose one of the following:**

   > 0 - Transparent
   >
   > 1 - Solid
   >
   > 2 - Dash
   >
   > 3 - Dot
   >
   > 4 - Dash-Dot
   >
   > 5 - Dash-Dot-Dot
   >
   > 6 - Inside Solid

If you choose any style from 2 to 5, set the BorderWidth property to 1. Otherwise, Visual Basic displays the BorderStyle you selected as a solid line.

Changing the size and position of lines

When you create a line, try to draw the line as the exact size you need. (What's the point of drawing a long line when you know that you really need a short one?) Visual Basic provides two ways to change the size and position of a line:

✔ You can use the mouse.

✔ You can change the X1, X2, Y1, and Y2 properties in the Properties window.

The mouse is the quickest and sloppiest way to change the size and position of a line. But if you insist on using the mouse, follow these steps:

1. **Click on the line that you want to change.**

   Visual Basic displays a blue rectangle at each end of the line. These rectangles are called *handles*. (Because clicking on a single line can be an exercise in frustration, you can also move the mouse above the line, hold down the mouse button, move the mouse below the line, and release the mouse button.)

2. **Move the mouse over one of these handles until the mouse pointer turns into a crosshair.**

3. **Hold down the mouse button and move the mouse to adjust the line. When the line takes the shape you want, release the mouse button.**

If you prefer not to soil your hands by touching the mouse, you can use a more refined method favored by people of distinction everywhere: Use the Properties window. To change the size of a line using the Properties window, follow these steps:

1. **Click on the line you want to change.**

2. **Open the Properties window. (Press F4, choose View⇨Properties Window, or click on the Properties Window icon on the toolbar.)**

3. **Double-click on the X1 property and type a new value.**

4. **Double-click on the Y1 property and type a new value.**

5. **Double-click on the X2 property and type a new value.**

6. **Double-click on the Y2 property and type a new value.**

   Figure 10-5 shows the X- and Y-coordinates of a line.

Figure 10-5:
How the X1,
X2-, Y1-,
and Y2-
coordinates
affect a
line's
position.

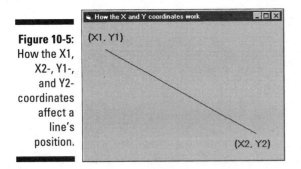

How the X and Y coordinates work

(X1, Y1)

(X2, Y2)

Changing the size of circles, rectangles, and other shapes

Happily, changing the size of circles, rectangles, and other shapes is much easier than changing the size of a line. You can use the mouse or the Properties window to change the size of a shape. To change the size of a shape using the mouse, follow these steps:

1. **Click on the shape you want to change.**

   Visual Basic displays black handles around the shape.

2. **Move the mouse over one of these handles until the mouse pointer turns into a double arrow.**

3. **Hold down the mouse button and move the mouse. When the object is the shape you want, release the mouse button.**

For those who prefer to use a keyboard at the expense of ease and convenience, you can change the size of a shape also by using the Properties window. To change the size of a shape by using the Properties window, follow these steps:

1. **Click on the shape you want to change.**

2. **Open the Properties window. (Press F4, choose <u>V</u>iew➪Properties <u>W</u>indow, or click on the Properties Window icon on the toolbar.)**

3. **Double-click on the Height property and type a new value.**

4. **Double-click on the Width property and type a new value.**

Filling Shapes with Colors and Pretty Patterns

The inside of a shape is usually empty, blank, and boring. For more excitement than most people's hearts can handle, you can change the color and pattern of the inside of a shape. Visual Basic provides eight patterns that you can use to fill the inside of a shape. The pattern is defined by the FillStyle property. The color of the pattern is defined by the FillColor property. Figure 10-6 shows the eight patterns that Visual Basic provides for filling the inside of a shape.

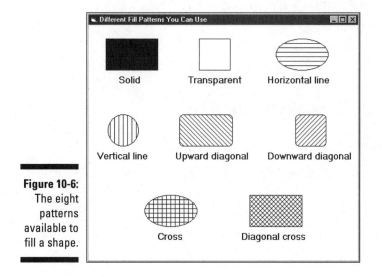

Figure 10-6: The eight patterns available to fill a shape.

To define the fill pattern of a shape, follow these steps:

1. **Click on the shape whose inside pattern you want to change.**

2. **Open the Properties window. (Press F4, choose <u>V</u>iew⇨Properties <u>W</u>indow, or click on the Properties Window icon on the toolbar.)**

3. **Click on the FillStyle property and choose one of the following:**

   0 - Solid

   1 - Transparent

   2 - Horizontal Line

   3 - Vertical Line

   4 - Upward Diagonal

   5 - Downward Diagonal

   6 - Cross

   7 - Diagonal Cross

To change the color of a shape's fill pattern, follow these steps:

1. **Click on the shape whose pattern color you want to change.**

2. **Open the Properties window. (Press F4, choose <u>V</u>iew⇨Properties <u>W</u>indow, or click on the Properties Window icon on the toolbar.)**

3. **Double-click on the FillColor property in the Properties window and click on the Palette tab.**

4. **Click on the color you want.**

   Visual Basic obeys instantly.

Changing the Background Color of Shapes

In addition to changing the color of the fill pattern inside a shape (fill color) and the line color that makes up a shape (border color), you can also change a shape's background color (back color). Confused? Take a look at Figure 10-7 for clarity.

Figure 10-7:
The
background
color of a
shape
compared
to its border
color and
fill pattern
color.

Border color

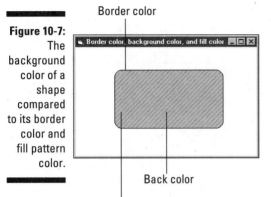

Back color

Fill color (the color of the lines)

Before you can change the background color of a shape, you must set the shape's BackStyle property to Opaque. (The default is Transparent, which means that the shape is invisible. If the shape is invisible, changing the color isn't going to do a thing.)

To change the background color of a shape, follow these steps:

1. **Click on the shape whose background color you want to change.**

2. **Open the Properties window. (Press F4, choose View⇨Properties Window, or click on the Properties Window icon on the toolbar.)**

3. **Click on the BackStyle property and set the value to Opaque.**

4. **Double-click on the BackColor property in the Properties window and click on the Palette tab.**

5. **Click on the color you want.**

   Visual Basic instantly obeys.

Try Changing an Object's Size for Yourself

The following sample program lets you change a circle's thickness by using the horizontal scroll bar. To see for yourself, create three objects with the following property settings.

If you don't feel like creating the program listed below, just load and run the SHAPE.VBP file off the enclosed CD-ROM.

Object	Property	Setting
Form	Caption	The Shrinking/Growing Circle
Shape1	Name	shpCircle
	Height	1455
	Left	1440
	Shape	3 (Circle)
	Top	1080
	Width	1695
HScroll1	Name	hsbCircle
	Height	255
	Left	720
	Max	20
	Min	1
	Top	360
	Width	3255

Double-click on the horizontal scroll bar and type the following in the Code window:

```
Private Sub hsbCircle_Change()
   shpCircle.BorderWidth = hsbCircle.Value
End Sub
```

To run the program, press F5. Then click on the horizontal scroll bar and watch the circle grow before your eyes. Amazing! Astound your friends! Be the hit of your next cocktail party! Visual Basic reveals it all!

Part III
Making Menus

The 5th Wave   By Rich Tennant

YOU'RE NOT A CYBERHOLIC... if you look for the Soup of the Day in the Format menu.

In this part . . .

Pull-down menus are a fancy way to organize all the options available in your program. That way, if users want to do something with your program, they just have to choose the right pull-down menu and pick the appropriate command.

This part of the book shows you how to make pull-down menus in your own programs. Believe it or not, making your own menus is actually simple. (The hard part is making your program actually work the way you want it to, which is something that even eludes the grasp of the Microsoft programmers.)

Chapter 11

Creating and Editing Pull-Down Menus

· ·

In This Chapter

▶ Creating menus and menu titles

▶ Adding separator bars

▶ Using shortcut keys and check marks

▶ Dimming or making menu commands disappear

· ·

*G*enerally, every menu bar contains the following menu titles: File, Edit, Window, and Help. (See Figure 11-1). The File menu appears on the far left, the Edit menu appears next, the Window menu appears next to last, and the Help menu appears last. In between the Edit and Window menus are menu titles unique to a particular program.

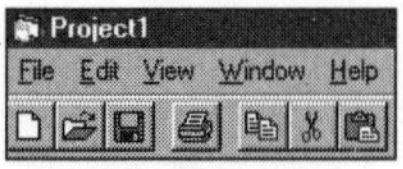

Figure 11-1:
A typical list
of pull-
down
menus.

Every menu consists not only of menu titles but also menu commands, as shown in Figure 11-2. The menu titles appear at the top of the screen in a menu bar, and the menu commands appear in pull-down menus.

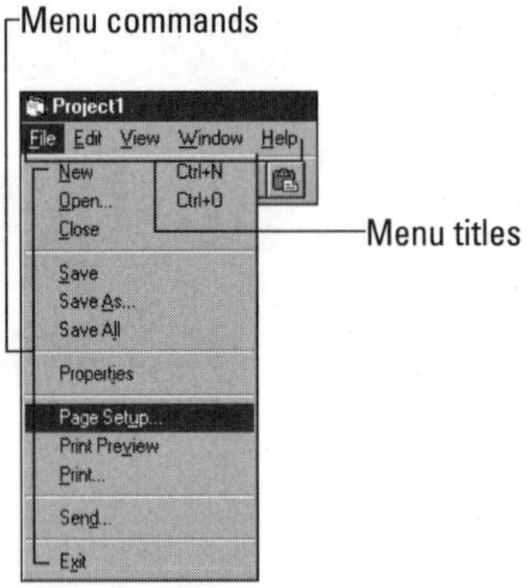

Menu commands

Menu titles

Figure 11-2:
Menu titles
and menu
commands.

The Basic Elements of a Menu Bar

Before creating menus, decide how many menu titles your program needs and where each command belongs in your menu titles.

Visual Basic can create menus for you if you use the VB Application Wizard to help you create your program (as I explain in Chapter 3).

The File menu (refer to Figure 11-2) needs to contain commands directly related to file operations, such as opening, closing, saving, and printing files, as well as quitting the program so that you can go to the kitchen and get something to eat.

The Edit menu, shown in Figure 11-3, needs to contain commands related to editing (duh), such as Undo (and Redo), Cut, Copy, Paste, Clear, and Select All.

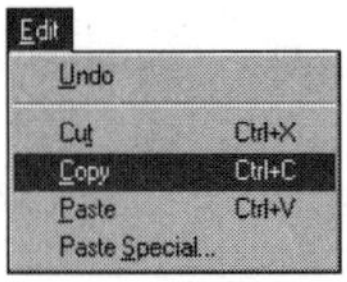

Figure 11-3:
A typical
Edit menu.

The Window menu, shown in Figure 11-4, needs to contain commands related to opening, closing, arranging, and switching among different windows.

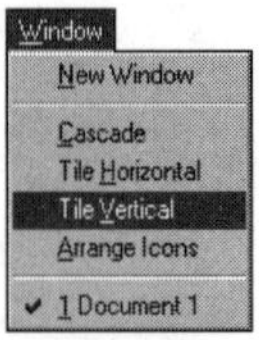

Figure 11-4:
A typical
Window
menu.

The Help menu, shown in Figure 11-5, needs to contain commands for getting help from the program. Typical help commands include a table of contents to the help system, an alphabetical index, propaganda about product support, and a useless About command that displays information the programmers think looks cute on the screen.

Figure 11-5:
A typical
Help menu.

Any other menus you sandwich between the Edit and the Window menu titles need to clearly organize the type of commands hidden underneath.

For example, many word-processing programs have a Tools menu title that displays commands for grammar checking, hyphenation, macro creation, and other commands that 99 percent of the working population of America is never going to use.

If your menu titles are unique to your particular program (in other words, they're not the standard Edit or Window menu titles found on other programs), try to make your menu titles descriptive — that way users will have a better idea where to find a specific command.

Making Menus for Your User Interface

To create and edit menus, you have to open the Menu Editor window, which appears in Figure 11-6. (If you use the VB Application Wizard, Visual Basic can create standard pull-down menus for you automatically, but you still need to use the Menu Editor window to edit your menus.)

In the name of freedom and confusion, Visual Basic provides three ways to display the Menu Editor window:

  ✔ Press Ctrl+E.

  ✔ Choose Tools➪Menu Editor.

  ✔ Click on the Menu Editor icon on the toolbar. (Refer to Figure 11-6.)

You can create one set of pull-down menus for each form. So if your program contains two forms, you can have a completely different menu for each form. Of course, having multiple menus may confuse users, but if you're a typical programmer who generally doesn't care what users think, this isn't going to bother you one bit.

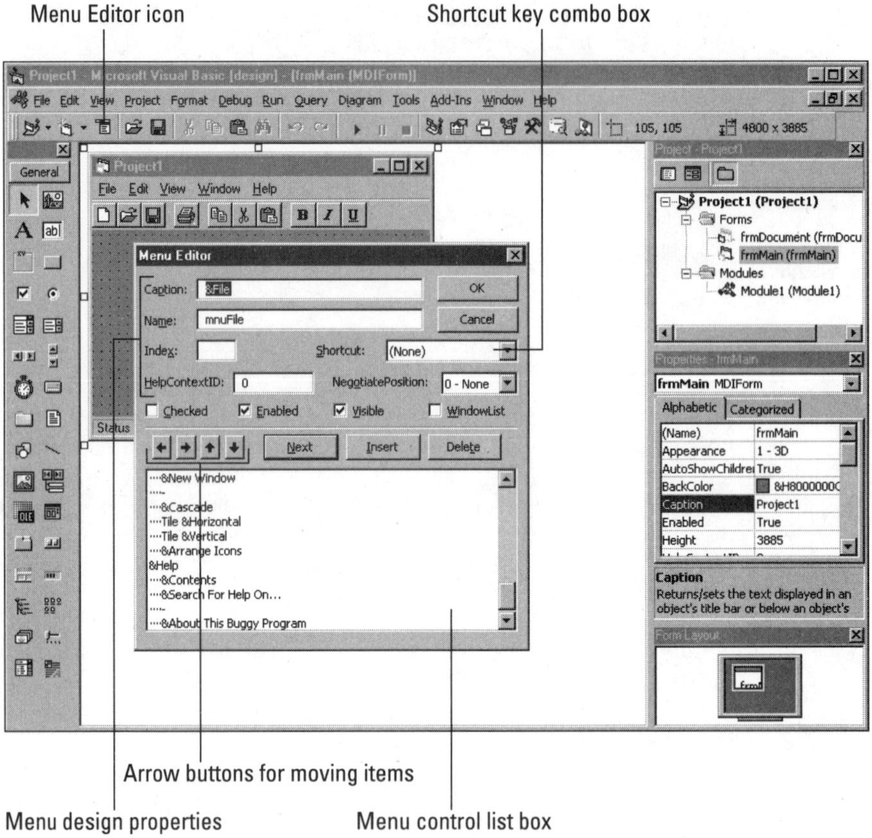

Menu Editor icon   Shortcut key combo box

Figure 11-6:
The Menu
Editor
window for
creating
pull-down
menus.

Arrow buttons for moving items

Menu design properties   Menu control list box

The Menu Editor window is where you define everything to create your menus. The first two things you have to define for all your menu titles are their names and their captions.

Naming menus

Every menu title and menu command has a caption and a name. The caption is what appears on the screen. The name never appears on the screen; you use the name to identify which menu command the user chooses.

Captions can be up to 40 characters long, including numbers, spaces, punctuation, and the underscore character (_). Of course, the longer your caption is, the more space the caption is going to gobble up on the screen.

Because captions appear on the screen, you can use an ampersand (&) in your captions, such as &File or T&able. Why do you want to do such a silly thing? An ampersand in front of any letter makes that letter underlined in the caption, as you can see in Figure 11-7.

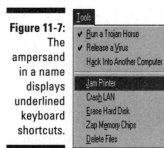

Figure 11-7:
The ampersand in a name displays underlined keyboard shortcuts.

When a letter is underlined in a *menu title,* users can pull down that menu by pressing and holding down the Alt key and pressing whatever letter is underlined. If a menu title is named &Window, the caption appears on the screen as W̲indow, and users can pull the menu down by pressing Alt+W. Offering this option can help users choose menu titles by using these keyboard shortcuts rather than using the mouse.

When the ampersand underlines a letter in a *menu command* caption, users can choose the caption simply by typing the underlined letter without pressing Alt. So if a menu command caption is named &New, the caption appears on the screen as N̲ew. Users can choose that caption by first pulling down the menu and then pressing N.

Names, like captions, can be up to 40 characters long, including numbers and the underscore character. Because names never appear on the screen, you can make them as long as you want until you reach the magic number of 40.

Unlike captions, names cannot include spaces, punctuation, or words that the editors at IDG Books Worldwide, Inc., deem offensive and, hence, may harm sales of this book.

For menu names, Visual Basic recommends that the name begins with mnu, as in the following examples:

- ✔ mnuFile
- ✔ mnuWindow
- ✔ mnuFileOpen

Visual Basic doesn't care whether you use uppercase or lowercase consistently. If you really want to, you can use the following names for menus:

- MNufiLEmNuwINDow
- MNUfileOPEN

Such names are not only hard to read, but the scattered casing also makes you look illiterate. So for consistency (and to protect your image), the best method is to adopt Microsoft's style and stick with this style whenever you use Visual Basic.

To identify menu commands that appear under certain menu titles, include the menu title as part of a menu command's name. For example, if the menu title File is named mnuFile, menu commands (such as the Open, Save, and Exit commands) that appear in the File menu should have names like mnuFileOpen, mnuFileSave, and mnuFileExit.

Making menu titles

Creating pull-down menus for your Visual Basic programs is a two-step process:

- First you create the menu titles that appear in the menu bar.
- Next you create the menu commands that appear under each menu title.

To create menu titles that appear in the menu bar at the top of a form, follow these steps:

1. **Click on the form to which you want to add menu titles.**

2. **Open the Menu Editor window by pressing Ctrl+E, choosing Tools⇨Menu Editor, or clicking on the Menu Editor icon on the toolbar.**

3. **In the Caption text box of the Menu Editor window, type the menu title that you want to have appear on the screen, including any ampersands.**

   As you type, Visual Basic displays your caption in the Menu control list box.

4. **Press Tab to move the cursor to the Name text box.**

5. **Type your menu name, beginning with mnu followed by the menu caption itself, such as mnuFile or mnuFilePrint.**

   You can mix uppercase and lowercase, but for consistency with Visual Basic programmers around the world, stick with the style mnuFileExit where you use uppercase letters to identify separate words such as File and Exit.

6. **Press Enter or click on Next to create the next menu title.**

7. **Repeat Steps 3 through 6 until you create all the menu titles that you want to have appear at the top of the screen in the menu bar.**

8. **Click on OK.**

   Visual Basic displays your menus at the top of the form.

Adding and deleting menu titles and commands

Creating menu titles is fairly straightforward. Unfortunately, nothing in life is permanent, and that can include your menu titles. For that reason, Visual Basic gives you the option of adding or deleting menu titles.

To add another menu title to a form, follow these steps:

1. **Click on the form to which you want to add another menu title.**

2. **Open the Menu Editor window by pressing Ctrl+E, choosing Tools➪Menu Editor or clicking on the Menu Editor icon on the toolbar.**

3. **Click on the menu title that you want to appear to the right of your new menu title.**

4. **Click on Insert.**

   Visual Basic pushes the previously highlighted menu title down and highlights a blank line, as shown in Figure 11-8.

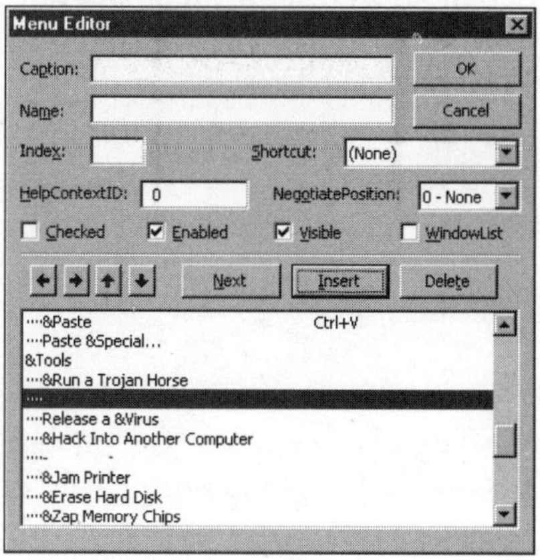

Figure 11-8:
Inserting a new menu title in the Menu control list.

5. **Click on the Caption text box and type your new menu title caption, such as &Tools or Forma&t.**

6. **Press Tab to move the cursor to the Name text box and type your new menu name (such as mnuTools or mnuFormat) and then press Enter.**

7. **Click on OK.**

To delete a menu title, follow these steps:

1. **Click on the form from which you want to delete a menu title.**

2. **Open the Menu Editor window by pressing Ctrl+E, choosing Tools⇨Menu Editor, or clicking on the Menu Editor icon on the toolbar.**

3. **Click on the menu title you want to delete.**

4. **Click on Delete.**

   Visual Basic deletes the highlighted menu title.

5. **Click on OK.**

When you delete a menu title or menu command, any BASIC code you've written for that particular menu command still exists, so you'll have to delete this code as well.

Creating Menu Commands under Menu Titles

After you create the menu titles that appear in the menu bar at the top of a form, the next step is to create the commands to appear underneath each menu title.

In the Menu control list box, all flush left items are menu titles that appear in the menu bar. Indented items are menu commands that appear below a menu title.

To create menu commands, follow these steps:

1. **Click on the form to which you want to add menu commands.**

2. **Open the Menu Editor window by pressing Ctrl+E, choosing Tools⇨Menu Editor, or clicking on the Menu Editor icon on the toolbar.**

   Visual Basic obediently opens the Menu Editor window.

3. **Click underneath the menu title where you want to display the menu commands.**

   For example, if you want to put menu commands underneath the File menu title, click underneath the File menu title.

4. **Click on Insert.**

5. **Click on the Caption text box and type the menu command's caption, such as &Save or &Print.**

6. **Press Tab to move the cursor to the Name text box.**

7. **Type the menu command's name, such as mnuFileSave or mnuFilePrint.**

8. **Click on the right-arrow button to indent the menu command.**

   This indentation shows you that an item is a menu command and not a menu title. (How's that for similar but confusing terms?)

9. **Click on OK.**

Moving Menu Titles and Commands

When you create pull-down menus, you can always edit and change them at a later time. Visual Basic gives you four ways to move your menu titles and commands around:

- ✔ Up
- ✔ Down
- ✔ Indent right
- ✔ Indent left

In the Menu Editor window, Visual Basic provides four arrow buttons that enable you to move items up, down, right, or left (see Figure 11-6). Moving an item up or down in the Menu control list box simply rearranges that item's position on the menu bar or in a pull-down menu.

To move an item up or down in the Menu control list box, follow these steps:

1. **Click on the form containing the menu titles or commands that you want to rearrange.**

2. **Open the Menu Editor window by pressing Ctrl+E, choosing Tools⇨Menu Editor, or clicking on the Menu Editor icon on the toolbar.**

3. **Click on the item in the Menu Editor window that you want to move up or down.**

4. Click on the up-arrow button to move the item up, or click on the down-arrow button to move the item down.

5. Click on OK when you're done goofing around.

When within the Menu Editor window, indenting an item to the right turns a menu title into a menu command. (See Figure 11-9). Likewise, while within this window, indenting an item to the left turns a menu command into a menu title.

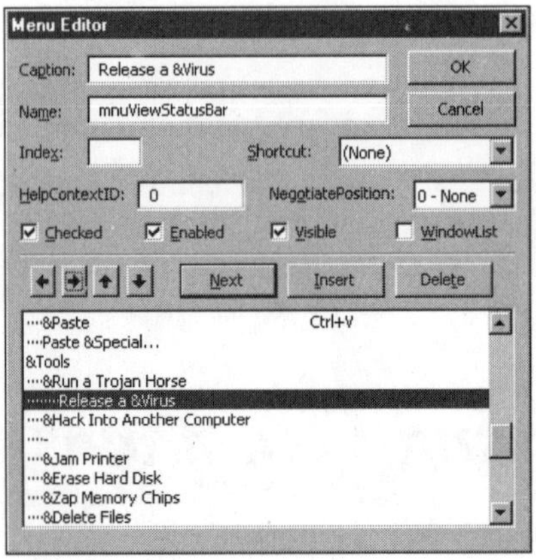

Figure 11-9:
The effect
of indenting
an item to
the right.

To indent an item left or right in the Menu control list box, follow these steps:

1. Click on the form containing the menu titles or commands that you want to rearrange.

2. Open the Menu Editor window by pressing Ctrl+E, choosing Tools⇨Menu Editor, or clicking on the Menu Editor icon on the toolbar.

Visual Basic obediently opens the Menu Editor window.

3. Click on the item that you want to indent left or right.

4. Click on the right-arrow button to indent the item to the right, or click on the left-arrow button to indent the item to the left.

5. Click on OK.

Making Menus Pretty

Pull-down menus conveniently list commands where users can (hopefully) find them. To make your menus even easier to use, Visual Basic also lets you separate menu commands with separator bars, display check marks next to currently used menu commands, add shortcut keys so users don't have to use your pull-down menus at all, and dim or remove menu items altogether.

Putting separator bars in menus

Separator bars are lines in a pull-down menu that divide groups of commands, as shown in Figure 11-10. Generally, separator bars group related items so that users can find the command they want.

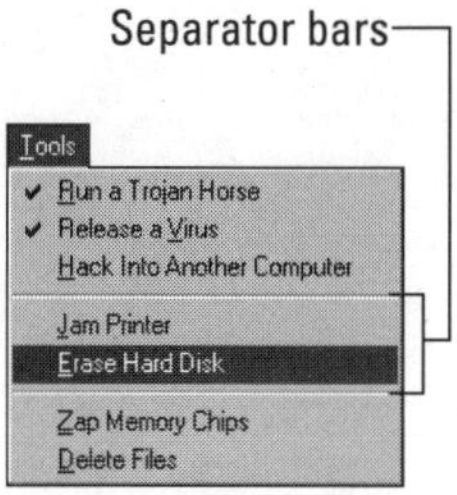

Separator bars—

Figure 11-10:
Typical
separator
bars in a
pull-down
menu.

To create a separator bar, follow these steps:

1. **Click on the form containing the menus to which you want to add separator bars.**

2. **Open the Menu Editor window by pressing Ctrl+E, choosing Tools⇨ Menu Editor, or clicking on the Menu Editor icon on the toolbar.**

3. **Click on the item in the Menu Editor window that you want to appear directly below the separator bar.**

4. **Click on Insert so that Visual Basic displays an empty line.**

   If necessary, you may have to click on the right- or left-arrow buttons to make the separator bar appear on the same level as the items the bar is dividing.

5. **Click on the Caption text box, type a hyphen (-), and press Tab to move the cursor to the Name text box.**

6. **Type any name you want to identify the separator bar.**

   Ideally, the name should include part of the menu title, such as mnuFileBar1 or mnuEditBar3.

7. **Click on OK to close the Menu Editor window.**

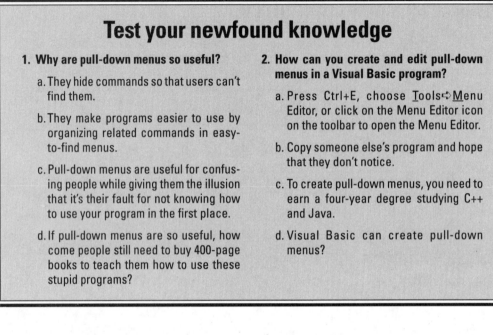

Test your newfound knowledge

1. **Why are pull-down menus so useful?**

   a. They hide commands so that users can't find them.

   b. They make programs easier to use by organizing related commands in easy-to-find menus.

   c. Pull-down menus are useful for confusing people while giving them the illusion that it's their fault for not knowing how to use your program in the first place.

   d. If pull-down menus are so useful, how come people still need to buy 400-page books to teach them how to use these stupid programs?

2. **How can you create and edit pull-down menus in a Visual Basic program?**

   a. Press Ctrl+E, choose Tools⇨Menu Editor, or click on the Menu Editor icon on the toolbar to open the Menu Editor.

   b. Copy someone else's program and hope that they don't notice.

   c. To create pull-down menus, you need to earn a four-year degree studying C++ and Java.

   d. Visual Basic can create pull-down menus?

Assigning shortcut keys

After a while, you are likely to get tired of using pull-down menus every time you want to pick a command. For commonly used commands, a good idea is to assign these commands to *shortcut keys,* such as Ctrl+S to choose the Save command or Ctrl+X to choose the Cut command. Such a shortcut key lets the user give a command without wading through multiple pull-down menus. Figure 11-11 shows some shortcut keys.

Figure 11-11: Examples of shortcut keys in a pull-down menu.

Shortcut keys appear on menus next to the commands they represent. In this way, users can quickly discover the shortcut keys for all your menu commands.

To assign a shortcut key to a menu command, you have to use the Menu Editor window again. Although you may want to make up your own shortcut keys, Visual Basic lets you choose from only a limited list of possible keys.

Visual Basic doesn't let you assign the same shortcut keys to different commands. If you try to, Visual Basic scolds you with an Error dialog box.

To assign shortcut keys to menu commands, follow these steps:

1. **Click on the form containing the menus to which you want to add shortcut keys.**

2. **Open the Menu Editor window by pressing Ctrl+E, choosing Tools⇨Menu Editor, or clicking on the Menu Editor icon on the toolbar.**

   Visual Basic displays the Menu Editor window.

3. **Click on the menu command for which you want to assign a shortcut key.**

4. **Click on the down-arrow button in the Shortcut list box.**

   Visual Basic displays a list of possible keystroke combinations you can use.

5. **Scroll through this list until you find the right keystroke combination.**

   Ideally, you want to choose keystroke combinations that are easy to remember, such as Ctrl+S for the Save command or Ctrl+X for the Cut command. Visual Basic displays your choice in the Menu control list box.

6. **Click on OK.**

Now when you click on your pull-down menus, shortcut keys appear next to some of the commands. Because you haven't written any BASIC code to tell these commands what to do, nothing happens if you press any of the shortcut keys.

Putting check marks next to menu commands

Check marks, which appear next to items on a menu, visually show that the items already have been selected (see Figure 11-12). These check marks are often useful in identifying which font, type style, or size is currently in use.

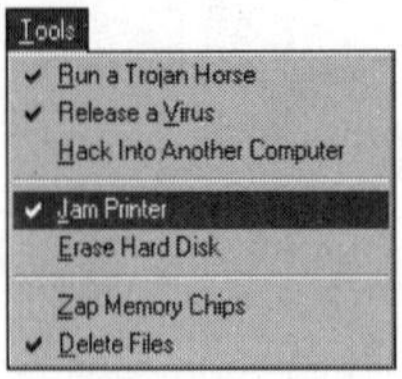

Figure 11-12:
Using
check
marks in a
pull-down
menu.

Tools
✓ Run a Trojan Horse
✓ Release a Virus
   Hack Into Another Computer
✓ Jam Printer
   Erase Hard Disk

   Zap Memory Chips
✓ Delete Files

If you want to make any default choices in your pull-down menus, you can
have check marks appear when your program runs.

Check marks can appear next to menu commands only and not menu titles.
If you try to put a check mark next to a menu title, Visual Basic screams and
displays the error message Can't put check mark here.

To add check marks to menu commands, follow these steps:

1. **Click on the form containing the menus to which you want to add
   check marks.**

2. **Open the Menu Editor window by pressing Ctrl+E, choosing
   Tools⇨Menu Editor, or clicking on the Menu Editor icon on the
   toolbar.**

3. **Click on the menu command from the Menu Editor window that you
   want a check mark to appear next to.**

4. **Click on the Checked check box.**

5. **Click on OK.**

If you put check marks next to your menu commands, you're going to want
to remove the check marks eventually. To do this, you have to use (gasp!)
BASIC code.

To remove a check mark that's next to a menu command, just set the
command's Checked property to False. The following example removes a
check mark from a menu command named mnuFont12:

```
mnuFont12.Checked = False
```

To add a check mark using BASIC code, just set the menu command's
Checked property to True. The following example adds a check mark next to
a menu command named mnuFontHelvetica:

```
mnuFontHelvetica.Checked = True
```

Dimming menu commands

Sometimes using certain commands doesn't make sense. For example, until you select a block of text, having the Cut or Copy commands as options is pointless. To prevent users from choosing menu commands that aren't available, you can dim the commands, as shown in Figure 11-13. That way, the commands still appear in the menus, but the user can't choose them.

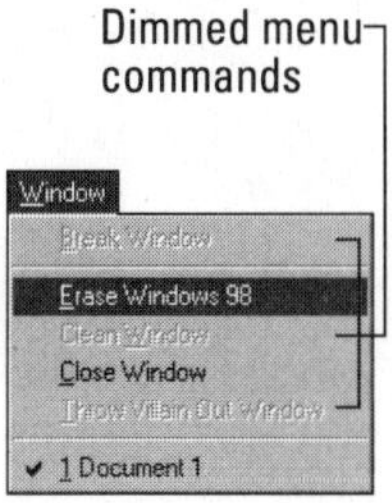

Dimmed menu commands

Figure 11-13:
An example of dimmed menu commands.

Window
Break Window
Erase Windows 98
Clean Window
Close Window
Throw Villain Out Window
✔ 1 Document 1

To dim a menu item, follow these steps:

1. **Click on the form containing the menu commands that you want to dim.**

2. **Open the Menu Editor window by pressing Ctrl+E, choosing Tools⇨Menu Editor, or clicking on the Menu Editor icon on the toolbar.**

   Visual Basic cheerfully displays the Menu Editor window.

3. **Highlight the menu item that you want to dim.**

4. **Click on the Enabled check box to remove the check mark (see Figure 11-14).**

5. **Click on OK.**

If you dim a menu command, eventually, you're going to want to undim the command. To do so, you have to use BASIC code. To undim a menu command, set the command's Enabled property to True. The following example undims a menu command named `mnuEditCut`:

```
mnuEditCut.Enabled = True
```

To dim a menu command while your program is running, use BASIC code. Just set the menu command's property to False. The following example dims a menu command named `mnuEditCopy`:

```
mnuEditCopy.Enabled = False
```

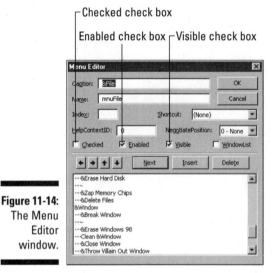

Checked check box

Enabled check box ┌Visible check box

Figure 11-14:
The Menu
Editor
window.

Making menu commands disappear

Rather than dim a menu command, you can make the command disappear. For example, some programs remove all menu titles except File and Help from the menu bar until the user opens or creates a file. (After all, displaying an Edit menu when you have nothing to edit is pointless.)

To remove a menu item, follow these steps:

1. **Click on the form containing the menu commands you want to make invisible.**
2. **Open the Menu Editor window by pressing Ctrl+E, choosing Tools⇨Menu Editor, or clicking on the Menu Editor icon on the toolbar.**
3. **From the Menu Editor window, highlight the menu item that you want to make invisible.**
4. **Click on the Visible check box to remove the check mark (see Figure 11-14).**
5. **Click on OK.**

After you make a menu command invisible, eventually you're going to have to make the command visible. To do so, you have to use BASIC code. To make a menu command visible, set the command's Visible property to True. The following example makes a menu title named mnuEdit visible:

```
mnuEdit.Visible = True
```

To make a menu command invisible while your program is running, use BASIC code and set the menu item's property to False. The following example makes a menu title named mnuTools disappear:

```
mnuTools.Visible = False
```

Just remember that all these fine points of beautifying your menus make your program easier to use and give your program that professional look. As any professional programmer can tell you, if a program looks good, users assume that any error they come across must be their fault. And that's the real reason programmers spend so much time creating a user interface — so that users aren't going to blame the programmers when the program fails catastrophically.

Chapter 12

Submenus, Growing Menus, and Pop-Up Menus

· ·

In This Chapter

▶ Creating submenus

▶ Dynamically growing menus

▶ Creating pop-up menus

· ·

A typical menu bar displays a list of menu titles at the top of the screen. Selecting one of the menu titles displays a pull-down menu.

Unfortunately, a menu bar can hold only a limited number of menu titles, and a pull-down menu can hold only as many commands as can appear on the screen simultaneously. So what happens if you write a killer application that requires more commands than can possibly appear on the menu bar or in multiple pull-down menus? The solution is to use submenus (or to redesign your program).

Creating Submenus

Submenus are often used to bury a command several layers deep within a series of pull-down menus. If organized properly, submenus clearly show the relationship between various topics. If organized improperly, your program is going to look just as confusing as the most popular commercial programs that millions of people are forced to use every day.

For example, many programs have a Format menu title. Under this Format menu may be commands such as TypeStyle, Font, and Size. Choosing Font often displays a submenu listing all the possible fonts available, as shown in Figure 12-1.

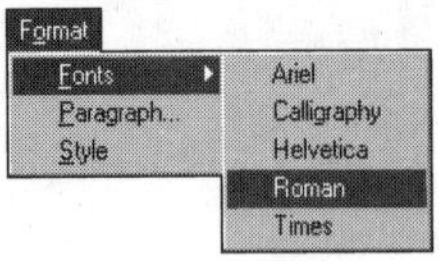

Figure 12-1:
A Format
pull-down
menu
offering a
Font
command
and a
submenu of
different
font types.

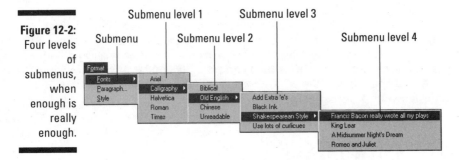

Visual Basic lets you create up to four levels of submenus, as shown in Figure 12-2. Although this number of submenus can be handy, most programs use only one level of submenus to avoid burying commands so deeply that no one can find them again. Rumor has it that the Watergate tapes, Jimmy Hoffa's body, and the location of the Holy Grail reside somewhere in a well-known program's submenus.

Figure 12-2:
Four levels
of
submenus,
when
enough is
really
enough.

Whenever a menu item displays an arrowhead symbol, the symbol indicates that a submenu exists for that item. When you create submenus, Visual Basic displays this arrowhead symbol automatically. Figure 12-3 shows an example of the arrowhead symbol.

Figure 12-3:
The
arrowhead
symbol
indicates the
existence of
a submenu.

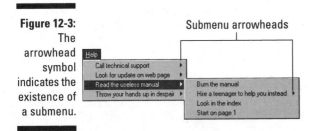

The Menu Editor window is the only place where you can define submenus. Any item that appears flush left appears as a menu title in the menu bar. Items indented once appear on the pull-down menus, items indented twice appear on the first submenu level, items indented three times appear on the second submenu level, items indented four times appear on the third submenu level, and items indented five times appear on the fourth and last submenu level.

To create submenus, follow these steps:

1. **Click on the form on which you want to create submenus.**

2. **Open the Menu Editor window by pressing Ctrl+E, choosing Tools⇨Menu Editor, or clicking on the Menu Editor icon on the toolbar.**

3. **In the Menu Control list box, highlight the menu item that you want to make into a submenu.**

4. **Click on the right-arrow button to indent the item.**

5. **Click on OK.**

Each level of indentation (submenu level) is represented by four dots (. . . .) in the Menu Control list box.

If you want to move submenus up a level (such as from submenu level 3 to submenu level 2), you can. Just follow these steps:

1. **Click on the form containing the submenus that you want to modify.**

2. **Open the Menu Editor window by pressing Ctrl+E, choosing Tools⇨Menu Editor, or clicking on the Menu Editor icon on the toolbar.**

3. **In the Menu Control list, highlight the menu item box that you want to move up a level.**

4. **Click on the left-arrow button to indent the item to the left.**

5. **Click on OK when you finish playing around.**

Rather than using multiple levels of submenus, most of the really cool programs use dialog boxes. (See Chapter 13 to find out all about dialog boxes.) A *dialog box* lets users make multiple choices all at once instead of making choices one at a time through many submenu levels. While submenus are fine for choosing a few options, dialog boxes are better for choosing lots of options.

Then again, what's the point of offering submenus if even Microsoft recommends against doing so? This is just one of the many ways that Microsoft gives you the freedom to write hard-to-use user interfaces so that your programs can never pose a real threat to Microsoft's own programs.

Changing Menu Captions While Your Program Is Running

In certain cases, changing the caption of a menu command while the program is running is necessary. The most common menu command that changes is the Undo command in the Edit menu. After choosing the Undo command, some programs may toggle Undo to display the Redo command.

To change a menu caption, you have to use BASIC code. Just find the name of the menu item that you want to change and set the item's Caption property to a new caption. The following example changes the mnuEditUndo caption to Redo:

```
mnuEditUndo.Caption = "Redo"
```

The following example changes the mnuEditUndo caption back to Undo:

```
mnuEditUndo.Caption = "Undo"
```

When changing menu captions, you can use the ampersand (&) symbol to display a menu command hot key. (You can read more about hot keys in Chapter 11.) For example, the following code changes the mnuEditUndo caption to Undo where the capital letter U appears underlined:

```
mnuEditUndo.Caption = "&Undo"
```

Designing Dynamically Growing Menus

If you use many Windows-based programs (such as Microsoft Word), you may notice an odd feature: Each time you load a program, the File menu displays a list of the last four or five files you worked on, as shown in Figure 12-4. If you ever open two or more windows in the same program, you may notice that the Window menu also lists the names of the files currently open.

To create a *dynamically growing menu,* you have to create empty spaces in your menu. To do this, use the Menu Editor window and create BASIC code to add items to make the items visible.

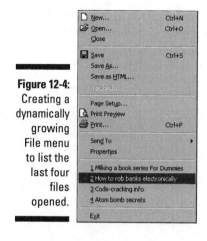

Figure 12-4:
Creating a
dynamically
growing
File menu
to list the
last four
files
opened.

To create a dynamically growing menu, follow these steps:

1. **Click on the form where you want to create a dynamically growing menu.**

2. **Open the Menu Editor window by pressing Ctrl+E, choosing Tools⇨Menu Editor, or clicking on the Menu Editor icon on the toolbar.**

3. **Click below the last menu command under the menu title to which you want to add new items.**

   For example, if you want to add new items under the File menu, click below the last menu command under the File menu title.

4. **Click on Insert to add the item.**

5. **Click on the right-arrow button to indent the empty lines so that they appear as menu commands below the menu title.**

6. **Leave the Caption text box empty and press Tab.**

7. **In the Name text box, type the same name for each of these empty lines, such as** mnuFileMRU.

8. **Type 0 in the Index text box for the first empty line.**

   Each time you add another empty line, increase the number in the Index text box by 1. You want the first empty line Index text box to contain 0, the second to contain 1, the third to contain 2, and so on.

9. **Click in the Visible check box to clear the check box.**

10. **Press Enter.**

11. Repeat Steps 3 through 10 until you create four or five empty lines below the last menu title in the Menu Editor Control list box.

Make sure that each empty line has a different number in its Index text box.

12. Click on OK.

The preceding steps create a dynamically growing menu, but to actually add items to this menu, you have to use BASIC code. The following example shows how to add an item to give the illusion of a dynamically growing menu:

```
Private Sub Form_Load()
    mnuFileMRU(0).Caption = "&1 C:\VB\HELLO.VBP"
    mnuFileMRU(0).Visible = True
End Sub
```

The second line of the preceding Form_Load event procedure sets the caption of the first empty line to 1 C:\VB\HELLO.VBP. The third line makes this item visible on the pull-down menu.

Creating Pop-Up Menus

Pop-up menus (also called context menus) are often used to quickly display a list of commands on the screen. Any menu or submenu can appear as a pop-up menu. Pop-up menus are usually programmed to appear when the user presses the right mouse button. Figure 12-5 shows an example of a pop-up menu.

X- and Y-coordinates measured from the upper left-hand corner

New	Ctrl+N
Open...	Ctrl+O
Close	
Delete file by mistake	
Save	
Save As...	
Save All	
Pretend to save file	
Properties	
Page Setup...	
Print Preview	
Print...	
Print and jam printer	
Send...	
Crash computer	
Exit	

Figure 12-5: An example of a pop-up menu.

To create a pop-up menu, you have to use the BASIC command `PopupMenu`. The following example displays the mnuEdit menu as a pop-up menu when the user clicks the right mouse button:

```
Private Sub Form_MouseDown(Button As Integer, Shift As _
          Integer, X As Single, Y As Single)
  If Button = 2 Then    ' Right mouse button pressed _
    PopupMenu mnuEdit  ' Pops up the mnuEdit menu
  End If
End Sub
```

Instead of using the number 1 to represent the left mouse button and the number 2 to represent the right mouse button, you can use the variables vbPopupMenuLeftButton and vbPopupMenuRightButton, respectively.

To create a pop-up menu, follow these steps:

1. **Click on the form containing the menu that you want to turn into a pop-up menu.**

2. **Press F7, choose _View_⇨_Code_, or click on the View Code icon in the Project Explorer window.**

   The Code Editor window appears.

3. **Click in the Object list box and choose Form.**

4. **Click in the Procedure list box and choose MouseUp.**

   Visual Basic displays an empty Private Form_MouseUp procedure.

5. **Type the following code below the** `Private Sub Form_MouseDown` **statement and above the** `End Sub` **statement:**

```
If Button = vbPopupMenuRightButton Then
  PopUpMenu (type the menu name here such as mnuEdit)
End If
```

If for some odd reason you want to make a menu pop up by pressing the left mouse button, substitute the vbPopupMenuRightButton variable with the vbPopupMenuLeftButton variable instead.

Defining the location of pop-up menus

Normally, the pop-up menu appears wherever the mouse pointer happens to be. However, if you want pop-up menus to appear in a specific location on the screen, you can specify the exact coordinates.

For example, the following PopupMenu BASIC command displays a pop-up menu named mnuTools at X-coordinate 500 and Y-coordinate 650:

```
PopupMenu mnuTools, 500, 650
```

For those people who are finicky about where the pop-up menu appears relative to the mouse pointer, you can specify whether the menu appears to the left, to the right, or dead center of the mouse. Use one of the following commands:

```
PopupMenu mnuEdit, 0 ' Left aligned
PopupMenu mnuEdit, 4 ' Center aligned
PopupMenu mnuEdit, 8 ' Right aligned
```

Using numbers to specify right or left alignment can be easy to type but ultimately confusing to understand what the code actually does. To simplify matters, Visual Basic lets you use honest-to-goodness English phrases that represent the above numbers, such as the following:

```
PopupMenu mnuEdit, vbPopupMenuLeftAlign ' Left aligned
PopupMenu mnuEdit, vbPopupMenuCenterAlign ' Center aligned
PopupMenu mnuEdit, vbPopupMenuRightAlign ' Right aligned
```

Essentially, these statements tell Visual Basic, "Hey stupid, whenever you see the words vbPopupMenuRightAlign, substitute the number 8 instead."

Using the old method in a Visual Basic procedure looks like the following:

```
Private Sub Form_MouseDown(Button As Integer, Shift As _
          Integer, X As Single, Y As Single)
  If Button = 2 Then       ' Right mouse button pressed
    PopupMenu mnuEdit, 4  ' Old, confusing way
  End If
End Sub
```

Now here's what the modern, easy-to-read method using English looks like:

```
Private Sub Form_MouseDown(Button As Integer, Shift As _
          Integer, X As Single, Y As Single)
  If Button = vbPopupMenuRightButton Then
    PopupMenu mnuEdit, vbPopupMenuCenterAlign
  End If
End Sub
```

In case your mind is racing ahead already to new possibilities, you can left-, center-, or right-align a menu around a specific X-coordinate. For example, if you want to center-align the pop-up menu around a specific X-coordinate, do the following:

```
PopupMenu mnuTools, 4, 500, 650
```

or

```
PopupMenu mnuTools, vbPopupMenuCenterAlign, 500, 650
```

This example displays the pop-up menu at the X- and Y-coordinates of 500 twips and 650 twips, respectively.

If you change the units of measurement on a form from twips to inches or centimeters, you may have to change the X- and Y-coordinate values as well to correspond to your new scale. (See Chapter 6 in case you want to define different units of measurement for your form.)

Defining the right mouse button to work with pop-up menus

Normally, pop-up menus work like ordinary pull-down menus. To choose a command, you just click on the command with the left mouse button. However, because the right mouse button is used about as often as you use your wisdom teeth, you may want to give users the capability to use either the left or right mouse button.

The following code example activates the right mouse button:

```
PopupMenu mnuEdit, 2
```

To replace numbers with English, you can substitute the following:

```
PopupMenu mnuEdit, vbPopupMenuRightButton
```

By default, Visual Basic assumes that you always want to use the left mouse button with any pop-up menu.

Trick question: How do you define both center-alignment and right-button activation? The answer is to use the Or operator, as shown in the following:

```
PopupMenu mnuEdit, 2 Or 4
```

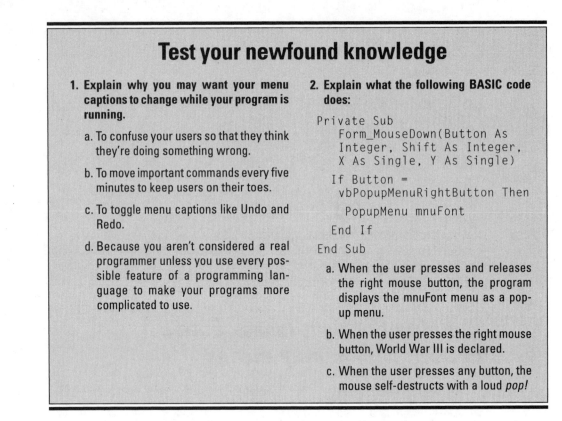

Test your newfound knowledge

1. Explain why you may want your menu captions to change while your program is running.

    a. To confuse your users so that they think they're doing something wrong.

    b. To move important commands every five minutes to keep users on their toes.

    c. To toggle menu captions like Undo and Redo.

    d. Because you aren't considered a real programmer unless you use every possible feature of a programming language to make your programs more complicated to use.

2. Explain what the following BASIC code does:

```
Private Sub
   Form_MouseDown(Button As
   Integer, Shift As Integer,
   X As Single, Y As Single)

   If Button =
   vbPopupMenuRightButton Then

      PopupMenu mnuFont

   End If
End Sub
```

    a. When the user presses and releases the right mouse button, the program displays the mnuFont menu as a pop-up menu.

    b. When the user presses the right mouse button, World War III is declared.

    c. When the user presses any button, the mouse self-destructs with a loud *pop!*

To use English instead of numbers, you can use the following:

```
PopupMenu mnuEdit, vbPopupMenuRightButton Or
         vbPopupMenuCenterAlign
```

Most popular programs (such as WordPerfect, Excel, and Paradox) use submenus, dynamically growing menus, and pop-up menus. But for less-complicated programs, such as games, you probably aren't going to need all these different menu features.

Fortunately, most users are already familiar with all these menu features, so when a pop-up menu or submenu appears on the screen, the user is not going to be shocked. The secret is to use these features only if you have to. Remember, the more fancy features you add to your program, the more programming concerns you have to worry about. (Now aren't you glad you decided to find out how to program your computer?)

Chapter 13

Dialog Boxes

• •

• •

*P*ull-down menus certainly make life easier for users (provided, of course, that the users know how to use the menus). In addition to pull-down menus, nearly every program also uses dialog boxes.

Dialog boxes are those tiny windows that pop up on the screen. Most of the time, the computer uses dialog boxes to let the user know what the computer is doing, such as "Now printing page 4 of 67" or "Windows 98 just crashed again and here's an application error number that you won't understand anyway."

However, dialog boxes also let the computer ask questions of users, such as "Cancel printing?" or "Do you really want to exit out of Windows?" A fancy dialog box may be crammed full of options so that the user can make multiple choices all at one time. Just as most Windows-based programs use similar pull-down menus (File, Edit, Help), these programs also use similar dialog boxes.

Creating a Simple Dialog Box

A dialog box displays a brief message on the screen along with one or more command buttons. Dialog boxes typically contain the following four parts, as shown in Figure 13-1.

  ✔ A title bar

  ✔ A message

  ✔ An eye-catching icon

  ✔ One or more command buttons

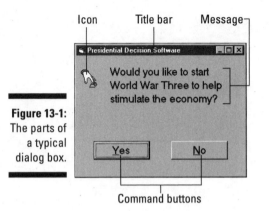

Icon Title bar Message

Figure 13-1:
The parts of
a typical
dialog box.

Command buttons

The title bar identifies the purpose of the dialog box, such as About This Program. The message contains text that appears in the dialog box, such as "Are you sure that you want to start World War III?" The icon provides visual information about the dialog box's importance. The number and type of command buttons can vary from one to three.

The simplest dialog box is one that displays a message on the screen and provides an OK command button so that the user can make the dialog box go away.

The following BASIC code creates the simple dialog box displayed in Figure 13-2:

Figure 13-2:
The
Another
Windows
Crash
dialog box.

```
Private Sub Form_Load()
  MsgBox "Get a Macintosh", ,"Another Windows Crash"
End Sub
```

This simple dialog box does nothing more than appear on the screen and then disappear when the user clicks on OK.

Adding icons to a dialog box

Icons can help grab a user's attention to your dialog box. Visual Basic uses four icons. (See Figure 13-3.)

- **Critical Message:** Alerts the user to an extremely important question, such as "If you continue, you are going to erase all the files on your hard disk. Are you sure that you want to do this?"

- **Warning Query:** (A question mark.) Highlights less-threatening questions, such as "Do you really want to exit from Microsoft Word?"

- **Warning Message:** (An exclamation mark.) Emphasizes warnings that the user needs to know about, such as "You are about to replace all 79 pages of your document with a period!"

- **Information Message:** Makes otherwise drab and boring messages look interesting, such as "Printing all 3,049 pages of your document may take a long time. Click on OK if you want to go through with this."

Icon	Name	Numerical Value	Visual Basic Constant
⊗	Critical Message	16	vbCritical
⑦	Warning Query	32	vbQuestion
⚠	Warning Message	48	vbExclamation
ⓘ	Information Message	64	vbInformation

Figure 13-3:
The four icons for dialog boxes and their numerical values.

To add an icon to a dialog box, just add the numeric value of the icon between the dialog box message and the title bar text, as follows:

```
Private Sub Form_Load()
  MsgBox "It crashed again!", 16, "Windows Error Message"
End Sub
```

This code creates the dialog box shown in Figure 13-4.

Normally, Visual Basic lets you display only one of four possible icons in a dialog box. If this seems limiting and downright boring, you can create your own dialog box from scratch. To do this, create a separate form, set the form's BorderStyle property to Fixed Dialog, and draw command buttons and an image box directly on this form. You can then draw an image box on the form and load any type of icon you want.

Figure 13-4:
A dialog
box
containing
the Critical
Message
icon.

Just remember that creating a dialog box by using a separate form requires you to draw the command buttons, label, and image box, and to write BASIC code to make the whole dialog box work. If you just want to create a dialog box quickly and easily, use the MsgBox command instead.

Defining the number and type of command buttons in a dialog box

Dialog boxes can contain from one to three command buttons. A numerical value represents each command button. Table 13-1 lists the six command button combinations.

Table 13-1	Command Button Combinations Available in Visual Basic	
Displays	**Value**	**Visual Basic Constant**
OK button	0	vbOKOnly
OK and Cancel buttons	1	vbOKCancel
Abort, Retry, and Ignore buttons	2	vbAbortRetryIgnore
Yes, No, and Cancel buttons	3	vbYesNoCancel
Yes and No buttons	4	vbYesNo
Retry and Cancel buttons	5	vbRetryCancel

To define a command button combination, choose the combination you want and type the numerical value of the combination or the Visual Basic constant between the dialog box's message text and title bar text, such as

```
Private Sub Form_Load()
  MsgBox "File not found", 2, "Error Message"
End Sub
```

or

```
Private Sub Form_Load()
  MsgBox "File not found", vbAbortRetryIgnore, "Error
          Message"
End Sub
```

Which command button did the user select in a dialog box?

If a dialog box just displays an OK command button, clicking on that OK command button usually makes that dialog box go away. However, dialog boxes with two or more command buttons give users a choice. When dealing with multiple command buttons on a dialog box, you have to write BASIC code to figure out:

✔ Which button the user chose

✔ What your program should do depending on which button the user chose

The seven possible buttons a user can choose are represented by the numerical values in Table 13-2.

Table 13-2	Command Buttons a User Can Choose	
Button Selected	*Numerical Value*	*Visual Basic Constant*
OK	1	vbOK
Cancel	2	vbCancel
Abort	3	vbAbort
Retry	4	vbRetry
Ignore	5	vbIgnore
Yes	6	vbYes
No	7	vbNo

To make your program determine which command button a user chose, you have to set a variable equal to the MsgBox BASIC code, as shown in the following line:

```
Reply = MsgBox("File not found", 2, "Error Message")
```

This code displays a dialog box with the Abort, Retry, and Ignore command buttons. If the user clicks on Abort, the value of Reply is 3. If the user clicks on Retry, the value of Reply is 4. If the user clicks on Ignore, the value of Reply is 5.

Note: Whenever you assign a variable to represent the value chosen from a dialog box, you must use parentheses to enclose the dialog box parameters.

Commonly Used Dialog Boxes

While a simple dialog box may be sufficient occasionally, you may want to use a more complicated, yet more common, dialog box such as

- ✔ Open
- ✔ Save As
- ✔ Color
- ✔ Font
- ✔ Print

Before you can use one of these common dialog boxes, you may have to load the Common Dialog Box icon into the Visual Basic Toolbox. To do this, follow these steps:

1. **Choose Project⇨Components or press Ctrl+T.**

   A Components dialog box appears.

2. **Click on the Controls tab.**

3. **Make sure that a check mark appears in the Microsoft Common Dialog Control 6.0 check box. If a check mark does not appear, click on the check box.**

4. **Click on OK.**

   The Visual Basic Toolbox displays the Common Dialog Box icon, as shown in Figure 13-5.

To display one of the five commonly used dialog boxes in your program, follow these steps:

1. **Click on the Common Dialog Box icon in the Visual Basic Toolbox.**

2. **Move the mouse anywhere on the form. Hold down the mouse button and move the mouse down and to the right. Let go of the mouse button.**

   This draws the Common Dialog Box icon on the form, as shown in Figure 13-5.

If you double-click on the Common Dialog Box icon in the Visual Basic Toolbox, Visual Basic draws the Common Dialog Box icon on the form for you automatically.

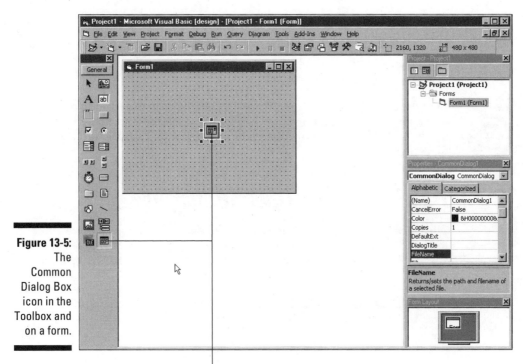

Figure 13-5:
The
Common
Dialog Box
icon in the
Toolbox and
on a form.

Common Dialog Box icon

Test your newfound knowledge

1. Why do you want to display an icon in a dialog box?

a. In case an illiterate computer user wants to use your program.

b. To catch the eye of the user and pro vide a visual cue. For example, a Criti cal Message icon can warn users that something terrible is about to happen if they don't do something immediately.

c. To see if the user is smart enough to realize that the dialog box has nothing important to say.

2. To use the predefined Open, Save As, Color, Font, or Print dialog box, what must you do first?

a. Buy the Visual Basic manuals that used to come with the program for free.

b. Create a new form, draw three com mand buttons, two check boxes, one list box, and a partridge in a pear tree.

c. Save your file and exit Visual Basic.

d. Make sure that you have drawn the Common Dialog Box icon on your form.

Where you place the Common Dialog Box icon on a form is irrelevant because the icon is always invisible when your program runs. Putting the Common Dialog Box icon on a form essentially tells Visual Basic, "Okay, this icon gives you the magical power to display the Open, Save As, Print, Color, or Font dialog box whenever I tell you to."

Because you need only one Common Dialog Box icon per form to display the different types of common dialog boxes, you don't have to change the icon's name. Just use the default name that Visual Basic gives the icon, which is `CommonDialog1`.

Displaying the Open dialog box

The *Open dialog box,* shown in Figure 13-6 lets users choose a drive, directory, and file to open. The user also has the choice of displaying only specific file types, such as those matching the *.TXT or *.EXE criteria.

Figure 13-6:
The Open
dialog box.

To display the Open dialog box, you need only one magic BASIC command that looks like this:

```
CommonDialog1.ShowOpen
```

If you want to define the list of files that the Open dialog box displays, you have to use something technical called a filter. A *filter* tells Visual Basic what types of files to display, such as all those with the TXT or BAT file extension.

A filter consists of two parts: the label that appears in the list box and the filter itself. Table 13-3 lists some examples of labels and filters. For added clarity, labels usually include the filter they use.

Text files, for example, usually have the file extension TXT, but sometimes they have the file extension ASC. So the label "Text Files (*.TXT)" lets you know that the dialog box shows only text files with the TXT file extension (and not text files with the ASC file extension).

Table 13-3	Labels and Filters
Label	*Filter*
All Files (*.*)	*.*
Text Files (*.TXT)	*.TXT
Batch Files (*.BAT)	*.BAT
Executable Files (*.EXE)	*.EXE

To define your labels and filters, use BASIC code, as in the following example:

```
CommonDialog1.Filter = "All Files (*.*)|*.*|Text Files _
          (*.TXT)|*.TXT|Batch Files(*.BAT) _
          |*.BAT|Executable Files
(*.EXE)|*.EXE"
```

This code also establishes the filter order, which you can utilize with the corresponding filter index number. In the above example, the All Files filter is first, and so has a filter index number of 1. After you define the filter, you have to tell Visual Basic which filter to display by default. Again, you use BASIC code:

```
CommonDialog1.FilterIndex = 1
```

This code line displays "All Files (*.*)" in the List Files of Type list box. Or you can choose the following:

```
CommonDialog1.FilterIndex = 4
```

This line displays "Executable Files (*.EXE)" in the List Files of Type list box.

The order in which you define your filter (using the `CommonDialog1.Filter` command) determines the FilterIndex number. For example, if you change the filter to

```
CommonDialog1.Filter = "Text Files (*.TXT) _
          |*.TXT|All Files(*.*)|*.*"
```

the following code displays "Text Files (*.TXT)" in the List Files of Type list box:

```
CommonDialog1.FilterIndex = 1
```

How to create an Open dialog box

Obviously, if your program is going to store data in a file, the program is going to have to open a file at some point. Because nearly every program needs to open files, make your life easy and use the Open dialog box.

To actually display an Open dialog box, you need to write BASIC code, such as

```
Private Sub mnuFileOpen_Click()
  CommonDialog1.Filter = "Text Files (*.TXT)
         |*.TXT|All Files (*.*)|*.*"
  CommonDialog1.FilterIndex = 1
  CommonDialog1.ShowOpen
End Sub
```

This event procedure tells Visual Basic:

1. When the user clicks on the Open command underneath the File pull-down menu, follow the instructions sandwiched in between the first and last lines of the `Private Sub mnuFileOpen_Click()` **event procedure.**

2. The second line tells Visual Basic what types of files to display in the Open dialog box.

3. The third line tells Visual Basic to display files matching the first list of files defined by the `Filter` property. In this case, the third line tells the Open dialog box to display `*.TXT` text files.

4. The fourth line tells Visual Basic to display the Open dialog box on the screen, displaying only files with the .TXT file extension.

At this point, the Open dialog box looks nice and seems to work, but because you haven't written any BASIC code to tell the dialog box what to do, the box doesn't do a thing but look pretty.

Which file did the user choose from an Open dialog box?

After you display an Open dialog box, the next big question is to find out which file the user chose. When the user clicks on a file displayed by the Open dialog box, Visual Basic stores the filename in the Filename property of the Common dialog box. So if you want to retrieve the filename that the user clicked on, you need to set a variable to store the filename property, such as

```
WhatFile = CommonDialog1.filename
```

So the complete event procedure may look like this:

```
Private Sub mnuFileOpen_Click()
Dim WhatFile As String
   CommonDialog1.Filter = "Text Files (*.TXT)|*.TXT|All _
          Files (*.*)|*.*"
   CommonDialog1.FilterIndex = 1
   CommonDialog1.ShowOpen
   WhatFile = CommonDialog1.filename
End Sub
```

The CommonDialog1.filename property contains both the filename and the directory that the file is stored in, such as C:\MyDocuments\Secrets\ Resume.txt. If the user clicks the Cancel command button in the Open dialog box, the filename property is set to " " (no text).

Displaying a Save As dialog box

A Save As dialog box is nearly identical to the Open dialog box. However, the text of the title bar is not the same. (The Open dialog box's title bar says "Open" and the Save As dialog box's title bar says "Save As".)

The only BASIC command you need to use to display a Save As dialog box is

```
CommonDialog1.ShowSave
```

However, you may also want to use filters to display certain types of files, such as

```
Private Sub mnuFileSaveAs_Click()
   CommonDialog1.Filter = "Text Files (*.TXT)|*.TXT|All _
          Files (*.*)|*.*"
   CommonDialog1.FilterIndex = 1
   CommonDialog1.ShowSave
End Sub
```

Which file did the user choose from a Save As dialog box?

Like the Open dialog box, the Save As dialog box stores the filename in the Filename property of the Common dialog box. So if you want to retrieve the filename on which the user clicked, you need to set a variable to store the filename property, such as

```
WhatFile = CommonDialog1.filename
```

So the complete event procedure may look like this:

```
Private Sub mnuFileSaveAs_Click()
Dim WhatFile As String
    CommonDialog1.Filter = "Text Files (*.TXT)|*.TXT|All _
            Files (*.*)|*.*"
    CommonDialog1.FilterIndex = 1
    CommonDialog1.ShowSave
    WhatFile = CommonDialog1.filename
End Sub
```

The Save As dialog box doesn't actually save files on its own. To save a file under a different name, you have to write additional BASIC code that tells your computer to save a file onto a disk.

Rather than use Visual Basic's Open and Save As dialog boxes, try experimenting with a free File dialog box control that offers more flexibility and features while being smaller to use. You can download this `FileDialog` control from the CCRP Web site at `www.mvps.org/ccrp`. (Note that an independent group of programmers created this `FileDialog` box control, so if it doesn't work, don't blame Microsoft.)

Displaying a Color dialog box

The Color dialog box lets users choose colors or mix their own, as shown in Figure 13-7.

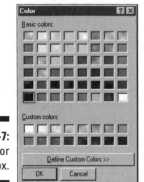

Figure 13-7:
The Color
dialog box.

To display a Color dialog box, you have to use two magic BASIC commands:

```
CommonDialog1.Flags = cdlCCRGBInit
CommonDialog1.ShowColor
```

The first line tells Visual Basic that the Common dialog box, defined by `CommonDialog1,` can be used to retrieve a color from the Color dialog box.

The second line tells Visual Basic to display the Color dialog box.

For example:

```
Private Sub Command1_Click()
   CommonDialog1.Flags = cdlCCRGBInit
   CommonDialog1.ShowColor
End Sub
```

Which color did the user choose from the Color dialog box?

The Color dialog box stores the color the user chose in the Color property of the Common dialog box. So if you want to retrieve the color (which Visual Basic stores as a number) that the user clicked on, you need to set a variable to store the Color property, such as

```
WhatColor = CommonDialog1.Color
```

So the complete event procedure may look like this:

```
Private Sub Command1_Click()
Dim WhatColor as Long
   CommonDialog1.Flags = cdlCCRGBInit
   CommonDialog1.ShowColor
   WhatColor = CommonDialog1.Color
End Sub
```

Displaying a Font dialog box

The Font dialog box, shown in Figure 13-8, lets users choose different fonts, font styles, and point sizes. Each time the user chooses an option, this dialog box displays a sample so that the user can see whether the font, font style, or point size looks okay.

To display a Font dialog box, you have to use two magic BASIC commands:

```
CommonDialog1.Flags = cdlCFEffects Or cdlCFBoth
CommonDialog1.ShowFont
```

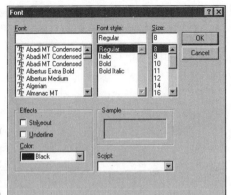

Figure 13-8:
The Font
dialog box.

The first line tells Visual Basic that the Common dialog box, defined by CommonDialog1, can be used to retrieve a font value from the Font dialog box.

The second line tells Visual Basic to display the Font dialog box. For example:

```
Private Sub Command1_Click()
  CommonDialog1.Flags = cdlCFEffects Or cdlCFBoth
  CommonDialog1.ShowFont
End Sub
```

Which options did the user choose from the Font dialog box?

The Font dialog box lets the user choose a variety of options, as Table 13-4 shows:

Table 13-4	Properties That Store Values from the Font Dialog Box
Property	*What Information It Contains*
Color	The selected color. To use this property, you must first set the Flags property to cdlCFEffects.
FontBold	Whether bold was selected.
Property	What information it contains.
FontItalic	Whether italic was selected.

Property	What Information It Contains
FontStrikethru	Whether strikethru was selected. To use this property, you must first set the Flags property to cdICFEffects.
FontUnderline	Whether underline was selected. To use this property, you must first set the Flags property to cdICFEffects.
FontName	The selected font name.
FontSize	The selected font size.

So the complete event procedure may look like this:

```
Private Sub mnuFormatFont_Click()
Dim TextColor As Long
Dim Bold As Boolean
Dim Italic As Boolean
Dim Underline As Boolean
Dim Strikethru As Boolean
Dim Font As String
Dim Size As Integer
   CommonDialog1.Flags = cdICFEffects Or cdICFBoth
   CommonDialog1.ShowFont
   TextColor = CommonDialog1.Color
   Bold = CommonDialog1.FontBold
   Italic = CommonDialog1.FontItalic
   Underline = CommonDialog1.FontUnderline
   Strikethru = CommonDialog1.FontStrikethru
   Font = CommonDialog1.FontName
   Size = CommonDialog1.FontSize
End Sub
```

Displaying a Print dialog box

A Print dialog box, shown in Figure 13-9, lets users choose the printer, the print range, and the print quantity.

To display a Print dialog box, use the following BASIC command:

```
CommonDialog1.ShowPrinter
```

For example:

```
Private Sub mnuFilePrint_Click()
   CommonDialog1.ShowPrinter
End Sub
```

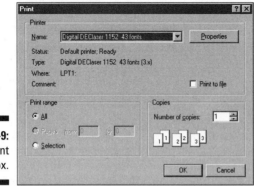

Figure 13-9:
The Print
dialog box.

To set the default value for the number of copies to print, you have to use the following BASIC commands:

```
CommonDialog1.Copies = 1
CommonDialog1.ShowPrinter
```

For example:

```
Private Sub Command1_Click()
    CommonDialog1.Copies = 1
    CommonDialog1.ShowPrinter
End Sub
```

Like the Open, Save As, Color, and Font dialog boxes, the Print dialog box looks like it works but really doesn't do anything until you write BASIC code to tell the box how to work after the user clicks on OK.

Using the common dialog boxes that I discuss in this chapter can give your programs that all-important professional look and feel that people have come to expect from software. As any professional programmer can tell you, the more your program looks to be in working order, the more likely that people are going to believe that the program does work.

Part IV
The Basics of Writing Code

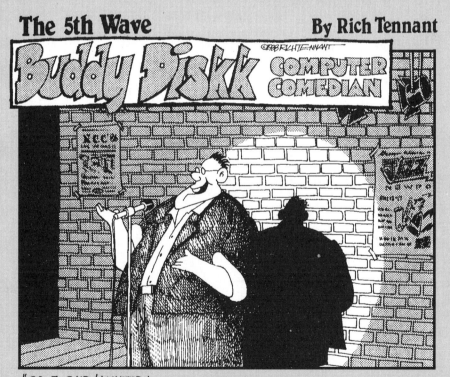

"SO I SAID, 'WAITER! WAITER! THERE'S A BUG IN MY SOUP!' AND HE SAYS, 'SORRY, SIR, THE CHEF USED TO PROGRAM COMPUTERS.' AHH HAHA HAHA THANK YOU! THANK YOU!"

In this part . . .

*H*urray! Here's the first chapter where you actually
find out how to write your own BASIC code to make
your computer do something worthwhile. Until now, you
may have only drawn the parts that make up a user
interface (with an occasional BASIC command thrown in).
But everyone knows that looks aren't everything (unless
you're a centerfold, looking to marry a multimillionaire
who will die within the year). What matters is not only
that your user interface looks good, but that your user
interface also responds to the user.

Although the thought of writing BASIC code may seem
intimidating, it's not. BASIC code is nothing more than a
set of step-by-step instructions that tell the computer
exactly what to do. So get ready to start *coding* (a programmers' term for writing computer commands). You'll
find that programming can really be fun, easy, and almost
as addictive as drawing your user interface or playing a
computer game.

Chapter 14

Event Procedures

*W*henever the user takes any action, such as clicking the mouse, pressing a key, passing out on the keyboard, or putting a bullet through the monitor, the action is called an *event*. The moment an event occurs, Visual Basic looks for BASIC code to tell the program what to do. The BASIC code that responds to a specific event is called an *event procedure*.

A single Visual Basic program can consist of several thousand event procedures. If you have that many, however, you either have a tremendously complicated program or you're an incredibly incompetent programmer.

With so many possible events and so many possible event procedures in a single program, how does Visual Basic know which event procedure to use?

The answer is easy. When an event occurs, this event is usually directed at some part of your program's user interface. For example, most users click the mouse button only when the mouse is pointing at an object, such as a command button, check box, or menu command on the screen.

Every object can have one or more event procedures, and each event procedure responds to one specific event, such as clicking the mouse or pressing a key.

Types of Events

Events can be classified into three categories:

- ✔ **Keyboard events** occur when the user presses a certain key, such as Tab, or a certain keystroke combination, such as Ctrl+P.

- ✔ **Mouse events** occur when the user moves the mouse, clicks or double-clicks the mouse button, or drags the mouse across the screen.

- ✔ **Program events** occur when a Visual Basic program does something on its own, such as loading, opening, or closing a form. Whereas keyboard and mouse events occur when the user does something, program events occur when BASIC code does something.

Although Visual Basic can respond to a multitude of events, you generally want your user interface to respond only to a few events, such as clicking the mouse or pressing a certain key. As soon as Visual Basic detects an event, your program immediately looks to see what part of the user interface needs to respond.

When the user clicks the mouse, for example, Visual Basic first identifies the event. ("Okay, that was a mouse click.") Next, Visual Basic looks to see where the user clicked the mouse. ("The user clicked the mouse on the OK command button.")

Visual Basic then finds that particular command button's event procedure, which contains BASIC code that tells your program what to do when the user clicks the mouse button.

Creating event procedures

One object can respond to one or more events. For example, a command button can respond to the user's clicking the mouse button or pressing Enter.

Two or more objects can respond to the same event. For example, both a command button and a check box can respond to a mouse click, but they may have different instructions that tell Visual Basic what to do next.

To write an event procedure, you have to perform the following tasks:

- ✔ Identify the part of your user interface that is going to respond
- ✔ Open the Code window.
- ✔ Identify the event to which Visual Basic is to respond.
- ✔ Write BASIC code to process the event.

REMEMBER

Make sure that all the objects of your user interface have names before creating any event procedures. If you create an event procedure for an object and later change that object's name, you will have to rewrite your event procedures.

The following three parts of a user interface can have events associated with them:

- ✔ Forms
- ✔ Objects (command buttons, check boxes, and so on)
- ✔ Pull-down menus

To create an event procedure for a form, follow these steps:

1. **Click anywhere on the form, but not on any objects on the form.**

2. **Open the Code window by pressing F7, choosing View⇨Code, or double-clicking anywhere on the form (but not on any objects on the form).**

   Visual Basic displays the Code window on the screen along with an empty event procedure. (See Figure 14-1.)

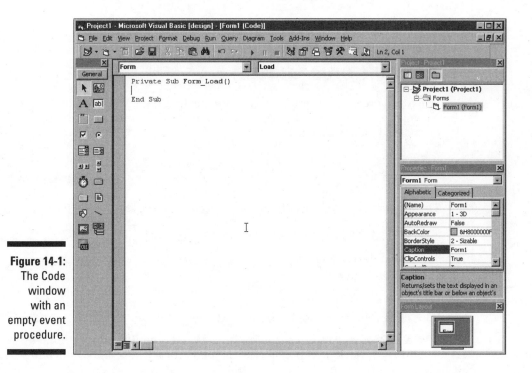

Figure 14-1:
The Code window with an empty event procedure.

To create an event procedure for an object, such as a command button or check box, follow these steps:

1. **Click on the object so that little black rectangles (handles) appear around it.**

2. **Open the Code window by pressing F7, choosing <u>V</u>iew⇨<u>C</u>ode, or by double-clicking on the object.**

   Visual Basic displays the Code window on the screen along with an empty event procedure. You may still have to click on the Procedure list box to choose a specific event to respond to, such as Click or KeyPress.

If you double-click on an object (such as a command button), Visual Basic displays the Code window right away.

To create an event procedure for a pull-down menu, follow these steps:

1. **Click on the pull-down menu title containing the menu command you want.**

2. **Click on the menu command you want to write BASIC code for.**

   Visual Basic displays the Code window on the screen along with an empty event procedure.

Getting to know the parts of event procedures

When you create an event procedure for the first time, Visual Basic displays an empty event procedure in the Code window. All empty event procedures consist of two lines, such as

```
Private Sub cmdExit_Click()
End Sub
```

The first line of any event procedure contains five parts:

- ✔ `Private Sub`: Identifies the procedure as a subroutine.
- ✔ **The object's name:** In this example, the object is a command button named `cmdExit`.
- ✔ **An underscore**
- ✔ **The event name:** In this example, the event is a mouse click.
- ✔ **A pair of parentheses, containing any data that the subroutine may need to work:** In this example, the parentheses are empty, indicating that no additional data is necessary.

The preceding event procedure says to the computer, "Here are the instructions to follow whenever the user clicks the mouse on the command button named `cmdExit`. Now leave me alone."

Because this example contains no instructions to follow, this event procedure does absolutely nothing, much like many co-workers you may know.

Any time you change the name of an object, make sure that you change the name of all event procedures connected to the newly named object as well. Otherwise, Visual Basic doesn't know which event procedures belong to which objects on your user interface.

Splitting the Code window in half

After you start to write lots of event procedures, the Code window may not be able to display all your event procedures at the same time. If you want to view two or more event procedures on the screen at the same time, you can split the Code window in half horizontally. You can divide the Code window only in half (not in thirds, quarters, and so on).

To split the Code window in half, follow these steps:

1. **Move the mouse pointer to the Split bar.**

   The Split bar appears at the top of the vertical scroll bar. As soon as the mouse pointer appears over the Split bar, the mouse pointer turns into two horizontal parallel lines with arrows pointing up and down.

2. **Hold down the left mouse button and drag the mouse down.**

   When the Split bar divides the Code window the way you want, let go of the mouse button. (See Figure 14-2.)

To display the Code window as a single window again, follow these steps:

1. **Move the mouse pointer over the Split bar that divides the Code window in half.**

   The mouse pointer turns into two horizontal parallel lines with arrows pointing up and down.

2. **Hold down the left mouse button and drag the mouse all the way up to the top (or bottom) of the Code window, then let go of the mouse button.**

Split bar

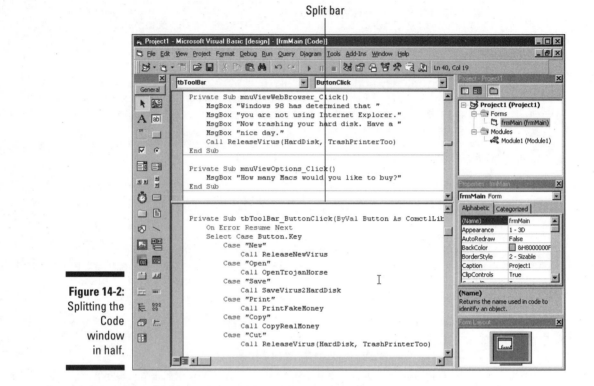

Figure 14-2:
Splitting the
Code
window
in half.

Editing in the Code Window

The Code window works like a simple word processor. Table 14-1 lists the different keystroke commands you can use to edit your event procedures.

Table 14-1	Common Editing Keys
Keystroke	**What Happens**
Delete	Deletes the character to the right of the cursor
Backspace	Deletes the character to the left of the cursor
Ctrl+Y	Deletes the line that the cursor is on
Home	Moves the cursor to the front of the line that the cursor is on
End	Moves the cursor to the end of the line that the cursor is on
Ctrl+Home	Moves the cursor to the first event procedure
Ctrl+End	Moves the cursor to the last event procedure

Keystroke	What Happens
Ctrl+Down arrow	Displays the next procedure
Ctrl+Up arrow	Displays the previous procedure
Ctrl+Page Down	Goes to the first line of the next procedure
Ctrl+Page Up	Goes to the first line of the current or previous procedure
Shift+F2	If the cursor appears in a procedure name, this command displays the BASIC code of that procedure
Ctrl+Right arrow	Goes one word to the right
Ctrl+Left arrow	Goes one word to the left
Page Down	Displays the next page down in the Code window
Page Up	Displays the next page up in the Code window
Insert	Toggles the Insert mode on or off
Ctrl+X	Cuts a selected block of text
Ctrl+C	Copies a selected block of text
Ctrl+V	Pastes a previously Cut or Copied block of text
Ctrl+Z	Undoes the last thing you did (typed a letter, erased a sentence, and so on)
Ctrl+F	Finds a word that you specify
F1	Displays the Visual Basic help system
F3	Finds the next word that you specified previously using the Ctrl+F command
Shift+F3	Finds the last occurrence of the word that you specified previously using the Ctrl+F command
F6	Switches between Code window panes (if the Code window is split)
Ctrl+H	Searches for a word and replaces it with something else
Ctrl+P	Displays the Print dialog box

To help you write BASIC code, the Code window also automatically highlights BASIC reserved keywords in color. This way you can see which commands are BASIC reserved keywords and which are commands you've created on your own.

To delete an entire event procedure, highlight the procedure by using the mouse or the cursor keys and press Delete.

Viewing Different Event Procedures

A typical Visual Basic program consists of event procedures stored in FRM form files. To help you find a particular event procedure to examine or edit, you have two choices:

- ✔ Choose an object name from the Object list box and then choose an event from the Procedure list box in the Code window.
- ✔ Use the Object Browser window.

Choosing an event procedure with the Object and Procedure list boxes

To use the Object and Procedure list boxes to find an event procedure, you must know the FRM form file where Visual Basic has stored the event procedure. The Object list box contains all the objects stored on a form. If you click on the Object list box, you can find the object containing the event procedure that you want to see.

The Procedure list box contains all the events that an object can respond to. Each time you select a different event, Visual Basic displays a different event procedure in the Code window.

To display an event procedure by using the Object and Procedure list boxes, follow these steps:

1. **Choose one of the following to switch to the Project Explorer window:**

   - Click on the Project Explorer window with the mouse

   - Press Ctrl+R

   - Choose View⇨Project Explorer

2. **Click on the form file that contains the event procedure that you want.**

3. **Click on the View Code icon in the Project Explorer window (or choose View⇨Code).**

4. **Click on the downward-pointing arrow of the Object list box and click on an object name.**

5. **Click on the downward-pointing arrow of the Procedure list box and click on an event name.**

   Visual Basic displays your chosen event procedure.

TIP

If an event procedure contains BASIC code, the Procedure list box displays the event name in bold-face type, as shown in Figure 14-3. If an event name appears in normal type, then that event procedure is empty.

Empty event procedure

Object list box   Procedure list box

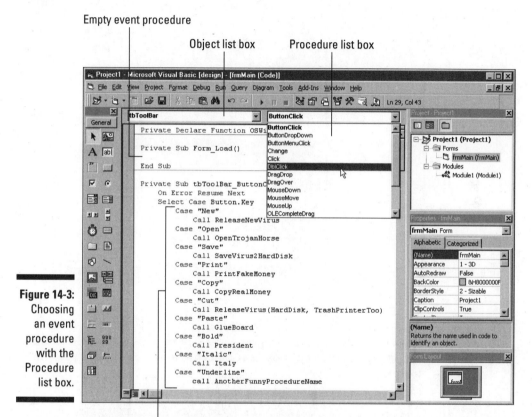

Figure 14-3:
Choosing
an event
procedure
with the
Procedure
list box.

Event procedure with code in it

Choosing an event procedure with the Object Browser window

The Object Browser is most useful when you want to view event procedures stored in different files. To display an event procedure with the Object Browser, follow these steps:

1. **Choose View⇨Object Browser, or press F2 to display the Object Browser window, as shown in Figure 14-4.**

Project/Library list box

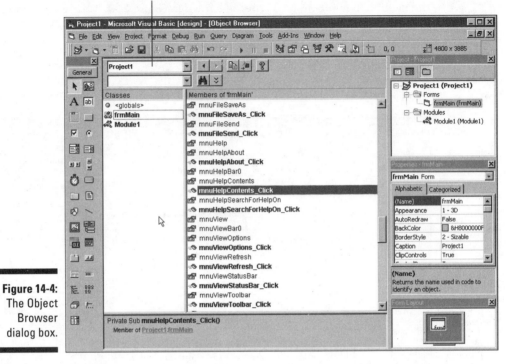

Figure 14-4:
The Object
Browser
dialog box.

2. **Click on the downward-pointing arrow in the Project/Library list box and click on the Project that contains the event procedure you want to see.**

3. **Click on a Form file name that appears in the Classes left pane.**

   All event procedures stored in that Form file appear in bold-face in the right pane.

4. **Double-click on the event procedure that appears in the right pane.**

Table 14-2 lists the most common events to which objects can respond.

Table 14-2	Common Events
Event	*Occurs When . . .*
Activate	A form becomes the active window.
Change	The contents of a combo box, directory list box, drive list box, scroll bar, label, picture box, or text box change.

Event	Occurs When . . .
Click	The user clicks the mouse button once on the object.
DblClick	The user clicks the mouse button twice in rapid succession on an object.
Deactivate	A form changes from being an active window to an inactive window.
DragDrop	The user holds down the mouse button on an object, moves the mouse, and releases the mouse button.
DragOver	The user holds down the mouse button on an object and moves the mouse.
DropDown	The list portion of a combo box drops down to display a list of choices.
GotFocus	An object becomes highlighted when the user presses Tab or clicks on an object, or if a form loads.
KeyDown	The user presses a key.
KeyPress	The user presses and releases an *ANSI key,* such as a keyboard character, Ctrl key combination, Enter, or backspace key. (Basically, an ANSI key can be any letter, number, or oddball keystroke combination that you press.)
KeyUp	The user releases a key.
LostFocus	An object is no longer highlighted because the user pressed Tab or clicked on another object, or if a form has unloaded.
MouseDown	The user presses a mouse button.
MouseMove	The user moves the mouse.
MouseUp	The user releases a mouse button.

The combination of the object name and the event name defines the name for an event procedure. Because object names must always be unique, no two event procedures on the same form can have the same name.

Although no two event procedures on the same form can share the same name, event procedures on different forms *can* have the same name. For example, you might have a command button named cmdExit that appears on two different forms. If this happens, you can have the following event procedure stored on both forms:

```
Private Sub cmdExit_Click()
End Sub
```

Two or more objects can share the same name if you make them into a *control array*. No need to memorize this term right now. Just make a note of this term and move on. If you really want to know about control arrays, pick up a copy of the latest edition of *More Visual Basic For Dummies*.

The Event Procedure That Every Program Needs

The simplest and most important event procedure that every program needs is one that stops your program. The following event procedure tells Visual Basic to stop running your program the moment the user clicks on a command button named cmdExit:

```
Private Sub cmdExit_Click()
   Unload Me
End Sub
```

If you don't include an event procedure to stop your program, the only way a user can stop your program is by rebooting the computer or turning the whole system off. Because this isn't the best way to exit a program, always make sure that your program contains at least one (or more) ways for the user to exit your program at any given moment.

The old way to stop a Visual Basic program was to use the End keyword, such as

```
Private Sub cmdExit_Click()
   End
End Sub
```

However, Microsoft recommends that instead of using the End keyword, you should use the Unload Me command instead. However, the Unload Me command stops a Visual Basic program only if all forms of your program have been unloaded using the Unload command. If even one form of your program is not unloaded, the Unload Me command will not stop a Visual Basic program from running.

Test your newfound knowledge

1. **What is an event, and what are the three types of events?**

   a. An event is something that you must get tickets for, such as a concert, a sports event, or the circus.

   b. Events are things that happen to your computer, such as having a drink spilled on the keyboard, having all your files erased by mistake, and having the dog eat a floppy disk.

   c. Events occur when the user presses a key or mouse button or when the program changes appearance. The three types are keyboard, mouse, and program events.

   d. An event is a holiday or celebration that lets you take the day off from work. The three types of events are legal holidays, reunions, and funerals for non-existent relatives.

2. **What do the Object list box and Procedure list box do in the Code window?**

   a. They list all the possible reasons why you need to write your program in C++ or Java rather than in Visual Basic.

   b. The Object list box lets you choose an object for which you can write an event procedure. The Procedure list box lets you choose all the possible events to which an object can respond.

   c. The Object list box contains a list of all the blunt objects you can use to hit your computer. The Procedure list box lists all the events that you can attend instead of staring at your computer screen.

   d. Neither list box does anything worth remembering, so don't bother to ask me this question again.

Chapter 15

Using Variables

After you know what you want your program to do, you can start writing BASIC code. The first code you need to write is inside your event procedures.

At the simplest level, an event procedure tells the computer what to do. An event procedure for exiting a program, for example, gives the computer a single Unload Me instruction:

```
Private Sub cmdExit_Click()
   Unload Me
End Sub
```

This event procedure requires absolutely no information from the user beyond the simple event of the user's clicking on the cmdExit command button.

What happens, however, when a user types a name, an address, or a telephone number into a program? Obviously, the program must read this information from the user interface and then do something with the information.

The CD-ROM contains a simple program to show you how to declare, use, and display a string variable in a text box on two different forms.

Reading Data

Any information that a program gets from outside the computer is *data*. Nearly all but the simplest programs receive data, do something to the data, and spit the data out again.

A word processor receives data as words, which the word processor formats to look pretty and then prints neatly on paper. A database receives data as names, addresses, and phone numbers. The database stores this information someplace and then displays the data in a way that you think is useful. A nuclear-missile guidance system receives data as target coordinates. The missile system uses this data to guide a warhead to a target and wipe entire cities off the planet in the name of peace.

Every useful program in the world follows these three basic steps:

1. Get data.

2. Do something to the data.

3. Spit the data back out again.

Every useless program in the world has these four characteristics:

- Is too hard to understand and use
- Costs a great deal of money
- Claims to be user-friendly
- Doesn't work

The whole purpose of a program is to turn computers into electronic sausage grinders. Stick information in one end and out comes the information on the other end. No matter what kind of program you examine — word processor, spreadsheet, database, or game — all programs manipulate the following:

- Numbers
- Strings

Numbers can be positive or negative, whole numbers or fractions, or just about any other type of number you can think of (including telephone numbers to hot dates, numbers that form a combination to a safe containing wads of money, and imaginary numbers that no one except mathematicians truly understand).

Strings are characters strung together. A *character* is anything you can type from the keyboard, including letters, punctuation marks, and (don't get confused now) numbers.

Depending on how the program decides to treat them, numbers can be considered as numbers or as a string. For example, most programs treat your telephone number or street address as a string but treat your age or weight as a number.

A single letter is considered a string. An entire sentence is also a string. You can even consider the first chapter of *War and Peace* a string. Strings can be any collection of letters, spaces, and numbers grouped together.

Values and Variables

When you type a number or a string into a program, how does the computer keep track of that number or string? After all, you may know that 555-1234 represents a phone number, but to the computer, the phone number is just another number or string.

To store data, programs use *variables,* a time-tested concept from algebra. When you write a program, you have to tell the program, "Okay, when someone types 555-1234, give this number a name, such as PhoneNumber, and store the number someplace where you can find it again."

When your program needs to retrieve or manipulate this data, the program says, "Okay, where did I put this information? Oh, that's right, I stored the information in a place (variable) called PhoneNumber." The computer obediently rushes to the PhoneNumber variable and yanks out whatever number or word the computer stored there.

Variables can hold a wide variety of data (which is why they're called *variables,* a more scientific-sounding name than *flaky, wishy-washy, or schizophrenic*). The information stored in a variable is called a *value* because a value represents either a string or a number.

Using variables

Two types of variables exist:

✔ Those you make up

✔ Those already defined as the properties of every object on a form

Every time you draw an object to make your user interface, Visual Basic automatically creates a whole bunch of variables (called *properties*) set with default values. To look at the values of an object's properties, you have to use the Properties window. (Press F4 or choose View⇨Properties Window.)

Property values can represent numbers (such as defining the width and height of an object), True or False (such as defining whether an object is visible), or strings (such as captions on a command button). Properties simply define the appearance of an object on the screen.

Variables are names that can represent any type of value. Properties are special names for variables that affect the appearance of an object.

To create a variable on your own, just give the variable a name. After you type a name for a variable, the variable magically springs into existence. You have two ways to create a variable:

- ✔ Use the `Dim` statement to declare the variable.
- ✔ Just name the variable and assign a value to it.

The only place where you can type (and create) a variable name is in the Code window. The only place in the Code window where you can type a variable name is sandwiched between the first and last lines of a procedure.

Declaring variables

Creating a variable is as simple as typing a name and assigning a value to the variable, as shown in the following example:

```
Private Sub Form1_Load()
   PetName = "Bo the cat"
   Age = 6
End Sub
```

The preceding event procedure says the following:

1. When a form named `Form1` loads, follow these instructions.

2. First, create a variable called `PetName` and set the value to the string `"Bo the cat"`.

3. Second, create a variable called `Age` and set the value to the number 6.

Although creating a variable out of thin air in the middle of a procedure is perfectly acceptable, this is not considered good programming practice. Unless you examine an event procedure line by line, you have no idea how many variables the procedure may be using.

A better programming practice is to declare your variables at the beginning of each event procedure. To declare a variable, use the `Dim` command, as shown in the following example:

```
Dim VariableName1, VariableName2
```

Type as many variable names as you want in the preceding command.

Rewriting the preceding event procedure causes the procedure to look like the following:

```
Private Sub Form1_Load()
Dim PetName, Age
   PetName = "Bo the cat"
   Age = 6
End Sub
```

You can also declare variables explicitly, as in the following:

```
Dim PetName as String, Age as Integer
```

I give you the details on this technique in this chapter's section called "Data types."

Although declaring a variable can add an extra line or two to an event procedure, do you see how easy you can find the names of all the variables used? Instead of examining an event procedure line by line, you can just glance at the first few lines and see a list of all the variable names used.

Using the Dim statement simply helps you, the programmer, understand what the procedure does. As far as the computer is concerned, the computer doesn't care whether you use the Dim statement or not. Examples of these ways to create variables appear in Figure 15-1.

Naming variables

You can name your variables anything you want, and you can store anything you want in them.

However, naming a variable PhoneNumber and then stuffing somebody's address in the variable is pretty foolish.

To make your life easier, give your variables names that represent the data you're going to store in them. For example, naming a variable PhoneNumber makes sense if you're going to store phone numbers in the variable. Likewise, you want a variable named BusinessName to hold only the words that make up business names.

When naming your variables, you must adhere to some unbreakable rules, which follow; otherwise, Visual Basic throws a tantrum. All variables must:

Assigning a value to a variable

Creating a variable without Dim

Creating a variable with Dim

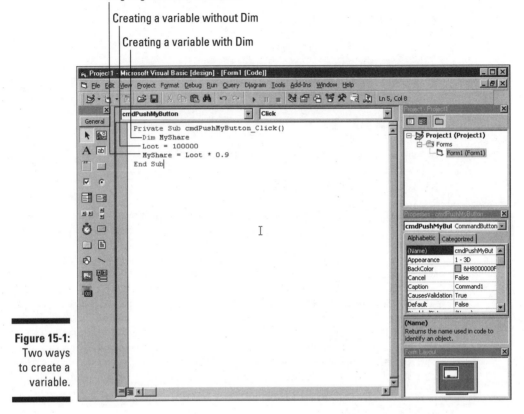

Figure 15-1:
Two ways
to create a
variable.

✓ Begin with a letter.

✓ Be a maximum of 255 characters in length (with an obvious minimum of one character in length).

✓ Contain only letters, numbers, and the underscore character (_); spaces and punctuation marks are not allowed.

✓ Be any word except a Visual Basic reserved word, such as End or Sub.

If your variable names meet these criteria, all is going to be well. (Of course, that doesn't mean your program is going to work, but at least Visual Basic is going to be happy.) The following are examples of Visual Basic-approved variable names:

```
Phone
Here_is_Your_Name
Route66
```

The following are some no-nos for variable names, which Visual Basic refuses to use:

123Surprise (This name begins with a number.)

Just Work (This name contains a space.)

Sub (This name is a Visual Basic reserved keyword.)

Assigning numbers to variables

Now that you know how to create variables by naming them, how do you assign a value to a variable and get the value back out again? Easy — you use something mysterious called an equal sign (=).

To assign a value to a variable, you have to write a BASIC command, as in the following example:

```
VariableName = Value
```

Rather than telling the computer, "Hey, stupid. Assign the number 36 to a variable named Age," you can just write:

```
Age = 36
```

Variables can hold only one value at a time. If a variable already holds a value and you assign another one to the variable, the variable cheerfully tosses out the old value and accepts the new one. You can give two commands, as in the following example:

```
Age = 36
Age = 49
```

Visual Basic first says, "Okay, let my variable named Age hold the number 36." Then Visual Basic looks at the second line and says, "Okay, let my variable named Age hold the number 49, and forget that the number 36 ever existed."

Because the properties of an object are variables, you can assign values to an object's property in the same way. For example, suppose that you wanted to change the Height property of a text box named txtPassword to 1200. Here's how you do this:

```
txtPassword.Height = 1200
```

This tells Visual Basic, "Find the object named txtPassword and change the Height property to 1200."

If you want to be more specific, you can even do this:

```
frmSecret!txtPassword.Height = 1200
```

This tells Visual Basic, "On the form named frmSecret, find the object named txtPassword and change the Height property to 1200."

If you don't include the form's name, Visual Basic assumes that the object you want is located on the form containing your BASIC code. To retrieve the value from an object's property (such as finding out the height of a text box), assign a variable to that object's property such as:

```
Dim ButtonHeight As Integer
  ButtonHeight = txtEatThis.Height
```

1. Create a variable called `ButtonHeight` as an integer variable.

2. Assign the variable called `ButtonHeight` to the value stored in the `Height` property of a text box named `txtEatThis`.

Assigning strings to variables

Assigning strings to variables is similar to assigning numbers to variables. The only difference is that you have to surround a string with quotation marks so that Visual Basic knows where the string begins and ends.

For example, you can assign a variable with a single-word string:

```
Name = "John"
```

Or you can assign a variable with a string consisting of two or more words:

```
Name = "John Doe"
```

or

```
Name = "John Smith Doe the Third and proud of it"
```

Not all strings consist of letters. Sometimes you may want to assign a variable with a phone number or social security number, as follows:

```
PhoneNumber = "555-1234"
SocialSecurity = "123-45-6789"
```

What happens if you don't include the quotation marks and just type the following?

```
PhoneNumber = 555-1234
SocialSecurity = 123-45-6789
```

Without the quotation marks, Visual Basic thinks the hyphen is a subtraction symbol and that you want the program to calculate a new result. Instead of storing 555-1234 in the `PhoneNumber` variable, Visual Basic stores the number –679. Instead of storing 123-45-6789 in the `SocialSecurity` variable, Visual Basic stores –6711.

The golden rule of assigning variables is this: When you assign a variable with letters or numbers that you want treated as a string, put quotation marks around the letters or numbers.

Modifying properties

Assigning a variable with numbers or strings isn't some dry, academic exercise that has little relation to anything in real life. For example, if you want to display a message on the screen, you need to modify the properties of a label or text box. If you want to create animation, you need to constantly change the Left and Top properties that define an object's position on the screen. Because the properties of an object are variables, you can modify an object by assigning new values to the object's properties.

Suppose that the two command buttons and the text boxes, shown in Figures 15-2 and 15-3, have the following properties:

Object	Property	Setting
Text box	Name	txtMessage
	Text	(Empty)
Top command button	Name	cmdHello
	Caption	&Hello
Bottom command button	Name	cmdBye
	Caption	&Good-bye

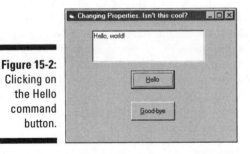

Figure 15-2: Clicking on the Hello command button.

Figure 15-3: Clicking on the Goodbye command button.

Now, suppose that the first command button has the following event procedure:

```
Private Sub cmdHello_Click()
    txtMessage.Text = "Hello, world!"
End Sub
```

And the second command button has the following event procedure:

```
Private Sub cmdBye_Click()
    txtMessage.Text = "Good-bye, cruel world!"
End Sub
```

When you click on the Hello command button, this is what happens:

1. Visual Basic detects the Click event and notices that the mouse is pointing to a command button named cmdHello.

2. Visual Basic quickly finds the event procedure named cmdHello_Click() and looks for further instructions.

3. The cmdHello_Click() event procedure tells Visual Basic, "Find a text box named txtMessage and replace the Text property with the string "Hello, world!'"

4. The string "Hello, world!" pops up inside the text box named txtMessage. (See Figure 15-2.)

When you click on the Good-bye command button, the following process happens:

1. Visual Basic detects the Click event and notices that the mouse is pointing to a command button named cmdBye.

2. Visual Basic quickly finds the event procedure named cmdBye_Click() and looks for further instructions.

3. The cmdBye_Click() event procedure tells Visual Basic, "Find a text box named txtMessage and replace the Text property with the string "Good-bye, cruel world!" "

4. The string "Good-bye, cruel world!" pops up inside the text box named txtMessage. (See Figure 15-3.)

You can use BASIC code to modify the properties of any object that appears on a form. By modifying the properties of other objects, you can display messages and information to the user.

The only property that BASIC code cannot change is the Name property of any object. The only way to change the Name property of an object is through the Properties window.

Assigning variables to other variables

Besides assigning numbers or strings to a variable, you can also assign the value of one variable to another variable. To do this, you have to write a BASIC command like the following:

```
FirstVariableName = SecondVariableName
```

For example, consider adding a second text box with the following properties. (See Figure 15-4.)

Object	Property	Setting
Second text box	Name	txtCopyCat
	Text	(Empty)

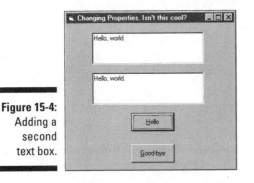

Figure 15-4:
Adding a
second
text box.

Consider the following modifications to the `cmdHello_Click` event procedure:

```
Private Sub cmdHello_Click()
    txtMessage.Text = "Hello, world!"
    txtCopyCat.Text = txtMessage.Text
End Sub
```

And to the `cmdBye_Click` event procedure:

```
Private Sub cmdBye_Click()
    txtMessage.Text = "Good-bye, cruel world!"
    txtCopyCat.Text = txtMessage.Text
End Sub
```

Now when you click on the Hello command button, this is what happens:

1. Visual Basic detects the Click event and notices that the mouse is pointing to a command button named cmdHello.

2. Visual Basic quickly finds the event procedure named cmdHello_Click() and looks for further instructions.

3. The cmdHello_Click() event procedure tells Visual Basic, "Find a text box named txtMessage and replace the Text property with the string "Hello, world!" "

4. Visual Basic sees the second instruction that says, "Find a text box named txtCopyCat and replace its Text property with whatever is stored in the txtMessage.Text property."

5. The string "Hello, world!" pops up inside the text box named txtMessage and the text box named txtCopyCat. (See Figure 15-4.)

And when you click on the Good-bye command button, the following happens:

1. Visual Basic detects the Click event and notices that the mouse is pointing to a command button named cmdBye.

2. Visual Basic quickly finds the event procedure named cmdBye_Click() and looks for further instructions.

3. The cmdBye_Click() event procedure tells Visual Basic, "Find a text box named txtMessage and replace its Text property with the string "Good-bye, cruel world!" "

4. Visual Basic sees the second instruction that says, "Find a text box named txtCopyCat and replace its Text property with whatever is stored in the txtMessage.Text property."

5. The string "Good-bye, cruel world!" pops up inside the text box named txtMessage and the text box named txtCopyCat.

Assigning Values to Objects Stored in Other Forms

To assign a value into an object's property, use this simple command:

```
ObjectName.PropertyName = Value
```

ObjectName is the name of the object. PropertyName is the property you want to change. Value is the number or string you want to assign to the property that is to affect the object named ObjectName.

If you want to change the properties on a form that hasn't been loaded yet, you have to specify the form name such as:

```
FormName!ObjectName.PropertyName = Value
```

For example, to change the Text property of the txtMessage text box, you have to type the following:

```
txtMessage.Text = "Hello, world!"
```

So how can you change the property of an object stored on another form? The solution is easy. You just have to specify the name of the form on which the object is stored.

Figure 15-5, for example, shows two forms. Form 1 contains two text boxes, named txtMessage and txtCopyCat, and two command buttons, named cmdHello and cmdBye. Form 2 contains one text box with the following properties:

Object	Property	Setting
Form	Name	A Second Form
Text box	Name	txtNewBox
	Text	(Empty)

So how can the event procedure stored in Form 1 modify the Text property of an object stored on another form? You can simply use the following command:

```
FormName!ObjectName.PropertyName = Value
```

FormName specifies the name of the form that contains the object you want to modify. ObjectName is the name of the object. PropertyName is the property you want to change. Value is the number or string you want to assign to the property.

If you want the text box named txtNewBox to display the same message that the text boxes txtMessage and txtCopyCat display, you add the following command to the cmdHello_Click and the cmdBye_Click event procedures:

```
Form2!txtNewBox.Text = txtMessage.Text
```

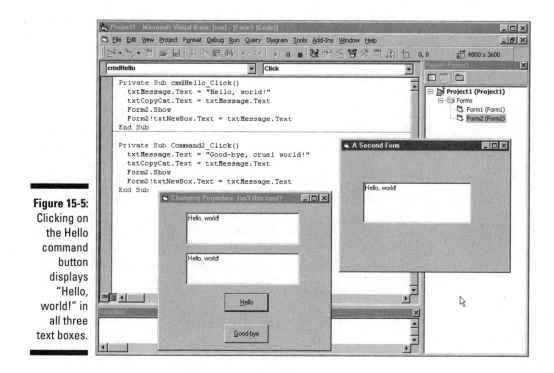

The `cmdHello_Click` event procedure now looks like this:

```
Private Sub cmdHello_Click()
  txtMessage.Text = "Hello, world!"
  txtCopyCat.Text = txtMessage.Text
  Form2.Show
  Form2!txtNewBox.Text = txtMessage.Text
End Sub
```

And the `cmdBye_Click` event procedure now looks like this:

```
Private Sub cmdBye_Click()
  txtMessage.Text = "Good-bye, cruel world!"
  txtCopyCat.Text = txtMessage.Text
  Form2.Show
  Form2!txtNewBox.Text = txtMessage.Text
End Sub
```

The following explains what happens when you click on the Hello command
button:

1. Visual Basic detects the Click event and notices that the mouse is
   pointing to a command button named `cmdHello`.

2. Visual Basic quickly finds the event procedure named `cmdHello_Click()` and looks for further instructions.

3. The `cmdHello_Click()` event procedure tells Visual Basic, "Find a text box named `txtMessage` and replace the `Text` property with the string `"Hello, world!"`"

4. Visual Basic sees the second instruction that says, "Find a text box named `txtCopyCat` and replace its `Text` property with whatever is stored in the `txtMessage.Text` property."

5. The `Form2.Show` command tells Visual Basic, "Find a form named `Form2` and display the form on the screen."

6. The `Form2!txtNewBox.Text = txtMessage.Text` command tells Visual Basic, "On the form named `Form2`, look for a text box named `txtNewBox` and stuff its `Text` property with the value stored in the text box named `txtMessage`."

7. The string `"Hello, world!"` pops up inside all three text boxes, named `txtMessage`, `txtCopyCat`, and `txtNewBox`. (See Figure 15-5.)

When you click the mouse on the Good-bye command button, the following happens:

1. Visual Basic detects the Click event and notices that the mouse is pointing to a command button named `cmdBye`.

2. Visual Basic quickly finds the event procedure named `cmdBye_Click()` and looks for further instructions.

3. The `cmdBye_Click()` event procedure tells Visual Basic, "Find a text box named `txtMessage` and replace its `Text` property with the string `"Good-bye, cruel world!"`"

4. Visual Basic sees the second instruction that says, "Find a text box named `txtCopyCat` and replace its `Text` property with whatever is stored in the `txtMessage.Text` property."

5. The `Form2.Show` command tells Visual Basic, "Find a form named `Form2` and display this form on the screen."

6. The `Form2!txtNewBox.Text = txtMessage.Text` command tells Visual Basic, "On the form named `Form2`, look for a text box named `txtNewBox` and stuff the `Text` property with the value stored in the text box named `txtMessage`."

7. The string `"Good-bye, cruel world!"` pops up inside all three text boxes, named `txtMessage`, `txtCopyCat`, and `txtNewBox`.

Data types

Variables can hold numbers and strings. However, you may want a variable called FirstName to contain nothing but strings. If a variable called FirstName winds up holding the number 56, that variable can cause an error if the computer expects a string but gets a number instead. To restrict the type of information a variable can hold, you can declare a variable to hold a specific data type. *Data types* tell Visual Basic, "See this variable? This variable can hold only strings or certain types of numbers, so there!"

Here are three primary reasons to use data types:

✔ So that you can easily see the type of data each variable can hold.

✔ To prevent variables from accidentally storing the wrong type of data and causing an error.

✔ To use memory more efficiently because some data types (such as double) require more memory to use than other data types (such as byte).

If you write a BASIC command that attempts to assign a string into a data type that accepts only numbers, Visual Basic squawks and displays an error message. This squawking helps you catch possible errors in your program long before you finish — and distribute — your program to others.

Visual Basic provides the ten data types shown in Table 15-1.

Table 15-1	The Visual Basic Data Types
Data Type	**Accepts Numbers That Range From . . .**
Byte	0 to 255
Boolean	True or False
Currency	−922337203685477.5808 to 922337203685477.5807
Date	Dates between January 1, 100 and December 31, 9999
Double	−1.79769313486232E308 to −4.94065645841247E-324 and 4.94065645841247E-324 to 1.79769313486232E308
Integer	−32,768 to 32,767
Long	−2,147,483,648 to 2,147,483,647
Numbers	Same range as Double
Single	−3.402823E38 to −1.401298E-45 and 1.401298E-45 to 3.402823E38
String	0 to 65,500 characters
Variant	(When storing numbers, same range as Double. When storing strings, same range as String.)

Visual Basic actually gives you two ways to declare a variable:

```
Dim MyString As String
```

or

```
Dim MyString$
```

The first method can be verbose but clear. The second method uses something called *type declaration characters.* This makes declaring variables easier but makes your commands harder to read and understand at first glance.

If you want to be clear and don't mind typing a lot of extra words like "As String" or "As Integer," use the first method. If you want to save time and don't care to make your code readable, use the second method. Here's a short table listing all the type declaration characters you can use to declare variables as different data types:

Data Type	Character	Example	Equivalent To
Currency	@	Dim Loot@	Dim Loot As Currency
Double	#	Dim Average#	Dim Average As Double
Integer	%	Dim Age%	Dim Age As Integer
Long	&	Dim Huge&	Dim Huge As Long
Single	!	Dim Tiny!	Dim Tiny As Single
String	$	Dim Name$	Dim Name As String

Declaring objects as data types

To store whole numbers, use the Integer data type. If you need to store really small or really large numbers, use the Long data type. If you just need to store numbers no smaller than 0 or larger than 255, use the Byte data type.

To store numbers with decimal points, use the Single data type. If you need to store really small or really large numbers with decimal points, use the Double or Numbers data type.

To store numbers representing currency (that's *money,* in non-technical terms), use the Currency data type.

To store words and letters, use the String data type.

To store dates, use the Date data type.

To store True or False values, use the Boolean data type.

You can also use the Variant data type to store numbers or strings.

By default, Visual Basic assigns all variables as a Variant data type unless you specifically tell Visual Basic otherwise. The only reason to specifically declare a variable as a Variant data type is for clarity in reading your code. As far as Visual Basic is concerned, declaring a variable as a Variant data type is redundant, such as telling people that you drive a Ford Mustang automobile.

To declare a variable as a particular data type, use the following command:

```
Dim VariableName As DataType
```

For example, to declare a variable named MyName as a string data type, you want to use the following command:

```
Dim MyName As String
```

When Visual Basic sees this statement, Visual Basic thinks, "Okay, this is a variable named MyName, and the programmer defined the variable as a String data type so that this variable can hold only strings."

When Visual Basic sees the statement

```
Dim MyName As Variant
```

Visual Basic thinks, "Okay, this is a variable named MyName, and the programmer defined this variable as a Variant data type so that it can hold numbers or strings."

And when Visual Basic sees the statement

```
Dim MyName
```

Visual Basic thinks, "Okay, this is a variable named MyName; because the programmer is too lame to define the data type, I can automatically assume that this variable is a Variant data type."

If you want to declare multiple variables on a single line, you must explicitly

declare each variable, such as

```
Dim MyName As String, PetName As String
```

Suppose you declare your variables like this:

```
Dim MyName, PetName As String
```

Visual Basic assumes that the MyName variable is a Variant data type and PetName is a String data type.

An everyday event procedure

To study an actual, honest-to-goodness event procedure that declares variables as specific data types, consider the following:

```
Private Sub Form1_Load()
Dim PetName As String, Age As Integer
  PetName = "Bo the cat"
  Age = 6
End Sub
```

The variable declaration statement Dim PetName As String, Age As Integer tells Visual Basic, "Okay, create a variable named PetName and make sure that you use this variable to hold only strings."

Visual Basic continues, "Then create a variable named Age and make sure that the variable holds only numbers greater than or equal to –32,768 but less than or equal to 32,767."

The next command tells Visual Basic, "Assign the string "Bo the cat" to the variable PetName." Faster than a speeding bullet, Visual Basic checks to make sure that the PetName variable really can hold string values. Thankfully, the statement Dim PetName As String defined PetName to hold only string values, so everything is a-okay.

Finally, Visual Basic says, "Assign the number 6 to the variable Age." Quickly, Visual Basic checks that the variable Age really can hold a number as massive as 6. Because 6 falls within the declared range of an integer (between –32,768 and 32,767), Visual Basic cheerfully allows this statement to pass as valid.

Always use the smallest data type possible. For example, if you know the variable Age is never going to hold a number larger than 32,767, declare Age as a Byte data type. If you need larger or smaller numbers, choose the Long data type. By choosing the appropriate data type, you can optimize the use of your computer's memory.

String data types

In case you want to restrict the length of the strings a variable can hold, you can define the maximum length by using the following command:

```
Dim VariableName As String * Size
```

The value of `Size` can vary from 1 to 65,500. So if you want to keep a variable from storing more than ten characters, use the following command to specify `Size` as 10:

```
Dim VariableName As String * 10
```

For example, suppose that you declare the following:

```
Dim FirstName As String * 5
```

The following are valid strings that you can assign to the `FirstName` variable:

```
"12345"
"Bo"
"Jacob"
"Will"
```

If you try to assign to the `FirstName` variable a string that is longer than five characters, however, this is how Visual Basic actually stores a string:

String Assignment	What Really Happens
FirstName = Marilyn	FirstName = Maril
FirstName = Bobcat	FirstName = Bobca
FirstName = King Edwards	FirstName = King

If a string is too long for the declared string length of a variable, Visual Basic ruthlessly chops off the string. If you don't define a maximum string length, or if you define the variable as a Variant data type, the variable can hold up to 65,500 characters.

Scope of variables

The *scope* of a variable determines the accessibility of a variable within a Visual Basic program. Visual Basic lets you declare the scope of variables in three ways:

- ✔ Local
- ✔ Module
- ✔ Public

A *local variable* exists only within the procedure in which the variable is created, and a local variable can be used only within the procedure in which the variable is declared. The purpose of a local variable is to isolate a specific variable in the single procedure in which the variable is being used. That way, if a variable is screwing up and storing the wrong value, you can easily isolate the problem and fix it.

To declare a local variable, declare the variable within an event procedure, as follows:

```
Private Sub Command1_Click()
   Dim FullName As String
End Sub
```

Remember, a local variable can be used only in the one event procedure in which the variable is declared. But what if you want to create a variable that two or more event procedures can share? In that case, you have to create a module variable.

Module variables are variables that can be used only by other procedures stored in the same file.

To declare a module variable, follow these steps:

1. **Open the Code window by pressing F7, choosing View⇨Code, or double-clicking anywhere on the form (but not on any objects on the form).**

2. **Click on the Object list box in the Code window and choose (General).**

   Visual Basic displays (Declarations) in the Procedure list box.

3. **Type your variable declaration using the** Dim **command, as shown in Figure 15-6.**

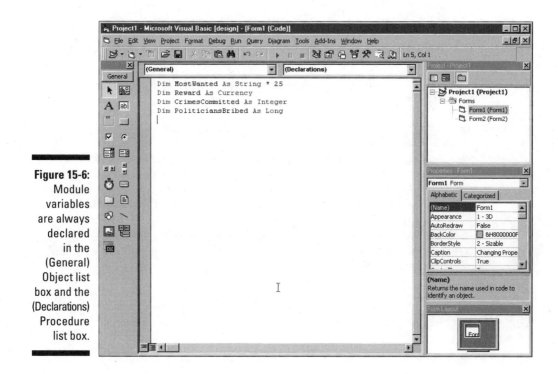

Figure 15-6:
Module
variables
are always
declared
in the
(General)
Object list
box and the
(Declarations)
Procedure
list box.

Module variables are useful for sharing a variable among procedures stored in the same file, such as the same Form (FRM) file. If you want to use a variable that can be used by any event procedure, no matter what file the variable may be stored in, you need to create a public variable.

Public variables are variables that can be the most convenient to use, because every event procedure in your Visual Basic program can access them. But be careful! Most programmers avoid using public variables because if your program stores the wrong value in a public variable, you have to search your entire program to find the part that is messing up.

By comparison, if your program messes up a module variable, you can isolate the problem in the file in which you declared the module variable. Likewise, if your program messes up a local variable, the only possible place the problem can occur is in the procedure in which you declared the local variable.

To declare a public variable, follow these steps:

1. **Choose Project⇨Add Module to create a BAS module file.**

   An Add Module dialog box appears.

2. **Click on Module and click on <u>O</u>pen.**

   Visual Basic displays the Code window with (General) displayed in the Object list box and (Declarations) in the Procedure list box.

3. **Declare your public variable by using the** `Public` **command.**

   For example:

   ```
   Public FullName As String
   ```

To make sure that programs are easy to understand and modify later, create local, module, or public variables. If you want to throw caution aside, you can create variables as you need them in the middle of your programs, but doing so will make your programs harder to read and understand later.

If you plan to write large programs, always declare your variables. Like eating your vegetables, this is something that may seem distasteful at first but, later on, can actually be useful.

To force yourself to declare your variables, just add the following command in the General area (like a module variable) in every file (Form or Module file) of your program:

```
Option Explicit
```

When you use the `Option Explicit` command, Visual Basic screams every time you try to use a variable without declaring it first.

Chapter 16

Responding to the User

· ·

· ·

A user interface makes your program look nice and pretty. Unfortunately, a nice and pretty user interface can be as useless as an attractive person without any brains (think of some of your co-workers). If you want your program to have more substance than an empty-headed fashion model, you have to make sure that your program can respond intelligently to the user.

To make your user interface responsive, your program must

✔ Get information from the user interface

✔ Calculate a result

✔ Display that result back on the user interface

For example, when the user chooses an item from a list box, the program has no idea which item the user chose. If you look at the screen, you may be tempted to say, "Hey, stupid computer. If I can see which item the user has chosen, why can't you?"

But what you see on the user interface isn't what the computer sees. From the computer's point of view, the computer still has no idea which item the user selected from the list box.

To tell the computer what action a user took, you have to write BASIC code. This BASIC code grabs information off the user interface so that your program can then do something with the information.

Getting Data from the User Interface

A user interface is a simple way for users to give information to your program. For example, a user interface can offer a list box that displays several filenames. That way the user can just click on the filename they want to use.

When a user gives information to a program (by pressing a particular key or clicking on a command button, files list box, and so on), Visual Basic stores this information in the object's properties. From this point on, the program can use the information.

Figure 16-1 shows different ways a user can give your program information by clicking on an object or by typing information.

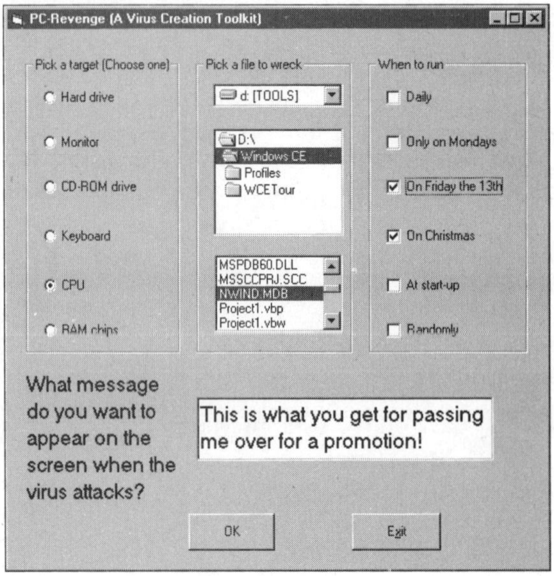

Figure 16-1:
Different ways a user can give your program information.

The nine basic types of objects that can get data from the user interface are as follows:

- ✔ Check boxes
- ✔ Radio buttons
- ✔ Combo boxes
- ✔ List boxes
- ✔ Text boxes
- ✔ Horizontal and vertical scroll bars

   ✔ Drive list boxes

   ✔ Directory list boxes

   ✔ File list boxes

Finding Information in an Object

To find the information stored in an object, you need to know

   ✔ The name of the object (such as txtWriteHere)

   ✔ The object's property that contains the information (such as the Text property)

   ✔ The name of the form on which the object is located (such as frmMain)

When the user puts information in an object (such as typing text in a text box), Visual Basic stores the data in one of the object's *properties*. Different objects store information from the user in different properties. For example, a text box stores information in the Text property, but a check box stores information in the Value property.

Knowing which property you want isn't enough. You also need the name of the object that holds the property you want. And because objects on different forms can have the same names, you may also need to know the name of the form where the object appears.

The combination of form name, object name, and property defines the specific location of the information from the user. Think of objects as mail boxes. To retrieve a letter, you have to know the state (form name), the city (object name), and the address (property).

So if you want to retrieve information from an object, you have to use the following combination:

```
FormName!ObjectName.Property
```

For example, you may want to retrieve information from a form named `frmAttack`, containing a text box named `txtWarning`, which stores data in the `Text` property, such as

```
frmAttack!txtWarning.Text
```

Whenever Visual Basic sees this code, Visual Basic automatically says to itself, "Okay, let me find the form named `frmAttack`, look for the object named `txtWarning`, and find the value stored in the `Text` setting. Ah, here is the value I want."

If you omit the form's name, Visual Basic looks only for objects that appear on the current form. If that's where you want to look, you can shorten this combination to the following:

```
ObjectName.Property
```

Getting data from text boxes

When a user types something in a text box, Visual Basic stores the information in the Text property. Typing in a text box is equivalent to assigning a value in the text box's Text property. (See Figure 16-2.)

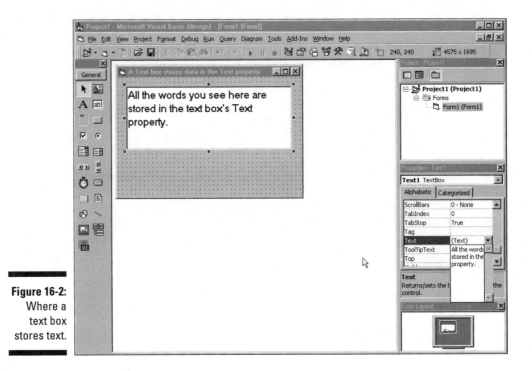

Figure 16-2:
Where a
text box
stores text.

If the user types "Greetings from Mars!" in a text box named `txtSecret`, this is the equivalent to the following BASIC code:

```
txtSecret.Text = "Greetings from Mars!"
```

Determining which radio button the user chose

A radio button can have one of two possible values stored in its Value property:

- ✔ True (selected)
- ✔ False (unselected)

An unselected radio button has the Value property set to False. Clicking on an unselected radio button changes the Value property to True.

A selected radio button has the Value property set to True. Clicking on a selected radio button changes the Value property to False.

To determine which radio button the user chose, you have to check the Value properties of all your radio buttons. For example, if the user chooses an unselected radio button named optStation, choosing the button is equivalent to the following BASIC code:

```
optStation.Value = True
```

If the user selects a different radio button (other than the radio button named optStation), this is equivalent to the following BASIC code:

```
optStation.Value = False
```

Determining which check box the user chose

A check box can have one of three possible values stored in the Value property:

- ✔ 0 - unchecked
- ✔ 1 - checked
- ✔ 2 - grayed

Figure 16-3 illustrates the possible values of check boxes.

An unselected check box has the Value property set to 0. Clicking on an unselected check box changes the Value property to 1.

Value property = 1 (Checked)

Value property = 2 (Grayed)

Value property = 0 (Unchecked)

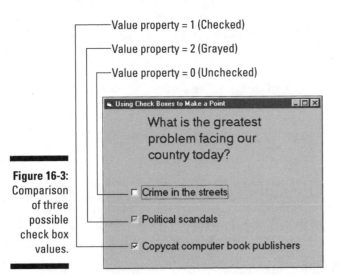

Figure 16-3:
Comparison
of three
possible
check box
values.

A selected check box has the Value property set to 1. Clicking on a selected check box changes the Value property to 0.

A grayed check box has the Value property set to 2. Clicking on a grayed check box changes the Value property to 0.

Note that a user can still click on a grayed check box, unlike a disabled check box which also looks gray.

A selected check box obviously means that the user chose the command represented by the check box. Likewise, an unselected check box means the user did not choose the command represented by the check box. A grayed check box can draw the user's attention that the grayed check box's command represents a special exception or feature.

You have only two ways to set a check box's Value property to 2 and have the check box appear grayed. The first approach is to change the Value property in the Property window when you design your program. The second way is to use BASIC code. The following BASIC code sets the Value property to 2 for a check box named `chkBold`:

```
chkBold.Value = 2
```

To determine which check box the user chooses, you have to review the Value properties of all your check boxes. For example, if a check box named `chkBold` is blank, this is equivalent to the following BASIC code:

```
chkBold.Value = 0
```

If the check box is selected, this is equivalent to

```
chkBold.Value = 1
```

If the check box is grayed, this is equivalent to

```
chkBold.Value = 2
```

Retrieving data from Drive, Directory, and File list boxes

When a user makes a selection from the Drive list box, Visual Basic stores the selection as a string in the Drive list box's Drive property. If a user clicks on c: in a Drive list box named drvWhichDrive, for example, this is equivalent to the following BASIC code:

```
drvWhichDrive.Drive = "c:"
```

When a user makes a selection from the Directory list box, Visual Basic stores the selection as a string in the Directory list box's Path property.

If a user clicks on c:\dos in a Directory list box named dirFolder, for example, this is equivalent to the following BASIC code:

```
dirFolder.Path = "c:\dos"
```

When a user makes a selection from a File list box, Visual Basic stores the file name as a string in the File list box's FileName property.

If a user clicks on autoexec.bat in a File list box named filGetFiles, for example, this is equivalent to the following BASIC code:

```
filGetFiles.FileName = "c:\dos\autoexec.bat"
```

Obtaining choices from a combo box

When a user chooses or types an item in a combo box, Visual Basic stores this information in the combo box's Text property. (See Figure 16-4.)

The text that a combo box displays is stored in the combo box's List property. When the user actually types an item or clicks on an item in the combo box, the user's choice is stored in the combo box's Text property.

If the user types or selects an item named "ASAP" in a combo box named cboPriorities, for example, this is equivalent to the following BASIC code:

```
cboPriorities.Text = "ASAP"
```

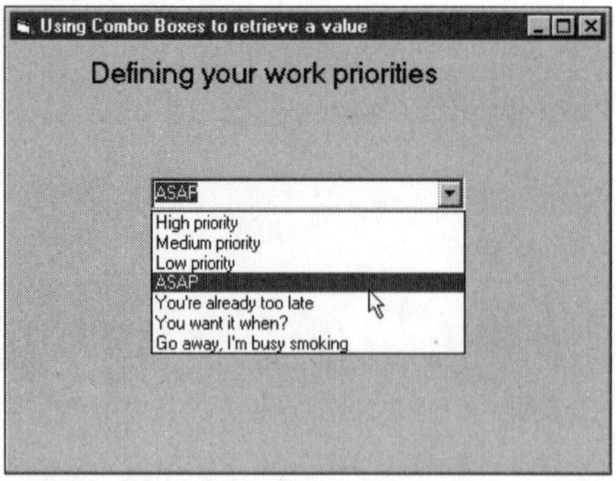

Figure 16-4:
The Text
property of
this combo
box
contains
the string
"ASAP".

Getting values from horizontal and vertical scroll bars

Scroll bars that are not part of a text box, list box, or combo box represent a number. This number is stored in the scroll bar's Value property.

The value that a scroll bar can represent is determined by the scroll bar's Min and Max properties. The lowest possible value is –32,768. The highest possible value is 32,767.

Scroll bars let users visually represent a value, rather than typing a number from the keyboard. Ideally, you want to use a scroll bar along with a label that shows the actual value of the scroll bar. That way, as users move the scroll box in the scroll bar, they can also see the value of the scroll bar changing, as shown in Figure 16-5.

Although scroll bars can represent a range of values, your program eventually needs to read a single value from the scroll bar. If you want to retrieve the value of a horizontal scroll bar named `hsbSensitivity`, for example, you have to set a variable to equal the Value property of the scroll bar. So if you have a variable named `MouseSensitivity` and a scroll bar named `hsbSensitivity`, you could use the following command:

```
MouseSensitivity = hsbSensitivity.Value
```

Retrieving data from a list box

A user can select one or more items from a list box depending on the list box's MultiSelect property. If the MultiSelect property is set to 0 (the default value) and a user selects an item, the list box stores the item in the Text property.

Test your newfound knowledge

1. What does the following BASIC command do?

```
WhatIsIt = chkBold.Value
```

a. The command tries to identify UFOs named `chkBold.Value`.

b. The command questions the need for anything named `chkBold.Value`.

c. The command makes the computer ask, "What do you want me to do? Tell me and then leave me alone. I'm feeling bold today."

d. The command yanks a number that's stored in the Value property of a check box named `chkBold` and stuffs the number in a variable named `WhatIsIt`. If the check box named `chkBold` is selected, the value of `WhatIsIt` is 1.

2. Examine the following command and explain what this code does.

```
FrmDataSheet!txtMessage.Text
= "Warning!"
```

a. The command tells Visual Basic, "Okay, look for a form named `frmDataSheet`, and on this form find a text box named txtMessage. When you find that, stuff the Text property with the string "Warning!""

b. The command tells everyone that the person who wrote this command probably had a good reason for not being present to help you interpret this command.

c. The command warns you that your computer is about to explode and you had better take cover immediately.

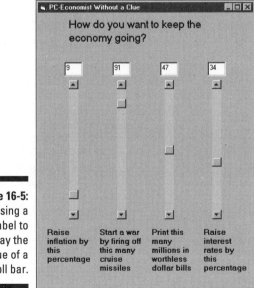

Figure 16-5:
Using a label to display the value of a scroll bar.

If the user selects an item named "Cat food" in a list box named lstGroceries, this is equivalent to the following BASIC code:

```
lstGroceries.Text = "Cat food"
```

If a list box's MultiSelect property is 1 or 2, users can hold down the Shift key and click on an item to select two or more items in the list box. Because a list box's Text property can hold only one string at a time, you can't store all the selections made by a user in the list box's Text property.

To retrieve data from a list box that allows multiple selections, you have to do the following:

1. **Create a second list box to temporarily store any selected items from the first list box.**

2. **Set this second list box's Visible property to False so that the list box isn't visible on the user interface.**

3. **Every time a user selects an item from the first list box, copy the item into the second (invisible) list box. (See Figure 16-6.)**

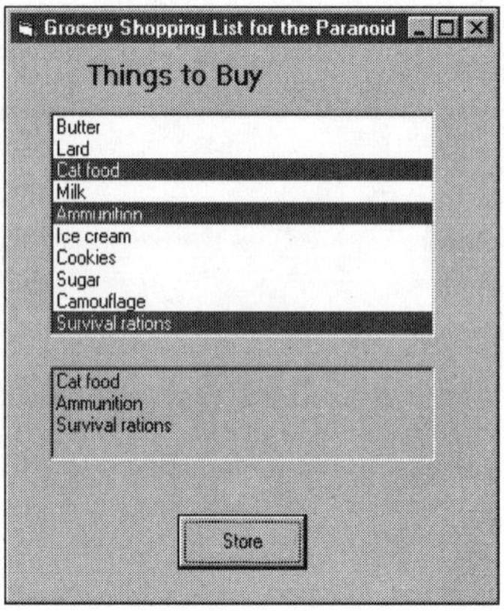

Figure 16-6:
Retrieving multiple items from one list box requires using a second (preferably invisible) list box.

> **Grocery Shopping List for the Paranoid**
>
> **Things to Buy**
>
> Butter
> Lard
> Cat food
> Milk
> Ammunition
> Ice cream
> Cookies
> Sugar
> Camouflage
> Survival rations
>
> Cat food
> Ammunition
> Survival rations
>
> Store

The invisible list box contains only those items selected from another list box, and stores all items in a List property. Items in a list are assigned an index number. The first item in the list is given an index number of 0, the second item in a list is given an index number of 1, and so on. To better understand this concept, create on a blank form two list boxes and a command button with the following properties:

If you don't feel like typing in the following program, just load the LISTBOXES.VBP program off the CD-ROM.

Object	Property	Value
First list box	Name	lstChoose
	MultiSelect	1 – Simple
Second list box	Name	lstTemp
	Visible	True
Command button	Name	cmdStore
	Caption	Store

If the Visible property of the second list box is False, the box is (obviously) invisible and you can't see what is happening. So, when you test the procedure, set the Visible property for the second list box to True so that you can see what happens. Then, after you've become *educated,* change the Visible property back to the original False setting.

The following procedure stores items in the lstChoose list box:

```
Private Sub Form_Load()
  lstChoose.AddItem "Butter"
  lstChoose.AddItem "Lard"
  lstChoose.AddItem "Cat food"
  lstChoose.AddItem "Milk"
  lstChoose.AddItem "Ammunition"
  lstChoose.AddItem "Ice cream"
  lstChoose.AddItem "Cookies"
  lstChoose.AddItem "Sugar"
  lstChoose.AddItem "Camouflage"
  lstChoose.AddItem "Survival rations"
End Sub
```

This loads the lstChoose list box with items for the user to select.

An event procedure to retrieve multiple selected items from the lstChoose list box may look like the following:

```
Private Sub cmdStore_Click()
  Dim I
  lstTemp.Clear
  For I = 0 To lstChoose.ListCount - 1
    If lstChoose.Selected(I) Then
      lstTemp.AddItem lstChoose.List(I)
    End If
  Next I
End Sub
```

This is how Visual Basic responds to the code:

1. The first line tells Visual Basic, "Follow these instructions whenever the user clicks on the command button named `cmdStore`."

2. The second line says, "Declare a variable called `I` and assume the data type is Variant."

3. The third line says, "Find a list box named `lstTemp` and clear out anything the box may be storing."

4. The fourth line says, "Set the value of `I` to `0`. Continue to count by one until the value of `I` equals the number of items displayed in the `lstChoose` list box."

5. The fifth line says, "If the user selected an item displayed in the `lstChoose` list box, follow the instructions in the sixth line."

6. The sixth line says, "Copy the item selected in the list box named `lstChoose` and put the copied item in the list box named `lstTemp`."

7. The seventh line says, "This is the end of all the instructions to follow for now."

8. The eighth line says, "Add one to the value of `I` and start back at line five."

9. The ninth line says, "This is the end of the instructions to follow when the user clicks on the command button named `cmdStore`."

These instructions do nothing more than copy all selected items from one list box into a second list box, which is invisible.

Each item in a list box (and a combo box, for that matter) is identified by an index number. The top item of the list is assigned an index number of 0, the second item from the top is assigned an index number of 1, and so on.

To get at the items stored in the list box named `lstTemp`, you have to use index numbers. The following command retrieves the top item stored in the `lstTemp` list box:

```
lstTemp.List(0)
```

The following command retrieves the second item from the top in the `lstTemp` list box:

```
lstTemp.List(1)
```

Each increase in the index number retrieves the next item further from the top.

Chapter 17

Math 101: Arithmetic, Logical, and Comparison Operators

. . . .

In This Chapter

▶ Adding, subtracting, multiplying, and dividing numbers

▶ Using the Not, And, Or, or Xor operators

▶ Comparing numbers and strings

▶ Comparing strings and operators

. . . .

*A*fter a program gets data from the user (either as a number or as a string), the next step is to do something with that data. If your program mimics an overworked clerical worker, the program may just lose the data and blame the loss on something else. But most likely, you want your program to calculate some sort of result with the data the program receives from the user.

To calculate a result, your program needs to get data from the user interface and then somehow change, modify, mutilate, or spindle that data. Changing anything involves an operation, so the special commands to work with data are called *operators*.

Visual Basic provides the following three types of operators:

✔ Arithmetic

✔ Logical

✔ Comparison

Arithmetic Operators

Arithmetic operators essentially turn your $2,000 computer into a $4.95 pocket calculator. These operators let you add, subtract, multiply, and divide numbers or variables that represent numbers. Table 17-1 shows the most common arithmetic operators.

Table 17-1	Arithmetic Operators
Operator	**What the Operator Does**
+	Adds two numbers
–	Subtracts two numbers
*	Multiplies two numbers
/	Divides two numbers and returns a floating-point (decimal) number, such as 3.14, 16.2, or 392.2398
\	Divides two numbers and returns an integer, such as 8, 16, 302, or 25
Mod (or modulo)	Divides two numbers and returns only the remainder
^	Raises a number to an exponential power
&	Adds (concatenates) two strings

Adding two numbers with the + operator

To add two numbers, use the addition operator (+), as shown in the following example:

```
X = 10
Y = 15.4
Sum = X + Y
```

In case these three BASIC commands mystify you, here's how they work:

1. The first command says, "Create a variable called X and set the value of X to 10."

2. The second command says, "Create a variable called Y and set the value of Y to 15.4."

3. The third command says, "Create a variable called Sum and set the value of Sum equal to the value of X plus the value of Y." In this case, the value of Sum equals 10 + 15.4, or 25.4.

Subtracting two numbers with the – operator

To subtract two numbers, use the subtraction operator (–), as shown in the following example:

```
Income = 2000
Taxes = 2500
Real_Income = Income - Taxes
```

Here's how Visual Basic interprets these three BASIC commands:

1. The first command says, "Create a variable called Income and set the value of Income to 2000."

2. The second command says, "Create a variable called Taxes and set the value of Taxes to 2500."

3. The third command says, "Create a variable called Real_Income and set the value of Real_Income equal to the value of Income minus the value of Taxes." In this case, the value of Real_Income equals 2000 - 2500, or –500.

Negating numbers with the – operator

The subtraction operator (–), used by itself, can turn a positive number into a negative number and vice versa. To negate a number, place the – operator in front of any number or variable, as shown in the following example:

```
Amount = 250
Balance = - Amount
```

This is how the tiny little brain of Visual Basic interprets these BASIC commands:

1. The first command says, "Create a variable called Amount and set the value of Amount to 250."

2. The second command says, "Create a variable called Balance and set the value of Balance to the negative value of Amount." In this case, the value of Balance is –250.

Multiplying two numbers with the * operator

To multiply two numbers, use the multiplication operator (*), as shown in the following example:

```
Hours = 25
Wages = 5.75
Salary = Hours * Wages
```

To see how Visual Basic understands these three BASIC commands, this is how they work:

1. The first command says, "Create a variable called Hours and set the value of Hours to 25."

2. The second command says, "Create a variable called Wages and set the value of Wages to 5.75."

3. The third command says, "Create a variable called Salary and set the value of Salary equal to the value of Hours multiplied by the value of Wages." In this case, the value of Salary equals 25 * 5.75, or 143.75.

Dividing two numbers with the / operator

To divide two numbers and calculate a floating-point (decimal) number, use the forward-slash division operator (/), as shown in the following example:

```
GamesWon = 104
TotalGames = 162
WinningPercentage = GamesWon / TotalGames
```

Visual Basic interprets these three BASIC commands as follows:

1. The first command says, "Create a variable called GamesWon and set the value of GamesWon to 104."

2. The second command says, "Create a variable called TotalGames and set the value of TotalGames to 162."

3. The third command says, "Create a variable called WinningPercentage and set the value of WinningPercentage equal to the value of GamesWon divided by the value of TotalGames." In this case, the value of WinningPercentage equals 104 / 162, or 0.6419753.

Dividing two numbers with the \ operator

To divide two numbers and calculate an integer, use the backslash division operator (\ ), as shown in the following example:

```
CrateCapacity = 72
Bottles_in_Crate = 1900
FullCrates = Bottles_in_Crate \ CrateCapacity
```

So how does Visual Basic interpret these three BASIC commands? Glad you asked. Here's how:

1. The first command says "Create a variable called CrateCapacity and set the value of CrateCapacity to 72."

2. The second command says, "Create a variable called Bottles_in_Crate and set the value of Bottles_in_Crate to 1900."

3. The third command says, "Create a variable called FullCrates and set the value of FullCrates equal to the value of Bottles_in_Crate divided by the value of CrateCapacity." In this case, the value of FullCrates equals 1900 \ 72, or 26.

Dividing two numbers often calculates a floating-point (decimal) number, so how does Visual Basic handle rounding? Consider the following example:

```
Operand1 = 2.5
Operand2 = 1.5
Result = Operand1 \ Operand2
```

Before Visual Basic performs a calculation using the \ operator, the operands are rounded to the nearest whole number. (If an operand is halfway between two whole numbers, such as 2.5 or 1.5, then the operand is rounded up.) In this example, Operand1 is rounded up to 3 and Operand2 is rounded up to 2; therefore, Result = 3 \ 2, or 1.5. Because the \ operator must return an integer, the value of Result is rounded down to 1.

Dividing with the modulo (Mod) operator

To divide two numbers and calculate the remainder, use the modulo operator (Mod), as shown in the following example:

```
CrateCapacity = 72
Bottles_in_Crate = 1900
LooseBottles = Bottles_in_Crate Mod CrateCapacity
```

For those curiosity seekers, this is how Visual Basic interprets these commands:

1. The first command says, "Create a variable called `CrateCapacity` and set the value of `CrateCapacity` to `72`."

2. The second command says, "Create a variable called `Bottles_in_Crate` and set the value of `Bottles_in_Crate` to `1900`."

3. The third command says, "Create a variable called `LooseBottles` and set the value of `LooseBottles` equal to the remainder of the value of `Bottles_in_Crate` divided by the value of `CrateCapacity`." In this case, the value of `LooseBottles` equals `1900 Mod 72`, or 28.

Calculating an exponential with the ^ operator

An *exponential* is a fancy mathematical term that means to multiply the same number by itself a certain number of times. For example, multiplying the number 2 four times is represented by 2^4, or 2 * 2 * 2 * 2.

Because you can't type 2^4, and typing 2 * 2 * 2 * 2 is a bit cumbersome, Visual Basic provides the caret operator (^), as shown in the following example:

```
2 ^ 4
```

Adding (concatenating) two strings with the & operator

Adding or *concatenating* two strings means smashing them together. For this operation, use the ampersand operator (&), as shown in the following example:

```
FirstName = "John "
LastName = "Doe"
FullName = FirstName & LastName
```

When concatenating strings, always make room for a space between the two strings. Otherwise Visual Basic just slams the two strings together as one word like "JohnDoe."

This is how Visual Basic follows these three BASIC commands:

1. The first command says, "Create a variable called `FirstName` and set the value of `FirstName` to `"John "` (note the space at the end)."

2. The second command says, "Create a variable called `LastName` and set the value of `LastName` to `"Doe"`."

3. The third command says, "Create a variable called `FullName` and set the value of `FullName` equal to the value of `FirstName` and the value of `LastName` smashed together." In this case, the value of `FullName` equals `"John"` & `"Doe"`, or "John Doe".

Besides concatenating strings using the ampersand character (&), you can also use the plus sign (+). However, you should use the ampersand character instead because the plus sign is also used with numerical addition. Using the ampersand simply makes your code easier to read.

Logical Operators

Logical operators manipulate True and False values. Visual Basic represents a value of True as –1 and a value of False as 0. Table 17-2 shows the most common logical operators.

Table 17-2	Logical Operators
Operator	*How to Use*
And	Variable1 And Variable2
Or	Variable1 Or Variable2
Xor	Variable1 Xor Variable2
Not	Not Variable

Using the Not operator

It's a sad commentary on the negative impact that television has on children when their vocabulary degenerates to the monosyllabic utterance, "Not!"

Of course, the computer world laid claim to Not long before MTV materialized. The `Not` operator simply changes a True value to False and a False value to True, as in the following example:

Variable Name	Value
Another_Computer_Book	True
Not Another_Computer_Book	False

For clarity, cool programmers like to use parentheses. If you use parentheses in the preceding example, it would look like this:

```
Not(Another_Computer_Book)
```

Using the And operator

The And operator compares the True or False values of two variables and calculates a new True or False value. This allows your program to make decisions, as the following example illustrates:

```
KicktheCat = CatPresent And CatMisbehaving
```

So when is the variable KicktheCat True or False? This depends on the True or False value of CatPresent and CatMisbehaving.

KicktheCat	CatPresent	CatMisbehaving
True	True	True
False	False	False
False	True	False
False	False	True

The And operator returns a True value only if both CatPresent and CatMisbehaving are True.

Using the Or operator

Like the And operator, the Or operator compares the True or False values of two variables and calculates a new True or False value. This allows your program to make decisions, as the following example illustrates:

```
LoafInside = GameOnTV Or WeatherBad
```

So when is the variable LoafInside True or False? This depends on the True or False values of GameOnTV and WeatherBad.

LoafInside	GameOnTV	WeatherBad
True	True	True
True	False	True
False	True	True
False	False	False

The Or operator returns a False value only if both GameOnTV and WeatherBad are False.

Using the Xor operator

As with the And and Or operators, the Xor operator compares the True or False values of two variables and calculates a new True or False value. This allows your program to make decisions, as the following example illustrates:

```
TellOffBoss = BossPresent Xor AtWork
```

So when is the variable TellOffBoss True or False? This depends on the True or False value of BossPresent and AtWork.

TellOffBoss	BossPresent	AtWork
True	True	False
True	False	True
False	True	True
False	False	False

The Xor operator returns a False value if both BossPresent and AtWork are True or if both are False.

Comparison Operators

Comparison operators compare two numbers or strings to see whether the numbers or strings are equal to, not equal to, greater than, or less than one another. Table 17-3 shows the most common arithmetic operators.

Table 17-3	Comparison Operators
Operator	**Meaning**
<	Less than
<=	Less than or equal to
>	Greater than
>=	Greater than or equal to
=	Equal to
<>	Not equal to

Comparing numbers and strings

As the following example illustrates, comparison operators compare the values of numbers and strings in order to return a value of True or False:

```
Age = 18
MinimumAge = 21
Pass = (Age >= MinimumAge)
```

This is how Visual Basic interprets these three BASIC commands:

1. The first command says, "Create a variable called Age and set the value of Age to 18."

2. The second command says, "Create a variable called MinimumAge and set the value of MinimumAge to 21."

3. The third command says, "Compare the value of Age and see whether the value is greater than or equal to the value of MinimumAge. If the value of Age is greater than or equal to the value of MinimumAge, create a variable called Pass and set the value of Pass to True. If the value of Age is not greater than or equal to the value of MinimumAge, create a variable called Pass and set the value of Pass to False."

Comparing numbers is fairly easy, but comparing strings is a bit trickier. When comparing strings, Visual Basic calculates the ANSI character code value of each letter.

ANSI character codes

At the simplest level, computers understand only two numbers: zero and one. You can represent all numbers with zeros and ones; such numbers are called *binary numbers.*

Since computers only understand numbers, not letters, humans created a simple system where certain numbers represent certain letters, punctuation marks, and characters. So the number 97 represents the letter a, the

number 65 represents the letter A, and the number 33 represents an exclamation mark (!).

To make sure that all computers use the same numbers to represent the same letters and punctuation marks, the American National Standards Institute (ANSI) defined an ANSI Character Set that specifies which number represents which letter or punctuation mark.

Comparing strings with the = and <> operators

Two strings are equal only if they are absolutely identical. As you can see in the following example, the equal to operator (=) always calculates a False value unless the operator compares two identical strings, such as "a" = "a":

Operation	Value of Operation
"a" = "a"	True
"a" = "A"	False
"a" = "aa"	False

In the next example, however, you see that the not equal to operator (<>) always calculates a True value unless this operator compares two identical strings, such as "Abott" <> "Abott":

Operation	Value of Operation
"A" <>"a"	True
"Abott" <> "Abott"	False

Visual Basic always treats uppercase and lowercase letters as completely different entities when comparing strings.

Comparing strings with the >, >=, <, and <= operators

When comparing strings, Visual Basic calculates the ANSI character code for each letter in each string, beginning with the first letter. The string whose character has the higher ANSI character code is considered greater.

For example, the letter *A* has an ANSI character code of 65 and the letter *a* has an ANSI character code of 97. So consider the following line:

```
Flag = ("Air" < "aardvark")
```

Because the first letter in "Air" has a lower character code number than the first letter in "aardvark", Visual Basic considers the value of "Air" to be less than "aardvark", so the value of Flag is going to be True.

Now consider the following example:

```
Flag = ("air" < "aardvark")
```

Here the value of Flag is False. How does Visual Basic decide whether "air" is less than "aardvark"? First, Visual Basic calculates the ANSI character code for the first letter of each string. Because both begin with *a*, Visual Basic looks at the second letter. Because *i* has a higher ANSI character code than *a*, "air" is considered greater than "aardvark" and Flag is therefore False.

Test your newfound knowledge

1. **What is the difference between the / operator and the \ operator?**

   a. One is called a forward slash and one is called a backslash. Other than that, they both look like typos.

   b. The / operator divides two numbers and the \ operator puts them back together again.

   c. The / operator calculates a floating-point (decimal) number, such as 3.54, and the \ operator calculates an integer, such as 5 or 34.

   d. The / operator doesn't work at all, so you have to use the \ operator instead.

2. **Is the following statement True or False?**

   "aeroplane" < "airplane"

   a. False, because I don't know what to think; besides, the answer hasn't been the letter (a) for a long time.

   b. True, because the second letter in aeroplane is less than the second letter in airplane.

   c. True and False, because I'm hedging my bets.

   d. False, because an aeroplane is an old-fashioned way of saying airplane, so both strings are exactly the same.

Consider one final example:

```
Flag = ("air" < "airplane")
```

In this example, the value of Flag is True. The first three letters of each string are identical, but the fourth letter is not. Because "air" doesn't have a fourth letter and "airplane" does, "airplane" is considered greater and Flag is therefore True.

Precedence

With all these operators crowding your BASIC commands, what happens if you lump them all together on one line, like this:

```
Mess = 4 / 7 + 9 * 2
```

If you guessed that the value of Mess is 18.57143, congratulations! But how does Visual Basic handle this? First, Visual Basic calculates those operators that have higher priority, or *precedence*.

Not all operators are equal. Some have a higher precedence than others, which means that they demand attention first, just like crying babies. Table 17-4 lists the order in which Visual Basic pays attention to the various operators. The higher an operator appears in Table 17-4, the higher that operator's precedence, so the exponential operator (^) has higher precedence than the less than operator (<).

Table 17-4	Precedence of Operators
Operator	*Type of Operator*
Exponential (^)	Arithmetic
Negation (-)	Arithmetic
Multiplication and Division (* and /)	Arithmetic
Integer division (\ )	Arithmetic
Modulo (mod)	Arithmetic
Addition and Subtraction (+ and -)	Arithmetic
String concatenation (&)	Arithmetic
Equality (=)	Comparison
Inequality (<>)	Comparison

(continued)

Table 17-4 (continued)

Operator	Type of Operator
Less than (<)	Comparison
Greater than (>)	Comparison
Less than or equal to (<=)	Comparison
Greater than or equal to (>=)	Comparison
Like	Comparison
Is	Comparison
Not	Logical
And	Logical
Or	Logical
Xor	Logical
Eqv	Logical
Imp	Logical

How does Visual Basic calculate the value of Mess in the following equation?

```
Mess = 4 / 7 + 9 * 2
```

To help you understand how Visual Basic calculates a result, these are the steps Visual Basic follows:

1. Multiplication and division have a higher precedence than addition, so Visual Basic looks at the multiplication and division operators first.

2. Because multiplication and division have the same precedence, Visual Basic starts with the one furthest to the left. So Visual Basic calculates the value of 4 / 7 and comes up with 0.57143. Now the equation has been simplified to

```
Mess = 0.57143 + 9 * 2
```

3. Visual Basic sees that the multiplication operator has a higher precedence than the addition operator, so Visual Basic calculates the value of 9 * 2 and comes up with 18. The equation is now

```
Mess = 0.57143 + 18
```

The final value of Mess is 18.57143.

What if you really wanted Visual Basic to add the two numbers first before doing any division or multiplication? For clarity, and to make sure that calculations come out the way you intend, enclose particular operations in your equations in parentheses, as shown in the following example:

```
Mess = 4 / (7 + 9) * 2
```

This is how Visual Basic calculates the result:

1. The parentheses tell Visual Basic to add 7 + 9 first, which creates the following equation:

```
Mess = 4 / 16 * 2
```

2. Because the division and multiplication operators have the same precedence, Visual Basic begins with the leftmost operator. Visual Basic calculates 4 / 16, and comes up with 0.25. The equation is now

```
Mess = 0.25 * 2
```

3. Finally, Visual Basic multiplies these numbers and assigns the value of 0.5 to the variable Mess.

Whenever you use two or more operators, use parentheses to provide clarity and to ensure that Visual Basic calculates everything in the exact order you want.

To help you better understand precedence, the enclosed CD-ROM provides a program that shows you how precedence works when using parentheses and when omitting parentheses while calculating a numeric result.

Chapter 18
Strings and Things

● ●

In This Chapter

▶ Converting the case of strings

▶ Using parts of strings to search for and replace other strings

▶ Converting strings into numbers and numbers into strings

▶ Converting strings into ASCII values

● ●

*I*n addition to manipulating numbers, your program can manipulate strings as well. *Strings* are any combination of letters, numbers, or symbols that you want the program to treat literally.

For example, computers blindly interpret phone numbers and social security numbers as mathematical expressions. A typical computer interprets the phone number 123-4567 as the expression, "Subtract 4567 from the number 123."

To tell your program to treat strings literally, always surround your strings with quotation marks, "like this". So if you want to assign the string 123-4567 to a variable, you use quotation marks, as in the following example:

```
Private Sub Count()
   Phone = "123-4567"
End Sub
```

If you forget to add the quotation marks, Visual Basic stupidly tries to interpret the string of numbers as an actual command. In this case, Visual Basic would try to subtract 4567 from 123.

After you designate particular data as a string, Visual Basic provides all sorts of weird ways to examine, manipulate, and mutilate the string.

Manipulating Strings

You are not limited to using strings exactly as they originally appear. You can modify them in many ways. You can convert the case of a string, use parts of a string to look for and replace other strings, and shorten a string by removing extra spaces.

Counting the length of a string

A string is only as long as the number of characters (including spaces) that the string contains. To count the length of a string, use the following BASIC command:

```
VariableName = Len("String")
```

For example:

```
Private Sub Command1_Click()
Dim Name As String
Dim NameLength As Integer
  Name = "Bo the cat"
  NameLength = Len(Name)
End Sub
```

In this case, the length of the string "Bo the cat" is 10 (eight letters and two spaces), so this value is assigned to the variable called NameLength.

Converting from uppercase to lowercase

To convert a string to all lowercase letters, use the following BASIC command:

```
LCase("String")
```

For example:

```
Private Sub Form_Click()
Dim Name As String, LowerCase As String
  Name = "DOESN'T THIS LOOK OBNOXIOUS?"
  LowerCase = LCase(Name)
End Sub
```

In this case, the value of LowerCase is the following string:

```
doesn't this look obnoxious?
```

Notice that the LCase command affects only letters. (How *do* you present a lowercase question mark, anyway?)

To convert a string to all uppercase letters, use the following BASIC command:

```
UCase("String")
```

For example:

```
Private Sub Form_Click()
Dim Name As String, UpperCase As String
   Name = "whisper when you speak"
   UpperCase = UCase(Name)
End Sub
```

In this case, the value of UpperCase is the following string:

```
WHISPER WHEN YOU SPEAK
```

Reversing strings

The newest string manipulation command in Visual Basic reverses strings, which can be useful for playing with *palindromes* (phrases that appear the same written forward as they do backward). To reverse a string, use the following BASIC command:

```
StrReverse("String")
```

For example:

```
Private Sub Form_Click()
Dim Phrase As String
   Phrase = "Madam, I'm Adam"
   Phrase = StrReverse(Phrase)
End Sub
```

In this case, the value of Phrase is the following string:

```
madA m'I ,madaM
```

Extracting characters from a string

Sometimes a string contains more information than you want. For example, you may have stored a person's full name in a variable called FullName, as in the following:

```
FullName = "John Doe"
```

To extract characters starting from the left of the string, use the following BASIC command:

```
Left(FullName, N)
```

The preceding command says, "See that string over there called FullName? Yank out *N* number of characters, starting from the left." For example:

```
Private Sub Form_Click()
    Dim FullName As String, First As String
    FullName = "John Doe"
    First = Left(FullName, 4)
End Sub
```

In the preceding example, the value of First is John.

To extract characters starting from the right of the string, use the following BASIC command:

```
Right(FullName, N)
```

This command says, "See that string over there called FullName? Yank out *N* number of characters, starting from the right." For example:

```
Private Sub Form_Click()
    Dim FullName As String, Last As String
    FullName = "John Doe"
    Last = Right(FullName, 3)
End Sub
```

In this example, the value of Last is Doe.

Another command for extracting characters from a string is the Mid command, such as:

```
Mid(FullName, X, Y)
```

This command says, "See that string over there called `FullName`? Count *X* number of characters from the left, and rip out the next *Y* number of characters. For example,

```
Private Sub Form_Click()
Dim FullName As String, Middle As String
   FullName = "John Q. Doe"
   Middle = Mid(FullName, 6, 2)
End Sub
```

In this example, the value of `Middle` is `Q.` (including the period).

Finding part of a string with another string

If one string is buried in the middle of another string, you can find the location of the burial string by using the following BASIC command:

```
InStr("TargetString", "WantedString")
```

This command returns a number defining the exact location from the left where the `"WantedString"` begins inside the `"TargetString"`. For example:

```
Private Sub Form_Click()
   Dim FullName As String
   Dim Location As Integer
   FullName = "John Plain Doe"
   Location = InStr(FullName, "Plain")
End Sub
```

In this case, the value of `Location` is 6.

If the string you want isn't located inside the string you're searching for, the `InStr` command returns 0.

When you search for a string within another string, you have to search for the exact uppercase or lowercase string. For example, the following command returns a value of 0:

```
InStr("John Plain Doe", "PLAIN")
```

In this case, `"Plain"` is not the same string as `"PLAIN"`, so `InStr` returns 0. Essentially, a zero is the Visual Basic way of saying, "Sorry, I can't find your exact string anywhere."

Replacing part of a string with another string

In case you get the creative urge to write your own word processor in Visual Basic (complete with search and replace features), you can do so with the following BASIC command:

```
Mid("TargetString", Position) = "NewString"
```

This command says, "See that string called TargetString? Find the value defined by Position, count that number of characters from the left, and insert the string called NewString."

Of course, you have to be careful when inserting a new string into an existing one. For example, consider the following code:

```
FullName = "John Plain Doe"
Mid(FullName, 6) = "Vanilla"
```

Here's how Visual Basic interprets this code:

First, Visual Basic assigns the string "John Plain Doe" to the variable called FullName.

Next, Visual Basic looks at the string "John Plain Doe", finds the sixth character from the left, and inserts the string "Vanilla" replacing the original string beginning with the sixth character. So the following is what happens:

John Plain Doe	(Original string)
^	(Sixth character from the left)
John Vanillaoe	(New string)

After you tell Visual Basic to replace part of a string with another one, Visual Basic gets overzealous and wipes out anything that gets in the way of the new string.

Trimming spaces from strings

Strings aren't always nice and neat. Sometimes spaces lie in front of or behind the string, as the following examples illustrate:

```
"          This is an example of leading spaces"
"This is an example of trailing spaces          "
```

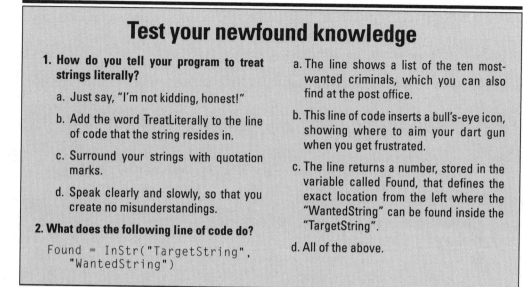

Test your newfound knowledge

1. How do you tell your program to treat strings literally?

a. Just say, "I'm not kidding, honest!"

b. Add the word TreatLiterally to the line of code that the string resides in.

c. Surround your strings with quotation marks.

d. Speak clearly and slowly, so that you create no misunderstandings.

2. What does the following line of code do?

```
Found = InStr("TargetString",
    "WantedString")
```

a. The line shows a list of the ten most-wanted criminals, which you can also find at the post office.

b. This line of code inserts a bull's-eye icon, showing where to aim your dart gun when you get frustrated.

c. The line returns a number, stored in the variable called Found, that defines the exact location from the left where the "WantedString" can be found inside the "TargetString".

d. All of the above.

To strip away leading spaces, use the following BASIC command:

```
LTrim("TargetString")
```

For example:

```
Private Sub Form_Click()
  Dim FullName As String
  FullName = "          John Doe"
  FullName = LTrim(FullName)
End Sub
```

The value of FullName is "John Doe" with the leading spaces removed.

To strip away trailing spaces, use the following BASIC command:

```
RTrim("TargetString")
```

For example:

```
Private Sub Form_Click()
  Dim FullName As String
  FullName = "John          "
  FullName = RTrim(FullName)
  FullName = FullName & " " & "Doe"
End Sub
```

In the preceding example, the RTrim command removes the trailing spaces so the value of FullName is just plain "John". Then the last command adds the value of FullName ("John") to a blank space (" ") and the string "Doe" to create the string "John Doe".

In case you have both leading and trailing spaces, you can combine the two commands like this:

```
LTrim(RTrim("TargetString"))
```

This command says, "First, remove all trailing spaces and then remove all leading spaces." For an even simpler method, use the following BASIC command instead:

```
Trim("TargetString")
```

For example:

```
Private Sub Form_Click()
  Dim FullName As String
  FullName = "        John Dull        "
  FullName = Trim(FullName)
  FullName = FullName & " " & "Doe"
End Sub
```

The Trim command removes both the leading and trailing spaces in one quick stroke, then the last command adds the string "John Dull" to a blank string (" ") and the string "Doe" to create "John Dull Doe".

Converting Strings and Values

Visual Basic handles numbers and strings differently. There may come a time, however, when you need to convert a string into a number so that you can use the string for calculations. Or you may need to convert a number into a string so that you can manipulate the string. You also may need to convert a string into the equivalent ASCII or ANSI value.

Converting a string into a number

What if you have a text box in which users can type their hourly wages? Unfortunately, the Text property of any text box stores data as a string, not as a number. To convert this string into a number, you have to use one of the following BASIC commands:

```
CDbl("TargetString")
```

```
CSng("TargetString")
```

The first command says, "Take the string called TargetString and convert TargetString to a Double data type."

The second command says, "Take the string called TargetString and convert TargetString to a Single data type."

For example:

```
Private Sub Form_Click()
   Dim GetNumber As Double
   GetNumber = CDbl(txtHourlyWage.Text)
End Sub
```

The following is how Visual Basic interprets this code:

1. The first statement says, "Declare a variable called GetNumber as a Double data type."

2. The second statement says, "Get the string stored in the Text property of a text box called txtHourlyWage and convert the string to a number that's a Double data type."

3. Finally, the value stored in the txtHourlyWage.Text property is assigned to the GetNumber variable.

If the user types **6.25** in the txtHourlyWage text box, the value of GetNumber is 6.25.

If the user types **6.25 Hourly wage** or **My hourly wage is 6.25** in the txtHourlyWage text box, Visual Basic chokes and screams about a type mismatch error because neither CDbl nor CSng knows how to handle characters.

Converting a number into a string

What if you have a number and need to convert it into a string so that you can do fancy string manipulations to the number? Then you have to use the following BASIC command:

```
CStr(Number)
```

This command says, "Take the number represented by Number and turn this number into a string."

For example, Visual Basic considers these to be two completely different creatures:

```
10          ' This is a number
"10"        ' This is a string
```

The following converts a number into a string:

```
CStr(10)    ' The string " 10"
CStr(10.5)  ' The string " 10.5"
CStr( - 10) ' The string "-10"
```

When Visual Basic converts a number into a string, the string has an extra leading space if the string is a positive number or a minus sign (–) if the string is a negative number.

Converting a string into an equivalent ASCII value

As a programmer, you have to practically memorize the ASCII table at some point, so you may as well find a copy of one and hang it near your computer somewhere so that you can find this table easily.

An ASCII table shows the codes that computers use to represent most of the characters you need. For example, the letter A has an ASCII value of 65, and the letter a has an ASCII value of 97.

Whenever you need the ASCII value of a one-character string, you can use this BASIC command:

```
Asc("Character")
```

The following shows how to convert a character into its ASCII value:

```
X = Asc ("A")   ' X = 65
X = Asc ("a")   ' X = 97
```

Converting an ANSI value into a string

Microsoft Windows doesn't use the ASCII table. Instead, Windows uses the ANSI table, which is practically the same as the ASCII table anyway. (You can read about the ANSI table in Chapter 17.)

To use an ANSI value, use the following BASIC command:

```
Chr("Character")
```

The only time you need to use the ANSI value of anything is for special control codes, such as for line feeds, carriage returns, and new lines.

The following commands shows common ANSI values:

```
LineFeed = Chr(10)
FormFeed = Chr(12)
Carriage = Chr(13)
```

By using all these fancy string-manipulation commands, you can make sure that your strings look exactly the way you want them to before displaying them in a text box or label. Either that, or you can just have fun playing with words and numbers and pretend you're doing serious research on your job.

To show you how Visual Basic can manipulate strings, examine the ELIZA.VBP program on the enclosed CD-ROM. This program is similar to the famous ELIZA artificial intelligence program that mimics a psychiatrist who simply echoes back portions of what the user types in.

Chapter 19

Defining Constants and Using Comments

● ●

In This Chapter

▶ Naming and calculating constants

▶ Declaring the scope of constants

▶ Creating and using the three types of comments

● ●

A *constant* is a fixed value that never changes, no matter what happens to your program. Numbers, strings, and dates can be constant values.

But why bother using constants? Several good reasons exist, none of which make any sense until you start writing your own programs.

For example, suppose that you want to write a program that pays employees according to the current minimum wage. If the minimum wage is $5.95, you have to type the number 5.95 everywhere in your program.

Unfortunately, the number 5.95 means nothing in itself. Even worse, if the minimum wage changes from $5.95 to $6.25, you have to change 5.95 to 6.25 everywhere in your program.

To overcome these problems, you can use constants. A constant is simply a word that represents a specific value. A constant not only uses plain English to describe what the value means, but a constant also lets you change values quickly and easily throughout an entire program.

Naming Constants

Constant names must meet the following criteria. They must

- Begin with a letter
- Be 40 characters or fewer
- Contain only letters, numbers, and the underscore character (_); punctuation marks and spaces are not allowed
- Be any word except a Visual Basic reserved keyword

To make constant names stand out, use all uppercase letters. For example, the following are acceptable constant names:

```
AGE
MY_BIRTHDAY
MINIMUM_WAGE
LIFEBOAT_CAPACITY
```

To provide additional information about the type of data a constant represents, use a three-letter prefix as part of the constant name such as:

```
intAGE      (int represents an Integer data value)
curMINIMUM_WAGE      (cur represents a Currency data value)
sngGPA     (sng represents a Single data value)
```

Table 19-1 provides Microsoft's list of suggested three-letter prefixes for naming constants (or variables, for that matter).

Table 19-1		Three-Letter Prefixes for Naming Constants and Variables
Data Type	**Prefix**	**Example**
Boolean	bln	blnIsItDeadYet
Byte	byt	bytThisNumber
Currency	cur	curCEOBonus
Date (Time)	dtm	dtmAnniversary
Double	dbl	dblHeight
Integer	int	intTotalNumber
Long	lng	lngWidth
Single	sng	sngAverage
String	str	strMyName
Variant	vnt	vntWhatEver

Declaring Constants

Before you can use a constant, you have to *declare* the constant. To declare a constant, you just give the constant a name and assign it a specific value, such as any of the following:

- ✔ Numbers
- ✔ Strings
- ✔ Dates

The following code declares number, string, and date constants:

```
Private Sub Command1_Click()
   Const intAGE = 21
   Const strCOMPANY = "Acme Manufacturing"
   Const dtmCHRISTMAS = #25 December 1995#
End Sub
```

Place all constant declarations at the top of your event procedures. Instead of typing one constant declaration on each line, you can smash them all together and separate them with commas, as illustrated in the following code:

```
Private Sub Command1_Click()
   Const intAGE = 21, strCOMPANY = "Acme Manufacturing"
End Sub
```

Note that *number constants* are only numbers, *string constants* are anything enclosed in quotation marks (" "), and *date constants* are dates surrounded by the pound sign (#).

Here are some of the ways in which dates can display:

```
#12-25-95#
#December 25, 1995#
#Dec-25-95#
#25 December 1995#
```

Calculating constants

Constants normally represent a fixed value. However, constants can also be mathematic values based on other constants. For example:

```
Const intRETIREMENT_AGE = 65
Const sngHALFWAY_THERE = intRETIREMENT_AGE / 2
```

In this case, the value of the constant `intRETIREMENT_AGE` is 65 and the value of the constant `sngHALFWAY_THERE` is 65/2, or 32.5.

Using constants

After you declare a constant, you can use the constant just like any other value. Consider the following:

```
Const curMINIMUM_WAGE = 5.75
Salary = curMINIMUM_WAGE * 20
```

Here's how Visual Basic interprets this code:

1. The first command says, "Create a constant named `curMINIMUM_WAGE` and set the value of `curMINIMUM_WAGE` to `5.75`."

2. The second command says, "Multiply the value of `curMINIMUM_WAGE` by `20` and store this value in the variable called `Salary`." In this case, the value of `curMINIMUM_WAGE` is 5.75, so you multiply 5.75 by 20, which equals 115. Then Visual Basic stores this value in `Salary`.

Scope of Constants

Visual Basic lets you declare the scope of constants in the following three ways:

- Local
- Module
- Public

Local constants

You can use a *local* constant only within the procedure in which you declare the constant. The purpose of local constants is to isolate specific constants in a single procedure where they are used.

Declare a local constant within an event procedure, as in the following:

```
Private Sub Command1_Click()
  Const intSPEED_LIMIT = 55
End Sub
```

You can use a local constant only in the one event procedure in which you declare the constant. However, what if you want to create a constant that two or more event procedures can share? In that case, you have to create a module constant.

Module constants

A *module* constant can be used only in an event procedure stored in the same file.

To declare a module constant, follow these steps:

1. **Open the Code window by pressing F7, choosing View⇨Code, or double-clicking anywhere on the form.**
2. **Click the Object list box in the Code window and choose (General).**
3. **Click the Procedure list box and choose (Declarations).**
4. **Now type your constant declaration using the Const statement, as in the following:**

```
Const intDRINKING_AGE = 21
```

Module constants are useful for sharing a constant value among one or more event procedures, but isolating the constant to only those event procedures stored in the same file. If you want a constant that *any* procedure in your program can use, you need to create a public constant.

To help you identify module constants buried in your code, Microsoft recommends that you put the letter *m* in front of your constant name such as:

```
Const mintDRINKING_AGE = 21
```

Public constants

A *public* constant (also called a global constant) can be the most convenient to use because every procedure in your Visual Basic program can access such a constant. However, cool programmers use public constants only when absolutely necessary; cluttering up your program with public constants that only a few procedures ever use is bad programming practice.

Using public constants is poor programming etiquette because changing a public constant can affect your entire program. Experienced programmers may blush in embarrassment for you if they catch you using public constants needlessly, and you may never get invited to any of the really great programmer parties as a result.

You need to declare public constants in a .BAS (module) file. To declare a public constant, follow these steps:

1. **Open the Project window.**

    To do this, press Ctrl+R and click on the .BAS (module) file where you want to put the public constant. (If you need to create a .BAS file, click the Module icon or choose Module from the Insert menu.)

2. **Open the Code window by pressing F7, choosing View⇨Code, or double-clicking anywhere on the form.**

3. **Click on the Object list box in the Code window and choose (General).**

4. **Click on the Procedure list box and choose (Declarations).**

5. **Type your public constant using the** Public **command, as in the following:**

```
Public Const AGE_LIMIT = 18
```

To help you identify public (or global) constants buried in your code, Microsoft recommends that you put the letter *g* in front of your constant name such as:

```
Const gsngHEIGHT_LIMIT = 21.67
```

If you want to see a list of all the global constants that Visual Basic has already defined for you, follow these steps:

1. **Choose Help⇨Index.**

    A dialog box appears.

2. **Click the Index tab.**

3. **Type** Constants **in the Type in the keyword to find text box.**

4. **Under the Constants category, click on Visual Basic.**

5. **Click Display.**

    Visual Basic displays the Visual Basic Constants window, as shown in Figure 19-1.

6. **Click on the constant category that you want to view, such as Button Constants.**

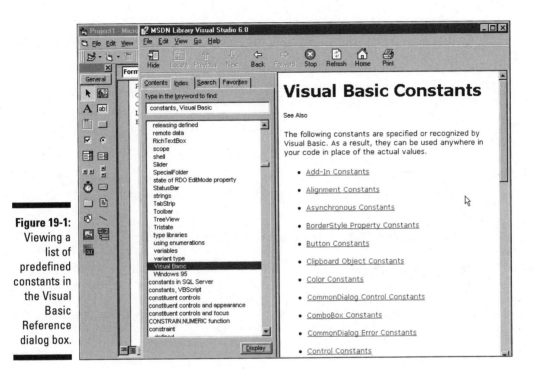

Figure 19-1: Viewing a list of predefined constants in the Visual Basic Reference dialog box.

Using Comments

When you're coding your program (note the proper use of the word *coding*), the way your program works may be clear to you. Unfortunately, if you put your program aside and try to modify it five years later, you may have forgotten why you wrote certain commands and even how some of those commands work.

For just this reason, add plenty of comments to your programs. *Comments* are short descriptions that programmers add to their program to explain what certain commands mean or to explain what is supposed to happen in a particular part of the program.

As far as the computer is concerned, comments do absolutely nothing to help or hinder the way your program works. However, from a programmer's point of view, comments help explain how and why a program functions.

Creating comments

Visual Basic lets you create comments by using the apostrophe (') symbol, followed by anything you care to type. The following, for example, is a valid comment:

```
Private Sub Command1_Click()
  ' This event procedure does absolutely nothing
End Sub
```

As far as Visual Basic is concerned, the computer ignores anything that appears to the right of the apostrophe symbol.

Comments can appear on separate lines or they can appear as part of another line, as in the following example:

```
Private Sub Command1_Click()
  X = Y * 2    ' Y represents the number of employees
End Sub
```

You can also cram several comments together on multiple lines:

```
Private Sub Command1_Click()
  Y = 200     ' Y represents the number of employees
  X = Y * 2
  ' X represents the number of employees who would like
  ' to slash the tires on the boss's car.
End Sub
```

Just remember that the computer ignores anything that appears to the right of the apostrophe symbol and considers it a comment.

Commenting for readability

The main reason for using comments is to make your programs easy to understand. For this reason, most cool programmers put comments at the beginning of every procedure.

These comments explain what data the procedure gets (if any) and what calculations the procedure performs. By just looking at the comments, anyone can quickly see what the procedure does without needing to decipher several lines of cryptic BASIC code. For example, can you figure out what the following event procedure does?

```
Private Sub Command1_Click()
  A = SQR(B ^ 2 + C ^ 2)
End Sub
```

To make the procedure's function easier to understand, add a bunch of comments at the top of this procedure:

```
Private Sub Command1_Click()
  ' The following equation uses the Pythagorean theorem
  ' for calculating the length of a side of a right
  ' triangle if the lengths of two sides are known. In
  ' this case, the length of one side of the triangle is
  ' represented by B and the length of the second side of
  ' the triangle is represented by C.
  A = SQR(B ^ 2 + C ^ 2)
End Sub
```

If several people share the responsibilities for writing procedures, you can use comments to note the name of the programmer and the date each procedure was last modified. (That way, you know who to blame when the procedure doesn't work.) For example:

```
Private Sub Command1_Click()
  ' Programmer: JOHN DOE
  ' Last modified: 1/1/80 (our computer clock doesn't work)
  A = SQR((B ^ 2 + C ^ 2))
End Sub
```

Of course, if you get too wordy, your comments can be more intrusive than helpful — like billboards along the highway. Just remember: Provide enough information to be helpful, but not so much that people nod off to sleep while reading your comments. You're not writing a classic novel here, just a brief description that other people can understand.

Test your newfound knowledge

1. **Why do you want to add comments to your program?**

   a. To summarize and explain how your BASIC code works.

   b. To exercise your literary skills and prove that programmers can write, too.

   c. To prove that you have something to say besides BASIC commands.

   d. So that you can leave cryptic messages for other programmers to decipher.

2. **Comment on the simplicity and brevity of this lesson.**

   a. All right! Now I can quit and go home early.

   b. Why can't all the lessons in this book be this simple and short?

   c. I still can't write a program, but I know how to use comments. Maybe I need to get a job as a commentator.

   d. Comments are cool. If we can write comments in our programs, does that mean we can write programs with our word processors?

Comments for legibility

If your program contains lots of BASIC code, you can use comments and
blank lines to make your code easy to read. For example, to make each
chunk more easily seen, separate chunks of code:

```
Private Sub Command1_Click()
    Const dblINTEREST_RATE = .055   ' 5.5% interest rate

    Dim Msg As String               ' Declares Msg as a string
                                        ' variable
    BankBalance = 500
    BankBalance = BankBalance * dblINTEREST_RATE

    ' Subtract bank fees
    BankFees = BankBalance * 2
    BankBalance = BankBalance - BankFees

    ' Display a message box saying that the user owes the
    ' bank a certain amount of money.
    Msg = "Please pay this amount: " & -BankBalance
    MsgBox Msg, vbCritical, "Amount You Owe"
End Sub
```

As the preceding example shows, you can insert hard returns to add blank
lines between chunks of code, thereby enabling yourself to see more easily
what each chunk actually does.

Stripping out all comments and blank lines gives you the following equivalent, but uglier, version:

```
Private Sub Command1_Click()
    Const INTEREST_RATE = .055
    Dim Msg As String
    BankBalance = 500
    BankBalance = BankBalance * INTEREST_RATE
    BankFees = BankBalance * 2
    BankBalance = BankBalance - BankFees
    Msg = "Please pay this amount: " & -BankBalance
    MsgBox Msg, vbCritical, "Amount You Owe"
End Sub
```

Notice how this new version seems cramped and cluttered, much like your
bathroom counter or your garage.

Comments for disability

With comments, you can not only add explanations about your program and visually break up your code but also temporarily disable one or more BASIC commands.

For example, as you're writing a program, you may find that a command isn't working as you want it to. To test how your program works without this command, you have two choices:

- ✔ Erase the command.
- ✔ Comment the command out.

If you erase a command and then decide you need it, you have to type the command all over again. If you *comment the command out,* however, you only have to erase the apostrophe symbol in order to put the command back in.

The following example contains a fairly long line of numbers:

```
Private Sub Command1_Click()
   X = 3.14 * 650 - (909 / 34.56) + 89.323
End Sub
```

If you erase the second line, typing the line again can be a real pain in the neck. However, you can just comment the line out, as follows:

```
Private Sub Command1_Click()
   ' X = 3.14 * 650 - (909 / 34.56) + 89.323
End Sub
```

Remember, the computer ignores anything that appears to the right of the apostrophe symbol. So, to the computer, this procedure now looks like the following:

```
Private Sub Command1_Click()
End Sub
```

Placing the apostrophe in front of this statement turns the statement into a comment and disables this new comment as a BASIC command. By removing the apostrophe symbol, you can quickly turn the comment back into a real-life BASIC command.

By using comments wisely, you can ensure that you or another programmer can easily understand any programs you write. Then again, if you really want to sabotage a programming project, add comments that don't make any sense or leave them out altogether and see what happens.

If you want to comment multiple lines of code quickly, follow these steps:

1. **Highlight the lines of code you want to turn into a comment.**

2. **Choose View⇨Toolbars⇨Edit.**

    The Edit toolbar appears as shown in Figure 19-2.

Comment Block icon

Uncomment Block icon

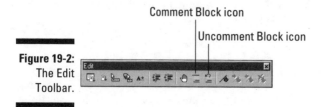

3. **Click on the Comment Block icon.**

    Visual Basic adds an apostrophe to the front of each line that you highlighted in Step 1.

To uncomment blocks of code, just repeat the above three steps except click on the Uncomment Block icon on the Edit toolbar in Step 3.

Chapter 20

Killing Bugs

• •

• •

*E*ven if you've written millions of different programs before, you are still going to make a mistake at one time or another. You may misspell a word or forget to type a command. So no matter how carefully you write your program, the program may not work exactly as you design it to. The problems hindering your program from working are *bugs*.

Every program in the world has bugs, including Netscape Navigator, WordPerfect, Lotus 1-2-3, Quicken, and Microsoft Windows 98. The only difference between the bugs in your program and the bugs in a commercial program is that nobody is paying you to eliminate bugs in your program. However, with a fair amount of planning, application design, and just plain common sense, you can avoid quite a few bugs.

Don't worry. Many bugs are relatively harmless. These minor bugs normally aren't going to prevent you from using a program correctly, but they may slow down your computer or display odd colors or objects on the screen at random times.

Major bugs are more devastating. For example, a major bug allegedly blew up one of NASA's multimillion-dollar weather satellites because someone mistyped a single command in the program.

Nobody is perfect, so no program can be guaranteed to be completely bug-free. Even an experienced professional with a doctorate in computer science regularly writes bug-ridden programs.

Bugs are a fact of life, like cockroaches in a kitchen. You may never get rid of them all, but you can kill as many as possible along the way.

Why computer problems are called bugs

The first computer in the world used mechanical relays instead of modern electronics. One day the computer stopped working for no apparent reason. The scientists checked their programming (the program was supposed to have worked), the electric cord (it was plugged in), and the wires inside the computer (they were still connected).

Eventually, someone noticed that a moth had gotten smashed in one of the relays, preventing the relay from closing all the way. Because the moth's dead body prevented the computer from working, problems with computers were henceforth known as bugs (which is a lot easier to say than Chihuahuas, so we should be glad that a dog didn't get smashed in the first computer).

Types of Bugs

The art of killing bugs is known as *debugging*. Before you can kill a bug, you first have to find the bug. With small programs, such as ones that display `Hello, world!` on the screen, you have only so many places a bug can hide. With large programs, a bug can be hiding anywhere, and this can be as frustrating as trying to find a single tsetse fly in a high-rise apartment building.

To make hunting for bugs easier, computer scientists classify bugs in three categories:

- ✔ Syntax errors
- ✔ Run-time errors
- ✔ Logic errors

Syntax errors

A *syntax* error is a bug that occurs when you misspell a command. If you type INTTEGER instead of INTEGER, for example, Visual Basic is going to have no idea what INTTEGER means and isn't going to even bother trying to run the rest of your program.

When Visual Basic runs across a syntax error, Visual Basic politely highlights the misspelled word on the screen to show you exactly what the problem is. Just type the correct spelling and run your program again.

Even one syntax error is going to keep your program from running. When you finally get your program to run for the first time, you know that your program is completely free of syntax errors. Then you have to worry only about run-time and logic errors.

Run-time errors

A *run-time* error occurs when your program gets data that the program doesn't quite know how to handle. A run-time error is more subtle than a syntax error. Your program may be riddled with run-time errors, but you may never know this until you actually run your program.

To simulate a run-time error in your own life, pull into the drive-through window at your nearest Burger King. When the cashier asks, "May I help you?" order a Big Mac. Because the cashier expects you to order something from Burger King's menu, this person has no idea how to respond to your question and is likely to suffer a run-time error.

For an example of a run-time error in a program, consider this formula for calculating a result:

```
TaxRate = TaxesOwed / YearlyIncome
```

This equation normally works — unless the `YearlyIncome` equals 0. Because dividing any number by 0 is impossible, the program stops running if the value in `YearlyIncome` is 0.

To discover a run-time error, you must test your program for every possible occurrence: from someone pressing the wrong key to some idiot typing a negative number for his or her age.

Because the number of things that can ever go wrong is nearly infinite (Murphy's Law), you can understand why every large program in the world has bugs. (Now isn't this a comforting thought to remember the next time you fly in a computer-controlled airplane?)

Logic errors

The trickiest type of bug is a *logic* error. A logic error occurs when the program doesn't work correctly because you gave the program the wrong commands or the commands you issued are out of sequence with other commands. Huh? How can you give a program the wrong commands when you're the one writing the program? Believe it or not, entering the wrong commands is easy.

Anyone raising teenagers knows that when you tell them to mow the lawn or clean up their rooms, they may do the task — but not quite the way you wanted the task accomplished. Instead of mowing the lawn in neat rows, a teenager may move around in circles and give up. Or instead of cleaning a room by picking up dirty clothes and tossing out papers, a teenager may shove the whole mess under the bed or out into the hallway.

In both cases, the teenager followed your instructions, but your instructions weren't specific enough. If a teenager can find a loophole in your instructions, he or she will, and a computer is no different.

Because you thought you gave the computer the right commands to follow, you have no idea why your program isn't working. Now you have to find the one spot where your instructions aren't clear enough. If you have a large program, this may mean searching the entire program, line-by-line. (Isn't programming fun?)

Bug Hunting

Basically, you need to go through four steps to hunt down and kill bugs in your program:

1. **Realize that your program has a bug.**
2. **Find the bug.**
3. **Find what's causing the bug.**
4. **Squash the bug.**

Realizing that your program has a bug

The best way to discover bugs in your program is to let unsuspecting individuals use your program. (In the world of commercial software, these unsuspecting individuals are often called *paying customers*.)

The more people you find to test your program, the more likely that these guinea pigs are going to uncover bugs you never knew existed. Bugs can be as glaring as ones that cause the computer to crash, or they can be as sneaky as ones that round off numbers to the wrong decimal place.

After you conclude that your program has a bug, you have to track the bug down. (For the optimists in the group, you can call your program's bugs *undocumented features*.)

Finding the bug

Finding where a bug is hiding is the toughest part. The simplest (and most tedious) way to find a bug's hiding place is to run your program and examine it line-by-line. The moment the bug appears, you know exactly which line caused the bug.

For small programs, this approach is acceptable. For large programs, this is crazy.

As a faster alternative, just examine the parts of your program in which you think the bug may be hiding. If your program doesn't print correctly, for example, the bug may be in your BASIC code that tells the computer how to print.

Finding what's causing the bug

After you isolate where you think the bug is hiding, you have to figure out what is causing the bug in the first place.

Suppose that your program is to print your name on the screen but is printing your social security number instead. The program may seem to be *printing* everything correctly but is simply getting the wrong type of information to print.

By using your incredible powers of deductive reasoning, you realize that the bug is (probably) wherever your program first tries to print your name.

Squashing the bug

After you find the cause of your bug, you've reached the time to correct your program. But be careful! Sometimes correcting one bug introduces two or three more by mistake. Huh? How can that be?

Compare bug squashing to repairing a problem with the plumbing in your house. The easiest solution may be to tear out a wall and put in new pipes. This may solve the plumbing problem, but tearing out a wall can also tear out electrical wires inside the wall. So now you've fixed your plumbing problems but also created a new electrical problem. If you put up a new wall with electrical wiring, you may inadvertently block a vent for the central air-conditioning. Move the wall back 3 feet, and now the roof may be too weak in the middle to hold up the wall. See — your small plumbing "bug" has just multiplied.

So when fixing a bug, be careful. Sometimes rewriting a huge chunk of code is easier than trying to fix a bug within the code.

The best way to avoid bugs is to not have any in the first place. Of course, that's like saying to avoid money problems, just make sure you always have enough money.

Because bugs appear in even the best of programs, the most you can hope for is to reduce the number of bugs that can pop up in your programs. Here are some tips that may help:

✔ To avoid bugs, write (and test) lots of tiny programs and paste them together to make one huge program. The smaller your programs, the easier isolating any bugs is going to be. In military terms, this is known as the *divide and conquer* method.

✔ Test your program each time you modify it. If your program worked fine until you changed three lines, the problem probably can be isolated to those three lines.

✔ Have someone you can pin the blame on. If your program refuses to work, blame your spouse, your dog, or your favorite deity. This isn't going to help fix your program, but blaming someone or something else can make you feel better for a moment or two.

How Visual Basic Tracks and Kills Bugs

Visual Basic provides two primary ways to help you track and kill bugs: stepping and watching.

✔ *Stepping* means that you go through your program line-by-line and examine each instruction. After each line runs, look to see what the program did. If your program works the way you wanted it to, the line is okay. If not, you just located a bug.

✔ *Watching* lets you see what data your program is using at any given time. If you watch for specific data, such as a name or phone number, you can see whether your program is storing, printing, or modifying the specific data correctly.

By stepping through a program line-by-line and watching to see what data your program is using, you can find any bugs in your program.

Stepping through a program line-by-line

If you have absolutely no idea where your bug may be, you need to examine your entire program line-by-line. To step through a program, Visual Basic provides three commands:

- Debug➪Step Into (or press F8)
- Debug➪Step Over (or press Shift+F8)
- Debug➪Step Out (or press Ctrl+Shift+F8)

The Step Into command runs through your entire program one line at a time, including every line stored in every procedure in your program.

The Step Over command runs through your entire program but whenever Visual Basic runs into a procedure, Visual Basic skips over the instructions that make up that procedure.

The Step Out command is used with the Step Into command. The Step Into command shows you, line-by-line, how a procedure is working. However, if you suddenly decide that you don't want to examine how a procedure is working, line-by-line, use the Step Out command.

 You can combine the three commands at any time. First, use the Step Into command to examine your program line-by-line. Next, use the Step Out command to get out of any procedures that the Step Into command starts displaying. Finally, use the Step Over command to skip over any procedures that you're positive already work.

To use the Step Into or Step Over commands, follow these steps:

1. **Press F8 or Shift+F8, or choose** **Debug**➪**Step Into or Step Over.**

   Visual Basic displays and outlines a line in your program, as shown in Figure 20-1.

2. **Choose Run➪End when you want to stop.**

Watching your variables

Stepping through your program line-by-line can be even more useful if you watch how your program handles data at the same time. To help you see what values your variables contain at any given time, Visual Basic provides a Watch window.

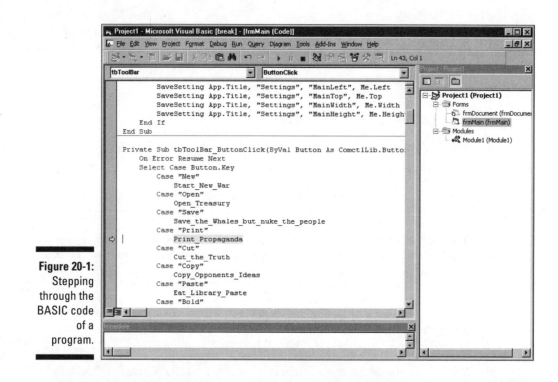

```
Project1 - Microsoft Visual Basic [break] - [frmMain (Code)]
File  Edit  View  Project  Format  Debug  Run  Query  Diagram  Tools  Add-Ins  Window  Help
                                                                            Ln 43, Col 1
tbToolBar                        ButtonClick
            SaveSetting App.Title, "Settings", "MainLeft", Me.Left
            SaveSetting App.Title, "Settings", "MainTop", Me.Top
            SaveSetting App.Title, "Settings", "MainWidth", Me.Width
            SaveSetting App.Title, "Settings", "MainHeight", Me.Heigh
        End If
    End Sub

    Private Sub tbToolBar_ButtonClick(ByVal Button As ComctlLib.Butto
        On Error Resume Next
        Select Case Button.Key
            Case "New"
                Start_New_War
            Case "Open"
                Open_Treasury
            Case "Save"
                Save_the_Whales_but_nuke_the_people
            Case "Print"
                Print_Propaganda
            Case "Cut"
                Cut_the_Truth
            Case "Copy"
                Copy_Opponents_Ideas
            Case "Paste"
                Eat_Library_Paste
            Case "Bold"
```

Project - Project1

- Project1 (Project1)
  - Forms
    - frmDocument (frmDocume
    - frmMain (frmMain)
  - Modules
    - Module1 (Module1)

Immediate

Figure 20-1:
Stepping through the BASIC code of a program.

Test your newfound knowledge

1. What is a bug?

a. A mistake that prevents a program from working correctly.

b. An ugly little creature with six or more legs and a hard shell that crunches when you step on it.

c. A moth that kills itself by crashing into your computer.

d. Something little boys eat to frighten little girls.

2. How does Visual Basic help trap bugs?

a. By coming loaded with several bugs of its own.

b. With glue and bug bait.

c. By making programming so difficult that you can't write a bug if you want to.

d. By stepping through your program and watching to see whether the program handles data correctly.

The Watch window tells Visual Basic, "These are the variables I want to examine. Show me the contents of these variables as I step through my program line-by-line."

To use the Watch window to watch your variables, follow these steps:

1. **Open the Code window by pressing F7, choosing View➪Code, or clicking on the View Code icon in the Project Explorer window.**

2. **Highlight the variable that you want to watch and choose Debug➪Add Watch.**

   An Add Watch dialog box appears, as shown in Figure 20-2.

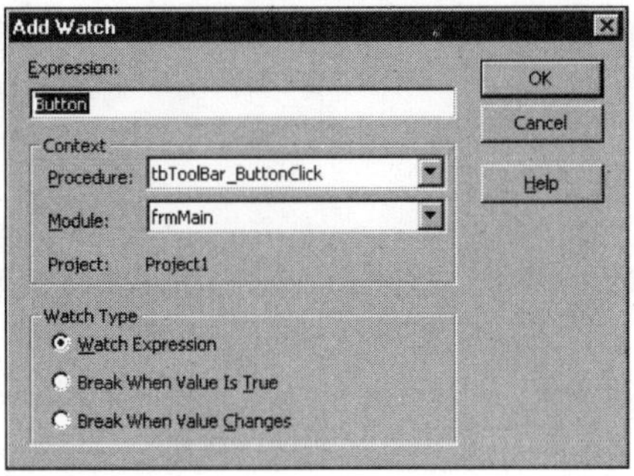

Figure 20-2:
The Add Watch dialog box for debugging your program.

3. **Click on OK.**

4. **Press F8 or Shift+F8 to choose the Step Into (if you want to examine the guts of a procedure) or Step Over (if you want to skip over the code trapped inside a procedure) commands.**

   The Watch window displays the value of your watched variable each time you choose the Step Into or Step Over command.

5. **Choose Run➪End or click on the End icon in the toolbar when you want to stop.**

Setting breakpoints

Both the Step Into and Step Over commands start from the beginning of your program and continue until they reach the end. This is acceptable for small programs, but the process can get tedious for large programs.

To skip over large sections of your program that you know (or hope) already work, you can set a breakpoint. A *breakpoint* tells Visual Basic, "Run the program up until you reach me. Then wait until I give you the Step Into, Step Over, or Run command."

To set a breakpoint, follow these steps:

1. **Open the Code window by pressing F7, choosing View➪Code, or clicking on the View Code icon in the Project Explorer window.**

2. **Click on the line where you want to set your breakpoint.**

3. **Press F9 (or choose Debug➪Toggle Breakpoint).**

After you set a breakpoint, press F5 to run your program until it reaches your breakpoint (see Figure 20-3). At this point, you can use the Step Into or Step Over commands along with the Add Watch command.

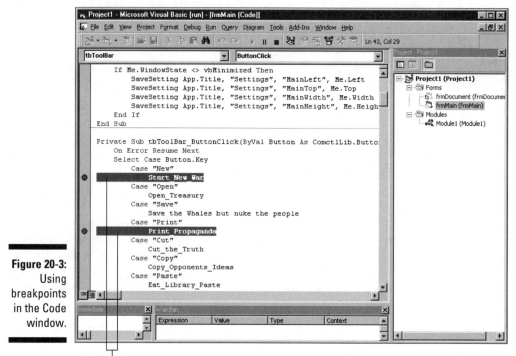

Figure 20-3:
Using breakpoints in the Code window.

Highlighted break point

To remove a breakpoint, just follow the above three steps again, clicking on the line that contains the breakpoint you want to remove.

To quickly remove all breakpoints in your program, press Ctrl+Shift+F9 or choose Debug➪Clear All Breakpoints.

Part V
Making Decisions (Something You Stop Doing When You Get Married)

The 5th Wave   By Rich Tennant

DOYNK SOFTWARE

"It's been reported that we went a little crazy trying to bring this product to market on time..."

In this part . . .

*P*rograms contain nothing more complicated than instructions that tell the computer what to do next. The simplest programs just contain one massive list of instructions that the computer follows, one instruction after another, like a shopping list.

But blindly following instructions doesn't make for a very useful program. Most programs need to receive data and then decide how to use the data.

This decision-making capability can make your computer seem alive, responsive, and intelligent. (Well, alive, anyway.) When a program can tell your computer how to make its own decisions, your computer can begin doing something useful.

Chapter 21

The If-Then and If-Then-Else Statements

- -

In This Chapter

▶ Specifying a condition

▶ Using If-Then and If-Then-End If statements

▶ Using If-Then-Else and If-Then-ElseIf statements

- -

*E*veryone has made decisions based on certain conditions, such as, "Don't worry, honey. If the ball game is over early, then I am going to mow the lawn." Or "If you stop feeding the cat, then maybe it won't keep getting fatter." Visual Basic is no different when making decisions is at hand. When you write a program, Visual Basic can check for certain conditions and then respond.

Conditions

A *condition* must represent a value that is either True or False. Conditions can be

▸ A single variable

▸ An expression

If a condition is a single variable, that variable must have a value that is either True or False. You can check the value of a variable in two ways. The first way is to specifically check if a variable is equal to True, as in the following example:

```
If TooHot = True Then
```

The second way (which is shorter to write) lets you eliminate = `True` and just write the following:

```
If TooHot Then
```

You don't have to specify whether this variable is equal to True because Visual Basic checks whether the value is True or False anyway.

If you want to specifically test whether a variable is False, you can do the following:

```
If TooCold = False Then
```

As a shortcut, eliminate = `False` and just write

```
If Not TooCold Then
```

If a condition is an expression, that entire expression must represent a value that is either True or False, such as

```
If Age >= 21 Then
```

In the above example, the condition is `Age >= 21`.

For this condition, if the value of `Age` is greater than or equal to 21, the expression is True. Otherwise, the expression is False.

In the following example, if the string stored in the `Text` property of a text box called `txtName` contains the string `"Captain Mike"`, the expression is True. Otherwise, the expression is False.

```
If (txtName.Text = "Captain Mike") Then
```

The parentheses in the preceding line of code don't affect your precious code one bit; they just help make the condition easier to identify.

In the following example, the expression `CatPresent And CatMisbehaving` evaluates to False:

```
CatPresent = False
CatMisbehaving = True
If CatPresent And CatMisbehaving Then
```

To make the condition in an If-Then statement easier to see, you can also surround the condition with optional parentheses, as in the following line of code:

```
If (CatPresent And CatMisbehaving) Then
```

Now that you understand what and how conditions work, you can find out how to plug them into an If-Then statement in the following section, "The If-Then Statement."

The If-Then Statement

To make decisions, Visual Basic uses something called an If-Then statement. An If-Then statement is the way Visual Basic checks whether a condition is True or False.

If the condition is True, Visual Basic follows a certain instruction. If the condition is False, Visual Basic ignores this instruction.

All of this may look rather wordy, so here's the condensed version of the statement:

```
If Condition Then Instruction
```

Essentially, this code tells Visual Basic that if a certain condition is True, Visual Basic needs to obey the instruction that follows.

Whatever the condition may be, the condition must always return a True or False value.

Here are a few real-life examples:

```
If Number > 25 Then txtNote.Text = "Full"
```

Here's how Visual Basic interprets this code:

1. This command says, "Check a variable called Number and see whether the value is greater than 25. If the value is greater than 25, then stuff the string "Full" into the Text property of a text box called txtNote."

2. "If the value of the Number variable is equal to or less than 25, then skip to the next instruction in your Visual Basic program."

```
If Hungry Or Bored Then Message = "Let's eat."
```

Here's how Visual Basic interprets this code:

1. This command says, "Check the value of a variable called Hungry and check the value of a variable called Bored. If either one has a value of True, then create a variable called Message and set the value equal to the string "Let's eat."

2. "If both the variable Hungry and the variable Bored are False, skip to the next instruction in your Visual Basic program."

The typical If-Then statement tests whether a certain condition is True or False and then follows a single instruction. But what happens if you want to test for a condition and then make the computer follow two or more instructions? In that case, you have to use a different form of the If-Then statement that is called the If-Then-End If statement.

The If-Then-End If Statement

The If-Then-End If statement lets Visual Basic check a single condition. If the condition is True, the program follows a bunch of instructions. Here's the proper If-Then-End If syntax:

```
If Condition Then
   Instruction1
   Instruction2
End If
```

Essentially, this code tells Visual Basic, "Check a condition; if the condition is True, then obey all the following instructions until you reach End If."

Here is an honest-to-goodness example:

```
If Electricity_is_Out = True Then
   Light_candles = True
   txtWarning.Text = "You just lost all your work."
End If
```

And here's how Visual Basic interprets this code:

1. The first line says, "Check the value for a variable called Electricity_is_Out. If the variable's value is True, then follow the next two instructions. If the value is False, then do nothing."

2. "Assign a value of True to the variable Light_candles."

3. "Assign the string "You just lost all your work." to the Text property of the txtWarning text box."

If-Then-Else Statement

The If-Then statement gives your program the capability to make decisions based on certain conditions. If this isn't the pinnacle of your computer programming career, hold on to your hats for the If-Then-Else statement.

The problem with using an If-Then statement or an If-Then-End If statement is that you may need too many of them to check for both True and False conditions. Is there an easier way? The answer, of course, is *yes!* Visual Basic offers something called an If-Then-Else statement.

The simplest If-Then-Else statement looks like this:

```
If Condition Then
    Instructions1
Else
    Instructions2
End If
```

This statement tells Visual Basic, "If the condition is True, then follow the first batch of instructions. If the condition is False, then follow the second batch of instructions."

Test your newfound knowledge

1. What is a condition?

a. Something that makes you want to scratch your scalp or between your toes.

b. An event that you use as an excuse for not doing something else, such as "My heart condition is bad today. I think I need to just stay inside and watch TV."

c. Something your parents threaten you with. "If you don't behave yourself, you're going to bed without any supper."

d. A variable or expression that evaluates to a True or False value.

2. What is the alternative to the following condition?

```
If MoneyGone = False Then
```

a. If MoneyGone Then "Complain about overseas competitors."

b. If MoneyGone Then "Reelect a new President."

c. If Not MoneyGone Then

d. If MoneyGone = True Or False Then

So how can you modify the following?

```
If Day > 15 Then txtReadMe.Text = "Bills are past due!"
If Day <= 15 Then txtReadMe.Text = "Pay your bills!"
```

Depending on the condition you use, you can rewrite these statements in two ways. If you use the condition `Day > 15`, you get the following:

```
If Day > 15 Then
   txtReadMe.Text = "Bills are past due!"
Else
   txtReadMe.Text = "Pay your bills!"
End If
```

But if you use the condition `Day <= 15`, you get the following:

```
If Day <= 15 Then
   txtReadMe.Text = "Pay your bills!"
Else
   txtReadMe.Text = "Bills are past due!"
End If
```

Both types of If-Then-Else statements are perfectly acceptable. Which statement you choose to use is just a matter of personal preference.

You can shove as many instructions as you want between the If-Then and Else lines and the Else and End If lines.

One possible drawback with an If-Then-Else statement is that if the first condition is False, Visual Basic blindly follows the second group of instructions. If you don't want this to happen, you have to specify a condition for the second set of instructions. To do that, you have to use an If-Then-ElseIf statement.

The If-Then-ElseIf Statement

An If-Then-ElseIf statement looks like the following:

```
If Condition1 Then
   Instructions1
ElseIf Condition2 Then
   Instructions2
End If
```

This code tells Visual Basic, "If `Condition1` is True, then follow the first set of instructions. But if `Condition1` is False, then check to see if `Condition2` is True. If `Condition2` is True, then follow the second set of instructions. If `Condition2` is False, then don't do anything at all."

With an If-Then-Else statement, the computer always follows at least one set of instructions. But with an If-Then-ElseIf statement, the computer could possibly ignore all instructions — much like a rebellious teenager.

For example:

```
If Day > 15 Then
   txtReadMe.Text = "Bills are past due!"
ElseIf Day > 10 Then
   txtReadMe.Text = "Pay your bills!"
End If
```

So what happens if the value of `Day` is 12?

1. Visual Basic checks the first condition and concludes that the expression 12 > 15 is False (because the value of `Day` is 12).

2. Then Visual Basic checks the second condition and concludes that the expression 12 > 10 is True, so Visual Basic assigns the string, "Pay your bills!" to the Text property of a text box called `txtReadMe`.

Here's the tricky part. What happens if the value of `Day` is 6?

1. Visual Basic checks the first condition and concludes that the statement 6 > 15 is False, so Visual Basic ignores the first set of instructions.

2. Next, Visual Basic checks the second condition and concludes that the statement 6 > 10 is False, so Visual Basic ignores the second set of instructions.

3. Finally, Visual Basic reaches the end of the If-Then-ElseIf statement. Because none of the statements were True, none of the instructions were followed.

To handle multiple possibilities, you need to add more ElseIf conditions.

Making multiple choices with If-Then-ElseIf

For checking multiple conditions, use multiple ElseIfs, as follows:

```
If Condition1 Then
   Instructions1
ElseIf Condition2 Then
   Instructions2
ElseIf Condition3 Then
   Instructions3
End If
```

This code tells Visual Basic, "If Condition1 is True, then follow Instructions1. But if Condition1 is False, check whether Condition2 is True. If Condition2 is True, then follow Instructions2. If Condition1 is False and Condition2 is False, then check to see whether Condition3 is True. If Condition3 is True, then follow Instructions3."

Once again, the possibility exists that all conditions are going to be False, so the computer may never follow any of the instructions.

You can use as many ElseIf lines as you need. Of course, the more you use, the more confusing your entire If-Then-ElseIf statement gets. ("Now if Condition3 is False but Condition4 is True, wait a minute, what's supposed to happen?")

Making sure that the computer follows at least one set of instructions

You can have a huge If-Then-ElseIf statement and still not have a single instruction that the computer follows. To make sure that the computer follows at least one set of instructions, add an Else statement at the end, as shown in the following:

```
If Condition1 Then
   Instructions1
ElseIf Condition2 Then
   Instructions2
Else
   InstructionsDefault
End If
```

This code tells Visual Basic, "If Condition1 is True, then follow the first set of instructions. But if Condition1 is False, check the value of Condition2. If Condition2 is True, then follow the second set of instructions. If all conditions are False, then go ahead and follow the last set of instructions."

Nesting If-Then statements

If you want, you can *nest* your statements (cram multiple If-Then statements inside one another), such as

```
If Age > 21 Then
   If Rating = 10 Then
     txtAction.Text = "Ask for a date."
   End If
Else
   txtAction.Text  = "Sorry, you're too young."
End If
```

If the value of Age were 23 and the value of Rating were 10, Visual Basic interprets this code as follows:

1. Visual Basic checks the first condition and concludes that the expression Age > 21 is True (because the value of Age is 23).

2. Then Visual Basic checks the second condition and concludes that the expression Rating = 10 is True, so Visual Basic assigns the string, "Ask for a date." to the Text property of a text box called txtAction.

If the value of Age were 23 but the value of Rating were only 9, Visual Basic interprets this code as follows:

1. Visual Basic checks the first condition and concludes that the expression Age > 21 is True (because the value of Age is 23).

2. Then Visual Basic checks the second condition and concludes that the expression Rating = 10 is False, so nothing happens.

Finally, if the value of Age were 13 and the value of Rating were 10, Visual Basic interprets this code as follows:

1. Visual Basic checks the first condition and concludes that the expression Age > 21 is False (because the value of Age is 13).

2. Visual Basic skips to the Else part of the If-Then-Else statement and stuffs the string "Sorry, you're too young." in the Text property of the text box called txtAction. Notice that in this case, the value of Rating is irrelevant.

Be careful when nesting If-Then statements inside one another because nested If-Then statements may act in ways that you didn't expect. For example, in the preceding code, if the value of Age were 23 but the value of Rating were only 9, you may be surprised to find that this code isn't going to put any string in the Text property of the text box called txtAction.

Chapter 22

The Select Case Statement

*T*he main problem with using massive If-Then-ElseIf statements, which I discuss in Chapter 21, is that these statements are ugly, hard to read and understand, and cumbersome to write. Consider the following:

```
If Caller = "Frank" Then
  txtReply.Text = "Yes!"
ElseIf Caller = "Matt" Then
  txtReply.Text = "Okay, but only if you buy."
ElseIf Caller = "Jeff" Then
  txtReply.Text = "I'm washing my hair tonight."
ElseIf Caller = "Steve" Then
  txtReply.Text = "This is a recording."
End If
```

So what's the alternative to an endless proliferation of ElseIfs that can be confusing to look at?

One alternative is to toss your copy of Visual Basic out the window and find someone to write your programs for you. But the more practical alternative is to use something called the Select Case statement.

The Select Case Statement

The *Select Case* statement looks like the following:

```
Select Case VariableName
   Case X
      Instructions1
   Case Y
      Instructions2
   Case Z
      Instructions3
End Select
```

This statement tells Visual Basic, "Look at the value of the variable called `VariableName`. If this value is equal to X, then follow `Instructions1`. If this value is equal to Y, then follow `Instructions2`. If this value is equal to Z, then follow `Instructions3`."

Replacing the multiple If-Then-ElseIf statement at the beginning of this chapter with the Select Case statement changes the code to look like the following:

```
Select Case Caller
   Case "Frank"
      txtReply.Text = "Yes!"
   Case "Matt"
      txtReply.Text = "Okay, but only if you buy."
   Case "Jeff"
      txtReply.Text = "I'm washing my hair tonight."
   Case "Steve"
      txtReply.Text = "This is a recording."
End Select
```

Notice the cleaner look and the elimination of repetitive words such as ElseIf and Then.

Depending on how many values you need to check, you can sandwich as many Case lines in a Select Case statement as you want.

Using the Select Case Statement with Comparison Operators

Normally, the Select Case statement requires an exact value to examine. However, by using comparison operators, such as <, <=, or <>, you can make the Select Case statement examine whether a variable falls within a range of values.

To make a Select Case statement use comparison operators, you have to use the magic reserved word is. Therefore, the following Select Case statement

```
Select Case Day
   Case is > 15
      txtReadMe.Text = "Bills are past due!"
   Case is > 10
      txtReadMe.Text = "Pay your bills!"
End Select
```

is equivalent to the following If-Then statement:

```
If Day > 15 Then
   txtReadMe.Text = "Bills are past due!"
ElseIf Day > 10 Then
   txtReadMe.Text = "Pay your bills!"
End If
```

Making Sure the Computer Follows at Least One Set of Instructions

Like the If-Then-Elself statement, the possibility that none of the instructions within the Select Case statement are going to be followed exists. To make sure that the computer follows at least one set of instructions, you have to use the magical Else command again. Take a look at the following example:

```
Select Case Day
   Case 1
      Instructions1
   Case 2
      Instructions2
   Case 3
      Instructions3
   Case Else
      InstructionsDefault
End Select
```

The preceding code tells Visual Basic, "If the value of Day equals 1, then follow the first set of instructions. If the value of Day equals 2, then follow the second set of instructions. If the value of Day equals 3, then follow the third set of instructions. If the value of Day doesn't equal 1, 2, or 3, then follow the last set of instructions."

Nesting Case Statements

Some of the simplest toys that amuse children to no end are those Chinese boxes stacked one inside the other. Each time you open a box, you find a smaller one inside. Eventually, you reach a point where no more boxes remain and you have to stop.

Normally an ordinary Select Case statement contains one or more groups of instructions, such as the following:

```
Select Case ID
  Case 123
    chkFrank.Value = True
  Case 124
    chkBob.Value = True
  Case 125
    chkMartha.Value = True
End Select
```

Rather than shoving boring old instructions inside a Select Case statement, however, you can shove If-Then and Select Case statements within a Select Case statement, as the following example illustrates:

```
Select Case IQ
  Case 120
    Select Case Age
      Case is <= 9
        txtAnalysis.Text = "You must be a smart kid."
    End Select
End Select
```

Here's how Visual Basic interprets this code:

1. The first line says, "Check the value stored in a variable called IQ. Then continue to the second line."

2. The second line says, "If the value of IQ is exactly equal to 120, continue to the third line. If the value of IQ is anything else (such as 119, 121, or 3), skip to the seventh line.

3. The third line says, "Check the value stored in a variable called Age. Then continue to the fourth line."

4. The fourth line says, "If the value stored in the variable called Age is equal to or less than 9, then continue to the fifth line. If the value of Age is anything greater than 9 (such as 13, 86, or 10), then skip to the sixth line."

5. The fifth line says, "Assign the string, "You must be a smart kid." to the Text property of a text box called txtAnalysis."

6. The sixth line says, "This is the end of one Select Case statement."

7. The seventh line says, "This is the end of another Select Case statement."

For kicks and grins, you can put an If-Then statement inside a Select Case statement or a Select Case statement inside an If-Then statement. (Some fun, huh?)

Although no theoretical limit exists as to how many If-Then or Select Case statements you can place inside one another, the fewer you use, the easier your code is going to be to figure out. As a general rule, if you have nested more than three If-Then or Case Select statements inside one another, you probably don't know what you're doing.

When nesting multiple statements, you should indent statements so that seeing where they begin and end is easier. For example, notice how confusing the following program appears without indentation:

```
Select Case Salary
Case 1200
If Name = "Bob" Then
txtReview.Text = "No raise this year, ha, ha, ha!"
ElseIf Name = "Karen" Then
txtReview.Text = "Okay, how about a 5% raise?"
End If
End Select
```

Here's what the same program looks like with indentation:

```
Select Case Salary
  Case 1200
    If Name = "Bob" Then
      txtReview.Text = "No raise this year, ha, ha, ha!"
    ElseIf Name = "Karen" Then
      txtReview.Text = "Okay, how about a 5% raise?"
    End If
End Select
```

From the computer's point of view, both programs are the same. But from a programmer's point of view, the program using indentation is much easier to read and understand.

Test your newfound knowledge

1. What is the limit to the number of control structures (If-Then or Select Case statements) you can nest?

   a. The limit is determined by the restrictions your government may place upon you.

   b. The limit is determined by the theoretical applications pursuant to the implications of Einstein's theory of relativity, as reworded by a lawyer.

   c. The limit is 65. If you go over that, you risk getting pulled over by a state trooper.

   d. No limit exists. But if you have too many nested control structures, your program is going to be harder to read and understand.

2. To make nested control structures easier to read and understand, what do you need to do?

   a. Avoid using nested control structures.

   b. Avoid programming altogether.

   c. Limit the number of nested control structures you use, and use indentation to make each If-Then or Select Case statement easy to find.

   d. Print in big, bold, block letters and use short statements like "See Dick run. Dick runs fast."

Part VI
Getting Loopy

The 5th Wave   By Rich Tennant

Re·al Pro·gram·mers

Real Programmers hate <u>decaffeinated</u> coffee.

In this part . . .

*E*very program contains instructions that tell the computer what to do. Sometimes these instructions are used only once, such as instructions that tell the computer what to do when the program loads.

But other times, the computer may need certain instructions over and over again. Rather than retyping these instructions each time, programmers invented something magical called *loops*.

Essentially a loop tells the computer, "See those instructions over there? Keep repeating them again and again a certain number of times, and then stop." By using loops, programmers spare themselves the tedium of repeatedly writing the same instructions — and saving time is what programmers know how to do best.

Chapter 23

The Do While and Do-Loop While Loops

• •

In This Chapter

▶ Using the Do While loop

▶ Finding out how often the Do While loop runs

▶ Examining how the Do-Loop While loop works and when to use it

• •

Do While loops don't do anything without checking if a certain condition is True first. If a certain condition is True, then the Do While loop goes ahead and does something. Otherwise, it jumps to the next instruction in the Visual Basic program.

You can find Do While loops in such everyday experiences as when office workers tell themselves, "Keep stuffing office supplies in my briefcase while no one is looking. The moment someone looks in my direction, stop and do something else."

A Do While loop looks like this:

```
Do While Condition
   Instructions
Loop
```

The condition must be a variable or an expression that represents a True or False value. A Do While loop can hold one or more instructions.

How the Do While Loop Works

The first time Visual Basic sees a Do While loop, it says, "Okay, is the value of the condition True or False? If it's False, ignore all the instructions inside the Do While loop. If it's True, follow all the instructions inside the Do While loop."

For example, the following code has a Do While loop:

```
Counter = 0
Do While Counter <> 5
    Counter = Counter + 1
    txtCounter.Text = CStr(Counter)
Loop
```

Visual Basic interprets the code like this:

1. The first line says, "Stuff the value of 0 (zero) inside a variable called `Counter`."

2. The second line says, "As long as `Counter` is not equal to 5, keep repeating all the instructions sandwiched between the `Do While` line and the `Loop` line."

3. The third line says, "Add 1 (one) to the value of the Counter variable."

4. The fourth line says, "Take the value of Counter, convert it into a String, and stuff it in the Text property of a text box called txtCounter."

5. The fifth line says, "This is the end of the Do While loop. Go back to the second line where the Do While loop begins as long as the condition that `Counter <> 5` is True."

Each time this loop runs, it increases the value of `Counter` by one. As soon as the value of `Counter` equals 5, the condition `Counter <> 5` suddenly becomes False and the Do While loop stops.

How many times does the Do While loop run?

If the condition of a Do While loop is False, none of the instructions inside the Do While loop runs. In that case, the Do While loop runs zero times.

If the condition of a Do While loop is True, the Do While loop runs at least once.

If the condition of a Do While loop is always True, the Do While loop repeats itself an endless number of times until you turn off the computer or the universe explodes in another Big Bang.

When a loop repeats itself endlessly, it is called an *endless loop*.

TIP

Endless loops send your program into infinity and keep it from working properly (because the loop never ends). To avoid an endless loop, make sure that at least one instruction inside your Do While loop changes the True or False value of the condition that the loop checks.

When to use a Do While loop

Use a Do While loop whenever you need to do the following:

- ✔ Loop zero or more times
- ✔ Loop as long as a certain condition remains True

How the Do-Loop While Loop Works

Do-Loop While loops essentially tell Visual Basic, "Go ahead and do something until a certain condition tells you to stop."

You can find Do-Loop While loops in such everyday experiences as when parents tell their kids, "Go ahead and do what you want, just as long as you don't bother me."

A Do-Loop While loop looks like the following:

```
Do
   Instructions
Loop While Condition
```

The condition must be a variable or an expression that represents a True or False value. A Do-Loop While loop can hold one or more instructions.

The first time Visual Basic sees a Do-Loop While loop, it says, "Let me follow all the instructions inside the loop first. After this, check whether the value of the condition is True or False. If it's False, stop. If it's True, repeat all the instructions inside the Do-Loop While loop again."

For example, the following code has a Do-Loop While loop.

```
Counter = 0
Do
   Counter = Counter + 1
Loop While Counter < 5
```

Visual Basic interprets the code like this:

1. The first line says, "Create a variable called `Counter` and set its value to 0."

2. The second line says, "This is the beginning of the Do-Loop While loop."

3. The third line says, "Take the value of `Counter` and add 1 (one) to it. Now store this new value in the `Counter` variable."

4. The fourth line says, "This is the end of the Do-Loop While loop. As long as the value of `Counter` is less than 5, keep repeating all the instructions sandwiched between the Do line and the Loop While line. Otherwise, exit the loop."

Each time this loop runs, it increases the value of `Counter` by one. As soon as the value of `Counter` equals 5, the condition `Counter < 5` suddenly becomes False and the Do While loop stops.

How many times does the Do-Loop While Loop repeat itself?

No matter what the condition of a Do-Loop While loop may be, it always runs at least once. As long as the condition remains True, the Do-Loop While loop can keep running until infinity (or until you neglect to pay your electricity bill).

To avoid an endless Do-Loop While loop, you have to make sure that at least one instruction inside your Do-Loop While loop changes the True or False value of the condition that the loop checks.

When to use a Do-Loop While loop

Use a Do-Loop While loop whenever you need to do the following:

- Loop at least once
- Loop as long as a certain condition remains True

Choose your loops carefully because loops may look similar but act differently. To avoid confusion, try to stick with one type of loop throughout your program so that it is easier for you to figure out how all your program's loops may work.

Test your newfound knowledge

1. What are two main differences between a Do While loop and a Do-Loop While loop?

   a. The words are in a different order, and they use a different number of consonants.

   b. The Do While loop runs zero or more times and repeats only if its condition is True. Regardless of its condition, the Do-Loop While loop runs at least once, and if its condition is True, it can run an infinite number of times.

   c. Both loops run endlessly, faster and faster, until your computer is flung up against a wall because they're running so fast.

   d. Four out of five dentists recommend the Do While loop, sugar-free chewing gum, and Crest toothpaste.

2. Why is it possible that a Do While loop runs zero or more times?

   a. Because it's the number one loop used by two out of three programmers employed at Microsoft, IBM, and Symantec.

   b. Nobody knows, but I remember seeing a segment on *Unsolved Mysteries*, asking viewers to call in if they had any information that might help resolve this question.

   c. Because it checks its condition before it runs even once.

   d. Because it uses steroids: So not only does it run once, it runs faster than any other loop that isn't doped up.

Chapter 24

The Do Until and Do-Loop Until Loops

In This Chapter

▶ Using the Do Until loop

▶ Finding out how often the Do Until loop repeats itself

▶ Examining how the Do-Loop Until loop works and when to use it

Do Until loops keep repeating until some condition becomes True, such as, "Keep stealing from the cash register until someone catches you."

A Do Until loop looks like this:

```
Do Until Condition
   Instructions
Loop
```

The condition must be a variable or an expression that represents a True or False value. A Do Until loop can hold one or more instructions.

How the Do Until Loop Works

The first time Visual Basic sees a Do Until loop, it says, "Let me check whether the value of the condition is True or False. If it's False, follow all the instructions inside the Do Until loop. If it's True, exit the Do Until loop."

For example, the following is a typical Do Until loop that counts:

```
Counter = 0
Do Until Counter > 4
  Counter = Counter + 1
Loop
```

Here's an explanation of the code:

1. The first line says, "Stuff the value of 0 inside a variable called Counter."

2. The second line says, "This is the beginning of the Do Until loop. As long as the value of Counter > 4 is False, keep repeating all the instructions sandwiched between the Do line and the Loop line. Otherwise, if the value of Counter > 4 is True (when Counter is 5), exit the loop."

3. The third line says, "Take the value of Counter and add 1 (one) to it. Now store this new value in the Counter variable."

4. The fourth line says, "This is the end of the Do Until loop."

Each time this loop runs, it increases the value of Counter by one. As soon as the value of Counter equals 5, the condition Counter > 4 suddenly becomes True and the Do Until loop stops.

How many times does the Do Until loop repeat itself?

The Do Until loop can run zero or more times. This loop keeps repeating itself until its condition becomes True.

Notice that this is the opposite of the Do While and Do-Loop While loops. These two loops keep running as long as their condition is True. The Do Until loop keeps running until its condition *becomes* True. (This is the same thing as saying that the Do Until loop keeps running as long as its condition is False.)

To avoid an endless Do Until loop, make sure that at least one instruction inside your Do Until loop changes the True or False value of the condition that the loop checks.

When to use a Do Until loop

Use a Do Until loop whenever you need to do the following:

- Loop zero or more times
- Loop until a certain condition becomes True

The Do Until loop works like the following two Do While loops:

```
Do While Not Condition        Do While Condition = False
   Instructions                  Instructions
Loop                          Loop
```

How the Do-Loop Until Loop Works

Do-Loop Until loops not only sound like you're stuttering, but they keep repeating until a condition becomes True.

A Do-Loop Until loop looks like this:

```
Do
   Instructions
Loop Until Condition
```

The condition must be a variable or an expression that represents a True or False value. A Do-Loop Until loop can hold one or more instructions.

The first time Visual Basic sees a Do-Loop Until loop, it says, "Follow all the instructions inside the loop once. Then check whether the value of the condition is True or False. If it's True, stop. If it's False, follow all the instructions inside the Do-Loop Until loop again."

For example, the following is a typical Do-Loop Until loop that counts:

```
Counter = 0
Do
   Counter = Counter + 1
Loop Until Counter > 4
```

Here's what this code means:

1. The first line says, "Stuff the value of 0 inside a variable called Counter."

2. The second line says, "This is the beginning of the Do-Loop Until loop."

3. The third line says, "Take the value of Counter and add 1 (one) to it. Now store this new value in the Counter variable."

4. The fourth line says, "This is the end of the Do-Loop Until loop. As long as the value of Counter is 4 or less, keep repeating all the instructions sandwiched between the Do line and this Loop Until line. Otherwise, exit the loop."

Each time this loop runs, it increases the value of Counter by one. As soon as the value of Counter equals 5, the condition Counter > 4 suddenly becomes True and the Do-Loop Until loop stops.

How many times does the Do-Loop Until loop repeat itself?

No matter what the condition of a Do-Loop Until loop may be, it always runs at least once. As long as the condition remains False, it keeps running until its condition becomes True.

Notice that this is the opposite of the Do While loop and the Do-Loop While loop. These two loops keep running as long as their conditions are True. The Do-Loop Until loop, on the other hand, keeps running as long as its condition is False.

To avoid an endless Do-Loop Until loop, make sure that at least one instruction inside your Do-Loop Until loop changes the True or False value of the condition that the loop checks.

Test your newfound knowledge

1. If you need to loop until a certain condition becomes True, which type of loop would you use?

   a. Either a Do Until loop or a Do While Not loop.

   b. A loop twisted in the shape of a pretzel.

   c. A loop-the-loop.

   d. Have you noticed that if you stare at the word loop long enough, it starts to look funny?

2. When do you use a Do Until loop and when do you use a Do-Loop Until loop?

   a. Whenever I need to confuse myself on how different loops work.

   b. When I get mixed up and use the wrong loop by mistake.

   c. I use the Do Until loop if I need to loop zero or more times. I use the Do-Loop Until loop if I need to loop at least once.

   d. When I can't remember how to use a Do While loop. Can you explain it to me again?

When to use a Do-Loop Until loop

Use a Do-Loop Until loop whenever you need to do the following:

- ✔ Loop at least once
- ✔ Loop until a certain condition becomes True

The Do-Loop Until loop is equal to the following two Do-Loop While loops:

```
Do                          Do
   Instructions                Instructions
Loop While Not Condition    Loop While Condition = False
```

When creating loops, always make sure that they eventually end and that they do exactly what you want them to do. If anything goes wrong with your program, look to see if your loops are causing the problem first.

Chapter 25

For Next Loops That Can Count

● ●

In This Chapter

▶ Using the For Next loop

▶ Counting backward and forward

▶ Using the Step increment

● ●

*I*f you want to loop until a certain condition becomes True or False, use one of the following principles:

	As long as Condition = True	As long as Condition = False
Loops at least once	Do Loop While *condition*	Do Loop Until *condition*
Loops zero or more times	Do While *condition* Loop	Do Until *condition* Loop

All four of these types of loops keep running until a certain condition becomes True or False. But if you already know how many times you want a loop to run, use a For Next loop.

A For Next loop looks like the following:

```
For Counter = Start To End Step X
   Instructions
Next Counter
```

The counter is a variable that represents an integer. Start represents the first number assigned to the value of the counter. End is the last number assigned to the value of the counter. Step is the interval to count by. If Step is omitted, the interval defaults to 1.

How the For Next Loop Works

If you want to loop exactly three times, you can use the following code:

```
For X = 1 To 3
   Instructions
Next X
```

Here's what this code means:

1. The first line says, "Create a variable called X and set its value equal to 1. Keep looping as long as the value of X is either 1, 2, or 3. The moment the value of X is no longer one of these values, stop looping."

2. The second line is where you can shove one or more instructions (including additional For Next loops if you want).

3. The third line says, "Okay, get the next value of X (by adding 1 to the value of X) and go back to the first line. At this point, the value of X is now 2."

The following line tells Visual Basic to loop three times:

```
For X = 1 To 3
```

By default, Visual Basic counts by one. For grins and laughs, you can use any combination of numbers that you want, such as

```
For X = 1209 To 1211
   Instructions
Next X
```

This For Next loop also loops three times, although it's not as easy to tell that just by looking at it:

The first time, X = 1209.

The second time, X = 1210.

The third and last time, X = 1211.

You can count by such bizarre numbers if these numbers somehow make sense to your program. For example, you can count by employee numbers:

```
For EmployeeNumber = 11250 To 11290
   ' Use the value of EmployeeNumber to search a database
   ' of employees and print their background information
Next EmployeeNumber
```

In this case, the instructions inside your For Next loop use the value of `EmployeeNumber` to find a specific employee.

If you just need to loop a particular number of times, such as five, use the simplest and most straightforward method, as shown in the following:

```
For X = 1 To 5
   Instructions
Next X
```

Only if your numbers must be used inside your For Next loop should you resort to bizarre, hard-to-read counting methods, such as

```
For Counter = 3492 To 12909
   Instructions
Next Counter
```

Counting Backward and Forward

Normally, the For Next loop counts forward by 1s. However, if you want to count by 5s, 10s, 13s, or 29s, you can. To count by any number other than 1, you have to specify a Step increment. For example:

```
For counter = start To end Step increment
   Instructions
Next counter
```

Adding the `Step` increment instruction tells Visual Basic, "Instead of counting forward by ones, count by the value of the increment that follows the word `Step`." If you wanted to count by 16s, you would use the following code:

```
For X = 0 To 32 Step 16
   Instructions
Next X
```

This For Next loop actually loops just three times:

The first time, X = 0

The second time, X = 16

The third time and last time, X = 32

If you want, you can even count backward. To count backward three times, you could use the following code:

```
For X = 3 To 1 Step -1
  Instructions
Next X
```

Here's what the preceding code means:

1. The first line says, "Create a variable called X, set its value to 3, and count backward by –1."

2. The second line contains one or more instructions to follow.

3. The third line says, "Choose the next value of X. Because we're counting backward by –1, the new value of X will be X –1. The second time, X will be 2."

Although Visual Basic doesn't care about how you count, always choose the simplest method whenever possible. That way, you and any other programmers can quickly see how many times a For Next loop keeps looping.

Count backward or by unusual numbers (increments of 3, 5, 16, and so on) only if instructions in a For Next loop need the numbers. Otherwise, you only make your program harder to read.

So what happens if you write a For Next loop like the following?

```
For J = 1 To 7 Step 5
  Instructions
Next J
```

Here's what this code means:

1. This For Next loop repeats itself twice. The first time, the value of J is 1.

2. The second time, the value of J is 1 + 5 (remember, the value of Step is 5), or 6.

3. Before it can repeat a third time, the loop changes the value of J to 6 + 5, or 11. Because 11 is greater than the specified range of J = 1 To 7, the For Next loop refuses to loop a third time and quits.

Use Caution When Using a For Next Loop with the Step Increment

A For Next loop must create its own variable to do its counting. For example, the following code creates a variable called XYZ that counts by 10s:

```
For XYZ = 1 To 50 Step 10
   Instructions
Next XYZ
```

And the next code creates a variable called TUV that counts by increments of 1.5:

```
For TUV = 1 To 7 Step 1.5
   Instructions
Next TUV
```

For Next loops usually count by whole numbers, such as 1, 2, 5, or 58, so it's not difficult to determine the number of loops there will be. The first code example just shown counts by 10, so the number of times it will loop is pretty easy to figure out. (It loops five times.)

The second example, however, counts in increments of 1.5; because of this decimal increment, it's harder to tell how many times it will loop. (It loops five times.) When using the Step increment, use whole numbers so that you can see the number of loops more easily.

When using a For Next loop, *never* (and I repeat, *never*) change the value of the counting variable within the loop. The loop will get messed up, as the following example illustrates:

```
For X = 1 To 5
   X = 3
Next X
```

Here's what happens:

1. The first line says, "Create a variable called X and set its value to 1."

2. The second line says, "Assign the value of 3 to a variable called X."

3. The third line says, "Add 1 to the value of X. Because X is equal to 3, now make X equal to 4."

Because X always equals 4 at the end of each loop, this For Next loop becomes an endless loop, which never stops. So when using For Next loops, make sure that none of the instructions inside the loop changes the counting variable. Otherwise, you'll be sorry. . . .

When to Use a For Next Loop

Use a For Next loop whenever you want to loop a specific number of times.

Just to show you that it is possible, you can also use other types of loops to count. The following two loops will loop exactly six times:

```
X = 0                      For X = 1 To 6
Do While X < 6                 Instructions
  X = X + 1                Next X
  Instructions
Loop
```

Notice how simple and clean the For Next loop is compared to the Do While loop. There are an infinite number of ways to write a program that works (and an even greater number of ways to write programs that don't work), but the simplest way is usually the best.

Test your newfound knowledge

1. How many times will the following For Next loop repeat itself?

```
For ID = 15 To 1 Step -1
        Instructions
Next ID
```

a. Fifteen times.

b. One time, but fifteen times as fast.

c. Zero or more times, or something like that. Wait a minute. I think I'm in the wrong lesson.

d. None, because only history can repeat itself.

2. What is the main advantage of a For Next loop over a Do While loop?

a. A Do While loop is more complicated to use, and a For Next loop doesn't work at all.

b. It all depends on your point of view, man. Like, all things are good if we only love one another and live in peace and harmony.

c. You can specify how many times you want a For Next loop to repeat itself.

d. There is no advantage to learning Visual Basic. You should be learning C++ or Java instead.

Try a For Next Loop for Yourself

If you don't want to type any code right now, just run and study the source code for this chapter, stored on the enclosed CD-ROM.

This sample program runs through a For Next loop and prints the value of X on the screen each time it loops. To create this program for yourself, use the settings defined in the following table:

Object	Property	Setting
Form	Caption	A For Next Loop Example
Command1	Caption	Next X
	Name	cmdNext

Type the following in the Code window:

```
Private Sub cmdNext_Click()
  For X = 1 To 10 Step 2
    Print X
  Next X
End Sub
```

This program does nothing more exciting than loop five times and print the value of X on the form each time.

Chapter 26

Nested Loops and Quick Exits

● ●

In This Chapter

▶ Using nested loops

▶ Making nested loops work

▶ Exiting quickly from loops

● ●

*F*or the ultimate in flexibility and complexity, you can jam loops inside other loops to create an endless series of loops. Whenever you have one loop stuffed inside another loop, it's called a *nested loop*. So which loop runs and completes first? The answer is simple.

Using Nested Loops

When you have nested loops, the loop inside finishes first as shown in the following example:

```
Do While Employee = "Supervisor"
  For J = 1 To 5
    Instructions
  Next J
Loop
```

Now, here's what this code means:

1. The first line says, "Create a variable called Employee and check to make sure its value is equal to "Supervisor". If it is, move to the second line. If it isn't, don't even bother looking at the For Next loop inside; simply skip to the fifth line."

2. The second line says, "Create a variable called J and set its value to 1."

3. The third line says, "Follow these instructions, whatever they may be."

4. The fourth line says, "Increase the value of J by 1 and jump back to the first line again. Keep doing this until the value of J is greater than 5."

5. The fifth line says, "This is the end of the Do While loop. Keep repeating as long as the variable Employee is equal to "Supervisor"."

In the preceding example, the For Next loop finishes before the Do While loop. The For Next loop also runs one complete time through for every time you go through the Do While loop.

Making Nested Loops Work

Naturally, Visual Basic gives you the complete freedom to cram as many loops inside one another as you want. When creating nested loops, indent each loop to make it easier to see where each loop begins and ends. For example, notice how confusing the following nested loops look without indentation:

```
Do While Name = "Sam"
Do
For K = 20 To 50 Step 10
Do
Do Until Sex = "Male"
'  Change some variables here
Loop
Loop While Age > 21
Next K
Loop Until LastName = "Doe"
Loop
```

This is what the same code looks like with indentations:

```
Do While Name = "Sam"
  Do
    For K = 20 To 50 Step 10
      Do
        Do Until Sex = "Male"
          '  Change some variables here
        Loop
      Loop While Age > 21
    Next K
  Loop Until LastName = "Doe"
Loop
```

From the computer's point of view, both nested loops work the same. But from a programmer's point of view, the nested loops using indentation are much easier to read and understand.

With so many nested loops, make sure that the inside loops don't accidentally mess up the conditions or counting variables of the outer loops. Otherwise, you may create an endless loop and have to examine all your loops to find the problem.

Another problem that can prevent nested loops from running is if they are tangled, as in the following example:

```
For K = 1 To 4
   For J = 2 To 20 Step 2
Next K
   Next J
```

In this example, the two For Next loops intertwine because the first For Next loop ends before the second, inner For Next loop can end. Fortunately, if you run the above BASIC code, Visual Basic catches this mistake so this type of problem is easy to correct.

Quick Exits from Loops

A Do loop continues running until a certain condition becomes True or False. A For Next loop continues running until it finishes counting. But what if you need to exit a loop prematurely? In that case, you can bail out of a loop by using the magic Exit command.

To bail out of a Do loop, use the Exit Do command, as shown in the following example:

```
X = 0
Do While X < 6
   X = X + 1
   If X = 4 Then Exit Do
Loop
```

This Do While loop continues looping as long as the value of a variable called X is less than 6. The moment the value of X equals 4, Visual Basic runs the Exit Do command.

The Exit Do command bails Visual Basic out of the loop, even though the value of X is still less than 6.

To bail out of a For Next loop, use the following:

```
Exit For
```

For example:

```
For Y = 1 To 100
   If Y = 50 Then Exit For
Next Y
```

Normally this For Next loop repeats 100 times but the second line tells Visual Basic to bail out of the For Next loop as soon as the value of Y equals 50 — even if the value of Y is still less than 100.

Usually (notice the emphasis on *usually*), a good idea is to provide a way to bail out of a loop prematurely, just in case the user needs to do something else. However, make sure that using Exit Do or Exit For doesn't kick you out of the loop before you want it to. Otherwise, you'll have another bug to hunt and track down.

If you use the Exit Do/For commands within a loop nested inside another loop, the Exit Do/For commands exit out of only the current loop and then return control to the outer loop.

Test your newfound knowledge

1. What is the limit to the number of loops you can nest?

a. Theoretically, the number is infinity. Practically, the number is as many as you feel like typing, although the more nested your loops are, the harder it is to see what each one does.

b. The number of loops is limited to your yearly allotment, as defined by Microsoft when you send in your registration card.

c. Five.

d. Discovered by Einstein, the limit to the number of nested loops is equal to the same value that represents the speed of light.

2. To make nested loops easier to read and understand, what should you do?

a. Avoid using loops, control structures, variables, or anything else that requires thinking.

b. Absolutely nothing. If people can't understand my nested loops, that's their problem.

c. Avoid indentation, because only amateurs need to rely on such editing tricks to write programs.

d. Use plenty of indentations to make the beginning and ending of each loop easy to find.

Part VII

Writing Subprograms (So You Don't Go Crazy All at Once)

THE GREAT THING ABOUT OBJECT-ORIENTED PROGRAMMING IS, IT'S MADE SOFTWARE DEVELOPMENT AS EASY AS PUTTING ONE FOOT IN FRONT OF THE OTHER.

In this part . . .

*N*ow is the time to find out how to divide your Visual Basic program into smaller programs so you can create programs that are easier to write, modify, and understand. Rather than write one huge, monolithic program (which is like carving a mansion out of a single piece of granite), subprograms let you create miniature programs and paste them together to make one larger program (like using bricks to build a house).

By dividing one large program into several smaller ones, you can test each part of your program before moving on to writing another part of the program. By conquering each task of your program one by one, you can also maintain your sanity so that you don't go nuts trying to create one monster program in one sitting.

Chapter 27

General Procedures (Subprograms That Everyone Can Share)

In This Chapter

▶ Creating general procedures

▶ Naming general procedures

▶ Using general procedures

*P*rocedures are small programs that make up a single larger program, much like bricks make up an entire wall. Visual Basic has two types of procedures: event procedures and general procedures.

An *event procedure* is part of a user interface object, such as a command button, check box, or scroll bar. Event procedures run only when a certain event occurs to a certain object, such as clicking the mouse on a command button or a check box.

A *general procedure* isn't attached or connected to any specific objects on the user interface. A general procedure doesn't do anything until an event procedure (or another general procedure) specifically tells it to get to work.

So do you need event procedures? Yes. Event procedures make your user interface responsive. Do you need general procedures? No. General procedures exist solely for the programmer's convenience.

If two or more event procedures contain nearly identical instructions, typing the same instructions over and over would be repetitive. Even worse, if you needed to modify the instructions, you would have to change these instructions in every event procedure that used those same instructions.

As an alternative, you can use general procedures. The whole purpose of general procedures is to hold commonly used instructions in one place. That way, if you need to modify the instructions, you change them in just one place.

How to Create a General Procedure

After you've drawn all the objects that make up your user interface, Visual Basic automatically creates empty event procedures for all your user interface objects.

Unfortunately, Visual Basic doesn't create a single general procedure for you; you have to create it yourself. You can create and save general procedures in two types of files:

- ✔ FRM (form) files
- ✔ BAS (module) files

When you save a general procedure in an FRM (form) file, that general procedure can be used only by event or general procedures stored in that same FRM file. (The one exception is that any part of your program can use a general procedure that is stored in an FRM form file, but only if that form file is loaded into memory at the time.) When you save a general procedure in a BAS (module) file, however, the general procedure can be used by any event or general procedures that make up your Visual Basic program.

If you save your general procedures in a BAS file, you can create a library of useful general procedures that you can plug into any other Visual Basic programs you write. If your general procedures are useful for only one specific program, store them in an FRM file.

To create and save a general procedure in an FRM (form) file, follow these steps:

1. **Click on a form file in the Project Explorer window and then press F7; choose View⇨Code; or click on the View Code icon to open the Code window.**

2. **Select (General) in the Object list box.**

3. **Choose Tools⇨Add Procedure.**

   Visual Basic displays the Add Procedure dialog box, as shown in Figure 27-1.

4. **Select the Sub radio button, type your procedure name in the Name box, and press Enter or click on OK.**

   Visual Basic displays an empty general procedure.

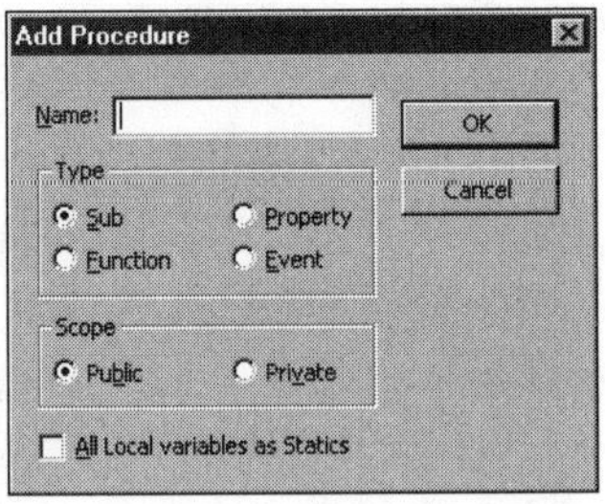

Figure 27-1:
Creating a
general
procedure
with the
Add
Procedure
dialog box.

To create and save a general procedure to a new BAS (module) file, follow these steps:

1. **Choose Project⇨Add Module.**

   An Add Module dialog box appears.

2. **Click on the Module icon and then click on Open.**

3. **Choose Tools⇨Add Procedure.**

   Visual Basic displays the Add Procedure dialog box (see Figure 27-1).

4. **With the Sub radio button selected, type your procedure name in the Name box, and press Enter or click on OK.**

   Visual Basic displays an empty general procedure.

To create a general procedure and save it to an existing BAS file, follow these steps:

1. **Choose View⇨Project Explorer, press Ctrl+R, or click on the Project Explorer icon on the toolbar.**

2. **Click on the module file where you want to save your general procedure; then click on the View Code icon.**

   Visual Basic displays the Code window for that particular BAS module file.

3. **Choose Tools⇨Add Procedure.**

   Visual Basic displays an Add Procedure dialog box.

4. **With the Sub radio button selected, type your procedure name in the Name box, and press Enter or click on OK.**

   Visual Basic displays an empty general procedure.

How to Name General Procedures

Unlike with event procedure names (which identify the object name and the event), you can name general procedures anything you want, with the following restrictions:

- The name must be 40 characters or fewer.
- The name must begin with a letter and can consist of only letters, numbers, and the underscore character (_).
- The name can't be a reserved word that Visual Basic already uses such as End, Sub, or Private.

Ideally, you want to use names for your general procedures that describe what they do. For example:

```
CubeRoot
Ask4Password
DisplayWindow
```

These complete procedure names would appear in the Code window as follows:

```
Public Sub CubeRoot()
End Sub
```

and

```
Public Sub Ask4Password()
End Sub
```

and

```
Public Sub DisplayWindow()
End Sub
```

Notice that a complete general procedure name consists of four parts:

- Public (or Private)
- Sub
- Your general procedure name
- A pair of parentheses ()

The word `Public` tells Visual Basic that the general procedure is public. So, if the general procedure is stored in a BAS file, any event or general procedures stored in other FRM or BAS files can use it. (If you don't want procedures stored in other files to use your general procedure, just use the word `Private` instead.)

The word `Sub` identifies your subroutine as a procedure. (If you replace the word `Sub` with the word `Function`, you can create a general function. I explain functions in Chapter 29.) Your procedure name is the name that event procedures and other general procedures use to call your general procedure. *Calling* a procedure means telling a particular procedure, "Okay, do something now!"

The pair of parentheses is called the *argument list* (which you can read about in Chapter 28). The simplest general procedures have an empty argument list, represented by an empty pair of parentheses.

How to Use a General Procedure

A general procedure contains one or more instructions. When another procedure wants to use those instructions that are stored in a general procedure, it calls this general procedure by name.

You can call a procedure in two ways. You can state the procedure's name:

```
ProcedureName
```

Or, you can state the procedure's name along with the word `Call`:

```
Call ProcedureName
```

If you want to use a general procedure that is stored in another FRM form file, you can call it by specifying the form name and then the procedure name, such as

```
FormName.ProcedureName
```

Or you can state the procedure's name along with the word `Call`:

```
Call FormName.ProcedureName
```

Your computer doesn't care which method you use. But whatever method you choose, use it consistently — your program's easier to read that way.

Stating only the procedure name is simpler than using the word Call, but the latter helps identify all the procedure calls in your program. For example, consider the following general procedure stored in a form called frmMainForm:

```
Public Sub Warning()
   MsgBox "Your computer will blow up in 3 seconds!", 16,
          "Warning!"
End Sub
```

This general procedure simply displays a dialog box with the message "Your computer will blow up in 3 seconds!" as shown in Figure 27-2.

Figure 27-2:
A dialog
box created
by a
general
procedure.

If an event procedure, stored in a different form, wanted to use or call this general procedure, it would look like the following:

```
Public Sub cmdAlert_Click()
   frmMainForm.Warning
End Sub
```

If the event procedure used the Call method of calling a procedure, it would look like this:

```
Public Sub cmdAlert_Click()
   Call frmMainForm.Warning
End Sub
```

Both of these event procedures are equivalent to the following:

```
Public Sub cmdAlert_Click()
   MsgBox "Your computer will blow up in 3 seconds!", 16,
          "Warning!"
End Sub
```

Although this example is simple, you can see that, if you cram two or more instructions inside a general procedure, you won't have to type these same instructions over and over again in multiple places. Instead, you can just call a single general procedure.

Test your newfound knowledge

1. Why would you need to use a general procedure?

   a. Because a more specific procedure won't do the job.

   b. To store commonly used instructions in one place so that the procedure is easy to modify.

   c. To keep your event procedures from getting lonely.

   d. There's no reason to use general procedures — cool programmers have no need of such crutches.

2. What are the two ways to use, or call, a general procedure?

   a. Telephone or mail a letter.

   b. State the general procedure's name or insert the word Call before the general procedure's name.

   c. See your favorite psychic and participate in a séance.

   d. Get your local hog-calling contest winner to shout real loud for you.

Chapter 28

Passing Arguments

● ●

In This Chapter

▶ Sending arguments to a procedure

▶ Passing arguments by value

▶ Quitting a procedure early

● ●

*W*hen a procedure calls a general procedure, it does so by name. Calling a general procedure by name essentially tells that general procedure, "Hey, get busy and start doing something."

Many times, the called general procedure needs no further instructions when its name is called. Sometimes, though, the called general procedure needs additional information before it can do anything.

Any procedure can call a general procedure and give it data to work with. This data is called an *argument*. Essentially, the first procedure is saying, "Don't argue with me. Here's all the information you need to get busy. Now get to work."

Why Use Arguments?

An argument is data — numbers, strings, or variables (which represent a number or string) — that a general procedure needs to work with. By using arguments, you can write a single, nonspecific procedure that can replace two or more specialized general procedures.

For example, you can create two general procedures, as follows:

```
Public Sub DisplayWarning()
  txtReadMe.Text = "Warning! Nuclear meltdown has
             occurred!"
End Sub
```

and

```
Public Sub DisplayCaution()
  txtReadMe.Text = "Caution! Turn off the reactors now!"
End Sub
```

To use either procedure, you call them in one of two ways:

- DisplayWarning or Call DisplayWarning
- DisplayCaution or Call DisplayCaution

However, creating two procedures that do almost the same thing is tedious and wasteful, which makes it a perfect technique to use in a job you don't like.

Instead of writing near-duplicate copies of the same procedure, you can replace both of those procedures with a single one, such as the following:

```
Public Sub Display(Message As String)
  txtReadMe.Text = Message
End Sub
```

This new procedure says, "Create a variable called Message that holds any string that another procedure will give me. Whatever this value may be, stuff it in the Text property of the text box called txtReadMe.

Using a general procedure, you can choose the type of text by calling the Display procedure like this:

```
Display ("Warning! Nuclear meltdown has occurred!")
```

or

```
Display ("Caution! Turn off the reactors now!")
```

Sending Arguments to a Procedure

To call a procedure and send an argument to it, you can use one of three methods:

- ProcedureName Argument
- ProcedureName (Argument)
- Call ProcedureName (Argument)

Suppose you had the following general procedure:

```
Public Sub Display(Message As String)
   txtReadMe.Text = Message
End Sub
```

To call the preceding procedure and display the message "Warning! Nuclear meltdown has occurred!", you can use one of three methods:

✔ Display "Warning! Nuclear meltdown has occurred!"

✔ Display ("Warning! Nuclear meltdown has occurred!")

✔ Call Display ("Warning! Nuclear meltdown has occurred!")

All three methods are equivalent, as shown in Figure 28-1.

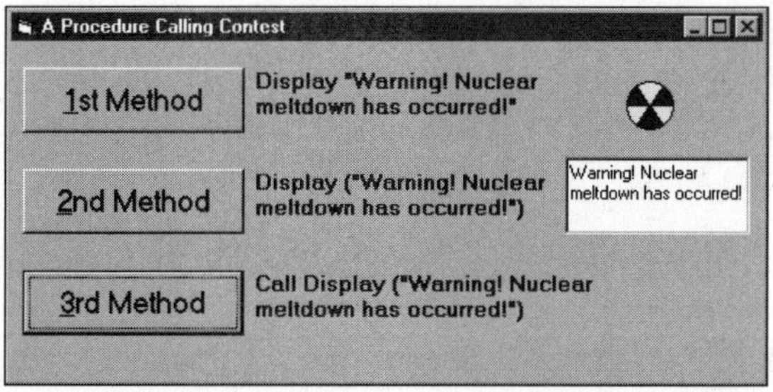

Figure 28-1:
Calling a
general
procedure
in three
different
ways.

Now here's what calling the Display general procedure does:

1. First it tells Visual Basic, "Find a general procedure named Display and send it one argument." In this case, the one argument is the string, "Warning! Nuclear meltdown has occurred!"

2. Visual Basic finds a general procedure called Display. The Display procedure says to assign whatever argument it gets to the variable Message.

3. Then the Display procedure says, "Stuff the value of Message into the Text property of the text box called txtReadMe. Because the value of Message is the string "Warning! Nuclear meltdown has occurred!", stuff this value into the Text property."

If you call the procedure in the following way:

```
Display ("Caution! Turn off the reactors now!")
```

the Text property of the text box called txtReadMe gets stuffed with the string "Caution! Turn off the reactors now!"

By using the same procedure but feeding it different arguments, you replace two specialized general procedures with a single general procedure.

Accepting Arguments

Before a general procedure can accept arguments, you have to define the procedure's argument list. Essentially, this list defines how many arguments the general procedure can take.

For example, to define a general procedure that won't take any arguments, you use a pair of empty parentheses, as follows:

```
Public Sub NoBackTalk()
End Sub
```

To call this procedure, you can choose one of two ways:

  ✔ NoBackTalk

  ✔ Call NoBackTalk

To define an argument list that takes one argument, you do the following:

```
Public Sub BackTalk(Something)
End Sub
```

In this case, the variable called Something is by default a Variant data type (see Chapter 15 for more information about data types), which can represent a number or string. To call this procedure and give it the argument 4, you can do one of the following:

  ✔ BackTalk 4

  ✔ BackTalk (4)

  ✔ Call BackTalk (4)

To define an argument list that takes two or more arguments, you have to specify a variable for each argument and separate each by a comma. For example, the following defines three arguments:

```
Public Sub Chatty(Message, Reply, Gossip)
End Sub
```

This argument list defines three arguments that can represent a number or a string. To call this procedure and give it the arguments 30, "Hello", and 12.9, you must do one of the following:

✔ Chatty 30, "Hello", 12.9

✔ Call Chatty (30, "Hello", 12.9)

There is no practical limit to the number of arguments that a procedure can accept. However, the longer your argument list is, the more complicated your procedure must be and the more likely you may get confused trying to understand exactly what your procedures do.

Defining argument types

Besides defining the number of arguments in an argument list, you have the option of defining the type of data each argument must represent.

For example, you can define an argument to represent only one of the following data types (see Chapter 15 for more information about data types):

✔ Integer

✔ Long

✔ Single

✔ Double

✔ Currency

✔ String

You have to define argument types in the argument list. For example:

```
Public Sub Convert(Fahrenheit As Integer, Celsius As Integer)
```

The preceding line of code defines two arguments, both of which must represent an integer. The following code shows the only procedure call that works:

```
Public cmdTest_Click()
Dim X, Y As Integer
Dim A, B As String
Dim M, N As Single
   Call Convert(X, Y)        ' This would work
   Call Convert(A, B)        ' Neither A nor B are Integers
   Call Convert(M, N)        ' Neither M nor N are Integers
   Call Convert("Hello", X)  ' "Hello" is not an Integer
End Sub
```

The main reason to specify an argument's type is to prevent your procedure from trying to work with incorrect data. For example, if your procedure expects a string but gets an integer, your program can crash. Even worse, it may run correctly but contain the wrong information. In this case, you have created a bug called a logic error. (For more about logic errors, check out Chapter 20.)

Although you don't have to declare an argument's type, doing so is a good idea, just to help prevent any bugs from breeding inside your precious code.

Problems with sending arguments

Two problems may occur when calling procedures. One problem is when the number of arguments sent doesn't match the number of arguments defined by the procedure. The other problem occurs when the types of arguments sent don't match the types of arguments defined by the procedure.

Giving the wrong number of arguments

When you define a procedure with an argument list, the argument list defines the number of arguments it needs to run. If you call this procedure and don't give it the correct number of arguments, the procedure doesn't work. For example:

```
Public Sub ArgueWithMe(Flame)
End Sub
```

This procedure expects one argument, which can be a number or a string. None of the following calls to this procedure works, because the number of arguments is not one:

- ✔ ArgueWithMe
- ✔ ArgueWithMe 9, "Shut up!"
- ✔ Call ArgueWithMe("Why?", "Go away!", 4500, "Okay.")

Giving the wrong type of arguments

Likewise, when calling a procedure, always make sure that the arguments have the same data types as the types defined in the argument list. For example:

```
Public Sub ArgueWithMe(Flame As String)
End Sub
```

This procedure expects one argument, which must be a String data type. None of the following calls to this procedure work because the arguments are not String data types:

✔ ArgueWithMe(78.909)

✔ ArgueWithMe(9)

✔ Call ArgueWithMe(34)

Passing arguments by value

To further protect your procedures from messing around with each other's variables, you can pass arguments by value. Normally, when you pass an argument to a procedure, the new procedure can change the argument's value. This is like giving somebody a drink and having them spit in it and hand it back to you.

If another procedure needs certain data, but you don't want that other procedure to risk changing the data used by other parts of your program, you can *pass an argument by value.* So, you give a procedure an argument, and the procedure can change the argument all it wants. However, any changes it makes to this variable are limited within that particular procedure. This situation is like pouring part of your drink into another cup and giving it to another person. If that person decides to spit in his or her cup, your drink remains uncontaminated.

To define an argument as passed by value, you use the ByVal keyword in the argument list, like this:

```
Public Sub ShowMe(ByVal Name As String)
```

You never need to use the ByVal keyword to call a procedure.

Suppose you have an event procedure such as the following:

```
Private Sub Command1_Click()
Dim MyString As String
   MyString = "John Doe"
   ShowMe MyString
   txtMessage.Text = MyString
End Sub
```

and a general procedure such as the following:

```
Public Sub ShowMe (ByVal Name As String)
   Name = UCase(Name)
   txtNewMessage.Text = Name
End Sub
```

Visual Basic follows the instructions in the Command1_Click( ) event procedure in the following way:

1. When the user clicks on a command button named Command1, Visual Basic starts to follow the instructions in the Private Command1_Click( ) event procedure.

2. The second line in the Command1_Click( ) event procedure tells Visual Basic to declare a variable called MyString that can only hold string values.

3. The third line stuffs the string "John Doe" into the MyString variable.

4. The fourth line calls the general procedure called ShowMe and sends it the value of the MyString variable as a single argument.

5. Visual Basic immediately jumps to the general procedure called ShowMe. The ByVal keyword tells Visual Basic that any changes it makes to the argument received are isolated within the ShowMe general procedure.

6. The first line of the ShowMe general procedure defines a new variable called Name and defines it to hold a string.

7. The second line of the ShowMe general procedure says to use the UCase keyword to turn all the letters of the Name variable into uppercase and store the result back in the Name variable. In this case, the value of the Name variable is now "JOHN DOE".

8. The third line of the ShowMe general procedure says to display the Name value in the Text property of a text box named txtNewMessage. In this case, the txtNewMessage text box displays "JOHN DOE".

9. The fourth line of the ShowMe general procedure says this is the end of the general procedure; now go back to the procedure that was originally called the ShowMe general procedure. This information tells Visual Basic to jump back to the fifth line of the Command1_Click( ) event procedure.

10. The fifth line of the Command1_Click( ) event procedure says to take the value of MyString and stuff it in the Text property of a text box named txtMessage. In this case, the txtMessage text box displays "John Doe".

11. The sixth line of the Command1_Click( ) event procedure tells Visual Basic to stop thinking anymore.

If you remove the ByVal keyword from the ShowMe general procedure, the txtMessage text box in Step 10 displays "JOHN DOE". The ByVal keyword simply keeps the general procedure from messing up variables used by other procedures.

To specify that an argument be passed by value, you must put the ByVal keyword in front of each argument:

```
Public Sub BlackBox(ByVal X As Integer, Y As Integer)
```

In the preceding example, only the argument X is passed by value. The Y variable is not. To specify that the Y argument also be passed by value, you have to do the following:

```
Public Sub BlackBox(ByVal X As Integer, ByVal Y As Integer)
```

Quitting a Procedure Prematurely

Normally, a procedure runs until all its instructions are followed. However, you may want to exit a procedure before it finishes.

To exit a procedure prematurely, you have to use the following code:

```
Exit Sub
```

For example, you may have a procedure like the one that follows:

```
Public Sub EndlessLoop()
   X = 0
   Do
      X = X + 1
      If (X = 13) Then
         Exit Sub
      End If
   Loop Until X = 25
End Sub
```

Normally, this loop would keep repeating until the value of X equals 25. However the If-Then statement inside the Do-Loop causes this procedure to end when X equals 13.

Try Passing Arguments Yourself

If you want to try your hand at a passing argument, head over to the CD. There you find a sample program that lets you type text in a text box and see how passing a variable by value (using the ByVal keyword) causes the variable's value to change only within that particular procedure. This program is stored under the name CALL.VBP.

Test your newfound knowledge

1. Explain why argument passing is useful in writing programs.

a. Argument passing is like passing the buck. Programmers do this all the time to avoid taking responsibility when their project is behind schedule.

b. Passing arguments lets you write one general-purpose procedure to replace two or more specialized procedures.

c. Arguments let you give wrong information to your procedures, so they have twice as many chances of wrecking your entire project.

d. Argument passing is like scream therapy. Each side argues for its own point until both sides are exhausted, which prevents people from shooting each other at work.

2. Explain what the following argument list means:

```
Public Sub Confusion(ByVal
Catch As String, X As Integer,
Z)

End Sub
```

a. Crud, I have to review this section all over again.

b. Now I finally understand why programmers look and act the way they do, if they have to spend eight hours a day deciphering cryptic commands like this.

c. Someone didn't comment the code correctly to make this argument easy to understand.

d. The procedure expects three arguments. The first argument is called Catch, is passed by value, and must be a String data type. The second argument is called X and must be an Integer data type. The third argument is called Z and can be any data type.

Chapter 29

Functions, a Unique Type of Subprogram

*F*unctions return a single value. Procedures on the other hand, return zero or more values. When you need to calculate only a single value, use a function. When you need to calculate zero or more than two values, use a procedure.

A typical function looks like the following:

```
Public Function FunctionName(ArgumentList)As DataType
   FunctionName = SomeValue
End Function
```

The word `Public` tells Visual Basic that if the function is stored in a BAS file, that this function can be used by all event and general procedures in your Visual Basic program. (If the function is stored in an FRM file, this function can be used only by event and general procedures stored in that same FRM file.)

The word `Function` defines the subprogram as a function. The `FunctionName` can be any valid Visual Basic name, preferably one that describes what the function does. The `Argument List` can contain zero or more arguments. The `DataType` defines what type of data the function returns, such as an integer or string.

Visual Basic includes several built-in functions that you can use in your programs. Table 29-1 lists a few of these built-in functions.

Table 29-1 Some Commonly Used Visual Basic Functions	
Built-In Visual Basic Function	*What It Does*
Abs (number)	Returns the absolute value of a number
Date	Returns the current system date
LCase (string)	Converts a string to lowercase
Sqr (number)	Returns the square root of a number

How to Create a Function

You can create and save functions in two types of files:

- FRM (form) files
- BAS (module) files

When you save a function in an FRM (form) file, that function can be used only by procedures or functions stored in that same FRM file. (The one exception is that any part of your program can use a function stored in an FRM form file, but only if that form file is loaded into memory at the time.) When you save a function in a BAS (module) file, the function can be used by any procedures or functions that make up your Visual Basic program.

If you save your functions in a BAS file, you can create a library of useful functions that you can plug into any other Visual Basic programs you write. If your functions are useful for only one specific program, store them in an FRM file.

To create and save a function in an FRM (form) file, follow these steps:

1. **Click on a form file in the Project Explorer window and then press F7, choose View⇨Code, or click on the View Code icon to open the Code window.**

2. **Select (General) in the Object list box.**

3. **Choose Tools⇨Add Procedure.**

   Visual Basic displays the Add Procedure dialog box.

4. **Click the Function radio button. Then type your function name in the Name box, and press Enter or click on OK.**

   Visual Basic displays an empty function.

To create and save a function to a new BAS (module) file, follow these steps:

1. **Choose Project⇨Add Module.**

   An Add Module dialog box appears.

2. **Click on the Module icon and then click on Open.**

3. **Choose Tools⇨Add Procedure.**

   Visual Basic displays the Add Procedure dialog box. (See Figure 27-1.)

4. **Click the Function radio button. Then type your function name in the Name box, and press Enter or click on OK.**

   Visual Basic displays an empty function.

To create a function and save it to an existing BAS file, follow these steps:

1. **Choose View⇨Project Explorer, press Ctrl+R, or click on the Project Explorer icon on the toolbar.**

2. **Click on the module file where you want to save your general procedure. Then click on the View Code icon.**

   Visual Basic displays the Code window for that particular BAS module file.

3. **Choose Tools⇨Add Procedure.**

   Visual Basic displays an Add Procedure dialog box.

4. **Click the Function radio button. Then type your function name in the Name box, and press Enter or click on OK.**

   Visual Basic displays an empty function.

Assigning a Value to a Function

Somewhere inside the function, you must assign the function's name to a value or an expression, such as the following:

```
Public Function YardsToMeters(Yards As Single) As Single
Const Conversion = 0.9
  YardsToMeters = Yards * Conversion
End Function
```

If you don't assign a value to a function's name, the function can't return any value — and the whole point of using functions is to return a value.

You can also define the specific data type of the value that a function returns, such as Integer, String, or Currency. For everything you've ever wanted to know about data types, check out Chapter 15.

The three main differences between a function and a procedure are as follows:

✔ A function can return only one value. A procedure can return zero or more values.

✔ Somewhere inside the function, the function's name must be assigned a value. You never have to do this with a procedure.

✔ You can define the data type that a function represents. You cannot define a procedure to represent a data type (but you can define the data types of a procedure's argument list).

Calling Functions

Calling a function is different than calling a procedure. Because functions represent a single value, you call a function by assigning the function name to a variable:

```
Public Function YardsToMeters(Yards As Single)
Const Conversion = 0.9
   YardsToMeters = Yards * Conversion
End Function


Private Sub cmdConvert_Click()
Dim Meters As Single
   Meters = YardsToMeters(CSng(txtYards.Text))
   txtMetric.Text = CStr(Meters)
End Sub
```

This event procedure says, "When the user clicks on a command button called cmdConvert, do the following:"

1. Create a variable called Meters and define this variable to hold only Single data type.

2. Take whatever value is stored in the Text property of a text box called txtYards and use the value as an argument for the YardsToMeters function.

3. The `YardsToMeters` function takes `txtYards.Text` as its argument, multiplies the argument by `0.9`, and stores this new result in the `YardsToMeters` function name. The result stored in the `YardsToMeters` function name gets stuffed into the `Meters` variable.

4. The value stored in the `Meters` variable gets converted into a string and stuffed into the `Text` property of a text box named `txtMetric`.

Note the differences in calling procedures and calling functions. When calling a procedure, you can use one of three methods:

- ✔ `ProcedureName ArgumentList`
- ✔ `ProcedureName(ArgumentList)`
- ✔ `Call ProcedureName(ArgumentList)`

You have only one way to call a function:

```
Variable = FunctionName(ArgumentList)
```

Because a function name represents a single value, you can use a function name in any mathematical expression, such as

```
Variable = FunctionName(ArgumentList) + Variable
```

So a procedure that calls a function called `YardsToMeters` may look like this:

```
Private Sub cmdConvert_Click()
Dim Meters As Single, NewValue As Single
   NewValue = (YardsToMeters (Meters) + 32) * 4
End Sub
```

Defining a Function as a Certain Data Type

Because a function returns a single value, you can specify what data type that value represents.

Take a look at the following, for example:

```
Public Function YardsToMeters(Yards) As Single
Const Conversion = 0.9
   YardsToMeters = Yards * Conversion
End Function
```

This defines the value of `YardsToMeters` as a `Single` data type. You can define a function to represent any one of the following:

- Integer
- Long
- Single
- Double
- Currency
- String

No matter what data type a function represents, any variables assigned to the function must be of the same data type. For example:

```
Public Function YardsToMeters(Yards) As Single
Const Conversion = 0.9
   YardsToMeters = Yards * Conversion
End Function

Private Sub cmdConvert_Click()
Dim Meters As Single
   Meters = YardsToMeters(CSng(txtYards.Text))
   txtMetric.Text = CStr(Meters)
End Sub
```

In this example, the variable `Meters` is defined as a `Single` data type, and the `YardsToMeters` function is also defined as a `Single` data type.

If `Meters` is defined as the following:

```
Dim Meters As String
```

the line

```
Meters = YardsToMeters(CSng(txtYards.Text))
```

can't work because `Meters` is a `String` data type, and `YardsToMeters` returns a `Single` data type value. Because `Meters` expects a string but `YardsToMeters` gives `Meters` a number, the program won't work.)

Defining argument types

Arguments are data (numbers, strings, or variables, which represent a number or a string) that a function needs to be able to work.

In addition to defining the number of arguments in an argument list, you have the option of defining the type of data each argument must represent.

For example, you can define an argument to represent only one of the following:

- ✔ Integer
- ✔ Long
- ✔ Single
- ✔ Double
- ✔ Currency
- ✔ String

To define an argument type, you have to define the type in the argument list:

```
Public Function Convert(Fahrenheit As Integer, Celsius As
         Integer)
```

This example defines two arguments and both must represent an Integer data type. The following shows the only procedure call that can work:

```
Private Sub cmdTest_Click()
Dim X, Y, Z As Integer
Dim A, B, C As String
Dim L, M, N As Single
   Z = Convert(X, Y)  ' This would work
   C = Convert(A, B)  ' Neither A nor B are Integers
   L = Convert(M, N)  ' Neither M nor N are Integers
   Z = Convert("Hello", X)  ' "Hello" is not an Integer
End Sub
```

The main reason to specify an argument's type is to prevent a function from working with the wrong type of data. For example, if your function expects an integer but gets a string, your program can crash. Even worse, your program may create a logic error. Although you don't have to declare an argument's type, you should — just to prevent any bugs from wrecking your program.

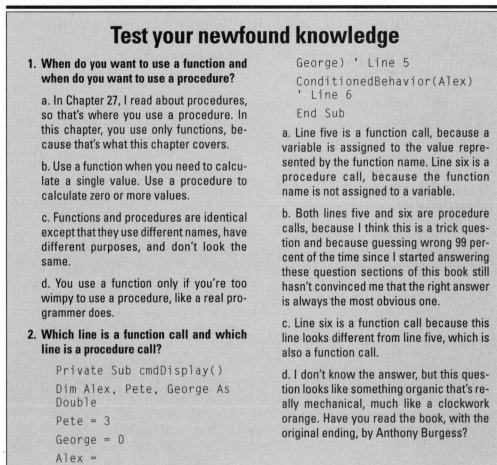

Test your newfound knowledge

1. When do you want to use a function and when do you want to use a procedure?

a. In Chapter 27, I read about procedures, so that's where you use a procedure. In this chapter, you use only functions, because that's what this chapter covers.

b. Use a function when you need to calculate a single value. Use a procedure to calculate zero or more values.

c. Functions and procedures are identical except that they use different names, have different purposes, and don't look the same.

d. You use a function only if you're too wimpy to use a procedure, like a real programmer does.

2. Which line is a function call and which line is a procedure call?

```
Private Sub cmdDisplay()
Dim Alex, Pete, George As
Double
Pete = 3
George = 0
Alex =
ClockworkOrange(Pete,
George) ' Line 5
ConditionedBehavior(Alex)
' Line 6
End Sub
```

a. Line five is a function call, because a variable is assigned to the value represented by the function name. Line six is a procedure call, because the function name is not assigned to a variable.

b. Both lines five and six are procedure calls, because I think this is a trick question and because guessing wrong 99 percent of the time since I started answering these question sections of this book still hasn't convinced me that the right answer is always the most obvious one.

c. Line six is a function call because this line looks different from line five, which is also a function call.

d. I don't know the answer, but this question looks like something organic that's really mechanical, much like a clockwork orange. Have you read the book, with the original ending, by Anthony Burgess?

Problems sending arguments

Two types of problems may occur when calling functions. One problem is when the number of arguments sent doesn't match the number of arguments defined by the function.

Another problem is when the types of arguments sent don't match the types of arguments defined by the function.

Giving the wrong number of arguments

When you define a function with an argument list, the list specifies the number of arguments that the function needs to run. If you call this function and don't give the function the right number of arguments, the function isn't going to work. For example:

```
Public Function Flame(Mail)
End Function
```

This function expects one argument, which can be a number or a string. None of the following calls to this function work, because the number of arguments is not one:

- ✔ X = Flame
- ✔ X = Flame(9, "Shut up!")
- ✔ X = Flame("Why?", "Go away!", 4500, "Okay.")

Giving the wrong type of arguments

Likewise, when calling a function, always make sure that the arguments have the same data types as the types defined in the argument list:

```
Public Function Flame(Mail As String)
End Function
```

This function expects one argument, which must be a String data type. None of the following calls to this function can work because the arguments are not String data types:

- ✔ X = Flame(78.909)
- ✔ X = Flame(9)
- ✔ X = Flame(34)

Quitting a Function Prematurely

Normally, your function runs until all the function's instructions have been followed. However, you may want to exit a function before the function is finished.

To exit a function prematurely, you have to use the following code:

```
Exit Function
```

Before you exit a function, make sure that you also assign a value to the function name; otherwise, your program may not work correctly.

Try Using Functions Yourself

The following sample program lets you see how a function works. In this example, the function converts yards to meters.

In case you don't feel like typing everything out, this program is stored on the CD-ROM under the name FUNCTION.VBP.

Object	Property	Setting
Form	Caption	Converts Yards into Meters
Label1	Caption	Yards:
	Height	495
	Left	360
	Top	360
	Width	1215
Textbox1	Height	495
	Left	1680
	Name	txtYards
	Text	(Empty)
	Width	1215
Label2	Caption	Meters:
	Height	495
	Left	360
	Top	1320
	Width	1215
Textbox2	Height	495
	Left	1680
	Name	txtMetric

Object	Property	Setting
	Text	(Empty)
	Width	1215
Command1	Caption	&Convert
	Height	495
	Left	840
	Name	cmdConvert
	Top	2400
	Width	1215
Command2	Caption	E&xit
	Height	495
	Left	2520
	Name	cmdExit
	Top	2400
	Width	1215

Type the following in the Code window:

```
Public Function YardsToMeters(Yards) As Single
Const Conversion = 0.9
  YardsToMeters = Yards * Conversion
End Function

Private Sub cmdExit_Click()
  Unload Me
End Sub

Private Sub cmdConvert_Click()
Dim Meters As Single
  Meters = YardsToMeters(CSng(txtYards.Text))
  txtMetric.Text = CStr(Meters)
End Sub
```

Chapter 30

Getting Some Class with Object-Oriented Programming

*I*n an attempt to keep up with the latest programming fads, Visual Basic gives you the ability to use object-oriented programming to develop your next killer application. Of course, unless you know what object-oriented programming is and what this form of programming can do for you, this latest feature is about as useful as giving a chain saw to a monkey and expecting the monkey to build a tree house.

So before you get all excited about using object-oriented programming with Visual Basic, take some time to find out what the heck object-oriented programming is supposed to do for you in the first place.

What the Heck Is Object-Oriented Programming?

Despite the rigors of college computer science curriculums, programming is still more an art than a science, which means that even having a Ph.D. in computer science is no guarantee that you can write better programs than a high school dropout.

To help turn programming into a science, the computer industry has been trying to develop guidelines to help people write bug-free programs as quickly and easily as possible. The first attempt at this "Holy Grail" of programming was something called *structured programming,* which encouraged you to divide a program into subprograms where each subprogram performed exactly one function.

While structured programming helped people create programs that were easier to write and modify, a problem still remained. Different parts of a program often accessed the same data, such as a file stored on the disk. This meant that if you wanted to change the way the program accessed specific data, you had to exhaustively search through the entire program and find all the commands that accessed that data. Miss one command and you've just introduced a bug into your program. In case you understand pictures better than text, Figure 30-1 shows the difference between the way an object-oriented program works and a non-object-oriented program works.

So the latest focus in computer science revolves around *object-oriented programming,* often abbreviated as OOP as in "Oops, you just wasted four years of college studying structured programming."

The central idea behind object-oriented programming is to divide your program into isolated parts called (what else?) *objects*. Each object contains two parts:

- ✔ Data (called *properties* in Visual Basic)
- ✔ Commands for manipulating that data (called *methods* in Visual Basic)

So when your program wants to access data, your program just gives a command to the object that contains that data. Your main program never directly accesses the data but just gives commands to the object to access the data.

Figure 30-1: How object-oriented programming can make your programs easier to modify.

Non-object-oriented program	Object-oriented program
Commands for opening a file	[File object]
Commands for displaying a window	Commands for opening a file
Commands for resizing a window	Commands for renaming a file
Commands for renaming a file	Commands for saving a file
Commands for closing a window	[Window object]
Commands for saving a file	Commands for displaying a window
	Commands for resizing a window
	Commands for closing a window
BASIC commands can be stored anywhere throughout a program, making it difficult to know where to look first.	BASIC commands are isolated in objects, which are easy to locate and then modify.

If you ever need to change the way your program accesses specific data, you just have to modify the commands inside that object instead of modifying commands throughout your entire program. In this way, object-oriented programming helps isolate the commands that affect specific data, thereby reducing the chance of introducing new bugs into your program when you need to modify your program.

Object-oriented programming is being credited with making programs easier to write, modify, and reuse. However, object-oriented programming alone won't make your program useful or bug-free in any way. A poor programmer using object-oriented programming will still be less efficient than a great programmer who doesn't use object-oriented programming. Don't let the hype about object-oriented programming fool you into thinking your programs will run faster, work better, or sell more copies just because you used object-oriented programming.

Theoretical Stuff about Class Modules

Now that you have a general idea how objects work, you may be curious how objects work in Visual Basic. To create an object in Visual Basic, you have to create something called a *class module,* which has a file extension of .CLS, such as NOCLASS.CLS.

The class module defines

- ✔ The type of data the object can hold (but not any actual data itself)
- ✔ BASIC commands (the *methods*) for manipulating the data in that object

The types of data defined by an object is called the *properties* of an object. The BASIC commands that manipulate the data in an object are called the *methods* of an object. If the terms *properties* and *methods* don't seem to clarify anything, don't worry; you're not the only one who feels that way.

A class module acts like a cookie cutter because this type of module defines the object but doesn't contain any data itself, much like a cookie cutter defines the shape of a cookie but doesn't contain any cookie dough itself.

A typical class module, as shown below, consists of three parts:

- ✔ Variable declarations
- ✔ Property declarations
- ✔ Methods, which are BASIC commands, stored in procedures, that manipulate variables and properties

In the example class module code below, the variable declaration is the line `Private mvarMessage As String`.

The first property declaration begins with the line `Public Property Let Message (ByVal vData As String)` and the second property declaration begins with the line `Public Property Get Message() As String`.

The method begins with the line `Public Sub CorporateSpeak()`.

```
Private mvarMessage As String 'local copy

Public Property Let Message(ByVal vData As String)
  mvarMessage = vData
End Property

Public Property Get Message() As String
  Message = mvarMessage
End Property

Public Sub CorporateSpeak()
  Dim NewString As String, FrontString As String,
          TailString As String
  Dim Location As Integer, PickOne As Integer
NewString = ""
  TailString = ""
  PickOne = CInt((4 * Rnd) + 1)
  Select Case PickOne
    Case 1
      NewString = "manufacture high-quality, customer-
          empowered "
    Case 2
      NewString = "service and deliver world-class "
    Case 3
      NewString = "create product-driven, solution-
          oriented "
    Case Else
      NewString = "customize functional, creatively-
          packaged "
  End Select

  Location = InStr(mvarMessage, "make")
  If Location = 0 Then
    mvarMessage = "You need to type a mission statement
          that uses the word 'make' in it."""
```

```
    Else
       FrontString = Left(mvarMessage, Location - 1)
       TailString = Right(mvarMessage, Len(mvarMessage) -
              (Location + 4))
       mvarMessage = FrontString & NewString & TailString
    End If
End Sub
```

Declaring your variables

Declaring all variables used by your class at the beginning of your class is a good idea, just so you know what type of information your class is using. If you want to declare a variable that any part of your program can use to store or retrieve information, you can declare a public variable, such as:

```
Public MoneyStolen As Currency
```

If you declare a public variable, any part of your program (including other objects) can put data into the variable, which means debugging your program can be extremely difficult. In general, don't declare a public variable unless you have a really good reason to do so.

If you want to declare a variable that only your class needs to use, you can declare a private variable, such as:

```
Private Counter As Integer
```

Defining an object's properties

As far as the rest of your Visual Basic program is concerned, two types of properties exist:

✔ Properties that the program can assign a value to

✔ Properties that the program can retrieve a value from

For example, if you have a property called Direction and you want to assign a value to this property, you have to declare the Direction property in its class by using a property definition like this:

```
Private mWay As Integer
Property Let Direction(ByVal WhichWay As Integer)
   mWay = WhichWay
End Property
```

Visual Basic interprets the above code as follows:

1. The first line defines a private variable, called mWay, that can hold an integer value.

2. The second line tells Visual Basic, "Let another part of the program assign an integer value to the mWay private variable." To assign a value to an object's property, you use code such as the following:

```
Set m_Object = New cObject
m_Object.Direction = 5
```

These two lines of code tell Visual Basic to create an object using the Set and New keywords (you can find out more about these keywords, later in this chapter, in the section "Creating an object"), and then assign a value to the object's properties just like you assign a property to a text box or a label on a form.

3. The third line tells Visual Basic, "Whatever integer value gets assigned to the Direction property, store that value in the mWay private variable."

4. The fourth line tells Visual Basic, "This is the end of the property definition that lets another part of the program assign a value to a property."

To yank out information trapped in an object's property, you have to declare the Direction property in its class by using a property definition like this:

```
Property Get Direction() As Integer
    Direction = mWay
End Property
```

Visual Basic interprets the above code as follows:

1. The first line tells Visual Basic, "The Direction property of this object can only hold integer values."

2. The second line tells Visual Basic, "Assign the integer value stored in the mWay private variable to the Direction property."

3. The third line tells Visual Basic, "This is the end of the property definition so another part of your program can get a value from the property."

To actually yank out information stored in an object's property, you can use BASIC code, such as the following:

```
txtDirection.Text = CStr (mObject.Direction)
```

Note the subtle differences between the two property definitions. To allow another part of your program to define a value for an object's property, you need to

✔ Use the magical `Let` keyword.

✔ Define a variable and its data type in parentheses, such as `(WhichWay As Integer)`.

✔ Assign a private variable (declared earlier in the class module) to equal the value of the variable identified in parentheses, such as `mWay = WhichWay`.

To allow another part of your program to retrieve (or `Get`) a value from an object's property, you need to

✔ Use the magical `Get` keyword and assign a data type to the property such as an integer.

✔ Leave the parentheses empty, such as `()`.

✔ Assign the actual property name (such as `Direction`) to a private variable, such as `Direction = mWay`.

You need to use the `Property Let` and `Property Get` statements for each of your object's properties.

Writing an object's methods

After you declare any variables your object may need and define your object's properties, the next step is to write methods (procedures or functions) that do something with the data stored inside of your object.

Writing a procedure or function is fairly straightforward (for more information check out Chapters 27, 28, and 29). The main difference is that instead of using the `Private` keyword in front of your procedure or function declarations, you use the `Public` keyword such as:

```
Public Sub Move ()
  ' Some useful BASIC code goes here
End Sub
```

```
Public Function XLocation () As Integer
  ' Some useful BASIC code goes here
End Function
```

When you want to call an object's methods, you just use the object's name plus the object's method such as:

```
m_Object.Move
```

The above code tells Visual Basic, "Find an object called m_Object and call the procedure named Move." As far as your main program is concerned, the program has no idea how the Move procedure works.

Designing a class on paper

While you could rush right into writing the BASIC code that makes up a class module, you should take some time to design your class module first. What's the best way to design a class module? None. (Now aren't you glad you bought a book that told you that?)

Actually, the optimum design for a class module depends on how you plan to use the class module. The optimum design of a class module for one program may be horrible for another type of a program. To give you some pointers in designing classes, consider the following tips:

✔ To determine a class module's properties, decide the basic building block of data your program needs to manipulate. If you're writing a program to store information about employees, your class module needs to include properties that contain names, addresses, phone numbers, IQs, or felony records. If you're writing a video game where cartoon aliens pop up on the screen so you can shoot them, your class module may contain the X- and Y-coordinates of your cartoon alien's position on the screen.

✔ To determine a class module's methods, decide what your main Visual Basic program needs to do with the information stored in your class module. For example, a class module containing employee names and addresses may need methods that allow the main program to search, sort, and print employee data. Likewise, a class module containing cartoon alien X- and Y-coordinates may need methods that allow the main program to move, display, and blow up the alien.

✔ After you sketch out the type of properties and methods your class module needs to include, then you're ready to create an actual class module.

Creating a Class Module with the VB Class Builder

Because creating classes can be messy if you don't know what you're doing, Visual Basic provides a handy program called the VB Class Builder. Essentially, the VB Class Builder lets you define your class methods and properties, and then the VB Class Builder writes the BASIC code for you.

Of course, if you like doing things the hard way, you can still create class modules from scratch, but at least with the VB Class Builder, you don't have to if you don't want to waste your time.

 Rather than rush right into creating a class module, you should design your object's properties and methods on paper first. Only after you're satisfied that you've designed your objects correctly should you rush into creating a class module.

Creating a new class

You need to create a separate class module for every different object you want to use in your program. To create a class module (or to edit an existing class module), follow these steps:

1. **Choose Project➪Add Class Module.**

   An Add Class Module dialog box appears, as shown in Figure 30-2.

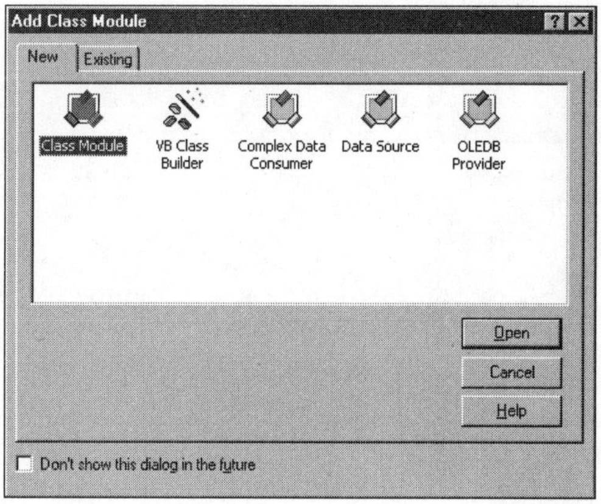

Figure 30-2:
The Add
Class
Module
dialog box
for creating
a class.

2. **Click on the VB Class Builder icon and click on Open.**

   The Class Builder window appears, as shown in Figure 30-3.

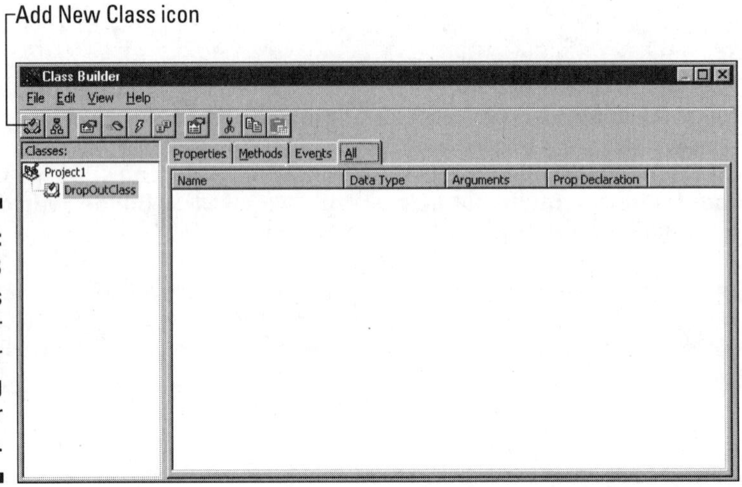

Add New Class icon

Figure 30-3:
The VB
Class
Builder
window for
creating
your
classes.

3. **Choose File⇨New⇨Class or click on the Add New Class icon on the toolbar.**

   A Class Module Builder dialog box appears, as shown in Figure 30-4. (If you just want to edit an existing class module, skip Steps 3 and 4, and just click on the class name that appears in the class window.)

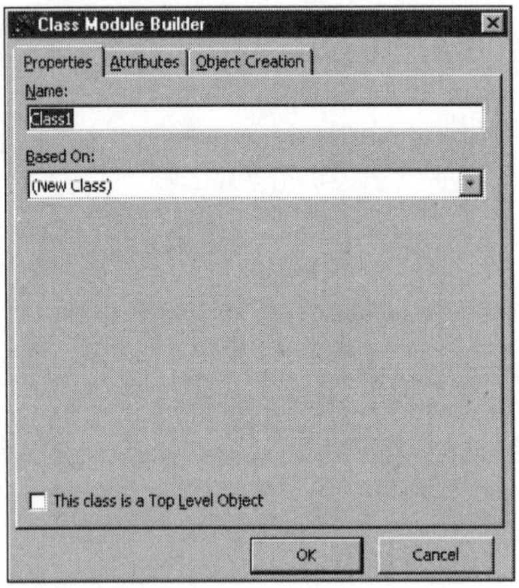

Figure 30-4:
The Class
Module
Builder
dialog box
for giving
your class a
name.

4. **Type a name for your class in the Name text box and click on OK.**

   If you don't choose a name, Visual Basic names your class something dull and generic like Class1.

The above steps only let you create and name a class module, but you still need to define properties and methods inside your class.

Creating properties for your classes

To define the properties for a class module, follow these steps (assuming that the VB Class Builder window is already displayed):

1. **Click on the class module where you want to define your properties.**

2. **Choose File⇨New⇨Property or click on the Add New Property to Current Class.**

   The Property Builder dialog box appears, as shown in Figure 30-5.

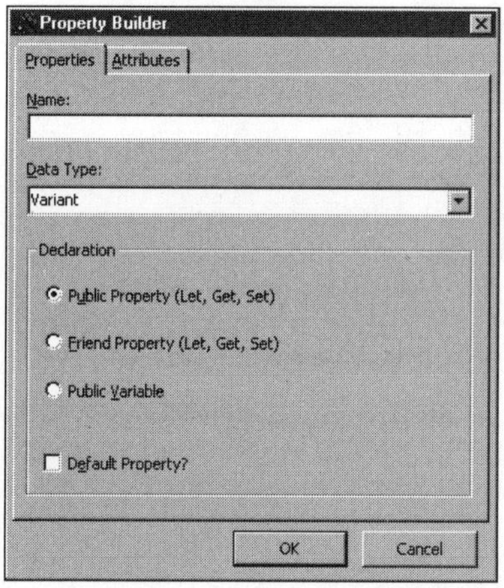

Figure 30-5:
The
Property
Builder
dialog box
for defining
an object's
properties.

3. **Type the name for your property in the Name text box.**

4. **Click on the downward-pointing arrow in the Data Type list box and choose a data type (such as Integer or Single) for your property.**

5. **Click on OK.**

Creating methods for your classes

To define the methods for a class module, follow these steps (assuming that the VB Class Builder window is already displayed):

1. **Click on the class module where you want to define your methods.**

2. **Choose File⇨New⇨Method or click on the Add New Method to Current Class.**

   The Method Builder dialog box appears, as shown in Figure 30-6.

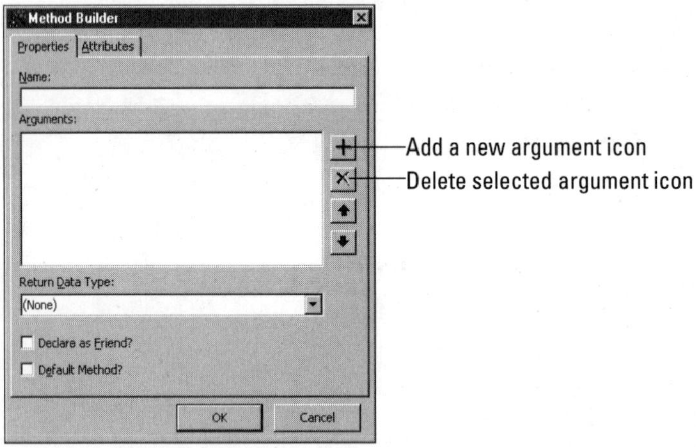

Figure 30-6:
The Method Builder dialog box for defining an object's methods.

3. **Type the name for your method in the Name text box.**

4. **Click on the Add a new argument icon (the plus sign), if your methods need arguments.**

   An Add Argument dialog box appears, as shown in Figure 30-7.

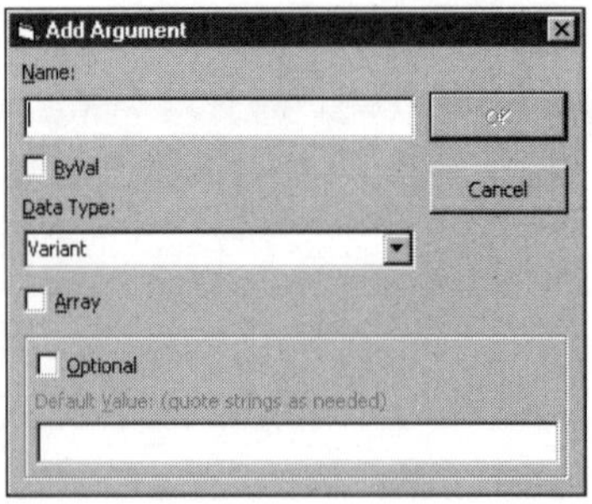

Figure 30-7:
The Add Argument dialog box.

5. **Type a name for your argument in the Name text box.**

6. **Click on a data type (such as Integer or Currency) in the Data Type list box.**

7. **Click on OK.**

8. **Click on the downward-pointing arrow in the Return Data Type list box and choose a data type.**

   (Skip this step if you don't want the method to return a value.)

9. **Click on OK.**

Quitting the VB Class Builder

When you're done creating or editing your class modules, you can get rid of the VB Class Builder window by one of these methods:

- Click on the close box of the VB Class Builder window
- Choose File➪Exit

If a dialog box appears, asking if you want to update your Visual Basic project, click on Yes. After the VB Class Builder window goes away, you can click on your newly created class module and view the BASIC code that Visual Basic kindly created for you automatically.

After you use the VB Class Builder to create a class module, you must still write code inside your class module to make it do something useful. Then you must write code in your main program to use the class module.

Using a Class Module in a Visual Basic Program

After going through all this trouble creating a class module, you still have to write BASIC code in your main program to actually use the program. Before you can use an object, you have to create one. After you create an object, then you can use that object's methods or store or retrieve information in that object's properties.

Creating an object

Even though you may have gone through the trouble of creating and defining your class module, you still have to create an object based on the design of your class module. In the world of object-oriented programming, creating an object is called creating an *instance*. (Once again, you can see that computer scientists are no better at choosing self-explanatory terms than other experts are in their fields.)

To create an instance of an object, you have to create an object to represent your class module using the Set and New keywords such as:

```
Set ObjectName = New ClassName
```

This is how Visual Basic interprets this single line of code:

1. The Set keyword tells Visual Basic, "Get ready to create an object."

2. The ObjectName variable is the name of your object.

3. The New keyword tells Visual Basic, "Create a new object based on the class module defined by ClassName."

Using an object

After you create an object, the final step is to use that object to

- ✔ Stuff a value into an object's property
- ✔ Retrieve a value out from an object's property
- ✔ Use an object's method to do something with the object's data

To stuff a value into an object's property, you just have to use the following code:

```
ObjectName.Property = Value
```

To retrieve a value out from an object's property, you have to use the following code:

```
Variable = ObjectName.Property
```

To use an object's method, you can use the following code:

```
ObjectName.Method
```

Try Class Modules Yourself

Naturally the best way to understand anything is to do what you don't understand yourself, so in case this entire chapter doesn't make a whole lot of sense, try the following program. This sample program demonstrates how a main program can create an object from a class module, call an object's method to manipulate the data, and then retrieve the data afterwards.

In this particular program, type your company's mission statement in the top text box, making sure that this mission statement includes the word "make," such as "We make cars." Then this program substitutes the word "make" for a more acceptable corporate term that makes no sense such as "manufacture high-quality, customer-empowered."

This program is stored on the CD-ROM so you don't have to type it all in if you don't want to. Just load the MISSION.VBP file.

If you get nothing else out of this chapter, just remember that object-oriented programming is supposed to help you organize your programs so that you have fewer chances of introducing bugs into any programs that you write or modify.

Object	Property	Setting
Form	Caption	Mission Statement Maker
	Height	3600
	Left	0
	Top	0
	Width	4800
Text1	Height	615
	Left	480
	MultiLine	True
	Name	txtInput
	TabIndex	0
	Text	(Empty)
	Top	360
	Width	3850
Text2	Height	615
	Left	480

(continued)

(continued)

Object	Property	Setting
	MultiLine	True
	Name	txtOutput
	Text	(Empty)
	Top	1440
	Width	3850
Command1	Caption	&Create
	Height	495
	Left	600
	Name	cmdCreate
	Top	2400
	Width	1575
Command2	Caption	E&xit
	Height	495
	Left	2640
	Name	cmdExit
	Top	2400
	Width	1575

Double-click on the two command buttons on the form and create the
following event procedures:

```
Private Sub cmdCreate_Click()
   Set DoubleSpeak = New CorporateTalk
   DoubleSpeak.Message = txtInput.Text
   DoubleSpeak.CorporateSpeak
   txtOutput.Text = DoubleSpeak.Message
End Sub

Private Sub cmdExit_Click()
   Unload Me
End Sub
```

Create a separate class module, give this module a name of CorporateTalk,
create a property named Message, and create a method named
CorporateSpeak. You will need to type code in the CorporateSpeak
method:

```
Private mvarMessage As String 'local copy

Public Property Let Message(ByVal vData As String)
  mvarMessage = vData
End Property

Public Property Get Message() As String
  Message = mvarMessage
End Property

Public Sub CorporateSpeak()
  Dim NewString As String, FrontString As String,
          TailString As String
  Dim Location As Integer, PickOne As Integer
  NewString = ""
  TailString = ""
  PickOne = CInt((4 * Rnd) + 1)
  Select Case PickOne
    Case 1
      NewString = "manufacture high-quality, customer-
          empowered "
    Case 2
      NewString = "service and deliver world-class "
    Case 3
      NewString = "create product-driven, solution-oriented
          "
    Case Else
      NewString = "customize functional, creatively-
          packaged "
  End Select

  Location = InStr(mvarMessage, "make")
  If Location = 0 Then
    mvarMessage = "You need to type a mission statement
          that uses the word 'make' in it."""
  Else
    FrontString = Left(mvarMessage, Location - 1)
    TailString = Right(mvarMessage, Len(mvarMessage) -
          (Location + 4))
    mvarMessage = FrontString & NewString & TailString
  End If
End Sub
```

Chapter 31

Managing Files

● ●

In This Chapter

▶ Determining how Visual Basic stores a program

▶ Playing with the Project Explorer window

▶ Adding Form, Module, and Class files

▶ Plugging ActiveX controls into your programs

● ●

*I*n the old days, a single program consisted of a single file. You just had to modify that one file and you could modify the entire program. But as programs have gotten more complicated, they now consist of two or more files that make up a single program. This chapter explains how Visual Basic manages these multiple files so you can keep track of them all.

How Visual Basic Stores a Program

When you use a word processor, you can type one sentence or 3,000 pages and your word processor can store all your text in a single file. However, when you use Visual Basic, Visual Basic always (yes, always) saves your program as two or more separate files. Table 31-1 lists the most common types of Visual Basic files you may see, along with their identifying three-letter file extension.

Table 31-1   Typical Visual Basic Files and Their File Extensions

File Type	Three-Letter File Extension	Sample File Name
Project file	.VBP	VIRUS.VBP
Form file	.FRM	MAINMENU.FRM
Module file	.BAS	LIBRARY.BAS
ActiveX control	.OCX	RICHTX32.OCX
Class file	.CLS	OBJECTS.CLS

Every Visual Basic program must contain exactly one Project (.VBP) file. The *Project file* lists all the separate files (Form files, Module files, ActiveX controls, and Class files) that make up a single Visual Basic program.

A *Form file* contains one window that makes up the user interface of your program along with the BASIC code that tells any button (check boxes and so on) on the window how to work. Most Visual Basic programs consist of one or more Form (.FRM) files.

A *Module file* contains BASIC code that performs some sort of calculation independent of the user interface. Visual Basic programs can contain zero or more Module (.BAS) files.

An *ActiveX control* is a miniature program that you can plug into your own program to add features. Some popular ActiveX controls let you quickly add word processing, charting, or spreadsheet features to your Visual Basic programs. You can buy ActiveX controls or write your own. A Visual Basic program may contain zero or more ActiveX (.OCX) controls.

A *Class file* contains BASIC code that defines different classes used by your Visual Basic program. A Class is simply a funny way to organize data that your program uses. (For more information about classes, see Chapter 30.) A Visual Basic program may contain zero or more Class (.CLS) files.

You can store your Project file in one folder and your other files (Form, Module, Class, or ActiveX files) in entirely different folders. However, if you don't store all files for a single program in the same folder, you may have difficulty modifying your program later if you can't find all the files that make up your program.

VBP Project Files

A *VBP project file* contains a list of all the FRM, BAS, CLS, and OCX custom control files that make up a single Visual Basic program. The Project Explorer window shows you all the files stored in a VBP project file, as shown in Figure 31-1.

To help organize your files, the Project Explorer window displays them as if they were stored within separate folders, such as

   ✔ Forms

   ✔ Modules

   ✔ Class Modules

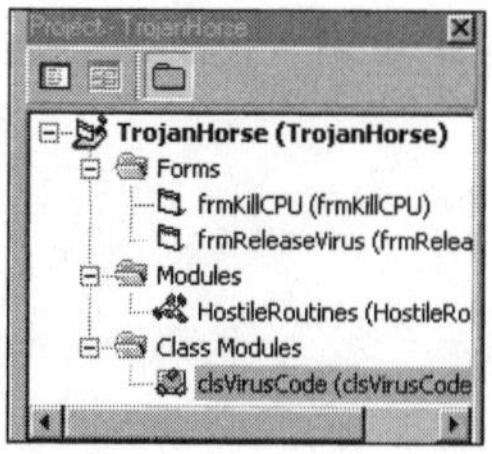

Figure 31-1:
The Project
Explorer
window
displays a
list of files
that make
up a single
Visual
Basic
program.

The Project Explorer window does not list all the ActiveX controls that your Visual Basic program uses. To see a list of ActiveX controls that a program uses, press Ctrl+T.

If you don't want to see all the files within a folder, double-click on the folder so that a Plus Sign icon appears to the left. Then, when you want to see a list of your files within a particular folder, double-click on that folder to display all the files again.

To create a new VBP project file, follow these steps:

1. **Choose File➪New Project or press Ctrl+N.**

   Visual Basic displays a New Project dialog box.

2. **Click on the type of program you want to create (such as a Standard EXE or ActiveX DLL) and click on OK.**

To load an existing VBP project file, follow these steps:

1. **Choose File➪Open Project, press Ctrl+O, or click on the Open Project icon.**

   Visual Basic displays an Open Project dialog box.

2. **Type or click on the name of the VBP project file you want to load and then click on Open.**

Whenever you load a VBP project file, Visual Basic automatically loads all the files listed in the VBP project file.

To save your Visual Basic project for all eternity (or until you erase the project from your hard disk), follow these steps:

1. **Choose File⇨Save Project or click on the Save Project icon on the toolbar.**

   If you haven't saved your files (such as FRM form or BAS module files), a Save File As dialog box appears.

2. **Type a name for each of your FRM Form files and click on Save.**

   After you save all your Form files, Visual Basic displays a Save Project As dialog box.

3. **Type a name for your VBP Project file and click on Save.**

Be sure to save your files before you try running your program. A program often has bugs that can crash your computer, which means that if you don't save your program before running it, you are going to lose all (yes, *all*) your changes if the computer crashes.

If you want Visual Basic to save any changes automatically before you run your program, follow these steps:

1. **Choose Tools⇨Options.**

   An Options dialog box appears.

2. **Click on the Environment tab.**

3. **Click on the Save Changes or the Prompt to Save Changes radio button and then click on OK.**

Adding files to a VBP project file

The more Visual Basic programs you write, the more useful certain parts of them are going to be for future programs you may write. Fortunately, Visual Basic makes it easy to take FRM Form, BAS Module, and CLS Class files from another Visual Basic program and add them to a new Visual Basic program.

To add an FRM Form, BAS Module, or CLS Class file to a VBP project file, choose Project and then choose the type of file you want to add, such as Add Form or Add Module.

If you add a Form, Module, or Class file from another Visual Basic program, make sure that you save the file under another name. If two or more Visual Basic programs share the same Form, Module, or Class file, any changes you make to that file will affect every Visual Basic program that uses that particular file.

Removing files from a project file

Sometimes you may want to remove a file permanently from a project file. To remove an FRM file, BAS file, or CLS file from a VBP project file, follow these steps:

1. **Press Ctrl+R; choose View➪Project Explorer; or click on the Project Explorer icon in the toolbar.**

2. **Click on the file (such as a Form, Module, or Class) that you want to remove.**

3. **Choose Project➪Remove.**

You can also right-click on a file in Step 2, and then left-click on the Remove command.

When you remove a file from a project file, the removed file still exists on your floppy or hard disk. Removing a file simply tells Visual Basic, "See that file over there? I don't want *that file* to be part of this particular program anymore, so get rid of it, but keep it saved on disk in case I want it back again." To erase or delete a file from your floppy or hard disk, use the Windows Explorer and erase the file off your floppy or hard disk for good.

Adding (Or Removing) ActiveX Controls

An ActiveX control is a miniature program that you can plug into your Visual Basic programs to give them added features without writing much BASIC code yourself. Because ActiveX controls can help you write a program quickly and easily, many people's Visual Basic programs are nothing more than globs of ActiveX controls that they've connected by using a little bit of BASIC code.

Although Visual Basic comes with several ActiveX controls, you can buy tons of them by mail order or through the Internet. Just be careful that you don't rely too much on ActiveX controls. If a company wrote an ActiveX control that doesn't work properly, then your Visual Basic program isn't going to work properly either.

Whenever you add a custom control to a VBP project file, the icon for that custom control appears in the Visual Basic Toolbox.

To add an ActiveX control to a VBP project file, follow these steps:

1. **Choose Project⇨Components or press Ctrl+T.**

   Visual Basic displays a Components dialog box that lets you add custom controls, as shown in Figure 31-2.

2. **Click in the check box of the ActiveX control that you want to use and then click on OK.**

   Visual Basic displays that custom control's icon in the Visual Basic Toolbox.

After you add an ActiveX control to your program, you still have to draw the ActiveX control on a form and then modify the properties or write BASIC code to make the control do anything.

Believe it or not, you can actually write your own ActiveX controls by using Visual Basic itself. (I explain ActiveX controls in more detail in the latest edition of *MORE Visual Basic For Windows For Dummies*, written by yours truly and also published by IDG Books Worldwide, Inc.) While writing these controls, just keep in mind that if you create a particularly useful feature in your program that you think others may find useful, you can save the feature as an ActiveX control and give or sell copies to other people.

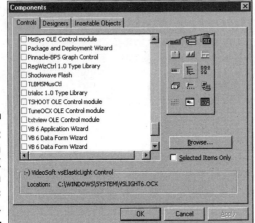

Figure 31-2:
Adding an
ActiveX
control to a
Visual Basic
project.

Part VIII
Database Files and Printing

"WE SHOULD HAVE THIS FIXED IN VERSION 2."

In this part . . .

Most people don't care about knowing how to use a database program, and even fewer people care about all the different file formats in which data may be trapped. So to cater to the majority of people, Visual Basic can cheerfully read, write, and modify information stored inside a variety of database file formats including Microsoft Access, dBASE, Paradox, and FoxPro.

In addition to providing employment for hundreds of computer book authors and publishers, the purpose of most programs is to store information and then print or display the information again. After all, what good would a database be if you had to keep typing names and addresses into your computer every time you turned on your computer? So in this part of the book, you find out all about creating, storing, and printing information for your Visual Basic programs.

Chapter 32
Creating Database Files

· ·

· ·

*I*n case you need to write a program that stores and retrieves organized information such as names and addresses or inventory part numbers and customer phone numbers, you have two choices. You can either write a Visual Basic program along with tons of BASIC code to store, retrieve, and organize information on your hard disk, or you can take the easy way out and just use a database file instead.

By using database files with Visual Basic, you can spend your time designing your user interface without worrying about the details in saving, retrieving, and sorting your data.

You can use one of two existing ways to create a database file. One, you can rush out and spend hundreds of dollars buying a separate database program with a weird name like Microsoft Access, Paradox, or FoxPro. Two, you can just use the Visual Basic special add-in program called the Visual Data Manager. Because this book is about doing things the easy way, this chapter focuses primarily on using the Visual Data Manager. After all, the program comes free with Visual Basic.

Databases For Dummies or (What the Heck Is a Database?)

Basically, a *database file* is nothing more than a special file designed to hold organized information. Just as a word processor file contains sentences and paragraphs, a database file contains information such as names, addresses, phone numbers, Social Security numbers, shoe sizes, secret passwords to sell to foreign agencies, and so on.

Typically a database file consists of the following parts, as shown in Figure 32-1.

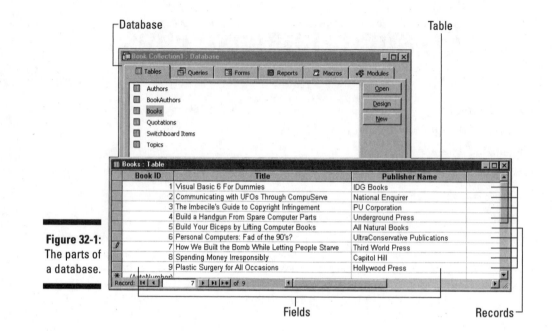

Database

Table

Figure 32-1:
The parts of
a database.

Fields

Records

✔ One or more tables

✔ Records

✔ Fields

The *database* is (usually) a single file that contains all your information.

Tables let you organize the information stored within a database. For example, rather than toss names and addresses into a database like throwing clothes in a hamper, tables let you store one set of names and addresses as Customers and another set of names and addresses as Suppliers, Mailing List, Hot Dates, or any other type of classification you can dream up. Every database must have at least one table.

Each table consists of one or more *records,* where a single record contains all the information about a single item such as a person's name, address, and phone number. In the real world, a person's business card is a record.

Each record consists of one or more *fields,* where a field contains a single bit of information such as a name, address, hat size, or marital status.

Organizing the Structure of a Database

Now that you have a general idea about the purpose of each part of a database file, you still need to decide exactly how you want to organize your information. Before creating a database, ask yourself, "What type of information do I need for the future?"

For example, if you're creating a database of business contacts, you may want to store names, phone numbers, e-mail addresses, and fax numbers. If you're creating an inventory list, you may want to store part numbers, part names, quantities left in stock, and the price per item.

After you decide what type of information you want to save, the next step is to create field names to identify each bit of information. Fields have two purposes in life:

✔ To store a chunk of information

✔ To provide a way to sort and search through a database

For example, if you want to store the name "John Doe," you can store the name by using one of the following two methods:

Method	Field Name	Actual Data
#1	Name	John Doe
#2	First Name	John
	Last Name	Doe

The first method stores a person's name as one complete chunk of information, which means that you can't search your database by first or last name.

The second method stores a person's name in two chunks of information, which can be more annoying to type in but allows you to search the database later by first or last name.

Neither method is right or wrong. The method you choose to use all depends on how you want to use your data. After you list all the fields in which you want to store your information, the next step is to decide if you want to divide your database into tables (categories). For example, if you're storing business cards, you may want to organize them according to Personal Contacts, Business Contacts, Contacts Who Owe Me a Favor, and so on. Figure 32-2 shows a typical database design.

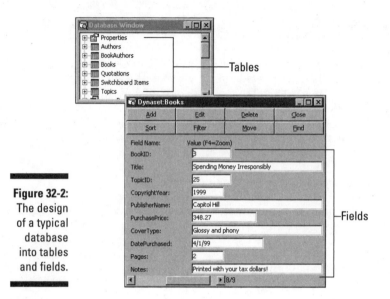

Figure 32-2:
The design
of a typical
database
into tables
and fields.

You don't have to divide your database into two or more tables. A database can consist of just one table if that's what you need.

Creating a Database File

After you design the structure of your database on paper, you can finally start designing your database on your computer. Although you can use a separate database program for this task (such as Microsoft Access or dBase), you may just want to use the Visual Basic add-in program called the Visual Data Manager.

Running the Visual Data Manager

To run the Visual Data Manager program, follow these steps:

1. **Load Visual Basic.**

2. **Choose Add-Ins⇨Visual Data Manager.**

   The Visual Data Manager window appears.

3. **Choose File⇨New.**

   A list of database file formats such as Microsoft Access, Paradox, and FoxPro appears.

4. **Choose <u>M</u>icrosoft Access➪Version <u>7</u>.0 MDB.**

   (Unless you need to create database files in another format because everyone else you know uses Paradox or FoxPro database files, use a Microsoft Access 7.0 database.) A dialog box appears.

5. **Type the name of your database file and click on <u>S</u>ave.**

   The Visual Data manager displays a Database Window.

6. **Point the mouse cursor on the Properties icon in the Database Window and click on the right mouse button.**

   A pop-up menu appears.

7. **Click on New <u>T</u>able.**

   The Table Structure dialog box appears.

8. **Type a name for your database table in the Table <u>N</u>ame text box.**

9. **Click on the <u>A</u>dd Field button.**

   An Add Field dialog box appears.

10. **Type the name of your field in the Name box, such as First Name, Employee ID, or Age.**

11. **Use the pull-down Type list box to choose the type of data you want to store in your field (such as Text, Currency, or Date/Time) and type the size of the data in the Size field); and then click on OK.**

12. **Repeat Steps 10 and 11 for each field you want to add, and then click on <u>C</u>lose when you finish.**

13. **Click on the <u>B</u>uild the Table button.**

    The Database Window displays your table as an icon.

After you create a table, you can always edit it later. To do so, simply point the mouse cursor over the Table icon in the Database Window, click the right mouse button, and choose Design.

Stuffing information into your database

After you create a database file, one or more tables, and one or more fields in each table to hold your information, you eventually need to stuff your database full of information such as people's names, phone numbers, or employee ID numbers.

You don't have to stuff a database with information. You may want to leave your database empty so someone using your Visual Basic program can stuff her own information into the database.

To stuff information into a database by using the Visual Data Manager program, make sure that the Visual Data Manager program is running and follow these steps:

1. **Move the mouse cursor over the Table icon in the Database Window, click with the right mouse button, and choose Open.**

   A dialog box appears.

2. **Click on Add.**

3. **Type the information you want to appear in each field.**

4. **Click on Update when you finish.**

5. **Click on Close.**

Exiting the Visual Data Manager

To exit the Visual Data Manager program, just choose File⇨Exit.

The Visual Data Manager is a simple program for creating databases. If you really need to create complicated databases, you are better off buying a separate copy of Microsoft Access and using that program to create your database files.

Chapter 33

Using Files from Database Programs You'd Rather Not Use

● ●

In This Chapter
▶ Connecting to a database file
▶ Displaying different records
▶ Searching for specific records

● ●

*I*f you're planning to store a great deal of data, you may as well store the data in a database file. Visual Basic can store and retrieve data in any one of the following four database formats:

- ✔ Microsoft Access MDB files
- ✔ Borland dBASE DBF files
- ✔ Microsoft FoxPro DBF files
- ✔ Borland Paradox DB files

If you have no clue as to what any of these files or databases are, consider yourself lucky.

Visual Basic comes with a separate program called the Visual Data Manager (see Chapter 32 for more information), which lets you create Microsoft Access database (MDB) files without shelling out the money to buy a real copy of Microsoft Access. If you want to create really sophisticated data-bases, you are better off buying a separate copy of that database program, such as dBASE, Microsoft Access, or Paradox.

What Are Database Files?

Whenever one of those fancy database programs such as Paradox, Access, or dBASE saves information, that program stores the information in a disk file. Because the disk file contains a bunch of data that somebody thinks is important, the file is called a *database file*. Essentially, a database file is like a Rolodex jammed with junk.

To organize the data in the file, a database file is made up of one or more records. A *record* is like a 3-x-5 index card. Each record contains fields, which contain the specific information (names, addresses, and stuff like that). Figure 33-1 shows an example of a record.

Figure 33-1:
A typical database record.

To organize this information further, database files let you organize data into tables. A table is a subset of your entire database. The table contains only specific information, such as the names of all the people who live in Oregon or the phone numbers of everyone you can't stand.

How to Connect to a Database File

When you want a Visual Basic program to store and retrieve information in a database file, you have to specify the following:

- ✔ Which database file to use
- ✔ Which recordset type to use

> ✔ Which database table to use
>
> ✔ Which database fields to display

Connecting to a database manually

To connect your program to a database file, follow these steps:

1. **Make sure that the database file to which you want to connect exists.**

   If not, you need to create the file by using a database program (such as Paradox or FoxPro) or the Visual Data Manager program.

2. **Click on the Data Control icon from the Visual Basic Toolbox and draw the data control on your form.**

   Figure 33-2 shows the Data Control icon on the Toolbox and drawn on a form. For more about how to use a data control, check out the section "Manipulating Different Records," later in this chapter.

3. **Open the Properties window. (Press F4; choose View⇨Properties Window; or click on the Properties Window icon on the toolbar.)**

4. **Double-click on the DatabaseName property.**

   Visual Basic displays the DatabaseName dialog box.

5. **Select the database file that you want to use, such as BIBLIO.MDB (which is the sample database that comes with Visual Basic) and click on Open.**

6. **Click on the Recordset Type property and click on the gray down-arrow button in the settings box.**

   Visual Basic displays a list of recordset types to choose from:

   > 0 - Table
   >
   > 1 - Dynaset
   >
   > 2 - Snapshot

7. **Click on a recordset type, such as 0 - Table.**

8. **Click the RecordSource property and click on the gray down-arrow button in the settings box.**

   Visual Basic displays a list of database tables you can choose from.

9. **Click on a database table (such as Titles, if you choose the BIBLIO sample database that comes with Visual Basic).**

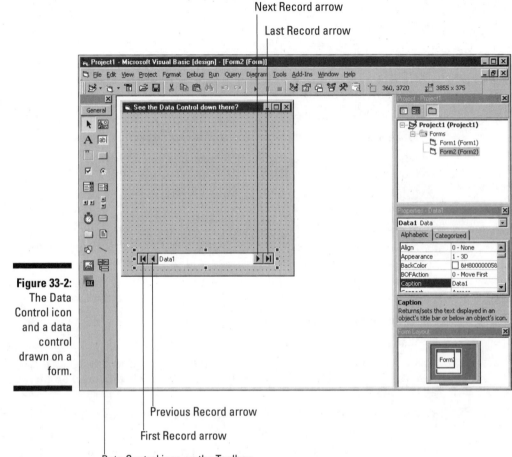

Next Record arrow

Last Record arrow

Previous Record arrow

First Record arrow

Data Control icon on the Toolbox

Figure 33-2:
The Data
Control icon
and a data
control
drawn on a
form.

If you're using Microsoft Access MDB files, choose the 0 - Table recordset type in Step 7. If you're using any other type of database, choose the 1 - Dynaset recordset type. If you need to read but not update data, go ahead and choose the 2 - Snapshot recordset type.

Connecting to a database using the VB Data Form Wizard

In case you'd rather not do everything the hard way, Visual Basic offers a VB Data Form Wizard, which can create a new form specifically for displaying data in your Visual Basic project.

To accept default settings for your data form, you can click the Finish button any time during the following steps.

To use the VB Data Form Wizard, follow these steps:

1. **Choose Project➪Add Form.**

   An Add Form dialog box appears.

2. **Click on the VB Data Form Wizard icon and click on Open.**

   The Data Form Wizard - Introduction dialog box appears, as shown in Figure 33-3. If you have created a form that you want to base your new form on, click on the down arrow in the list box to choose a profile to use.

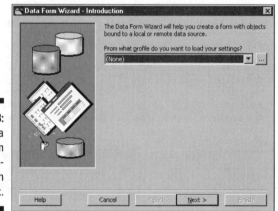

Figure 33-3:
The Data
Form
Wizard -
Introduction
dialog box.

3. **Click on Next >.**

   The Data Form Wizard - Database Type dialog box appears.

4. **Click on a database format (such as Access) and click on Next >.**

   The Data Form Wizard - Database dialog box appears.

5. **Click on the Browse button.**

   An Access Database dialog box appears.

6. **Click on the database file you want to use, click on Open, and click on Next >.**

   The Data Form Wizard - Form dialog box appears, as shown in Figure 33-4.

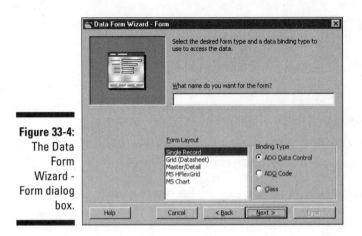

Figure 33-4:
The Data
Form
Wizard -
Form dialog
box.

7. **Type a name for your form and click on one of the following:**

   • **Single record:** Creates a form that displays one record at a time.

   • **Grid (Datasheet):** Creates a form that displays data in a spreadsheet (grid) format.

   • **Master/Detail:** Creates a Master record form that displays data in a single record format and a Detail record source in a spreadsheet (grid) format.

   • **MS HFlexGrid:** Creates a form that displays data in a spreadsheet (grid) format that merges and consolidates data by pivoting rows or columns.

   • **MS Chart:** Creates a form that displays your data as a chart.

8. **Click on Next >.**

   The Data Form Wizard - Record Source dialog box appears, as shown in Figure 33-5.

9. **Click on the downward-pointing arrow in the Record Source list box and choose the record you want to display.**

10. **Click on a field displayed in the Available Fields list box and click on the > button for each field you want to display on your form. Click on Next > when you're done.**

    The Data Form Wizard - Control Selection dialog box appears, as shown in Figure 33-6.

11. **Click in the check boxes for each type of button you want displayed on your form (such as an Add or Delete button), and then click Next >.**

    The Data Form Wizard - Finished! dialog box appears, as shown in Figure 33-7.

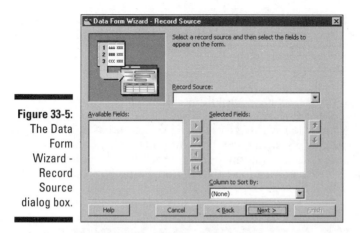

Figure 33-5:
The Data
Form
Wizard -
Record
Source
dialog box.

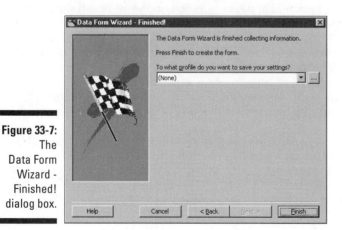

Figure 33-6:
The Data
Form
Wizard -
Control
Selection
dialog box.

Figure 33-7:
The
Data Form
Wizard -
Finished!
dialog box.

12. **Click on the three black dots to the right of the down arrow if you want to save your form as a profile for future use. Click Finish.**

    Visual Basic makes up your form.

13. **Click on OK.**

    Your form appears, ready for your editing or modifications.

 If you use the VB Application Wizard to create a skeleton program for you, you can create a form for displaying database information. By creating a program that displays database information with the VB Application Wizard, you don't have to go back later and use the VB Data Form Wizard.

Displaying Data Fields on the Screen

After you connect your program to a database file, the next step is to display the information stored in the fields of the database. (If you use the VB Data Form Wizard to create a form to display your data, you can edit your form and add or delete additional data fields.) Visual Basic gives you several ways to display database fields on a form:

- ✔ Check boxes
- ✔ Image and Picture boxes
- ✔ Labels and Text boxes
- ✔ List and Combo boxes
- ✔ Grids

Check boxes display Yes and No or True and False values. If a field has a Yes or True value, the check box appears selected on the screen. If the field has a No or False value, the check box appears blank.

Image and picture boxes enable you to display graphics, as long as the database file itself contains graphics.

Text boxes and labels display information such as names, addresses, phone numbers, and quantities.

List and combo boxes enable you to display multiple choices. The combo box gives users a chance to type in something that's not included in the combo box's list.

Grids let you display entire records as rows in a spreadsheet format.

Use a text box if you want to give the user the ability to change the displayed data. Use a label when you want to prevent a user from changing data.

To create a text box, label, check box, image box, combo box, list box, grid, or picture box to display a database field, make sure that you draw at least one data control on the form and then follow these steps:

1. **Draw the text box, label, check box, image box, combo box, list box, grid, or picture box on the form that contains the data control.**

2. **Open the Properties window. (Press F4; choose <u>V</u>iew⇨Properties <u>W</u>indow; or click on the Properties Window icon on the toolbar.)**

3. **Click on the DataSource property and click on the gray down-arrow button in the settings box.**

   Visual Basic lists the names of all the data controls on the form.

4. **Select a data control name (such as Data1).**

5. **Click on the DataField property and click on the gray down-arrow button in the settings box.**

   Visual Basic lists all the field names you can display. (Skip this step if you drew a grid in Step 1.)

6. **Click on a field name.**

When selecting a field name for a check box, make sure that the database field contains only Yes/No or True/False values. When selecting a field name for an image or a picture box, make sure that the database field contains only graphic images. Otherwise, Visual Basic becomes confused and won't know how to handle this data when your program is running.

Manipulating Different Records

When Visual Basic loads a database, Visual Basic makes the first record of the database the current record. Any commands you issue affect only that first database record.

Choosing different records is like thumbing through a library card catalog. (For those younger people who have never seen a library card catalog, think of thumbing through a CD music collection in a music store.)

Visual Basic provides two ways to make a different record the current record:

✔ Using the data control object
✔ Using BASIC code

Using the data control object to display the records in a database

The *data control object* has four arrows that let the user scroll through different records. Figure 33-2 shows these arrows.

The data control object is designed to look like the controls on a tape cassette or VCR. (Then again, how many people know how to program their VCR?)

The arrows on the far left and far right move to the first and last database record. The other two arrows move forward or backward, one record at a time.

The data control object lets a user choose a record. Just make sure that you have a text box or label on the screen to display the data from the current record. If you don't, the user is going to have no idea which record is current and is not going to be able to see or edit the data either.

Using BASIC code to display the records in a database

To display the *first record* by using BASIC code, issue the following command:

```
Data1.Recordset.MoveFirst
```

In all these commands, Data1 refers to the name of your data control object. If you change the name of the data control, you have to use your new name instead.

To display the *last record* in the database, use the following command:

```
Data1.Recordset.MoveLast
```

To display the *next record* in the database, use the command that follows:

```
Data1.Recordset.MoveNext
```

To display the *previous record* in the database, use the following command:

```
Data1.Recordset.MovePrevious
```

Adding a record

To add a record to a database, follow these steps:

1. **Create a new record, using the following code:**

```
Data1.Recordset.AddNew
```

2. **Put data in the fields of this newly created record by using the following code:**

```
Data1.Recordset.Fields("FieldName") = "NewData"
```

FieldName is the specific field you want to change in your database, and yes, you need the quotation marks surrounding the field name. *NewData* is the new information you want to store in the field, and can be a string or a number. If the information is a string, you need to place quotation marks around the information. If the information is a number, you don't need the quotation marks.

3. **Save the record to the database with the following code:**

```
Data1.Recordset.Update
```

Visual Basic always adds new records to the end of a database file.

Editing a record

To edit an existing record in a database, follow these steps:

1. **Display the record that you want to edit.**

2. **Use the following command to tell Visual Basic that you want to edit this record:**

```
Data1.Recordset.Edit
```

3. **Assign the new data to the specific field whose contents you want to change:**

```
Data1.Recordset.Fields("FieldName") = "NewData"
```

4. **Save the record to the database:**

```
Data1.Recordset.Update
```

Deleting a record

To delete a record from a database, find the record that you want to obliterate from the face of the earth and then use the following two BASIC commands:

```
Data1.Recordset.Delete
Data1.Recordset.MoveNext
```

This command says, "See the currently displayed record? Delete this record now and then display the next record so that the deleted record is no longer visible."

Counting the number of existing records

Sometimes knowing how many records a database file contains is handy. To calculate this value, use the commands that follow:

```
Dim TotalRecords As Long
Data1.Recordset.MoveLast
TotalRecords = Data1.Recordset.RecordCount
```

1. The first line says, "Create a variable called `TotalRecords`, and define this variable as a `Long` data type."

2. The second line says, "Move to the last record in the database."

3. The third line says, "Count the number of records and store this value in the variable called `TotalRecords`."

Finding a Specific Record

To find a specific record in a database, you have to use one of the following commands:

✔ `Data1.Recordset.FindFirst "criteria"`

✔ `Data1.Recordset.FindNext "criteria"`

✔ `Data1.Recordset.FindPrevious "criteria"`

✔ `Data1.Recordset.FindLast "criteria"`

The search criteria (or criterion, in case you think the singular form of criteria doesn't look silly) specifies which field to search and the specific data you want to find. For example, to find all the records containing information on people with the last name Jefferson, your search criteria may look like the following:

```
"LastName = 'Jefferson'"
```

Notice that the data you're searching for ('Jefferson') must appear surrounded by single quotation marks. If you fail to use single quotation marks, Visual Basic isn't going to know what you want to find and isn't going to do anything, out of spite. Of course, this example also assumes that a field called LastName exists.

If you try searching for data in a nonexistent field, you get an error message.

To find the *first record* that meets your search criteria, use a command like the following:

```
Data1.Recordset.FindFirst "LastName = 'Jefferson'"
```

After you find one record that meets your search criteria, you can search for another record that meets your criteria. To find the *next record* that meets your search criteria, use a command like the following:

```
Data1.Recordset.FindNext "LastName = 'Jefferson'"
```

To find the *previous record* that meets your search criteria, use a command like the following:

```
Data1.Recordset.FindPrevious "LastName = 'Jefferson'"
```

To find the *last record* that meets your search criteria, use a command like this:

```
Data1.Recordset.FindLast "LastName = 'Jefferson'"
```

Yanking data from a database field

Before you yank out information from a database field, find the record that you want by using the FindFirst, FindNext, FindLast, or FindPrevious command. Then yank information from the database field by using one of two methods:

✔ Create a text box or label and set the DataField property to the field you want.

✔ Use BASIC code to yank information out of a database and assign the information to a variable:

```
Dim Store As String
Store = Data1.Recordset.Fields("Fieldname").Value
```

1. The first line says, "Create a variable called Store and define this variable as a String data type."

2. The second line says, "Yank the data stored in the field called Fieldname and store the value in the Store variable."

Changing data in a database

To change the contents of a database field when the field is displayed in a text box, check box, image box, or picture box, just type or paste new information inside.

To change the contents of a database field by using BASIC code, use the following commands:

```
Data1.Recordset.Edit
Data1.Recordset.Fields("Fieldname").Value = NewValue
Data1.Recordset.Update
```

1. The first command tells Visual Basic, "I'm getting ready to change some data in a database."

2. The second command replaces the current value of the field "Fieldname" with the value stored in NewValue.

3. The third command says, "Save my changes to the database."

Any time you add, delete, or edit a record in a database using BASIC code, you have to use the magic Update command to update the database file.

Test your newfound knowledge

1. What are the steps you must follow to make your Visual Basic program use a database file?

a. First, create a database file using a separate database program such as Access or Paradox. Then draw the Data Control icon on a form, choose the database file name for the DatabaseName property of the Data Control icon, and choose a database table for the RecordSource property of the Data Control icon.

b. Buy a computer, take it back to the store because it doesn't work, hire a database programmer, fire the database programmer, and throw up your hands in despair.

c. Visual Basic can use database files? Hey, where can I find out more about this?

d. None. This is a trick question and I refuse to reveal my ignorance by selecting any of these choices.

2. What do the following lines of BASIC code do?

```
Data1.Recordset.AddNew
Data1.Recordset.Fields
("Question") = "Did you
ever
  accept money from overseas
  governments?"
```

```
Data1.Recordset.Fields
("Answer") = "Yes, but I
made them pay with American
money."
```

```
Data1.Recordset.Update
```

a. The first line erases any existing databases on your hard disk, the second and third lines are superfluous, and the fourth line wipes out the rest of the files stored on your hard disk.

b. The first line adds a new record to a database file; the second line stores the string "Did you ever accept money from overseas governments?" in the database field called "Question"; the third line stores the string "Yes, but I made them pay with American money." in the database field called "Answer"; and the fourth line updates the database with this new information, adding this new record at the end of the database file.

c. The first line confuses Visual Basic, the second line asks Visual Basic a question, the third line displays the Visual Basic answer as given under the advice of a lawyer, and the fourth line ignores the whole problem and hopes that everyone can forget what really happened.

d. Hey! You're making fun of somebody important, aren't you?

Placing a bookmark on a specific record

You can put a bookmark on a record so that you can quickly jump back to the record at any time. To create a bookmark, you have to create a variable and define this variable as a Variant or String data type. For example:

```
Dim MyBookMark1 As Variant
```

or

```
Dim MyBookMark2 As String
```

Each bookmark can point to only one record at a time.

To place a bookmark, display the record where you want to put it and then use the following command:

```
MyBookMark1 = Data1.Recordset.Bookmark
```

To jump back to a bookmark, use the following command:

```
Data1.Recordset.Bookmark = MyBookmark1
```

Note: Not all database files let you use bookmarks. Microsoft Access MDB files are always bookmarkable (is that a real word?), but other database types may not be, depending on whether an index exists for that particular database. (If you have no idea what an index is and don't care to know, feel free to ignore this whole discussion.) To determine whether a database file supports bookmarks, examine the Bookmarkable property, as in the following example:

```
If Data1.Recordset.Bookmarkable = True Then
   ' Can place bookmarks
ElseIf Data1.Recordset.Bookmarkable = False Then
   ' Cannot use bookmarks
End If
```

Be careful about database formats. Each time a company such as Microsoft upgrades their database program (such as Access), the new version of that database program may use a different file format. This means that Visual Basic may not be able to use the new, updated file format.

Chapter 34

Making Your Program Print Stuff

. . . .

. . . .

A program can suck in data, manipulate data, and display data on the screen. But eventually, your program may need to print stuff out. Visual Basic provides two ways to print stuff:

 ✔ Display data on a form and then print the form

 ✔ Send data directly to the printer using the Printer object

Printing a Form

Printing a form is the simplest method for printing out information. To print a form, use the following syntax:

```
FormName.PrintForm
```

This tells Visual Basic, "Find the form named FormName and send this form to the printer."

To print a form named frmAbout, use the following command:

```
frmAbout.PrintForm
```

You can print any form in your program, including invisible forms and minimized forms. The only drawback with printing forms is that the print resolution may not be very high.

Most screens display a resolution of 96 dots per inch (dpi). Most laser printers can print at resolutions of 300 or 600 dots per inch. For quick printing, the PrintForm command works well. But for higher resolution printing, print by using the Printer object instead.

Printing with the Printer Object

The *Printer object* is a temporary storage space that intercepts data, cleans up data, and then sends the clean version to the printer. To print a form using the Printer object, you essentially have to redraw your form on the Printer object, using BASIC code.

The advantage of the Printer object is that this object uses the resolution of your printer. The disadvantage is that you have to write lots of BASIC code just to print a simple form.

Before you print anything using the Printer object, you have to define the top/bottom page margins and the right/left page margins.

To define the *top* page margin, use the following syntax, where `TopValue` measures the size of the top margin:

```
Printer.ScaleTop = TopValue
```

To define the *bottom* page margin, use the syntax that follows, where `BottomValue` measures the size of the bottom margin:

```
Printer.ScaleBottom = BottomValue
```

To define the *left* page margin, use the following syntax, where `LeftValue` measures the size of the left margin:

```
Printer.ScaleLeft = LeftValue
```

To define the *right* page margin, use the following syntax, where `RightValue` measures the size of the right margin:

```
Printer.ScaleRight = RightValue
```

You may have to experiment with different values for your margins until they look the way you want.

Printing text on the Printer object

Before you can print text through the Printer object, you have to define the *X* and *Y* location where you want the text to appear.

To define this location, use this syntax:

```
Printer.CurrentX = XValue
Printer.CurrentY = YValue
```

These commands say, "Start printing all text at the location defined by the `CurrentX` and `CurrentY` properties."

To start printing at the upper-left corner of a page, use the following commands:

```
Printer.CurrentX = 0
Printer.CurrentY = 0
```

Test your newfound knowledge

1. Why would you want to have your Visual Basic program print anything?

   a. To waste paper and help contribute to global deforestation in Third World countries.

   b. So I can justify buying a $1,000 laser printer.

   c. To provide hard copies of any important information that my Visual Basic program may create.

   d. I can never justify a reason to print anything. Hasn't watching American politics taught you to never put down on paper anything that may implicate you in the future?

2. Why do you need to specify X- and Y-coordinates when printing text or drawing lines or circles?

   a. To make you feel like you actually learned something useful in high school geometry class.

   b. So you can tell Visual Basic exactly where you want your lines, circles, or text to appear on the printed page.

   c. The X- and Y-coordinates define the location of your printer in relation to your computer. If you define the X- and Y-coordinates incorrectly, your documents may start printing out from your toaster or air conditioner.

After you define where to start printing, the next step is to actually print some text. To print text on the Printer object, follow this syntax:

```
Printer.Print "Text string"
```

This command says, "Put a text string on the Printer object and print this text string at the location pre}qously defined by the `CurrentX` and the `CurrentY` properties."

Printing lines and circles on the Printer object

Printing plain text can be boring, so Visual Basic gives you the option to spice up your printouts with lines and circles. If this sounds like Visual Basic is turning your $2,000 computer and $1,000 laser printer into an Etch-A-Sketch, you're right.

Defining line thicknesses

Before you start drawing lines and circles, you have to define the draw width. The smaller the draw width, the thinner your lines are going to look.

To define the draw width, use the syntax that follows:

```
Printer.DrawWidth = Value
```

To define the skinniest draw width possible, use this command:

```
Printer.DrawWidth = 1
```

To define a fatter draw width, use this command:

```
Printer.DrawWidth = 5
```

For those who really care, the values of DrawWidth can vary from 1 to 32,767. A value of 1 specifies a line one pixel wide. A value of 32,767 specifies a line of 32,767 pixels wide, which is probably wider than you are going to ever need.

Printing a 1-pixel wide line on a 600 dots-per-inch laser printer may look different than if you print a 1-pixel wide line on a 300-dpi inkjet printer.

Drawing lines on the Printer object

To draw a line, use the syntax that follows, where x1 and y1 define the starting point of the line and x2 and y2 define the ending point:

```
Printer.Line (x1,y1) - (x2,y2)
```

Drawing circles on the Printer object

To draw a circle, use this syntax, where x and y are the center of the circle and Radius defines the circle's radius:

```
Printer.Circle(x,y), Radius
```

Printing Multiple Pages

Usually Visual Basic keeps printing your data until the printer runs out of room on the page. Then Visual Basic cuts your text off and starts printing a new page automatically.

However, if you want to control when Visual Basic starts printing a new page, use the following command:

```
Printer.NewPage
```

This command tells Visual Basic to start printing on a new page. (Wow! What are they going to think of next?)

Defining the Print Quality

Depending on your printer, you can specify a range of resolutions for printing. The magic command to control print resolution is

```
Printer.PrintQuality = x
```

In the preceding command, x represents a negative number between –4 and –1, or a positive number representing the specific resolution you want to use, measured in dots per inch. For example, the following list shows the print resolution of the negative numbers –4 to –1:

```
Printer.PrintQuality = -1          Draft resolution
Printer.PrintQuality = -2          Low resolution
Printer.PrintQuality = -3          Medium resolution
Printer.PrintQuality = -4          High resolution
```

In case you want to use the predefined Visual Basic constants, you can use them as follows:

Constant	Value	Print Resolution
vbPRPQDraft	−1	Draft resolution
vbPRPQLow	−2	Low resolution
vbPRPQMedium	−3	Medium resolution
vbPRPQHigh	−4	High resolution

If you're the type who likes to specify the exact print resolution to use, just specify a positive number. To define 300 dpi, which is what most cheap laser printers can produce these days, you want to use the following command:

```
Printer.PrintQuality = 300
```

Keeping a Page Count

When you're printing multiple pages, Visual Basic automatically keeps track of the page count in a property called Page. To use this page count, use the following BASIC command:

```
Printer.Page
```

When You Finish Printing

Use the following command to tell Visual Basic you've finished printing:

```
Printer.EndDoc
```

If you neglect to use this command, guess what? Visual Basic assumes this command exists anyway as the last command to the printer, so you really don't need to use this after all. However, for good programming practice, use this command so you know exactly when your program has finished printing.

In case you want to stop printing, you can tell Visual Basic, "Hey, I changed my mind. Stop printing." To stop the printer right away, use the following BASIC command:

```
Printer.KillDoc
```

As you can see, trying to torture Visual Basic into printing data can be cumbersome and tedious. If you have the time, write your own printing routines and reuse them for each program you write. As a quicker alternative, buy an ActiveX control called vsView from VideoSoft (www.videosoft.com). This ActiveX control makes it easy to add printing capabilities to your program without writing a lot of BASIC code.

Try Creating a Print Program Yourself

The following sample program prints a short message when you click the Click to Print command button. To create this program, use the settings specified in the following table:

Object	Property	Setting
Form	Caption	An Example of Printing
Command1	Caption	&Click to Print
	Name	cmdPrint

Type the following code in the Code window. If you don't want to give your fingers such a strenuous workout, just load the PRINTME.VBP file off the CD-ROM at the back of this book.

```
Private Sub cmdPrint_Click()
Dim TotalPages As Integer
Dim PageCount As String
  ' Specifies the text position to print
  Printer.CurrentX = 100
  Printer.CurrentY = 100
  Printer.Print "This appears at the top of the page"

  ' Specifies a line width and location
  Printer.DrawWidth = 3
  Printer.Line(100, 100)-(10000, 100)
  Printer.Line(100, 350)-(10000, 350)
  TotalPages = Printer.Page
```

(continued)

(continued)

```
    ' Specifies a line width and location
    Printer.Circle (2000, 3500), 450
    Printer.CurrentX = 2750
    Printer.CurrentY = 3500
    Printer.Print "This is a circle. Whee!"

    ' Specifies where to print the page count
    Printer.CurrentX = 1000
    Printer.CurrentY = 400
    PageCount = "TotalPages = " & Str$(TotalPages)
    Printer.Print PageCount
    Printer.EndDoc
End Sub
```

Printing a Visual Basic Project

While this chapter has explained how to make your Visual Basic program print out data while the program is running, you may have another question, "How the heck do I print out the source code to my Visual Basic project itself?"

Fortunately, after you take all the time and effort to write a program in Visual Basic, you can print the program out for posterity to admire. Visual Basic provides three ways to print out a Visual Basic project:

- ✓ Form Image: Prints your form exactly as the form appears on the screen.
- ✓ Code: Prints only your BASIC code.
- ✓ Form As Text: Prints the property values of all the forms and objects that make up your user interface.

To print a Visual Basic project, follow these steps:

1. **Choose File⇨Print or press Ctrl+P.**

   Visual Basic displays the Print dialog box.

2. **Click on the Current Module (to print only the highlighted file in the Project Explorer window) or the Current Project radio button (to print the entire Visual Basic project).**

3. **Click on one or more of the following check boxes: Form Image, Code, or Form As Text.**

4. **Make sure your printer is turned on and click on OK.**

Part IX
The Part of Tens

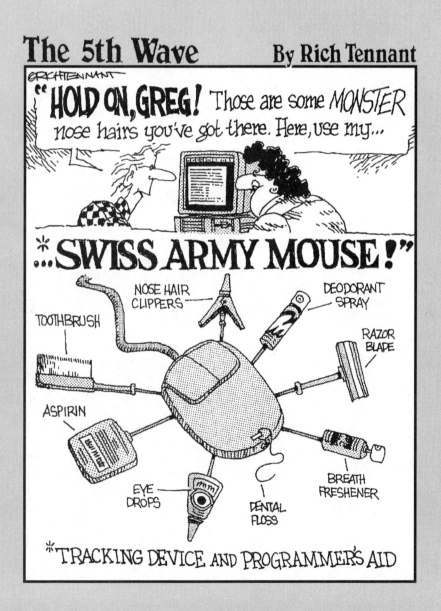

In this part . . .

*N*ow that you've made it this far in the book (or maybe you're one of those readers who jumps to the end of a great book), you're looking for a few ideas to help you write the best Visual Basic programs possible without losing your mind in the process.

With the help of this book and Visual Basic, you can now write your own programs or get a job writing programs for others. But no matter what you may plan to do with your programming skills, browse through this part of the book to pick up tips for making the most of your newly acquired Visual Basic programming skills.

Chapter 35

The Ten Visual Basic Topics That Didn't Fit Anywhere Else

● ●

In This Chapter

▶ Finding magazines and newsletters

▶ Visiting Visual Basic Web sites

▶ Joining a user group

▶ Attending technical conferences

▶ Writing your own DLL files

▶ Writing Visual Basic programs for the Macintosh and Linux

● ●

*N*ow that you've reached the end of this book (even if you just skipped to this section while browsing through this book in the bookstore), you may be wondering what to do next to continue your Visual Basic education without going through the process of trial and error and driving yourself crazy in the process.

You can pick up the latest edition of *MORE Visual Basic For Windows For Dummies* (written by yours truly and also published by IDG Books Worldwide, Inc.; order by calling 800-762-2974 or 415-655-3172). You can also use the following list of sources to find out more about Visual Basic and get help in creating the most powerful Visual Basic programs possible.

Buy, Read, or Steal Visual Basic Programmer's Journal

Every month, look for a fresh copy of *Visual Basic Programmer's Journal* at your favorite magazine stand or bookstore. This magazine comes loaded with articles exploring the intricate details of Visual Basic, reviews of Visual Basic add-ons, and samples of Visual Basic code that you can copy (steal) for your own use.

Unlike other magazines, one of the more useful features is the advertising. If you need an ActiveX control to make your programming task easier, then browse through the ads and you'll probably find what you need. For more information about this magazine, contact

Visual Basic Programmer's Journal
Fawcette Technical Publications
209 Hamilton Avenue
Palo Alto, CA 94301-2500
Tel: 415-833-7100
Fax: 415-853-0230
www.windx.com

Spend a Bundle of Money and Get a Visual Basic Newsletter

For more detailed information, buy a Visual Basic newsletter. The Cobb Group publishes monthly newsletters for a variety of programs, including Paradox, Microsoft Office, and Visual Basic. Although a year's subscription is about $60, the *Inside Visual Basic* newsletter provides plenty of source code examples that you can study, modify, and claim you wrote yourself to impress your boss, who doesn't know any better.

Another company, Pinnacle Publishing, Inc., publishes another Visual Basic monthly newsletter, *Visual Basic Developer,* that comes with source code examples on an enclosed floppy disk. Of course, this newsletter costs a bit more (about $179 a year), but if you can get your company to buy this for you, who cares about the price?

For more information on the two publications discussed in this section, contact

Inside Visual Basic
The Cobb Group
9420 Bunsen Parkway
Louisville, KY 40220
Tel: 502-493-3300
Fax: 502-491-8050
www.cobb.com

Visual Basic Developer
Pinnacle Publishing, Inc.
P.O. Box 72255
Marietta, GA 30007-2255
Tel: 770-565-1763
Fax: 770-565-8232
www.pinpub.com

Visit a Web Site Dedicated to Visual Basic

If you have access to the Internet, you can often find entire Web sites devoted to Visual Basic programming. While the number of specialized Visual Basic Web sites continue to grow, here's a short list of the more popular Web sites you may want to visit:

Carl and Gary's Visual Basic Home Page at the following Web address:

```
www.apexsc.com/vb
```

Chris & Tim's VB Programming Resources at the following Web address:

```
www.zetnet.co.uk/rad/index.html
```

VB Tips & Tricks Home Page at the following Web address:

```
www.vbtt.com
```

Attend a Visual Basic Technical Conference

Every few months, Microsoft and *Visual Basic Programmer's Journal* sponsor a Visual Basic Technical Summit somewhere around the world in the United States, Europe, and Asia. These conferences are great places to learn techniques from real-life Visual Basic programming experts, listen to the latest propaganda talks from Microsoft representatives, buy Visual Basic add-ons cheaply from vendors, and make lots of contacts in the Visual Basic world. For more information about these technical conferences, contact

Visual Basic Programmer's Journal
Fawcette Technical Publications
209 Hamilton Avenue
Palo Alto, CA 94301-2500
Tel: 415-833-7100
Fax: 415-853-0230
www.windx.com

Shop from Mail-Order Dealers

Don't buy Visual Basic or any Visual Basic add-on programs direct from the publisher. Most software publishers cheerfully charge full retail price for their programs, which makes as much sense as paying full sticker price for a used car.

Rather than buy direct from the software publisher, shop by mail order instead. Mail-order dealers give you even deeper discounts (up to 50 percent in some cases), with the added advantage of saving you from having to pay sales tax.

Two popular mail-order dealers are VBxtras and ZAC Catalog. Both companies specialize in selling Visual Basic add-ons at substantial discounts, so give them a call and ask for a free catalog.

For more information on these mail-order companies, contact

ZAC Catalog
1090 Kapp Drive
Clearwater, FL 33765-2111
Tel: 813-298-1181
Fax: 813-461-5808
www.zaccatalog.com

VBxtras
1905 Powers Ferry, Suite 100
Atlanta, GA 30339
Tel: 770-952-6356
Fax: 770-952-6388
www.vbxtras.com

Extend Visual Basic by Writing Your Own DLL Files

If you plan to write lots of Visual Basic programs, you need to organize your commonly used procedures in separate BAS module files. That way you can quickly plug in BAS module files to any Visual Basic programs you write.

Unfortunately, BAS module files can contain only Visual Basic commands. Because languages such as C++ and Pascal can be more flexible in digging into the guts of your computer and manipulating individual bits and bytes, many programmers write commonly used procedures in C++ or Pascal and store them in separate Dynamic Link Library (DLL) files. A DLL file contains commonly used procedures that you can share among different programs.

You can write a DLL file using C++, Pascal, or even Visual Basic. But no matter which language you use, a DLL file makes your programs run faster than if you just stored BASIC code in a BAS module file instead. (For more information about writing DLL files, pick up the latest edition of *MORE Visual Basic For Windows For Dummies*.)

Although using DLL files can be cumbersome, using these files is still easier than your other alternative, which is to use the Windows Application Programming Interface. (See the following section "Extend Visual Basic By Using the Windows API").

Extend Visual Basic By Using the Windows API

Visual Basic makes programming so easy because it insulates you from all the messy details needed to write Windows programs. But the price you pay for this insulation is a loss of flexibility that C++ programmers love to flaunt (as they slowly go mad, dealing with the complexities of Windows programming).

Eventually, you are likely to find Visual Basic's ease of use frustrating because you can't perform certain tasks. The quickest and easiest alternative is to buy an add-on program to give Visual Basic the features you want. But if you can't find such an add-on program, you are going to have to dig into the guts of Windows itself.

To help programmers write programs for Windows, Windows has many commands called the Microsoft Windows Application Programming Interface (API). Although these commands are complicated to learn and understand, the complexity of these commands gives you the ability to manipulate (and of course, crash) Windows to your heart's content.

If you like living dangerously, take the time to read about the Windows API. (You can find out more about the Windows API in the latest edition of *MORE Visual Basic For Windows For Dummies*.) Otherwise, just pretend this section never existed and skip to another part of the book.

Buy a Program to Create Help Files

Every good Windows program has an online help system so that panicky users can browse through a hypertext reference on the screen instead of wading through hundred-page manuals that don't make any sense anyway. If you're serious about writing Visual Basic programs, you are going to need to provide a help system with your programs, too.

Creating a help system isn't difficult, just incredibly dull and tedious. Fortunately, you can get a special program to make the process a little more enjoyable. Two popular help file creation programs are RoboHelp and ForeHelp, which let you design help screens as easily as writing a document in a word processor. When you're finished, each of these programs lets you test your creations by showing you exactly how your help screens are going to look when added to your own Visual Basic programs.

In today's competitive world of software development, a good help file is crucial to your program's professional appearance. Then again, if you don't care about making your programs easier to use, go work for any of the major software companies instead.

For more information on RoboHelp and ForeHelp, contact

RoboHelp	***ForeHelp***
Blue Sky Software	ForeFront, Inc.
7777 Fay Avenue, Suite 201	4710 Table Mesa Drive, Suite B
La Jolla, CA 92037	Boulder, CO 80303
Tel: 619-459-6365	Tel: 303-499-9181
Fax: 619-459-6366	Fax: 303-494-5446
`www.blue-sky.com`	`www.ff.com`

Buy a Program to Create Installation Disks

After you finish creating a program in Visual Basic, the final step is to distribute your program to others. While you can just copy your Visual Basic program onto a floppy disk and trust that the other person knows how to use the disk, you are better off using a special installation program instead.

Installation programs can guide someone, step-by-step, through the oftentimes complicated process of copying a program onto another computer. Visual Basic comes with an installation program called the Application Setup Wizard. However, you may want to buy a special installation program that offers you the chance to customize the installation with your own corporate logo, advertisements, or sound effects.

Two popular installation programs are InstallShield and PC-Install. Both programs can help you create foolproof installation programs for all your Visual Basic programs.

For more information on these installation programs, contact

PC-Install
20/20 Software, Inc.
8196 SW Hall Blvd., Suite 200
Beaverton, OR 97008
Tel: 503-520-0504
Fax: 503-520-9118
www.twenty.com

InstallShield
InstallShield Corporation
900 National Parkway, Suite 125
Schaumburg, IL 60173-5108
Tel: 847-240-9111
Fax: 847-240-9120
www.installshield.com

Write Visual Basic Programs for the Macintosh and Linux

When Microsoft first introduced Visual Basic back in 1991, programmers went nuts over it because they could design applications quickly and easily. So Microsoft promised that they would port Visual Basic to other operating systems so you could write Visual Basic programs for other computers.

After releasing Visual Basic for MS-DOS and then letting it die, Microsoft has done nothing but continue to hint of future releases of Visual Basic for other platforms. So if you want to use Visual Basic to write a Macintosh program, you can't.

However, you can use a Macintosh Visual Basic clone called (surprise!) Visual MacStandard Basic. Visual MacStandard Basic lets you visually draw your user interface and then write BASIC code to make it do something useful.

While Visual MacStandard Basic lacks many of the advanced features of Visual Basic 6.0, it does provide you with the ability to write Macintosh programs quickly and easily, just like Visual Basic 1.0 did for Windows back in 1991. So if you know how to program in Visual Basic, you can use your Visual Basic programming skills to write Visual MacStandard Basic programs for the Macintosh.

For the really adventurous, try XBasic, a BASIC compiler that runs under both Windows and Linux. While not as intuitive to use as Visual Basic, XBasic lets you write programs for Windows or Linux without resorting to learning C or C++. Since Linux may be the operating system of tomorrow, you can leverage your BASIC programming skills by writing Linux programs so you can insure job security for the future.

Visual MacStandard Basic
ZCurve Software
8206 Rockville Road #280
Indianapolis, IN 46214
www.zcurve.com

XBasic
Basmark Corporation
P.O. Box 40450
Cleveland, OH 44140
Tel: 440-871-8855
Fax: 440-871-1715
www.basmark.com

Appendix A

About the CD

● ●

*P*rovided that somebody didn't take a razor blade and slice out the plastic envelope attached to the back cover, you should find a compact disc (CD or, more specifically, CD-ROM) embedded inside a plastic envelope like a mosquito trapped in a block of amber. This CD contains the Visual Basic source code from the various exercises contained within the chapters of this book, along with a few bonus demo and trial programs provided by third-party companies. These demo or trial programs are Visual Basic ActiveX programs that you can add to your own programs, which can make your programming much easier.

The sample Visual Basic programs show actual working examples of the BASIC commands that I describe in different chapters. By studying this honest-to-goodness Visual Basic code, you can spend more time learning and less time typing tedious commands into your computer yourself.

System Requirements

Make sure that your computer meets the minimum system requirements listed below. If your computer doesn't match up to most of these requirements, you may have problems using the contents of the CD.

- ✔ A PC with a 486 or faster processor.
- ✔ Microsoft Windows 95/98/NT.
- ✔ At least 8MB of RAM installed in your computer. For best performance, I recommend that PCs have at least 16MB of RAM installed. (The more RAM, the better.)
- ✔ A CD-ROM drive — double-speed (2x) or faster.
- ✔ Visual Basic version 6.0 (earlier versions won't work with the enclosed CD, so there).

If you need more information on the basics, check out *PCs For Dummies,* 5th Edition, by Dan Gookin, and *Windows 98 For Dummies* by Andy Rathbone (both published by IDG Books Worldwide, Inc.).

How to Get to the Good Stuff

If you are running Windows 95, 98 or NT, follow these steps to get to the items on the CD:

1. **Insert the CD into your computer's CD-ROM drive.**

   Give your computer a moment to take a look at the CD.

2. **When the light on your CD-ROM drive goes out, double-click on the My Computer icon (which is probably in the top left corner of your desktop).**

   This action opens the My Computer window, which shows you all the drives attached to your computer, the Control Panel, and a couple other handy things.

3. **Double-click on the icon for your CD-ROM drive.**

   Another window opens, showing you all the folders and files on the CD.

To use the CD, follow these steps:

1. **Double-click on the file called License.txt.**

   This file contains the end-user license that you agree to by using the CD. When you finish reading the license, close the program (most likely NotePad) that displayed the file.

2. **Double-click on the file called Readme.txt.**

   This file contains instructions about installing the software from this CD. It may be helpful to leave this text file open while you are using the CD.

3. **Double-click on the folder for the software you are interested in.**

   Be sure to read the descriptions of the programs in the next section of this appendix (much of this information also shows up in the Readme file). These descriptions give you more precise information about the programs' folder names and about finding and running the installer program.

4. **Find the file called Setup.exe, or Install.exe, or something similar, and double-click on that file.**

   The program's installer walks you through the process of setting up your new software.

To run some of the programs on the *Visual Basic 6 For Dummies* CD-ROM, you may need to keep the CD inside your CD-ROM drive. This is a Good Thing. Otherwise, the installed program requires you to install a very large chunk of the program to your hard drive, which may keep you from installing other software.

What You Find

Sample Visual Basic code appears in separate folders, named according to the chapter they belong to. (See Table A-1 to find out what's in each folder.) For example, to find all the Visual Basic source code for Chapter 3, look for a folder on the CD named Chapter 3. You can load and run the source code directly off the CD or you can copy it to your hard disk. (Just remember that if you run the source code off the CD, you can't modify it.)

Table A-1	Folder Contents
Folder	*What's in It*
Chapter 3	Contains two programs, Hello1 and Hello2. By loading these files off the disk, you don't have to go through the tedium of typing BASIC code directly out of the book.
Chapter 4	Contains the final Hello program for you to examine and enjoy.
Chapter 5	Contains the Caption program that demonstrates how BASIC code can change the caption of an object displayed on the user interface.
Chapter 6	Contains the Forms and Buttons program that demonstrates how to use command buttons to modify the appearance of a form. (As a bonus, this sample program also demonstrates how to use dialog boxes, which you can find out about in Chapter 13).
Chapter 7	Contains the Boxes and Buttons program that demonstrates how to use check boxes, radio buttons, combo boxes, and list boxes.
Chapter 8	Contains the TextBoxes program that demonstrates how to use a password text box and an ordinary text box.
Chapter 9	Contains the ScrollBars program that demonstrates how to use scroll bars and display the scroll bar value on the screen.
Chapter 10	Contains the Shapes program that shows how to change a circle during run-time from the user interface.
Chapter 13	Contains the DialogBox program that shows how to use the built-in Visual Basic Common Dialog Box object.
Chapter 15	Contains the Variables program that shows how to change the properties of objects stored on different forms.
Chapter 16	Contains the ListBoxes programs that shows you how to use a Visual Basic list box.

(continued)

Table A-1 *(continued)*

Folder	What's in It
Chapter 17	Contains the Precedence program that shows you how precedence works when using parentheses and when omitting parentheses while calculating a numeric result.
Chapter 18	Contains the ELIZA program that demonstrates how to manipulate strings. ELIZA mimics a psychotherapist who simply echoes back anything you type, giving the illusion that the computer is actually responding to you.
Chapter 23	Contains the DoWhile program that demonstrates how a simple Do While loop works.
Chapter 25	Contains the ForNext program that demonstrates how a simple For Next loop works.
Chapter 28	Contains the Arguments program that shows how you can pass arguments among procedures.
Chapter 29	Contains the Functions program that shows you how a functions that converts yards to meters works.
Chapter 30	Contains the Mission program, which demonstrates how class modules work and how to use them within a Visual Basic program.
Chapter 34	Contains the PrintExample program that shows how you can print stuff from within a Visual Basic program.

What You Find in the ActiveX folder

The ActiveX folder contains all the trial ActiveX programs (see table A-2 for details) kindly provided by third-party companies eager to show you their wares and sell you the full-featured versions of their programs. While you can experiment with these trial versions, you can't use them within your own Visual Basic programs that you may distribute for sale.

Each trial ActiveX program comes with its own setup program (usually called SETUP.EXE). Just run this setup program by double-clicking on the SETUP.EXE file within Windows Explorer, or by clicking the Start button on the Windows taskbar, choosing Run, and choosing Browse until you find the SETUP.EXE program you want to run.

Some of the programs included on the Visual Basic 6 For Dummies CD were developed prior to the release of Visual Basic 6. These programs are noted as working with Visual Basic 4 and/or Visual Basic 5 only. However, all software included on the CD had been tested and does install and run with Visual Basic 6. Please visit the manufacturer Web site for each program (as noted in the Readme file on the CD) to check for Visual Basic 6 updates.

Table A-2	ActiveX Folder Contents
Program	*What It Does*
Crescent Internet ToolPak 4.1	If you want to create Internet applications, try this demo version of Crescent Internet ToolPak, which helps VB developers create applications that can browse the World Wide Web, send e-mail, execute FTP file transfers, and more. The Crescent Internet ToolPak simplifies accessing the alphabet soup of Internet standards such as IMAP4, TCP/IP Server, and FTP proxy support.
ElasticLight 6.0	This demo version can make your programs auto matically adjust to any screen resolution. So if you wrote your program on a super VGA monitor displaying an 800 x 600 screen resolution, but some- one runs your program on a plain old VGA monitor at 640 x 480 resolution, your program isn't cut off by the screen. This ActiveX control also adjusts the size of objects on your form (such as command buttons and radio buttons) if the user resizes a form.
HASHcipher	If you need secrecy, try this demo version of HASHcipher. This ActiveX control uses the Secure Hash Standard (SHS), developed by the U.S. Government's National Security Agency (NSA), to provide security through authentication. The algorithm specified by the Standard, the Secure Hash Algorithm, (SHA-1) is considered by many cryptographers to be the strongest hash algorithm available today and can be used in any application that requires authentication of a file or message.
InstallShield Express 2.02	Provides a more sophisticated installation program than the feeble one included with Visual Basic. InstallShield is the most popular installation program that commercial developers everywhere use, so join the bandwagon and try this trial version of InstallShield Express today!

(continued)

Table A-2 *(continued)* ActiveX Folder Contents

Program	What it Does
True DBList	The trial version of True DBList provides a set of customizable list and combo boxes for accessing information trapped in database files. Supports multiple columns; split group heading; multiple lines per record; alternate row color or style; in-cell graphics and text; data-sensitive color and font; and tons of other features that will make absolutely no sense to you until you try to torture yourself by accessing data with Visual Basic's built-in features.
True DBInput	The trial version of True DBInput provides data-aware ActiveX input controls for creating Visual Basic database applications. True DBInput includes scores of features to handle data entry and validation; intuitive customized display of dates, time, text, and numbers; plus other features to make sure your users don't type in invalid information into your database files.
VBAssist 5.0	The trial version of VBAssist contains various tools for helping you write Visual Basic programs faster and easier than before. With VBAssist you can quickly assign Tab Order to controls on a form, assign shortcut keys or accelerators to controls, place controls into exact positions on a form, along with other time-saving features.
VBPartner	This trial edition of VBPartner is an integrated add-in for Microsoft Visual Basic that includes 11 unique timesaving "Partners" that assist you with routine application design, error handling, and more by simplifying tedious development tasks.
VSData	This demo version of VSData enables your Visual Basic applications to access database files without using Visual Basic's own bulky database files that gobble up disk space and may offer way more features than your program needs.
VSDirect	This demo version of VSDirect provides routines for accessing Microsoft's DirectX technology for creating graphics, sound, and animation. Designed mostly for creating multimedia applications, VSDirect also includes routines for playing games over a modem link or network.

Program	What it Does
VSDocX	This demo version of VSDocX helps you create help files and printed documentation for your Visual Basic applications. Takes the hassle out of writing your program's documentation yourself, a task that most every programmer despises, as proven by the poor quality of computer manuals all over the world.
VSFlex 3.0	Visual Basic comes with an ActiveX control called MSFlexGrid, which is an older version of VSFlex. Like MSFlexGrid, this demo version of VSFlex lets you sort, merge, and group data in a grid. VSFlex also includes a string pattern matching ActiveX control for evaluating mathematical expressions or adding natural language capabilities to your programs.
VS-OCX 6.0	Provides notebook-style tabs along with a string parsing ActiveX control for advanced string manipulation. This demo version of VS-OCX also includes a more sophisticated screen resolution adapting control (similar to ElasticLight).
VSReports	VSReports enables your Visual Basic programs to create and print reports from Microsoft Access database files. By using this demo version of VSReports, you can avoid using Visual Basic's own bulky and cumbersome database reporting files.
VSSpell	Provides a spell-checker and a thesaurus for your Visual Basic applications. Perfect for creating the next generation of word processors to put Microsoft Word out of business.

If You Have Problems (of the CD Kind)

Because computers are notoriously finicky, picky, and downright unreliable at crucial times in our lives, you may be one of the unfortunate few plagued with problems while trying to use the enclosed CD.

If your computer has trouble reading the files off the CD, you may have a faulty CD. Despite our best efforts, occasionally a CD decides to follow the "dark side of the Force," turns corrupt, and tries to frighten people into thinking their computer problems are actually their fault.

If your computer can read other CDs okay but not the enclosed Visual Basic CD, please call the Hungry Minds Customer Care phone number, at 800-762-2974, and request a replacement CD.

If you don't have Visual Basic 6.0, you can't load any of the sample programs from the CD, even if you have an older version of Visual Basic, such as version 5.0 or 4.0. So check your version of Visual Basic by choosing Help⇨About Visual Basic. A dialog box appears to show you which version of Visual Basic you have.

Index

Wiley Publishing, Inc., End-User License Agreement

READ THIS. You should carefully read these terms and conditions before opening the software packet(s) included with this book "Book". This is a license agreement "Agreement" between you and Wiley Publishing, Inc. "WPI". By opening the accompanying software packet(s), you acknowledge that you have read and accept the following terms and conditions. If you do not agree and do not want to be bound by such terms and conditions, promptly return the Book and the unopened software packet(s) to the place you obtained them for a full refund.

1. **License Grant.** WPI grants to you (either an individual or entity) a nonexclusive license to use one copy of the enclosed software program(s) (collectively, the "Software" solely for your own personal or business purposes on a single computer (whether a standard computer or a workstation component of a multi-user network). The Software is in use on a computer when it is loaded into temporary memory (RAM) or installed into permanent memory (hard disk, CD-ROM, or other storage device). WPI reserves all rights not expressly granted herein.

2. **Ownership.** WPI is the owner of all right, title, and interest, including copyright, in and to the compilation of the Software recorded on the disk(s) or CD-ROM "Software Media". Copyright to the individual programs recorded on the Software Media is owned by the author or other authorized copyright owner of each program. Ownership of the Software and all proprietary rights relating thereto remain with WPI and its licensers.

3. **Restrictions On Use and Transfer.**

   (a) You may only (i) make one copy of the Software for backup or archival purposes, or (ii) transfer the Software to a single hard disk, provided that you keep the original for backup or archival purposes. You may not (i) rent or lease the Software, (ii) copy or reproduce the Software through a LAN or other network system or through any computer subscriber system or bulletin- board system, or (iii) modify, adapt, or create derivative works based on the Software.

   (b) You may not reverse engineer, decompile, or disassemble the Software. You may transfer the Software and user documentation on a permanent basis, provided that the transferee agrees to accept the terms and conditions of this Agreement and you retain no copies. If the Software is an update or has been updated, any transfer must include the most recent update and all prior versions.

4. **Restrictions on Use of Individual Programs.** You must follow the individual requirements and restrictions detailed for each individual program in Appendix A of this Book. These limitations are also contained in the individual license agreements recorded on the Software Media. These limitations may include a requirement that after using the program for a specified period of time, the user must pay a registration fee or discontinue use. By opening the Software packet(s), you will be agreeing to abide by the licenses and restrictions for these individual programs that are detailed in Appendix A and on the Software Media. None of the material on this Software Media or listed in this Book may ever be redistributed, in original or modified form, for commercial purposes.

Installation Instructions

The enclosed CD-ROM contains the Visual Basic source code from the various exercises contained within the chapters of this book along with a few bonus demo and trial programs provided by third-party companies. If you are running Windows 95, 98, or NT, follow these steps to get to the items on the CD:

1. **Insert the CD into your computer's CD-ROM drive.**

   Give your computer a moment to take a look at the CD.

2. **When the light on your CD-ROM drive goes out, double click on the My Computer icon (it's probably in the top left corner of your desktop.)**

   This action opens the My Computer window, which shows you all the drives attached to your computer, the Control Panel, and a couple other handy things.

3. **Double click on the icon for your CD-ROM drive.**

   Another window opens, showing you all the folders and files on the CD.

Notes

Notes